OVERWHELMED

Overwhelmed

LITERATURE, AESTHETICS, AND
THE NINETEENTH-CENTURY
INFORMATION REVOLUTION

Maurice S. Lee

PRINCETON UNIVERSITY PRESS
PRINCETON & OXFORD

Copyright © 2019 by Princeton University Press

Princeton University Press is committed to the protection of copyright and the intellectual property our authors entrust to us. Copyright promotes the progress and integrity of knowledge. Thank you for supporting free speech and the global exchange of ideas by purchasing an authorized edition of this book. If you wish to reproduce or distribute any part of it in any form, please obtain permission.

Part of chapter 1 appeared, in different form, in "Deserted Islands and Overwhelmed Readers," *American Literary History* 26:2 (2014), 1–27.

Part of chapter 2 appeared, in different form, in "Searching the Archives with Dickens and Hawthorne: Databases and Aesthetic Judgment after the New Historicism," *ELH* 79 (2012), 747–71.

Published by Princeton University Press
41 William Street, Princeton, New Jersey 08540
99 Banbury Road, Oxford OX2 6JX

press.princeton.edu

All Rights Reserved

LCCN 2019937195
First paperback printing, 2024
Paperback ISBN 9780691259246
Cloth ISBN 9780691192925

British Library Cataloging-in-Publication Data is available

Editorial: Anne Savarese and Lauren Bucca
Production Editorial: Sara Lerner
Jacket/Cover Design: Pamela Schnitter
Production: Merli Guerra
Publicity: Alyssa Sanford and Keira Andrews
Copyeditor: Kathleen Kageff

Jacket/Cover Credit: Wendy Wahl, *Branches Unbound*.
Exhibited at the Grand Rapids Art Museum, MI, 2011.

This book has been composed in Miller

To Nico, Matteo, and Marisa

CONTENTS

List of Figures · ix
Acknowledgments · xi

INTRODUCTION 1

CHAPTER 1   Reading   19
            Crusoe's Book(s)   21
            Coleridge's Anxiety of Authorship   32
            Carrying Out the Wealth of the Indies: Emerson   39

CHAPTER 2   Searching   57
            The New New Historicism   60
            Slavery and The Scarlet Letter   65
            The Office of Hawthorne and Company   70
            Dickens's Dream   78
            Notes, Queries, and Familiar Quotations   89

CHAPTER 3   Counting   108
            Quantity and Quality   112
            Stirring Enumerations in Treasure Island   124
            A Literary History of Adventure Novels   130
            Lost Worlds, Found Words   139
            Too Many Codas: Dark Continents, Repulsive
            Figures, Six Shooters, and Lost Arks   152

CHAPTER 4   Testing   165
            Subjects for Examination   166

Impersonality and Impersonation in
Our Mutual Friend   176

Fictions of Examination   184

US Correlations   203

"By What Standard Shall We Measure Men?":
Testing African Americans   211

Coda: Retaking the GRE   219

Notes · 223
Index · 265

FIGURES

1.1.	Inscription from copy of *Robinson Crusoe*	27
2.1.	Hablot Browne, "Mysterious Installation of Mr. Pinch," *The Life and Adventures of Martin Chuzzlewit*	81
2.2.	R. W. Buss, *Dickens' Dream*	87
3.1.	Graph of Thomas Macaulay's *Essay on History*	121
3.2.	Keyword frequencies for adventure novel corpus, 1820–1920	144
3.3.	Keyword frequencies for adventure novels, Group A	146
3.4.	Keyword frequencies for adventure novels, Group B	146
3.5.	Average adventure novel by decile	147
3.6.	Quantitative and textual terms by decile in *Peter and Wendy*	148

ACKNOWLEDGMENTS

THIS BOOK IS about literature and information, aesthetic pleasure and rational systems. If I had to guess about the earliest and most personal origins of what follows, I'd say that it comes partially from my mom, who writes fiction, and partially from my dad, who was a chemistry professor. I'm told that when they told my brother and me that they were divorcing, I insisted that the family play a board game together. (No one remembers exactly what game, though I like to think it was *Sorry!*) This book can be taken as a continuation of my efforts to reconcile literature and information, and I've been lucky to find some wonderful fellow players.

So many have contributed so much to this book that I'm nearly overwhelmed with gratitude. In the English Department at Boston University, Rob Chodat, Hunt Howell, Gene Jarrett (now at New York University), Laura Korobkin, Susan Mizruchi, and Joe Rezek were generous in responding to notions and drafts, as was Arianne Chernock in the History Department and Christina Dobbs in the School of Education. In their leadership capacities, Ann Cudd, Gina Sapiro, and James Winn helped create conditions for extended research, as did fellowships and grants from the Boston University Center for the Humanities and the Rafik B. Hariri Institute. Anne Austin made it possible for me to pursue my scholarship while also serving as department chair. Carl Weitkamp helped create a digital corpus of adventure novels, and Mary Kuhn and Reed Gochberg assisted with my research while producing their own impressive scholarship. Thanks also to participants in my graduate seminars, in which we experimented with some maturing thoughts.

Beyond my home institution, I have benefited from the expertise of librarians at the Houghton Library and American Antiquarian Society. I've enjoyed extended conversations with Jonathan Sachs, Chad Wellmon, and others at McGill University's Interacting with Print research group, where Andrew Piper offered some sage advice and good company at the intersections of information and literature. I also spent a blissful year in the Fellowship Program at the Radcliffe Institute for Advanced Study at Harvard University. Many thanks to Lizabeth Cohen, Judy Vichniac, and the Radcliffe staff for their support, to my amazing fellow fellows for expanding my mind, and to Robert Darnton, Sharon Marcus, and Adela Pinch for their specialized insights and generosity. The research opportunities with which I have been privileged would not have been possible without the support of Robert S. Levine, Samuel Otter, and Eric Sundquist, who have been for me models of professional grace.

Studying how information circulates has made me especially sensitive to the networks, events, conversations, and stray comments that have helped to shape this book. I'm grateful to hosts, panel organizers, paper respondents, colloquium participants, fellow travelers, and friends in the field who in one form or another provided opportunities for provocation. Special thanks to Branka Arsić, John Barnard, Lawrence Buell, Stuart Burrows, Christopher Castiglia, Amanda Claybaugh, Jeanne Cortiel, Elizabeth Maddock Dillon, Jonathan Elmer, David Faflik, Christopher Freeburg, Sean X. Goudie, Christopher Hanlon, Karin Hoepker, Carrie Hyde, Michael Jonik, Meredith McGill, Dana Nelson, Susan Scott Parish, John Plotz, Erik Redling, Geoffrey Sanborn, Stephanie Sobelle, Andrew Stauffer, Elisa Tamarkin, and Nathan Wolff. Thanks also to Gordon Hutner and readers at *American Literary History*, as well as to editors and evaluators at *ELH*, where portions of this book first appeared. Anonymous readers from Princeton University Press were also incisive and insightful in their reports, and Anne Savarese has been an absolutely marvelous editor, as have Sara Lerner and Kathleen Kageff, who shepherded and edited the manuscript with expert care.

There is some debate among information theorists about the semantic value of repetition. I hold that it matters, and I reaffirm my love to family and friends—Mom, Andrew, Yuko, Linda, Don, Dino, Philippe, Jen, Vince, Danno, Rob, Laura, Saya, Paul, Kelly, and Eloise. Most of all, this book is dedicated to Nico and Matteo, who enrich my life in more ways than I could ever have imagined, and to Marisa, who sustains me in so many ways and remains the love of my life. As I write these acknowledgments on a train from Barcelona to Madrid, I feel blessed to share our adventures together.

OVERWHELMED

Introduction

"CALL ME ISHMAEL" is not the first line of *Moby-Dick* (1851). Before we meet our itinerant narrator, before he shares a bed with Queequeg, before Ahab announces his fiery hunt, and before Melville piles on so much information about ships and marine life as to inspire some readers to abandon the book, a prefatory section presents two characters. The first is the school Usher, who dusts his grammars and dictionaries while introducing an etymological chart of the word *whale*. The second is the Sub-Sub-Librarian, who lists seventy-nine quotations about whales compiled from the Bible, Shakespeare, Milton, and Hawthorne, as well as scientific treatises, exploration narratives, and sailors' songs. We might contrast the rule-bound orderliness of the Usher with the rollicking researches of the Sub-Sub. The former presents philological information in an attempt to fix the meaning of whales, while the later assembles a multivalent archive gleaned from "the long Vaticans and street-stalls of the earth."[1] The unruliness of the Sub-Sub can be taken to accord with the untamable aesthetic of *Moby-Dick*, a book that mocks efforts to understand the world through systems, taxonomies, and facts. *Moby-Dick* in this way may seem to prefer literary extravagance to desiccated information. Yet for all their differences, both the Usher and the Sub-Sub-Librarian are information workers, while Melville's surfeit of information about shipping and cetology surpasses satire to register something like pleasure. Ishmael, Ahab, and boatloads of critics can obsessively interpret the wondrous white whale, itself a symbol of literature's unknowability, but Melville's prefatory materials foreground the point that literature and information are hard to disentangle. As an 1851 review of *Moby-Dick* noted of Melville's writings, "In one light they are romantic fictions, in another statements of absolute fact," and so it remains "quite impossible to submit such books to a distinct classification."[2]

It is indeed tempting to try to separate literature and information, romantic fictions and absolute facts, particularly if one valorizes aesthetic experiences that inhabit autonomous imaginative worlds. Information can be taken to puncture this dream and stand in disenchanting opposition to literature. Why do *Moby-Dick*'s lading lists and zoological categories seem out of place to some readers? Why is Thoreau's measuring of the pond in *Walden* (1854) sometimes mistaken for a joke? Why does the mixing of literature and information, myth and science, seem monstrous in Mary Shelley and Bram Stoker? Why did Trollope's artistic reputation suffer when he published a ledger detailing the earnings of his books? Or to think about how information systems might govern literary knowledge and practices: Is it odd to chart the number of pages one reads or writes in a year? Are standardized literature tests wrongheaded? What about critical claims based on data collected from thousands of digitized texts? Why do I sometimes feel demoralized in institutional libraries and chagrined when skimming the vastness of Google Books? Literature can seem incommensurate with information and information systems, though why this is so—and whether it is true—is difficult to say.

Maybe literature is like most objects of enchantment. What initially seems self-contained and engrossing is interrupted by recognitions of context and contingency, as if readers and their reading are always recapitulating some kind of fall into modernity. We might take this descent as a fall into knowledge, though it increasingly can feel like a fall into information. The difference between the two is not always clear, and one goal of this book is to work toward an understanding of information that is productive for literary critics at a time of methodological instability and professional insecurity. As a starting point, we might think of knowledge as the subject of epistemology, while information—a more recent and less disciplined concept—seems more the stuff of numbers, facts, classification, computational science, and media technology. To study information in these terms is to pivot away from philosophical questions about correlations between subjects and objects or the accuracy of language, and to focus instead on the possibilities of navigating the world through algorithmic processes, bureaucratic protocols, and data-based analysis. Such approaches seem to many far afield from literary studies if not downright anathema to its traditional commitments. However, a main claim of this book is that informational concepts and practices shape not only the internal thematics of literature but also the ways in which we make meanings from texts. Writers and readers, including literary critics, have frequently been inclined to resist the rise of information, and this, too, is part of the story.

If the fall of literature into information is disenchanting for some, it can feel especially precipitous when a superabundance of data and documents encroaches on aesthetic experience—when information overload and textual excess threaten to dispel literary pleasures of unity, beauty, and immersion. The predicted death of the codex in our digital age has not come to pass, but there is a sense (and some evidence) that readers are too distracted by multitudinous screens and texts to lose themselves in any single book, while the broad ascendency of data-based knowledge is continuing to supersede humanistic authority. To choose a pointed example, the use of computers to understand literature under the auspices of the digital humanities (or DH) has gone beyond the provision of electronic resources for conventional literary criticism and now includes the statistical analysis of thousands of texts generally termed *distant reading*. That is, literary criticism has come to entail not only the careful interpretation of single texts but also the algorithmic study of keywords and syntactical patterns across corpuses of books too large for anyone to read. For some commentators, distant reading is an outrageous sign of the times and an abdication of literary study's aesthetic commitments. Literature is not data, one hears, no more than one can count the angels on the head of a pin.[3] To turn literature into information, some fear, is to diminish it or capitulate to scientism and technological utopianism. At stake is not only the legitimacy of computation-based criticism but the very status of literature and literary studies in our information age.

How one regards the situation is probably more personal than rational argument cares to admit. I like to think of myself as a sanguine scholar open to the copious possibilities of the times, but I worry that I'm more like Ishmael at the start of *Moby-Dick*—buffeted by resentments and forebodings—and that this book pursues a set of questions stirred as much by anxiety as by wonder. What happens to literature and literary studies in an information revolution? What sorts of meaningful claims can aesthetics maintain in an age of data and science? How does one experience and interpret literature when overwhelmed by huge quantities of texts? Or more radically, what is gained and lost by treating literature as information? Clearly such questions are animated by digital developments of the last few decades, yet a historically minded scholar seeking intellectual orientation and some measure of emotional reassurance might notice that concerns about the relationship of information and literature also loomed in nineteenth-century America and Britain. This history can temper humanist alarms about the ascendency of information. It can provide guidance for thinking about and addressing current challenges to literary studies. It can feel so uncanny that a modern critic might doubt if his wonder and anxiety are his own.

Before Big Data and Big Tech, before DH and the dominance of STEM fields, the nineteenth century witnessed an unprecedented proliferation of information that shaped the content and uses of literature. As advances in publishing, distribution, and literacy drove the rapid expansion of print culture, the era's surfeit of texts, including works of literature, required what we now call information management—from bibliographic ordering and bureaucratic regulation to the quantification of literature and literary practices. It is not only that authors wrote about information overload (though they certainly did); the managing of literature within information systems influenced aesthetics, archival practices, reading habits, and the production of literary knowledge. All this happened at a time when literary studies was establishing itself as a discipline and the word *information* took on modern connotations, referring not only to edification and news (something one comes across in everyday life) but also to objective, reconfigurable data (something that functions within rule-bound systems). Debates over the fate of literature in our information age tend to swing between presentist celebration and despair, but they are powerfully conditioned by the nineteenth century, which encountered its own information revolution with wonder and anxiety. How readers and writers responded—and are responding—to the rise of information is the subject of *Overwhelmed*.

⁂

At the heart of this book is a revisionist argument about two loosely constructed domains. The first is what I call "the literary"—associated with beauty, subjectivity, interpretation, emotion, intuition, and the immersive pleasures of unified texts. The other is what I call "the informational"—characterized by instrumentalism, objectivity, transparency, bureaucratic impersonality, calculation, and reconfigurable data. Neither of these domains is internally coherent: interpretation and immersion can inhibit each other; bureaucracies are often opaque. Nor are they mutually exclusive: beauty can be instrumental; data spark feelings and intuitions. Much of what follows challenges hard distinctions between the literary and the informational, in part because differences between the two are less about ontological status (for instance, the type of text in question) and more about modes of understanding and practice (how we think about and what we do with a text). To say that the literary and the informational are porous, overlapping, and contingent is not to deny meaningful distinctions between them but rather to suggest that their relationship is most productively approached, not with formal analysis and brightly lined categories, but through the messy work of history.

That history, as I see it, is marked by the emergence of overdetermined dualisms. Terminology and dynamics shift unevenly over time, of course, but the literary and the informational remain recognizable confederations that generations of critics have set at odds, oftentimes tracing divisions to—and projecting them onto—the nineteenth century. New Critics invoked romantic legacies when defining literary aesthetics against information. The Frankfurt school went beyond Weber in positioning art against rationality and calculation. Poststructuralists rejected empiricism, positivism, and utilitarianism when drawing on Kantian and Nietzschean traditions, as did New Historicists, who emphasized the interpretation of singular phenomena over the objective analysis of large data sets. Other historians have traced the separation of science and literature into the romantic period, and even specious but persistent neurological notions of left-brain logic versus right-brain creativity are taken to begin in the nineteenth century, as if our very minds are split between information and art. Some recent literary scholarship challenges such dualisms—from work that draws on scientific methods, to statistical analyses in the digital humanities, to arguments from some quarters that critique should move toward (not against) empiricism and facts, to approaches that constrain interpretive license by dwelling on textual surfaces, denotations, and thin descriptions.[4] Yet the resistance that such scholarship can engender, particularly when rendering literature as data, indicates that, for all the talk of interdisciplinarity, the information/literature divide remains powerfully ingrained.

Something similar can be said of broader cultural formations that point toward an enduring habitus. In nineteenth-century literature, romantic and racialized characters stand outside informational modernity. Artist figures struggle as information workers—see, for example, Melville's Bartleby, George Gissing's Edwin Reardon, or Edith Wharton's Lily Bart. Unimaginative empiricists and utilitarian businessmen square off against, and sometimes manage to woo, feminine figures of aesthetic sensibility (Hawthorne's Roger Chillingworth and Hester Prynne, George Eliot's Edward Casaubon and Dorothea Brooke, or less disastrous pairings in Charles Dickens and Harriet Beecher Stowe that reinforce the dualisms they reconcile). Such common nineteenth-century fare can feel all too familiar these days. Though Steve Jobs may be idolized as a romantic genius and postmodernism can pursue dark obsessions with information, popular imaginings in our digital age still tend to juxtapose the informational and the literary. We have the emotionally stunted, fashion-challenged coder, the Dionysian artist who bucks bureaucratic order, and aestheticized women and racial others supposedly unfit for informational enterprises. When I was an undergraduate, we joked about "fuzzies" versus "techies," which was funnier before some people rode the rising tides of Silicon Valley and the STEM fields while others of us took our solitary way through the shadow of the valley of the humanities crisis. As much as one aspires to intellectual liberality, a critic might struggle with ungenerous feelings when the literary is not only defined against but subordinated to the informational. That such asymmetry turns out to have roots in one's chosen historical period adds irony to indignity and injury.

Yet as much as the nineteenth century shapes present-day dualisms between information and literature, its historical dynamics are less determined than our scholarly legacies and cultural stereotypes suggest. As print culture exploded in the nineteenth century, the outpouring of texts increasingly required organizational and analytic methods that rendered literature as information; and as they do today, readers and writers responded in diverse ways. Some resented the incursions of the informational into literary domains as easy access to print menaced tastemakers, statistics competed with aesthetic representations, and industrial publishing, standardized education, and the library movement threatened intimate relationships with books. Other people embraced the information revolution's influence on literature and literary practices. Authors imagined mastering superabundant information, as when artistically sensitive characters show a knack for navigating archives. Readers found calculative narratives enchanting, including detective fictions and adventure novels that involve probabilistic reasoning and informational savvy. Some literary critics adopted informational methods in bibliographic projects and pioneering statistical analyses. Reactions to the rise of information were richly mixed, as when Charlotte Brontë in *Villette* (1853) discusses factuality as necessary but subordinate to imaginative art, or when Edgar Allan Poe alternately celebrates and satirizes the growing authority of information in his age. The nineteenth century could champion an autonomous realm of aesthetics beyond the purview of system and logic, but even when the literary asserted its distinctiveness, it still worked—ambivalently, agonistically, collaboratively—within its information age. The watchwords here are entanglement instead of estrangement, accommodation as well as antagonism. To speak too generally, the literary/informational divide emerged unevenly in the nineteenth century, hardened in the middle of the twentieth, and is ripe for reconsideration today—not only in the name of revisionist history, but in the service of the future of literature.

Which is to say that the nineteenth century establishes the conditions for our possible negotiations between the literary and the informational—even if my gestures toward "rises" (instead of "origins") acknowledges trajectories beginning well before 1800, even if claims of present relevance (what's past is prologue) remains a last refuge for historicist scoundrels. The question of continuity versus change bears on all historical thinking but is especially weighty when assessing our digital revolution, which too often is viewed as a radical break. Proponents of continuity can go too far when they argue that daily newspapers are like the internet, or epistolary networks function like social media, or the telegraph is like Twitter. But nineteenth-century commentators believed that their era's vast productions of print and data would expand knowledge, increase efficiency, advance democracy, and enrich community life, even as they worried about information overload, unregulated communications, fake news, shrinking attention spans, and the decline of privacy. Our informational dreams and nightmares have a surprisingly deep past, for if physical pages are not digital texts and Poole's and Reuters are not Google, nineteenth-century discussions of information often feel familiar because they are part of a long revolution. Yuval Noah Harari has speculated that superabundant information drove the invention of literacy in the ancient world, while book historians have shown, in Robert Darnton's words, that "every age was an age of information."[5] The nineteenth century did not invent mass print, bibliography, statistics, and bureaucracy, but it witnessed the spread of information systems into new areas of life, including literary ones.

Overwhelmed focuses on literature, though it construes the category broadly. Not only did some unexpected archives assert their explanatory force, but the topic of excessive information can exert a kind of entropy in which inclinations toward close reading and author-centric inquiry give way to more capacious hermeneutic practices. Main objects of study in the chapters that follow include canonical nineteenth-century literary texts from the United States and Britain, and lesser-known novels about lost worlds, school life, and office work, as well as writings gathered from the street-stalls and databases of the earth (poems about libraries, comments on bibliomania, inscriptions scrawled in children's books). Major figures include Coleridge, Emerson, Hawthorne, Dickens, Charlotte Brontë, Fanny Fern, Frank Webb, and Robert Louis Stevenson—a transatlantic lineup attesting to the period's widening circulation of information and literature, though one more driven by thematic and theoretical connections than by efforts to mobilize transnationalism as a method. A trained Americanist such as me can, like a Henry James ingénue, mistake familiarities with Britain for more intimate knowledge, but studying superabundance can remind the anxious critic that mastery of even a narrowly defined field is impossible and that mutually illuminating competencies help to trace the transatlantic dynamics of nineteenth-century literature and information.

I wish I could say that my selection of authors and texts consistently reflects a grand strategy or set of principles, but my sense is that serendipity and chance have played unusually large roles in the composition of this book. I happened to be reading *Treasure Island* (1883) and watching *Raiders of the Lost Ark* (1981) with my kids when thinking about how numbers function in literature, and the endless connections of database searching led down many another unanticipated path. There is some truth to the trope of the wayward antiquarian stumbling upon a key document in the chaos of the archives, but if textual excess invites random encounters, patterns—intentional and otherwise—also figure. Some pairings of major authors in this book follow established lines of affinity, while many works were sought out because they engage an idiosyncratic theme. Authors such as Poe, Thoreau, Melville, Mary Shelley, George Eliot, Henry James, and W.E.B. Du Bois are deeply invested in informational projects but in the end have only cameos in this book for reasons no better than limited time and space. More worrisome, many of my primary texts were written by white men, which can indicate how women and people of color were discouraged from entering informational domains but might also point to some narrowness of reading on my part.[6] Chapter 2 will discuss how textual excess complicates any objective and comprehensive gathering of evidence, and so as broadly as this book samples from nineteenth-century literature, elaborations and corrections are surely in order.

If the nineteenth century created literary canons as a way to organize textual superabundance, it also witnessed the proliferation of documents that do not conform to such structuring.[7] Some objects of study in the chapters that follow come from what print historians call "informational genres," including those that, in Lisa Gitelman's words, "embrace the subjects and instruments of bureaucracy or of systematic knowledge generally."[8] I have been particularly drawn to unscrutinized materials that focus on literature and literary practices but do not take traditional literary forms. Surveys of reading habits and reports on publishing data, antiquarian journals and reference books, early statistical literary criticism and

Victorian standardized literature tests—such documents can contextualize canonical works in the service of high interpretation, but they also deserve attention in their own right as texts that straddle emerging boundaries between the literary and the informational. The facts they bear are often fascinating: among nine-year-old Chicago schoolgirls in 1897, for example, the most popular works of fiction were "Little Red Riding Hood," *Robinson Crusoe*, and *Little Women* in that order.[9] Equally important are the methods and forms of factuality with which informational genres order, analyze, and authorize the literature they treat. Making lists of best books and counting adverbs in Shakespeare struck many in the nineteenth century as misguided, though also telling (and, to me, more surprising) is how seriously some literary writers regarded informational projects, as when Emerson indexes his sprawling journals, or Webb weighs the costs and benefits of bureaucratic impersonality, or Charlotte Yonge and Louisa May Alcott critique standardized education.

As these materials suggest, *Overwhelmed* treats a lot of texts. An irony of the nineteenth century's information revolution is that efforts to control the explosion of print acted as a kind of accelerant, as when cultural authorities sought to regulate the era's profusion of books by issuing a profusion of books on "right reading." Similarly, a twenty-first-century literary critic intent on making sense of information overload can wind up studying a dizzying number of texts that both dramatize and exacerbate the glut. My excuse is that I find both explanatory power and wonder in overwhelming archives, and my hope is that by taking on as much as it does, this book shows how the nineteenth century's struggle with textual excess conditions the state of our criticism. The intensive reading of small numbers of texts remains at the core of literary studies, at least for now, but as in the nineteenth century, fantasies of escaping informational excess are just that.

So much literature, and so much scholarship! Current work on information in the humanities feels like an interdisciplinary colloquium in which conversations overlap and diverge in exciting and at times incoherent ways. We have excellent histories of the book that examine information overload in Britain and Europe from the fourteenth through eighteenth centuries.[10] Such work shows that superabundance matters—that even if the physical form of the codex has not changed much over the centuries, large quantities of texts make qualitative differences in how books are conceptualized and used. The foundations for similar claims have been laid by print historians who focus on nineteenth-century Britain and America, while literary critics have long studied how the period's accelerating production of texts transformed literary markets, authorship, and reading publics.[11] What has not received sustained attention is how literature under conditions of excess is shaped by the rise of information.

To take up this question is to join a developing synthesis of literary studies, media studies, the history of science, and information history and theory—fields coalescing unevenly around the topic of information increasingly understood as a thickly mediated, deeply historical, and theoretically complex phenomenon. Media studies came early to the subject, but because it tends to dwell on technological disruptions, especially film and the digital, when it does track information into the nineteenth century, it often privileges innovations such as telegraphy and radio over the "old"— and, in my mind, more influential—revolution of mass print.[12] Following Friedrich Kittler but resisting his sense of epistemic rupture, Gitelman and other media archaeologists are emphasizing continuities between new technologies and nineteenth-century informational genres.[13] Such work overlaps with cultural histories of information, and literature occasionally figures in the discussion, though typically as objects within information systems rather than as an entangled discourse that reflects on its own status.[14] A central premise of this book is that literature talks with—and back to—the informational.

Less integrated than book and media histories in discussions of nineteenth-century literature are histories of science that track developments in mensuration, calculation, and data analysis. When confronted with superabundant objects of study, most disciplines turn to numbers, which become more prevalent in the nineteenth century as sociology, ethnography, history, and the life sciences begin using quantitative methods.[15] During a period in which statistics grew into a science and statistical thinking spread through Anglo-American culture, readers and writers quantified the outpourings of print and sought to measure literary qualities. Because statistical logic subordinates individuality, interiority, and ambiguity to the calculative power of numbers, it is often regarded as antithetical or irrelevant to literary epistemologies and values. Yet as controversial as distant reading is today, we lack robust descriptions of similar practices as they emerged in the nineteenth century. Jerome McGann has recently worried that the digital humanities risks operating under an "increasingly attenuated historical sense," while Andrew Piper writes of literary studies and computational science, "We are talking not only past each other, but also past the past itself."[16] To study how literature was counted in the nineteenth century, and to reconstruct reactions to such counting, is to expand our historical understanding of DH and the debates that surround it today.

Closest to the aspirations of this book is literary criticism that can be roughly grouped in two clusters. The first focuses on the relationship between literature and information in and around the nineteenth century, including Mary Poovey's work on factuality and epistemology (primarily in Britain before 1820), Richard Menke's study of telegraphy (with an emphasis on Victorian realism), and a growing body of scholarship on information and literary modernism.[17] Such work situates the rise of information in different eras, does not share a single definition of the term (more on which below), and though it acknowledges the proliferation of data and texts, does not dwell on information overload. A second cluster of literary scholars examines the period's textual excess with an eye toward twenty-first-century concerns but remains more committed to book and print history than to information as an elaborated discourse. Here I'm thinking of Meredith McGill's *American Literature and the Culture of Reprinting, 1834–1853* (2003), Leah Price's *How to Do Things with Books in Victorian Britain* (2012), Ellen Gruber Garvey's study of reconfigurable scrapbooking, and Piper's work on the relationship between books and digital texts and between literary imagination and bibliographic forms.[18] Wandering the forests of relevant scholarship, I have felt a bit like Goldilocks—thankful for the resources I come across and sample but too particular to find any just right. This Media is too New! This era is too old! This book is insufficiently obsessed with information! Mindful of the ways in which Goldilocks has been chastened, it seems to me there is much to learn about how literature and information come fitfully into their own.

As should be apparent by this point, my own methodological commitments tend toward a historicism that remains dominant in literary studies, yielding among other things interpretations of texts animated by contexts of their time. Such readings should be regarded as case studies—strong in the ways of thick description and inference, susceptible to the dark forces of anecdotalism and subjectivity. One might wonder under conditions of superabundance what type of evidence-based argument is not to some degree a case study, though to contextualize and constrain their interpretive efforts, some of the chapters that follow move metacritically between close readings, broader literary histories, and statistical analyses (including a critique of confirmation bias in database searching and a modest experiment in distant reading). Multiscalar approaches are relatively rare in literary criticism, for if the field has long practiced a theoretical and interdisciplinary catholicity that runs from the fecund to the flaky, data-based scholarship in the digital humanities remains difficult to synthesize with other critical methods, in part because of abiding divisions between the literary and the informational.[19] This book is more a prehistory of the digital humanities and its reception than a project within its purview, though studying the entanglements of literature and information may benefit from similarly entangled approaches, despite and because of potential friction. One gambit of what follows is that the relationship between literature and information can be simultaneously historicized and performed.

Another point to emphasize at the outset of this book, and one reason work on information is difficult to organize, is that the only thing on which scholars of information agree is that no one agrees on what information is.[20] The purpose here is not to posit a rigid definition but rather to provide some theoretical coordinates from outside literary studies to suggest how approaching information from a humanist perspective differs from but is ultimately compatible with information theory, including its mathematical roots. More specifically, the history of information theory shows it to increasingly accommodate the kinds of interpretive, complex meanings valued by literary scholars. We have grounds for understanding information as an interdisciplinary concept with practical uses for humanists.

A common way of conceptualizing information in scholarly and everyday contexts entails some version of a hierarchical model. Raw data rise to the status of information when ordered, formed, and otherwise manipulated so as to communicate meaning and enact intentions. Information then reaches the level of knowledge when analysis, validation, ideology, and method render it sufficiently authoritative. Though information theorists seldom go so far, knowledge might progress toward something like wisdom, which is the hierarchy T. S. Eliot envisions in his now frequently quoted lines: "Where is the wisdom we have lost in knowledge? / Where is the knowledge we have lost in information?"[21] As most people tend to use the term, information occupies a middle ground between unprocessed data and more significant knowledge. Yet such distinctions are easily troubled—not simply because data is never raw, and not only because thresholds between epistemological states are difficult to identify, but also because information is not a stable thing or even a thing at all.

Scholars make this case when tracing the origins of information theory to Claude Shannon's "Mathematical Theory of Communication" (1948), an essay that proposes a series of theorems on the efficiencies and probabilities of transmitting information. For Shannon, who had a background in electrical engineering, information results from a process involving senders, messages, transmission technology, noise, and receivers. Because the communication of information requires the violation of signal patterns so as to register differences, Shannon defines a system's information potential as the measure of freedom possessed by a sender. Put another way, the amount of information a message contains is equivalent to how much it breaks a pattern, which can be regarded as its unpredictability or capacity to surprise a receiver. Shannon can thus help a literary critic regard information as constituting, not constraining, creative communication, as when Shannon cites Joyce's *Finnegans Wake* (1939) when discussing how complex vocabularies achieve high levels of potential surprise.

Further suggesting how mathematical accounts of information might be brought to bear on literary topics, the information philosopher Luciano Floridi mentions Poe's "The Raven" (1845) when glossing Shannon's point that utterly predictable messages, such as the bird's repetitive cry, carry no information.[22] Perhaps the claustrophobic, solipsistic unease of Poe's highly patterned and thus relatively predictable poem evokes the terror of an information vacuum: our deepest sorrows are beyond communication; information ("lore") will be forgotten; reading volumes will provide no succor; your chamber shall have Wi-Fi nevermore. Perhaps, too, Shannon can help explain Melville's Bartleby, whose repetitive responses, like the dead letters of the story, fail to transmit information—a critique of bureaucracies that perform no informational work, and a crisis for the narrator and reader of the tale who expect some measure of communication. To repeatedly "prefer not" is to make no distinctions, admit no differences, break no patterns, and thus send no signals, unless the lack of a signal itself signals the failure of information.[23] Be that as it may, the problem with Shannon's information theory is that semantics (that is, meaning) remains in his words "irrelevant to the engineering problem," which is why his theorems are best fitted for rule-bound actors such as mechanical ravens and scriveners who would fail the Turing test.[24] Crucially, Shannon helps us conceive of information as a process, not a thing, but in and of itself, his system remains of limited use for the meaning-making work of humanistic inquiry, as if information theory (to quote from "The Raven") bears "little relevancy" to the domain of the literary.[25]

However, information theorists following Shannon were quick to address the challenge of semantics, even if doing so foregrounded interpretation and culture while pressing mathematics into the background. In an influential 1949 article, Warren Weaver retained some of Shannon's resistance to semantics while also expanding his conceptual reach. As if to rebuke the protagonist of Henry James's *In the Cage* (1898), Weaver writes: "An engineering communication theory is just like a very proper and discreet girl accepting your telegram. She pays no attention to the meaning." But Weaver also speculates on the potential applicability of Shannon's theories to writing, performance, and the arts, ending his essay by acknowledging "one of the most significant but difficult aspects of meaning, namely the influence of context."[26] Weaver in this way recognized that the potentialities of information depend on its use in the social world.

Systems theorists working with information theory would continue to focus on such contingencies. Citing Weaver and defining information as "a difference that makes a difference," Gregory Bateson in 1972 adopted Shannon's criteria of pattern breaking (difference) while adding the requirement that it must also be meaningful (must "make a difference") by changing the state of another system. Bateson argued that abstract computational models struggle to register semantic specificities, and he referred to Shakespeare, Stevenson, and Henry Wadsworth Longfellow when suggesting that literature is especially adept at enacting the "seeming magic" of communication.[27] Niklas Luhmann would draw on Bateson's work when positing an even more dynamic model: "A meaning system obtains information from its environment. One might say that it interprets surprises. In turn, this particular information processing system is integrated into a network of systems that reacts to it."[28] For Luhmann, pattern violation is open to multiple hermeneutic possibilities (a system "interprets surprises"), while any meaning made from received information is in turn interpreted within a larger environment. Understood as such, information can be taken to occur within what Kittler has termed "discourse networks" or what are often referred to now as media ecologies, while messages under such conditions take on what Stuart Hall has called a "fluidity of meaning."[29] To a literary critic, such complexities are intuitive and welcome. Information is not some essential unit within a stable hierarchy; it involves the communication of meaning through various media connecting subjects and systems that make interpretations within rhetorical, temporal, social, and epistemological contexts.

One telling example of how the literary is difficult to keep out of information theory is the transcript of a 1950 Macy Conference session that included Shannon, Weaver, and Bateson, as well as the anthropologist Margaret Mead, the cyberneticist Norbert Wiener, and the mathematician Leonard Savage. Shannon presented on statistical approaches to cryptology, but discussion moved quickly from his probability models to literary and everyday examples—the verbal density of Joyce, attribution controversies in Shakespeare, the absurdity of reading Goethe's *Faust* in French, the meaningful redundancy of saying "I love you," the difference between humans and machines. There is some joshing about Shannon's disregard for semantics when he is asked about what book he used for his statistical experiments. Shannon: "I just walked over to the shelf and chose one." Savage: "There is the danger that the book might be about engineering." The group's turn toward meaning leaves Shannon behind as participants reflect on their lived experiences with language; and when Shannon is invited to comment at the end of the session, he admits: "I never have any trouble distinguishing signals from noise because I say, as a mathematician, that this is signal and that is noise. But there are, it seems to me, ambiguities that come in at the psychological level."[30] Ambiguity, psychology, the social world, love, our lived realities with language—information considered as semantically rich includes message and media, content and context, the sender's intention and the receiver's interpretation, the mysterious workings of the mind and heart. It's starting to sound like literature.

This is not to elaborate a history of information theory from the perspective of literary criticism, as does N. Katherine Hayles.[31] The simpler point is to challenge hard distinctions between the literary and the informational by sketching how information theory, including its mathematical foundations, comes to accommodate humanistic inquiry. As Geoffrey Nunberg has written regarding definitions of information, "the question we want to ask is phenomenological rather than lexicographical: not, What does 'information' mean? but rather, How is the impression of 'information' constituted out of certain practices of reading and the particular representations that support them?"[32] Mathematical approaches to information theory can be too narrow and abstract for some humanists, but Nunberg and other post-Shannon thinkers acknowledge how experience, culture, and history constitute the work of information.

Let me also add a final premise that draws together definitional questions and a primary concern of this book. Because communication systems, discourse networks, and media ecologies are made up of relations that have virtually no end, information can be robustly conceptualized as such only by acknowledging the dynamics of superabundance. Information, it seems to me, always entails the potential of overload and the imperatives of management. Its disarticulated surfeit exists under the assumption, though sometimes deferred or repressed, that it must be rendered knowable and usable through some kind of systematic processing. Much of what we do with information and literature—gather, classify, store, search, privilege, aggregate, analyze, validate, forget—implies an excess that must in some way be handled, if only to leave certain portions behind. To repurpose William James (whose pragmatism emphasizes differences that make a difference, and whose pluralism posits unending relations), information is not an ontological Thing but rather something that happens to communication, including literary texts. Grammar notwithstanding, information is a gerund, a formulation that governs the structure of this book.

Chapter 1, "Reading," recovers some roots of modern literary criticism by showing how some romantics respond to textual excess by variously resisting and adopting informational strategies of skimming and excerpting. A main concept here is what I call "deserted island reading," an ideal of immersive literary experience formed in opposition to mass print. The fantasy of losing oneself in a book unfolds across the legacy of *Robinson Crusoe* (1719), which projects an account of intensive hermeneutics from the eighteenth through the nineteenth centuries. Deserted island reading was especially attractive to romantics such as Coleridge, a founding figure of modern close reading whose aesthetics and interpretive practices were formed under the pressures of information. But whereas Coleridge offers an agonistic example of the relationship between information and literature, Emerson presents a more modulated case in which the prophet of subjectivity, intuition, and motility proves surprisingly open to informational modes of reading. Romanticism has long been associated with autonomous aesthetics, though Coleridge, Emerson, and others face up to a question that literary critics learned to bracket but have come to ponder anew: What happens to the reading of literature in an information revolution?

Chapter 2, "Searching," takes up a related methodological question: How can literary meaning be recovered under conditions of information overload? Revitalizing debates over New Historical evidentiary practices that have become exponentially more powerful with the rise of digital databases, this chapter discusses how the nineteenth century's expansion of archives and concomitant attention to bibliographic processes impelled some literary thinkers to assert a special authority in matters of archival searching. As if to vindicate the value of literary judgment, Hawthorne and Dickens imagine the aesthetic retrieval of exceptionally meaningful texts, though in doing so they turn away from close reading and toward the management of information. An obverse irony is evident in reference books designed to manage textual excess, including the antiquarian journal *Notes and Queries* (begun in 1849) and *Bartlett's Familiar Quotations* (first published in 1855), both of which privilege organization over aesthetics but cannot help but admit the pleasures of texts. Across the nineteenth century, readers and writers subjected literature to informational searching techniques—a concern this chapter projects into the twenty-first century with a statistical experiment that asks whether the influence of the slavery crisis on *The Scarlet Letter* (1850) can be settled with algorithmic searching.

The penetration of quantification into literary discourse is the subject of chapter 3, "Counting." Lovers of literature could resist information and wax nostalgic for the deserted island reading of their youths, but adventure novels of the long nineteenth century show how what I call "the accounting of literature" could also be aesthetically enchanting. British and American adventure novels from the period register a productive tension: guided by atavistic, preindustrial texts (ancient manuscripts, hieroglyphics, maps written in blood), characters flee from civilized realms marked by information overload only to impose informational modernity on the deserted islands and lost worlds they find. This chapter explores the limits and wonders of quantification by using a sustained multiscalar approach—a close reading of Stevenson's *Treasure Island*, a literary-historical argument that draws on a dozen transatlantic adventure fictions, and a distant reading project based on keyword frequencies in a corpus of 105 adventure novels. At issue is not only how nineteenth-century literature accommodated the rise of information but also the prospect that the digital humanities might begin to tell a deeper history of itself.

The fourth and final chapter, "Testing," sets aside questions of textual excess to discuss mass assessments and the production of literary knowledge—or perhaps more accurately, literary information. As the rise of liberal meritocracy in the Victorian period increasingly required bureaucratic impersonality and quantitative metrics, standardized literature tests negotiated between aesthetics and information during the formation of literary studies as a discipline. Literature exams from normal schools, the British Civil Service, and the US Bureau of Indian Affairs reflect broader controversies over what constitutes literary knowledge and whether it can be systematically assessed. Such concerns involve epistemological problems (how can one standardize and measure literary attainments?), as well as social questions (what is the role of literature and literary studies under liberal meritocracy?). Race, gender, and class inflect depictions of standardized examinations in novels by Dickens, Brontë, Trollope, Fern, Webb, Yonge, Alcott, and others. These and other texts anticipate aspects of our current crisis in the humanities—accountability through testing, the corporatization of education, and the instrumental value of the literary. Like previous chapters, "Testing" examines the distance between the nineteenth and twenty-first centuries—in this case by turning to the Common Core standards and the GRE subject test in English literature, present-day standardized efforts to render literary learning as information.

Reading, searching, counting, testing—this is what my book is about, though I am not an objective observer. Thus with real curiosity and in the spirit of performing the informational, here is another way of describing the contents of *Overwhelmed*. An enumeration of frequent terms and their variants in my manuscript (excluding endnotes and this introduction) indicates a range and proportion of interests that, for all the obvious limits of the exercise, do not feel to me untoward:

1. literature (790 occurrences)
2. reading (554)
3. information (552)
4. book (472)
5. text (287)
6. history (262)
7. novel (261)
8. exam (228)
9. standard (216)
10. aesthetic (212)
11. century (211)
12. print (210)
13. test (185)
14. writing (179)
15. critic (172)
16. America (167)
17. Emerson (154)
18. nineteenth (152)
19. account (150)
20. quantity (149)
21. number (145)
22. work (142)
23. Dickens (139)
24. like (123)
25. time (118)
26. scholar (112)
27. question (112)
28. practice (111)
29. Crusoe (111)
30. new (111)

Numbers 31–40: island (107), method (106), education (105), world (105), knowledge (100), modern (97), culture (96), data (94), England (91), search (90)

I also counted words associated with wonder (pleasure, joy, beauty, enchantment, etc.) and anxiety (worry, fear, suspicion, disenchantment, and so forth). This measure is blunt to the point of inconsequence, and yet I found myself relieved—and surprised by some joy—that the number of words associated with wonder exceed those of anxious language 363 to 142. That's nearly 72 percent wonder! In retrospect, the ratio seems to me a fair estimate of my moods when thinking about the subject of this book. If we have plenty of reasons to doubt the future of literature in our information age, encountering literature, even under duress, leaves open the possibilities of redemption. To be overwhelmed is to be overcome by both threatening and pleasurable plentitudes.

CHAPTER ONE

Reading

> *I have chosen my boat, and laid in my scant stores. I have selected a few books; the principal are Homer and Shakespeare—But the libraries of the world are thrown open to me—and in any port I can renew my stock.*
> —MARY SHELLEY, *THE LAST MAN* (1826)

> *Alas! the days of desolate islands are no more!*
> —EDGAR ALLAN POE, 1836 REVIEW OF *ROBINSON CRUSOE*

HERE'S SOMETHING SUPPOSEDLY FUN: If you were stranded on a deserted island and could have only one book, which would you choose? The appeal of this question for lovers of literature seems obvious enough, as most of us like to talk about books and express our aesthetic sensibilities. Less obviously fun is the deserted island gambit, which is actually quite grim. Do we need a shipwreck or plane crash and all our fellow travelers killed just to enjoy some close reading? It might feel that way sometimes, and not simply because formal explication has come to share explanatory power with historical context, theoretical mindfulness, and familiarities across the disciplines. Negotiations of this sort have been going on for half a century without leading to imagined extremes (the disintegration of texts, the end of the canon, the death of aesthetics, and so on). These days, a supposedly new anxiety haunts the prospects of literature. As our current information revolution reaches what can feel like terminal velocity, the most significant threat to the kind of attentive, interpretive, pleasurable reading generally associated with literature is the inconceivable quantity of texts so easily retrieved from digital databases, a superabundance that when managed with computational tools makes capacities for close reading seem measly by comparison. Every unread text on HathiTrust, every unclicked link on Google Books, every unheeded recommendation from Amazon can feel like an admonishment to those whose profession is textual mastery, sometimes—and absurdly—regarded as a combination of comprehension and comprehensiveness.

Under such conditions, careful reading may become a fading fetish, non-reading will extend its rich literary history, and Franco Moretti's statement from two decades ago appears increasingly prophetic: "Reading 'more' is always a good thing, but not the solution."[1] Literary scholars have good reasons to sense a sea change in our relations with texts, and yet for all the hand-wringing and euphoria over ongoing shifts in reading and interpretive practices, close reading has proven remarkably resilient under various literary-critical methods, and most scholars of literature still find themselves drawn to the scrutiny of specific works, just as most students still find themselves responsible for—and even excited about—individual texts.[2] When enthusiasm for our information revolution falters, and when one reflects on what makes literature meaningful and wonderful, one still might dream of a deserted island with just one book to command attention.

If fantasies of close reading and anxieties of textual superabundance are, as I'm suggesting, mutually constituted, then literary scholars who value intensive hermeneutics should not offhandedly reject methods of criticism that take up large numbers of texts. Over the last decade, reading has become a flood subject for historical, theoretical, and empirical inquiry, spurred in part by work in and around the digital humanities that presents the starkest alternatives to close reading today. Debates over the fate of books in our distracted age of screens often focus on how we are or should be or will be reading.[3] Katherine Hayles's "hyper reading" describes a hermeneutic that jumps Parkour-like among multiple sources of information.[4] The distant reading now practiced in various forms subjects thousands of texts to statistical analyses often performed by teams of scholars that do not read the writings they study. Data-mining projects algorithmically read for allusions, collocations, and topic clusters, while quantitative print histories and some aspects of "surface reading" share affinities with DH criticism.[5] If in the middle of the twentieth century, punch-card-driven stylometric analysis was largely regarded as a curiosity, today's computer-assisted literary study now enjoys a status that warrants more serious engagement, particularly as the internet supercharges worries over shallow knowledge and information overload and as commentators react fiercely to the very suggestion of conceptualizing literature as data.[6]

The disruptions of the digital have pushed literary scholars to pay renewed attention to reading, but it is also becoming increasingly clear that the nineteenth century anticipates twenty-first-century concerns over superabundance and the reading practices it generates. How reading fared under the proliferation of texts and information is a multifaceted question that this chapter takes up with three case studies: (1) an account of what I call "deserted island reading" in *Robinson Crusoe* (1719) and the novel's nineteenth-century reception; (2) a reconsideration of Samuel Taylor Coleridge's aesthetics in relation to textual excess, and (3) a look at Ralph Waldo Emerson's attitude toward extensive reading practices and his handling of large numbers of texts. These diachronic cases show how some literary thinkers approach reading as a negotiation between the literary and the informational. Taken together, they not only sketch a spectrum of responses to the challenge of information overload; they also trace a rough historical trajectory of reading that conditions twenty-first-century anxieties about the status of literature in our information age.

Crusoe's Book(s)

Before turning to the nineteenth century, a backward glance can acknowledge a longer history in which muddled continuities temper desires for clean narratives of origin and epistemic rupture. The nineteenth century was hardly the first to experience textual excess and information overload, a point rigorously demonstrated by historians of print such as Robert Darnton ("every age was an age of information"), Roger Chartier (we have inherited from the Middle Ages the "anxiety" of organizing books), Ann Blair (who traces concerns over textual superabundance from Seneca to medieval reference books to early modern notation systems), and Chad Wellmon (who studies the emergence of Enlightenment bibliography, including the trope of scholars being killed by falling bookshelves).[7] More specific to the question of how the proliferation of print and information influences conceptions of the literary, Lennard Davis, Michael McKeon, and especially Mary Poovey have focused on the eighteenth century, placing Daniel Defoe at a historical juncture where the mass production of texts and emergence of modern factuality begin shaping literature in a complex range of forms.[8] Poovey draws on Defoe's *Essay upon Projects* (1697) to discuss how informational methods undergird a liberal subjectivity fundamental to the rise of the novel, and she argues that *Roxana* (1724) as an exemplary print culture artifact points toward the construction of fiction as a genre. Poovey carries her arguments into the early nineteenth century where literary authorities, threatened by print culture, define disciplinary practices of close reading and canonization against the spread of facts and information. Nineteenth-century relations between the informational and the literary do indeed have much in common with those of the eighteenth, indicating not so much a moment of epistemic shift (as Friedrich Kittler and Geoffrey Nunberg would generally have it) as inflections in what Lisa Gitelman and Andrew Piper see as a more continuous evolution in print and media history.[9]

One inflection that distinguishes the nineteenth from the eighteenth century involves the application of informational methods to literature itself, a dynamic evident in *Robinson Crusoe* and its reception history. Indicating how information and its management spread irregularly across disparate domains, Defoe's novel does not extend its informational practices to the status of books themselves, though the nineteenth century worried over such possibilities, finding in *Crusoe* an object lesson and even totem for readers overwhelmed by mass print. Before the digital humanities, the Frankfurt school, and Weber's bureaucratized, rationalist modernity, nineteenth-century commentators on Defoe's deserted island novel wondered how literary reading could survive in an age of information.

Robinson Crusoe is famously packed with enumerated facts, but its treatment of books is oddly uneven. Marx and Weber were not wrong to see Crusoe as a proto-Enlightenment bookkeeper, and scholars from Ian Watt to Maximillian Novak and beyond have situated *Crusoe*'s investment in numbers within broader informational discourses of accounting and political economy.[10] Space, time, money, goods, animals, men, and Crusoe's own spiritual estate—such diverse and multiplying interests are all subject to Defoe's enumerations in a genre marked from its English origins by generative tensions between aesthetic enchantment and measurable materialism. Along with his robust will to inventory, Crusoe has "a competent Knowledge of the Mathematics," and Defoe himself studied under Charles Morton, who later became an influential mathematician and Baconian naturalist at Harvard College.[11] More than a merely practical accountant, Defoe appreciated computational schemes at a conceptual and imaginative level. In what seems today an otherwise straightforward section on double-entry bookkeeping in *The Complete English Tradesman* (1726), Defoe cannot help but admire an illiterate, innumerate shopkeeper who keeps his accounts by making notches on sticks and placing them in a series of shelves, drawers, and boxes, some of them painted with customers' faces. The man uses spoons as a kind of crude abacus, but because he owns only six, he invents for himself a base-six numeral system, which— Defoe insists with admiration—serves him perfectly well. As suggested by Crusoe's struggles to keep accurate records, *Robinson Crusoe* reflects

Defoe's long-standing interests in material and methodological aspects of bookkeeping, though books themselves are largely excluded from an informational worldview that, as McKeon has generally argued, lacks "quantitative completeness."[12]

Despite the presence of multiple volumes on the island, and excluding Crusoe's own metaliterary journal, only one text essentially matters in *Robinson Crusoe*. Crusoe initially lists the books he salvages from his shipwreck—"Books of Navigation," "three very good Bibles," "some *Portugueze* Books," "three Popish Prayer-Books," and (as if Defoe's interest in the specificity of formal realism has been exhausted) "several other Books" (59). Yet outside of the Bible, none of these volumes is mentioned again, even in the bill of lading Crusoe makes when leaving his island. Alberto Manguel has noted that Crusoe, unlike Defoe, is not an "assiduous reader."[13] Except, I think, in the case of the Bible, which Crusoe initially happens upon randomly but eventually comes to read closely: "I took the Bible, and beginning at the New Testament, I began seriously to read it, and impos'd upon my self to read a while every Morning and every Night, not tying my self to the Number of Chapters, but as long as my Thoughts shou'd engage me" (89). Self-imposed, regulated, linear study sounds like the Robinson we know (no flakey hyper reading for him), though importantly Crusoe refuses to tie himself to numbers, instead allowing inclination and even chance to determine his reading, which we see later when he engages in bibliomancy at moments when his calculative reason fails. Crusoe may lack exegetical sophistication, and he provides a nonscholarly model of heroism, but his hermeneutic practices are actually quite nuanced, alternating between comprehensive, systematic methods we might associate with informational discipline and more intuitive, serendipitous, imaginative interpretation—a dialectic of head and heart, works and grace, typical not only of Puritan autobiography and Protestant exegesis, but also (as we shall see) of emerging reading practices associated with textual excess.

Significantly less modulated than Crusoe's reading habits is the object of his reading insofar as *Robinson Crusoe*, its paradigmatic setting notwithstanding, actually does not think to dramatize the question: If you were stranded on a deserted island and could have only one book, which would you choose? A modern reader of *Crusoe* can imagine rich thematics arising from the load of salvaged texts. Will those popish prayer books compete with the Bible or become an occasion for Puritan commentary? (No, Crusoe's thoughts on Catholicism are mixed, but they are neither agonistic nor polemical.) Will those Portuguese books invite meditations on differences in language, culture, and nation? (No, that role, howsoever limited, is mainly reserved for Friday.) Will the navigation manuals prove crucial to Crusoe's return to civilization in a mode of scientific self-reliance and middle-class self-cultivation? (No, Crusoe had already learned navigation as a youth.) Does the multiplicity of Bibles raise questions about translation or scriptural authenticity or the materiality of texts? (No, Crusoe is neither an exegete nor a book historian.) That the Bible is the primary text on Crusoe's island should come as no surprise. For the vast majority of Defoe's contemporaries, and given the salvific trajectory of *Robinson Crusoe*, the Bible is the only possible answer to the deserted island question.

Or more precisely, and as indicated by a search of Google Books, the deserted island question was not a real question until the twentieth century, and even in that supposedly secular era, the most popular answer is the Bible.[14] All this is to say that Crusoe's "choice" of reading is not really a choice at all, for despite its initial inclusion on a list, the Bible is less the Book of Books and more the One and Only Text as the soon-to-be-forgotten other volumes on the island serve as temporary props to material realism, not alternate courses of reading. Like Shakespeare in *The Tempest* (c. 1611), Defoe conjures an island but is ultimately uninterested in differences between singular and multiple books.[15] Whereas his *Journal of the Plague Year* (1722) and *Essay upon Literature* (1726) ruminate on the circulation and quantity of printed information, thus showing Defoe to be (in Paula McDowell's words) "a theorist of mediation," the earlier *Robinson Crusoe* imagines a castaway reader who does not register the pressures and thus even the absence of textual superabundance—as if Defoe (to use Poovey's word) is "oblivious" to how the informational might differ from the literary, as if (to repurpose Kittler's comments on Goethe's *Faust*) "[t]he order of representations excludes the representability of the act of production," as if Defoe in *Crusoe* has yet to reckon the print culture that his novel is helping to invent.[16]

This is decidedly not the case for later readers of *Robinson Crusoe* who took the novel as something of a pharmakon—as a work both outside and inside print culture, as both a refuge from and participant in overwhelming profusions of texts and information. Rousseau in *Emile* (1762) repeatedly rages against the proliferation of print ("Always books! What a mania.... Europe is full of books"), and his hostility leads toward a deserted island fantasy when, wishing for a simpler, less textual time, he notoriously selects *Robinson Crusoe* as the only book for the young Emile's library.[17] Closer to home, a 1775 article in London's *Monthly Review* praised Defoe but bemoaned his ink-stained progeny: "the breed of De Foes has so much increased, of late years, that hundreds of them are to be found in the garrets of Grubstreet, where they *draw nutrition, propagate and rot*: and nobody minds them."[18] The eighteenth century did not witness a "Reading Revolution" that suddenly eschewed close reading, but the period's surfeit of texts engendered less-than-mindful practices—the sort of casual browsing and sporadic dipping that historians of reading call "extensive."[19] As George Crabbe complained in "The Library" (1781) when contrasting modern readers and writers to the "patient Fathers" of previous generations:

> Our nicer palates lighter labours seek,
> Cloy'd with a Folio-number once a week. . . .
> Abstracts, Abridgments, please the fickle times,
> Pamphlets and Plays, and Politics and Rhymes.[20]

Yet as much as superabundant print and extensive reading formed a self-reinforcing cycle, the perennially popular *Robinson Crusoe* was seen as impervious to information overload, standing instead as an exemplary case of enchanted, immersive, very literary reading. Samuel Johnson, who according to Boswell read and wrote with "impatience and hurry," listed *Crusoe* as one of three books he actually wished longer.[21] Sir Walter Scott also appreciated Defoe's novel as an anomaly in print culture. While Scott reckoned *Crusoe*'s amazing popularity ("It is computed that within forty years from [its] appearance . . . no less than forty-one different *Robinsons* appeared, besides fifteen other imitations"), he was most impressed by how consumers of *Crusoe* "read every sentence and word upon every leaf" instead of treating the narrative (to quote Henry James's later complaint about novel readers) as "an exercise in skipping."[22] Novels were routinely both praised and condemned for both absorbing and distracting readers, and the genre was especially traduced for dulling mental acuity.[23] *Crusoe*, however, was often seen as an exception that commanded close attention in markets flooded with print, which leads to an irony implying a difference between how the early eighteenth and nineteenth centuries tended to understand the relationship between information and literature: the most influential book about a deserted island is not itself concerned with deserted island reading but becomes over the course of a century an occasion for valorizing such reading.

Reflections on textual superabundance frequently figured in nineteenth-century appraisals of *Robinson Crusoe* as observers on both sides of the Atlantic enumerated the novel's many editions, translations, abridgments, and adaptations, sometimes (like Scott) using statistics to describe the unprecedented proliferation of the book. Yet despite—and because of—a lengthening print history that was becoming increasingly visible, *Robinson Crusoe* (as it did for Rousseau) stirred nostalgia for a time of fewer books and closer reading, especially as the nineteenth century followed the eighteenth in sentimentalizing childhood innocence. An 1859 review of a reprinting of *Crusoe* defined it as a classic in contrast to "the enormous multiplication of new novels," and when the reviewer recalled his own childhood enchantment with the book, he joined an ever-lengthening line of commentators who constructed their personal relationships with *Crusoe* over and against mass print.[24] Some recalled receiving the book as a gift from a loved one or happening upon a dusty edition in an out-of-the-way closet or bookshelf. Others described taking the volume into the woods (probably in one of the many pocket-sized editions designed for easy conveyance into nature or on coaches and trains). One man remembered being beaten by a teacher for attending to *Crusoe* instead of his lessons (an attempted escape from institutionalized reading), while another found consolation in the novel when being sent away to boarding school (Defoe "reached his hand down through a century and a half to wipe away bitter tears from my childish eyes").[25] An 1842 commentator spoke for many when he rhetorically asked, "Who of us . . . does not look upon Robinson Crusoe as an old friend, an intimate companion of our boyhood?"[26]

Shawn Thompson has shown how *Crusoe* in nineteenth-century America became a locus of nostalgia for lost youth, while Patricia Crain has demonstrated how immersive childhood reading in general became a metonym for childhood itself as books mediated the social construction of modern, possessive selfhood.[27] The irony is that many nineteenth-century adults who reflected on their reading of *Robinson Crusoe* acknowledged the disenchanting superabundance of mass print while excepting Defoe from such mediating power, as if their intensive, absorbing, emotional reading could transmute *Crusoe* to Crusoe. John Ruskin—who fiercely opposed mass print, bemoaned his era's "baffling proliferation of information," and likened great literature to gold that must be mined and smelted "syllable by syllable—nay, letter by letter"—recalled how the simple images and "plain facts" of *Crusoe* ushered him into a world of wonder.[28]

Other intimations of youthful relationships with *Crusoe* appear on the flyleaves of nineteenth-century editions of the novel and can, to some degree, reduce the risk that recollections of childhood reading (quoting Crain) primarily "serve adult memory."[29] Of the American Antiquarian Society's sixty-eight editions of *Crusoe* published between 1800 and 1860, twenty-four are catalogued as inscribed, though an inspection of physical

FIGURE 1.1. From Daniel Defoe, *Robinson Crusoe* (Philadelphia: Key and Mielke, 1831), second flyleaf. In the collections of the American Antiquarian Society.

copies shows that at least thirty-five bear at least one signature. In 1811, it was probably Oliver Coleman himself who wrote "Oliver Coleman His Book" twice in ink before drawing an elaborate personal insignia on the endpaper. Along with practicing capital "L's" on his flyleaves, Luther Anderson signed his 1828 edition of *Crusoe* three times, each with a differently styled "L"—one of multiple examples of young writers working out their signatures in the blanks of *Crusoe*. A majority of *Crusoe*'s owners appear to have been male, though Charlotte Gardiner received her 1831 edition as "A preasent [*sic*] from Amos Barter[?]." The first flyleaf has two "Charlotte H. Gardiner" signatures—one barely legible, one in better penmanship, which is also the case with the pair of "C. H. Gardiner" inscriptions on the second flyleaf. The ink appears to be the same for all these inscriptions, suggesting that Barter or some other adult provided a model for (or elucidation of) the young Gardiner's scrawl. However, the endpaper of the volume has "Charlotte H. Gardner" written in elegant print with different ink and a carefully decorated border (see figure 1.1), as if an older Gardiner decided to take the ownership of *Robinson Crusoe* into her own hands and hand.[30]

A scholar can make all sorts of conjectures about scenes of gifting, reading, writing, and possession. Does "Dr. J. W. Leon to Dudley Leon" suggest a distant father-son or uncle-nephew relationship or remind us that personal book inscriptions are actually publicly performed acts? What do we make of the status dynamics suggested by an 1831 children's version of *Crusoe* that was "Presented to Master R. J. M Chase by his well-wishing friend and instructress Phebe"?[31] What were the links between successive owners of a single volume of *Crusoe* (some of whom crossed out previous names, some of whom let the lineages stand)? Marginalia and inscriptions often raise more questions than answers, including concerns about critical projection. Might the urge to interpret childlike signatures on flyleaves as evidence of personal relationships with *Crusoe* actually point most, not toward recoverable histories, but toward the fantasies of a middle-aged humanist scholar hoping to salvage signs of intimate codex reading in an adulthood dominated by digital texts?

Most literary critics have learned how difficult deserted island fantasies are to maintain, but whereas John Guillory and Rita Felski attribute disenchantment to professionalization and the hermeneutics of suspicion, many nineteenth-century readers of *Robinson Crusoe* blamed their lost innocence on the sheer quantities of books encountered by modern adults.[32] An 1836 notice of a new Harper's edition of *Crusoe* generalized about first readings of the novel:

> The boy leaves all his ruder sports for that engrossing pleasure which he has never known before, which probably he never will experience again—and all that the adult and sober man may do, is to confirm the judgment, while he must regret the half-vanished pleasure, of his childhood.[33]

John Major's preface to his 1831 edition of *Crusoe* more explicitly figured the novel as an anachronism set against mass print and extensive reading practices, just as George Cruikshank's memorable illustrations to the edition—like almost all the hundreds of woodcuts and engravings accompanying nineteenth-century versions of the novel—carefully depict Crusoe's material possessions without including his store of books. In the spirit of deserted island reading, Major notes that *Crusoe* invites unusually close attention ("There are few books one can read through and through"), quotes a poetic homage to the novel (that "Classic of Boy-hood's bright and balmy hour"), and takes William Cowper's wistful lines as an epigraph to the volume ("'Twere well with most, if books that could engage / Their childhood, pleas'd them at a riper age").[34] For many male commentators in the nineteenth century, *Crusoe* marked "an epoch in a boy's life," commemorating (to tweak some language from Kant) their emergence from immaturity to enlightenment.[35] In this sense, and as chapter 3 will emphasize, modernity happens not only to cultures moving through history but also to individual readers who come of age by entering information-rich contexts. Such contexts entail Weberian disenchantment (calculation, positivism, instrumentality), as well as a sense that life is short and the possibilities of reading long.

Even Poe—a clear-eyed critic, expert manipulator, and frequent victim of print markets—could not resist indulging (and also deploying) a misty backward glance at *Robinson Crusoe*. Though astounded that Defoe "wrote no less than *two hundred and eight* works," though complaining that "[n]ot one person in ten—nay, not one person in five hundred" truly appreciates *Crusoe*, and though linking Defoe with Benjamin Franklin (that Weberian maven of information and print who owned a copy of *Crusoe* but never cut the pages), Poe speaks for his audience when recalling "those enchanted days of our boyhood, when we . . . labored out, line by line, the marvelous import of [*Crusoe*'s] pages."[36] Poe's memory of intensive reading survives—and is sharpened by—an acute sense of textual excess that, in his review of *Crusoe* and elsewhere, he renders in numerical forms.[37] As Poe wrote more generally in his "Marginalia" (1850), itself an effort to feed the mass print economy: "The enormous multiplication of books in every branch of knowledge, is one of the greatest evils of this age; since it presents one of the most serious obstacles to the acquisition of correct information, by throwing in the reader's way piles of lumber, in which he must painfully grope for the scraps of useful matter."[38] Defoe's novel itself may be unencumbered by anxieties of information overload, but for many in the nineteenth century (including those who read *Crusoe* as children's abridgments, some of which used only single-syllable words), the novel conjured dreams of deserted island reading while at the same time initiating youthful readers into more sprawling, more harried worlds of print.

Some mid-nineteenth-century novels further contrast the enchantments of *Robinson Crusoe* with the informational excesses of modernity. In James Fenimore Cooper's *The Crater* (1847), an island utopia in the Robinsonade tradition is spoiled when its population grows so large as to require a census, governmental bureaucracy, and a printing press. In Dickens's *David Copperfield* (1850), the young protagonist finds some solace by escaping into *Robinson Crusoe*, though inevitably he must make his way through an adult world of lawyers, clerks, and accountants. The fugitive slave Hannibal in Harriet Beecher Stowe's *Dred* (1856) keeps a copy of *Robinson Crusoe* in his pastoral but doomed maroon colony, while the old-fashioned Gabriel Betteredge of Wilkie Collins's *The Moonstone* (1868) retreats repeatedly to *Crusoe* when overwhelmed by the informational complexity of events. All these examples admire Defoe's novel while regarding it with varying degrees of irony insofar as the comforts afforded by the book are shown to be unsustainable shelters from modernity. When Ebenezer Scrooge remembers loving "Robin Crusoe" as a child before becoming a man obsessed with his ledgers, he can only stammer, "I wish . . . but it's too late now."[39]

Of all these examples, Annie Carey's It-Narrative, *The History of a Book* (1873), most insistently presents *Robinson Crusoe* as a mass print culture pharmakon.[40] In Carey's narrative, an old man accidently leaves a "New Book" in an auction house full of "very old books," "rare MSS," and "waifs and strays from the library of a learned and eccentric man."[41] The yellowed tomes, some of them vellum, initially dismiss the shiny newcomer as a dandy. But then they learn his title, "The Life and Adventures of Robinson Crusoe," which accords him respect as the relative of a venerable volume dubbed "Defoe Senior" (13). This launches Carey into a history of print presented in dialogue form as the older books relate a chronology stretching from antiquity to Gutenberg to Caxton, while the New Book describes modern printing practices, including information on production, circulation, sales, pricing, and library holdings. For all the focus on books, the contents of texts are almost entirely ignored in *The History of a Book* until Carey concludes her narrative with a poignant reflection on reading. Marveling at the overwhelming quantity of new books, an old manuscript assumes, "The people of these days must be very great readers" (173). But while the New Book admits that moderns do indeed "read an immense number of volumes in a short space of time," he complains that such reading is more the skimming of ephemera than the intensive study of canonical works. Here fears of textual excess come to the fore, but when a crusty old quarto calls the proliferation of print "worse, far worse than waste," an edition of Virgil cites Pliny the Elder to praise the wide availability of books, a position the company ultimately applauds. In keeping with Carey's intention to connect the modern print industry to its noble artisanal roots—and in contrast to the late Victorian "slow-print" movement that was fiercely opposed to mass print—*The History of a Book* uses *Crusoe* to bridge the gap between premodern and contemporary print cultures.[42]

And yet the continuity that Carey envisions is problematized at the end of her book when the old man returns with his grandson in tow to retrieve the forgotten New Book. As the books recur to their status as objects, the scene—knowingly, it seems to me—displays the attraction and impossibility of returning to a time before mass print. The grandson pays no notice to the many yellowed volumes in the room, but when spotting the new illustrated edition of *Crusoe*, he cries, "This for *me*—my very *own*. Why it really *is* 'Robinson;' see, here he is in his real skin coat. You are a jolly good grandpapa" (176). Experienced readers, as if in compensation for adult disenchantment, may appreciate the ironies here. The child is already on a first-name basis with his intimate companion Robinson, whereas we—having just read Carey's history of mediacy—know the difference of (and deference due to) older books such as Defoe Senior. "[T]he happy, impatient child" is blithely unaware of the wealth and burden of a textual excess that overwhelms reading capacities. He has no sense of what it means to choose one book and leave myriad others behind. We, however, can associate Crusoe's "real skin coat" with the vellum and leather-bound books in the auction house, who may eventually find readers though almost surely not ones as singularly focused as the enchanted child. That the volumes in the storeroom belonged to a dead antiquarian marks the passing of a time when books in general were scarce and scrutinized. Earlier in her narrative, Carey acknowledges the growing market for rare books, but whether the tomes of the antiquarian are destined to be auctioned by the yard or sold at premium prices to bibliophiles, they will likely exist as part of a lot or collection, not as companions to be intimately read in the woods or decorated with personal insignia. *Crusoe* alone, and only in the mind of the child, escapes the history of books in *The History of a Book*. Jolly good experienced readers can look on wistfully, though how to read—and write—after the fall into excess is a question Carey leaves unaddressed.

One final allusion to *Robinson Crusoe* can serve as a conclusion to this section. In *The Mastery of Books: Hints on Reading and the Use of Libraries* (1896), Harry Koopman, head librarian of Brown University and future president of the American Library Association, imagined a student's first visit to the stacks:

> Which will prove the master? Will it be the boy, with his undeveloped and untrained mind, his ignorance of his own strength and weakness, and his entire unconsciousness of the tremendous forces locked up in the quiet rows of volumes about him? Is it not certain that the books, with the terrible odds in their favor, will prove an overmatch for the raw student?

Koopman's aim is to arm maturing (presumptively male) readers for their battles with superabundance. After some calculations—reading one book a day for fifty years totals less than twenty thousand volumes, far fewer than the holdings of many libraries—Koopman subordinates "methodical reading" to "rapid reading," which he calls "the art of skipping needless words and sentences."[43] After providing this advice on extensive reading— and after discussing note taking, memorization, and other informational techniques—Koopman's final chapter, "Books on the Subject of Reading," provides a bibliography of fifty-two reading guides, forty-one of which were published after 1880, including books containing their own substantial bibliographies of books on the subject of reading. It is not quite a Borgesean catalog of all catalogs, but when presenting his list of lists of books about books (or if one prefers, his list of books that list books), Koopman never acknowledges the irony that a multitude of monographs at the turn of the nineteenth century attempted to order and in doing so exacerbated the problem of textual excess. Closer to this truth is Koopman's poem, "The Librarian of the Desert" (1908), which imagines a librarian journeying from the "mad turmoil" of the world to a "desert hush" where no "din or rush / Distracts the ear or eye." God waits in this austere space to succor the overwhelmed reader for whom books have become an encumbrance, except, of course, for the Bible, "Like a footprint on the strand / That has hardened into stone."⁴⁴ In addition to the Book of Books, Koopman recalls *Robinson Crusoe* when imagining deserted island reading.

Coleridge's Anxiety of Authorship

Coleridge first read *Robinson Crusoe* in 1778, six years after his birth and four years after the discontinuation of perpetual copyright in Britain. He reread the novel numerous times as a youth, sometimes sequestered in a favorite sunny nook, and he later wrote in the margins of *Crusoe* at the age of fifty-eight, "this is De Foe's Excellence, you become a Man while you read."⁴⁵ Recalling *Crusoe* as a passage into mature reading is, as we have seen, fairly typical of the time, though Coleridge's comments show no sign of the mass print anxieties that frequently accompany such nostalgia. What Coleridge's marginalia do include among their many detailed notes is a parsing of Defoe's masterful use of a semicolon, which Coleridge considers worthy of Shakespeare. As a practitioner and theorist, Coleridge remains a founding figure of close reading. His organicism, with its emphasis on literary forms growing toward unity according to internal designs, shaped Anglo-American romantic aesthetics, as well as seminal twentieth-century literary scholarship associated with the New Criticism's insistence on close reading as an alternative to what Cleanth Brooks and Robert Penn Warren called "mere information."⁴⁶ Coleridge has powerfully influenced traditions that set the literary and the informational at odds. Yet as much as he objects to disarticulated facts, narrow empiricism, mass print, and desultory reading, his thinking should not be too quickly conflated with autotelic aesthetics. Coleridge was a reluctant participant in the mediacy of his moment, formulating his hermeneutics over and against textual excess at a time when authors struggled to conceptualize expanding readerships and extensive reading practices.⁴⁷ For Coleridge and others in his romantic ambit, the era's information revolution posed a generative threat.

Situating Coleridge in print culture contexts is hardly new to the field of British romanticism where scholars have detailed how romantic authors in general and Coleridge in particular do not retreat in the face of industrial print but rather encounter it with degrees of animosity, uncertainty, acuity, and hope.⁴⁸ Scholars of US literature have been slower to recognize

Coleridge's active engagements with print, perhaps because Americanists under the field-defining sway of Perry Miller and F. O. Matthiessen have long been inclined to see Coleridge as a philosophical influence on New England transcendentalism, a trajectory continued by Laura Dassow Walls in her work on Coleridge's philosophy of science.[49] Coleridge was not wrong when he wrote in 1834, "I am a poor poet in England, but I am a great philosopher in America."[50] Nor is it unreasonable to think of him as an aesthetician, metaphysician, and theorist of scientific holism. When Coleridge praises intuition as that which "comprehends all truths known to us without a medium," a print culture scholar might take his transcendentalism to verge on magical thinking.[51] The complication is that Coleridge self-consciously struggles with his mediated condition and in doing so reflects on the relationship between the literary and the informational. Coleridge's misunderstanding of Kantian intuition as a purely unmediated intellectual sense can even indicate some amount of compensatory misprision, for elsewhere he recognizes (as does Kant) the capacity of mass print to simultaneously advance and obfuscate the Enlightenment project.[52] Wellmon has argued that Kant, Fichte, A. W. Schlegel, and (of special importance to Coleridge) Schelling found in transcendental reason a unifying solution to fragmented print ecologies, while Jonah Siegel has shown how British romantics posited authorial genius as a conceptual index for organizing huge collections of art.[53] But if romantic philosophers and aestheticians developed speculative responses to superabundance, Coleridge remained an author, editor, and publisher embedded in a less-than-ideal world of print.

In *Biographia Literaria* (1817) and beyond, Coleridge's views on his era's expanding print culture can be alternately rebarbative and receptive. He frequently worries that a literate but uncultivated public requires guidance when choosing books. As a literary historian, he tends toward narratives of declension: "In times of old books were as religious oracles; . . . as their numbers increased, they sunk" (1:57). Though Coleridge did appreciate some novels, he associated the genre with enfeebled popular tastes, perhaps because, as Nicholas Dames has generally noted, organic hermeneutics are better suited to lyric poetry than longer narratives with their inconsistent claims on attention.[54] Yet even after his conservative political turn, Coleridge could champion mass print—defending freedom of the press, hoping that circulating texts could encourage spiritual community, and (local quarrels notwithstanding) praising high-minded British periodicals for the gatekeeping function of their reviews.[55] Most optimistically, Coleridge found in art the potential to synthesize transcendental philosophy and romantic aesthetics under textual and informational excess. His poetry does not explicitly discuss mass print, but might the Ancient Mariner's tale—archaic, oral, immersive, inescapably holding one's attention—offer an alternative to the extensive reading practices of a world overflowing with print?[56]

Be that as it may, optimism is fleeting for Coleridge, who suffered mightily from information overload. Coleridge's 1818 introduction to his unfinished *Encyclopedia Metropolitan* project expresses an impossible desire for a unified system of human learning—one that orders all knowledge according to holistic scientific principles instead of disarticulated alphabetized entries in which "desired information is divided into innumerable fragments scattered over many volumes, like a mirror broken on the ground."[57] The problem was that Coleridge never managed to organize the multitude of pieces. Humphry Davy wrote of him, "His mind is a wilderness in which the cedar and the oak, which might aspire to the skies, are stunted in their growth by underwood, thorns, briers, and parasitical plants; with the most exalted genius, enlarged views, sensitive heart, and enlightened mind, he will be the victim of want of order, precision, and regularity."[58] Coleridge was widely regarded as a genius whose sheer capacity for reading books and retaining information retarded his poetic production. Coleridge himself acknowledged the problem when confessing his inability to handle his "Mass of miscellaneous Fragments" and when lamenting how his researches led only on to further researches across "an ever-widening Horizon" of texts.[59] As much as Coleridge's concept of unifying genius comes by way of romantic philosophy, it can also be taken as a defensive reaction to his era's glut of information.

It may not say much that *Biographia Literaria* represents Coleridge's best effort to consolidate his thinking, but if the book's constellations of philosophical idealism and aesthetic theory can be famously abstruse, Coleridge's views on mass print are relatively accessible and even practical to the point of cynicism. The often-neglected chapter "Advice to Young Authors Respecting Publication" recounts the troubles of running a journal (unreliable subscribers; the costs of paper and postage). It also complains about the desperate ledgers of authorship (research, paper, and printing expenses; the 30 percent of gross proceeds accorded to booksellers, whom Coleridge likens to warehouse managers). Coleridge recommends selling one's copyright (take fifty sure pounds rather than the chance for five hundred, especially if one is Coleridge). Any artist seeking idealistic affirmation will do better to turn to the 1800 preface to *Lyrical Ballads*, for *Biographia Literaria* advises aspiring writers to become doctors or lawyers instead—an admonition that some English majors today will no doubt find familiar. *Biographia Literaria* lacks the carefully orchestrated oscillations between transcendental idealism and empirical materialism that one finds in, say, Wordsworth's *Prelude* (1850), Melville's *Pierre* (1852), Thoreau's *Walden* (1854), Whitman's *Song of Myself* (1855), or some of Dickinson's poetry, but Coleridge remains a vatic philosopher self-consciously working in the real world of print. That he never realized that the publisher of *Biographia Literaria* was cheating him by overcharging his account for paper expenses only reinforces Coleridge's point that one must attend to the business of the publishing industry.[60]

Even worse than the economics of publishing for Coleridge is the decline of aesthetics under mass print:

> [A]las! the multitude of books and the general diffusion of literature, have produced . . . lamentable effects in the world of letters. . . . [L]anguage, mechanized as it were into a barrel-organ, supplies at once both instrument and tune. Thus even the deaf may play, so as to delight the many. . . . I have attempted to illustrate the present state of our language, in its relation to literature, by a press-room of larger and smaller stereotype pieces, which, in the present Anglo-Gallican fashion of unconnected, epigrammatic periods, it requires but an ordinary portion of ingenuity to vary indefinitely, and yet still produce something, which, if not sense, will be so like it as to do as well. Perhaps better: for it spares the reader the trouble of thinking; prevents vacancy, while it indulges indolence. (1:38–39)

As much as *Biographia Literaria* can feel like a maddeningly miscellaneous book, this attack on multiplicity, disarticulation, reconfiguration, and lassitude indicates deep coherences between Coleridge's metaphysics, aesthetics, and attitudes toward print. Just as Coleridge turned against David Hartley's mechanistic psychology, here he condemns the mass production and consumption of print. Just as he elsewhere subordinates Lockean empiricism to unifying reason, here he rejects passive hermeneutics and the dismemberment of literature, not only in the minds of readers, but in the print shop and marketplace. The passage goes on to condemn reviewers who quote truncated passages (a problem of excerption we will take up in chapter 2). To access one's intuition, realize totalities, and represent the unfolding of organic forms, one must engage in the kind of sustained reflection seldom attained by what Coleridge condescendingly calls the "mass of readers" (1:39). Theo Davis has explored from a phenomenological perspective what she calls romanticism's "poetry of attention," though challenges to aesthetic immersion can be as much about textual excess as about Heidegger.[61]

Coleridge would worry throughout his career that print culture debases reading habits, a concern shared by other intellectuals of the time as extensive reading became more prevalent (or at the very least, more visible). Coleridge complains in a letter from 1810 that reading among the populace has "by Newspapers, Magazines, and Novels, been carried into excess," and he fears that superficial literacy ("'Reading made easy'") vitiates the national mind.[62] Of the four types of readers Coleridge describes in his journals and mentions in his second lecture on Shakespeare, the first three suffer under information overload: "Spunges [sic]" absorb vast amounts of information that they then squeeze out in dirtier forms; "Sand Glasses" read mechanically and lack proper attention (using books for the "profitless measurement and dozing away of Time"); "Straining Bags" filter the flood of print materials but retain the bad instead of the good. Only the final type, "Great-Moguls' Diamond Sieves," can isolate priceless, self-illuminating gems from the slag of textual excess.[63] Such readers are rare in what Coleridge elsewhere calls "the present much-reading, but not very hard-reading age."[64] Yet *Biographia Literaria* hopes against hope to find a commensurate audience:

> In lieu of the various requests which the anxiety of authorship addresses to the unknown reader, I advance but this one; that he will either pass over the following chapter altogether, or read the whole connectedly. The fairest part of the most beautiful body will appear deformed and monstrous, if dissevered from its place in the organic Whole. (1:233–34)

For Bloomian critics, the anxiety of influence determines Coleridge's standing within literary history, but this passage points to an "anxiety of authorship"—inseparable from what Lucy Newlyn calls Coleridge's "anxiety of reception"—understood here within a history of literature marked less by flights across the high canon than by travels in the saturated lowlands of print.[65] Read me closely or do not read me at all, Coleridge enjoins us. Take me to your deserted island.

Coleridge's organicism and the hermeneutic it entails are for him incompatible with extensive reading practices, and other Anglo-American authors influenced by Coleridge share similar, if not always as explicitly or consistently theorized, concerns. Specific dynamics are of course diverse, but to gesture toward a family of romantic reactions to mass print, a schematic list of writers might include

1. Charles Lamb, Coleridge's lifelong friend and provider of books, who extravagantly displays his love of literature and distaste for informational texts in "Detached Thoughts on Books and Reading" (1822).
2. Poe—that market-menaced, sporadic transcendentalist—who plagiarizes Coleridge, bases his literary criticism on obsessive close reading, and mandates that a poetic masterpiece must be read in one sitting so as to apprehend its unities.
3. Thomas De Quincey, Coleridge's friend and competitor, who after being tricked as a youth into thinking that he had mistakenly ordered fifteen thousand volumes from a bookseller, imagines the publishing industry as a vast spider's web and suffers nightmares of an endless line of wagons dropping loads of books at his doorstep. De Quincey finds relief from the horror of superabundance in a kind of self-imposed deserted island reading, supposedly restricting himself to only *Lyrical Ballads* (1798) for a two-year period.[66]
4. The stubbornly austere, Crusoe-like Thoreau, who mocks "Easy Reading" and "'Little Reading'" in *Walden*, takes only a few volumes with him to the Pond, and proclaims, "Books must be read as deliberately and reservedly as they were written." When Thoreau writes in an 1853 journal entry, "I have now a library of nearly nine hundred volumes, over seven hundred of which I wrote myself," he is joking about his failure in a surplus print economy. (His publisher, having no room to store the unsold copies of *A Week on the Concord and Merrimack Rivers* [1849], had recently returned the remainders to Thoreau.)[67]

All these writers set intensive reading over and against mass print, which is not to say that they are immune to bibliomania, bibliophilia, and other excessive passions that both foreground and challenge (in Deidre Lynch's words) "the opposition between accumulating books and reading literature."[68] The desire for books can indeed heighten tensions between the informational practices of collectors (who list, enumerate, and monetize their books, sometimes with more emphasis on covers than contents), and the literary sensibilities of close readers (who, by many of their accounts, form more intimate, imaginative, aesthetic relationships with their texts). Such juxtapositions can extend to the different scholarly practices of print historians and literary critics, though clearly manifold correspondences point toward deeper affinities between parties that enjoy their books in multiple and nonexclusive ways. The careful purchases of the discerning collector differ from the profligacies of the hoarder, just as the aesthetic immersions of the close reader differ from the speed reader who absorbs information.

The fellowship between discriminating collectors and readers is evident throughout Brander Matthews's *Ballads of Books* (1887), an anthology of seventy poems about books that Matthews dedicates to bibliophiles everywhere.[69] Many of the poems equate heightened reading experiences with the physical enjoyment of books—even when catalogs of favorite authors threaten to render their writings as information, even when poems like John Ferriar's "The Bibliomania" (1809) and Robert Leighton's "Too Many Books" (1875) chide collectors who ignore the aesthetic qualities of literature. As John Guillory has argued, the cultural capital of the canon, like economies of rare books, is premised on the existence of surplus print materials against which to measure exceptional value. Similarly, fantasies of deserted island reading depend on the realities of textual excess. As with David Lodge's game of "Humiliation" in which literature professors confess to each other important texts they have not read, the deserted island question is only worth asking if people have read a lot of books.[70]

The subtended dynamics of superabundance and close reading are particularly evident in two novels from Mary Shelley. Scholarly accounts of reading in *Frankenstein* (1818) track larger critical trajectories—from Garrett Stewart's formal attentions to how Shelley disrupts constructions of ideal readers, to Patrick Brantlinger's more sociological account of how *Frankenstein* animates fears of mass audiences, to Shelley Jackson's hypertext novel *Patchwork Girl* (1995) and DH scholarship that takes *Frankenstein* as a case study for digital reading practices, to Michele Turner Sharp's analysis of how Shelley's novel reflects developments in the abstraction of information.[71] To shift the focus toward questions of superabundance, Shelley's Creature can embody Coleridge's concern in *Biographia Literaria* that the extensive reading associated with mass print makes literary passages "deformed and monstrous, if dissevered from . . . the organic Whole." Less metaphorically, Robert Walton and Victor Frankenstein can stand as dangerously desultory readers set loose as children among too many books, and even intensive models of reading are no better in *Frankenstein*, whether it is Victor immersed in his scientific studies or the Creature in his hovel poring over three books. If you're ever headed to a deserted island, maybe don't take Paracelsus or *Paradise Lost* (1667). Shelley dramatizes the point that readers should choose their books carefully under the guidance of thoughtful adults, which may help a literature professor convince STEM majors fulfilling their humanities requirements that *Frankenstein* makes a pretty good case for the value of liberal education. Still, it is hard to deny the sense that reading in *Frankenstein* leads to little good, an anxiety lurking in Shelley's last novel, which ends with a mutually constitutive fantasy of close reading and textual excess.

After surviving an epidemic more destructive than that of Defoe's *Journal of the Plague Year*, the voracious reader Lionel Verney of Shelley's *The Last Man* (1826) compares himself to Robinson Crusoe and, in an effort to cope with the apocalypse, eschews all books except for the most escapist. The novel begins with an allusion to Coleridge and seems in its conclusion to embrace an intensive hermeneutic when Verney prepares to leave Europe forever: "I have chosen my boat, and laid in my scant stores. I have selected a few books; the principal are Homer and Shakespeare." Shelley imagines a future of close reading not wholly unattractive, and yet Verney cannot entirely resist the appeal of superabundance. He adds, "But the libraries of the world are thrown open to me—and in any port I can renew my stock."[72] At the end of history with a single man left standing and all the world a deserted island, vast archives of books remain too attractive to leave behind, even if "renew" and "stock"—as opposed to, say, "increase" and "collection"—suggest that Verney will not be physically burdened with the books he comes to finish. A Kindle would preclude such hard choosing, and one fantasy of the digital age is that every reader can have it all. But the obverse fantasy of close reading—of attention, reflection, intimacy, discrimination, and the careful apprehension of unities—suggests that the love of books and their abandonment are not so easily disarticulated. Under the pressures of textual excess, Michel de Certeau was more correct than he intended when famously writing of reading, "each of the places through which it passes is a repetition of the lost paradise."[73]

Carrying Out the Wealth of the Indies: Emerson

The same year that he published "The American Scholar" (1837), Ralph Waldo Emerson wrote in his journal:

> I hate books, they are an usurpation and impertinence. I cannot once go home to truth and Nature for this perpetual clutter of words and dust of libraries. Yet take me at my word and burn my books and, like poor Petrarch, I might come to insanity for want of this fine wine of the gods.[74]

What would it mean to think about Emerson as a manager of information? Would a focus on print contexts and organizational systems displace or supplement his standing as a philosopher? Might his project seem less about epistemological motility, his rhetoric less about oratory, and his aesthetics less about ecstatic dialectics moving toward but never reaching unity? Considering his field-shaping legacy, would changing the center of Emerson's gravity alter—or reflect ongoing alterations in—nineteenth-century US literary history? And might an emphasis on information overload make it harder to conscript him as a forerunner of critical practices that privilege intensive reading? Emerson remains a crucial figure in transatlantic romanticism, but Coleridge's well-documented influence on him should not obscure the fact that Emerson is less enamored of close reading and more cavalier in his recourse to superabundant texts.

Here Defoe can serve again as a point of entry. In *Society and Solitude* (1870), Emerson generalizes about the childhood pleasures of reading *Robinson Crusoe*, but while he lists the novel among multiple works in his "encyclopaedia" of youthful wonders, he offers neither explications nor dreamy recollections of sequestering himself with Defoe.[75] As if to puncture the fantasies of deserted island reading enjoyed by devotees of *Crusoe* (Thoreau included), Emerson in an 1873 dedicatory speech at the Concord Free Public Library imagines how much better Crusoe's life would have been if he had had more books on his island. Perhaps Emerson forgets—or does not much care—that Crusoe's spiritual rise very much depends on his undivided attention to the Bible, but whatever the extent of Emerson's religious heterodoxy, he refuses to view *Robinson Crusoe* as an escape from textual excess. Mass print is often on Emerson's mind, for as much as his transcendental idealism seeks an unmediated relationship with Nature, and as much as his desires for originality can be read through romantic concepts of aesthetic autonomy, his working life as a reader, writer, and thinker involved the handling of multitudinous texts. To argue that the nineteenth-century information revolution shapes Emerson's attitudes toward intertextuality and influence is not only to continue the well-established tradition of detranscendentalizing Emerson; it is also to see how philosophical topics—epistemological limits, negotiations of the One and Many, postmetaphysical unfoldings of experience—remain bound up in Emerson's thought with the challenge of textual excess.

Throughout his career, Emerson views the proliferation of print with significant reservations, a reaction that Ronald and Mary Zboray trace more widely among New England transcendentalists, whom they call both "critics" and "creatures" of print culture.[76] At various moments, Emerson condemns "the spawn of the press" for its superficiality and partisanship, and he resents "the partial and noisy readers of the hour" who have no patience for reflective reading or writing.[77] He at times envisions a union of humanistic learning with "information and practical power," yet he harbors doubts as late as "The Progress of Culture" (1867) about the virtues of the telegraph and industrial print.[78]

Emerson's ambivalence about his era's information revolution is not that of a disaffected outsider. Having gained hard experience publishing his own works and serving as editor of the *Dial*, Emerson was wise to the ways of paper quality, copyright, reprinting, pricing, and distribution. Acting as Carlyle's unofficial American editor, Emerson wrote to him in 1843, "the cheap press has, within a few months, made a total change in our book markets." He even sounds perversely proud when reporting to Carlyle that British books in America are "instantly converted into a newspaper or coarse pamphlet, and hawked by a hundred boys in the streets of all of our cities for 25, 18, or 12 cents." Indicating a desire to reconcile print culture with the calling of the Poet, Emerson finds some compensation even in piracy: If Carlyle's works are to be "plundered" by American printers, they will still retain "a Worth unplunderable, yet infinitely communicable."[79] Easy enough to say for someone whose income relied more on lyceums and an inheritance than book sales, though like many of his contemporaries (as Meredith McGill has shown), Emerson recognized in the culture of reprinting both the potential power of reaching vast audiences and the dangers of uncontrollable circulation.[80]

Emerson's ambivalence about his era's information revolution is on display as early as "The American Scholar." The speech laments "the constant accumulation and classifying of facts," which require organization, which depends on categorization, which leads in turn to disarticulation so that the Ideal becomes "distributed to multitudes, . . . so minutely subdivided and peddled out, that it is spilled into drops, and cannot be gathered."[81] When Emerson likens men to dismembered body parts, life to a series of disconnected experiences, social groups to conveniently divided cakes, and empirical science to a discipline of dead taxonomies, he suspects that for things to be classified and ordered they must first be isolated, reified, and thereby diminished. At the same time, Emerson appreciates multiplicity (think of his Whitman-like love of lists and the parataxis of his style).[82] He is also moved, as Walls has emphasized, by comprehensive organizational schemes that intimate organic cohesion beneath seeming particularity—the Jardin des Plantes, the analogies of von Humboldt and Goethe, (less happily) the racial hierarchy of Johann Blumenbach, as well as the encompassing, centripetal personages of the Poet and other Representative Men.[83] The urge to bring unity out of multiplicity is a main feature of Coleridgean metaphysics and aesthetics, and how this might work in the context of superabundant print and information shapes Emerson's literary practices.

Emerson's intermittent complaints about books can be taken as an anxiety of influence or a preference for direct experience, but they are also driven by the rapid expansion of print culture, which Emerson—as a speaker and public intellectual—takes to be both an opportunity and a threat. "The American Scholar" famously scorns "the bookworm," "the book-learned class," and "bibliomaniacs of all degrees" (57). But after Emerson worries that books can tyrannize narrow minds, he adds that reading done rightly is salutatory. When he writes that "[m]eek young men grow up in libraries," it is unclear whether they are meek because they have spent their youth among books or whether libraries help them grow beyond meekness in the manner of "great and heroic men ... who had almost no other information than by the printed page" (59). As "The American Scholar" moves from dialectics toward synthesis, some general advice takes form: the scholar encountering superabundance must liberate his original genius while creatively reading texts. As if such demands are not challenging enough, Emerson concludes: "The scholar is that man who must take up into himself all the ability of the time, all the contributions of the past, all the hopes of the future. He must be an university of knowledges" (70). Inspiring perhaps, and even theoretically possible under an all-ordering subjectivity that discovers correspondences between the *me* and *not me*, but from the perspective of print culture, such aspirations are absurd. There are simply too many books, even good ones.

Emerson across his career increasingly reckons this reality and makes some surprising accommodations, especially in his later years when he seems more likely to acknowledge human limitations. Emerson's "Books" (1858), an instructively unenlivening article first appearing in the *Atlantic Monthly*, offers recommendations on what to read in a world awash with texts. Advice books on reading and stocking personal libraries had already existed for centuries, but Emerson's formulations reflect both the rise of popular interests in reading and also the development of statistical thinking, probability theory, and the quantification of texts. Emerson complains that in a library surrounded by tens of thousands of volumes "your chance of hitting the right one is to be computed by the arithmetical rule of Permutation and Combination," for finding a good book under such circumstances is like a lottery with "fifty or a hundred blanks to a prize."[84] Moreover, after noting that the Imperial Library of Paris contains eight hundred thousand volumes with an annual increase of twelve thousand more, Emerson writes, "It is easy to count the number of pages which a diligent man can read in a day, and the number of years which human life in favorable circumstances allows to reading; and to demonstrate, that, though he should read from dawn till dark, for sixty years, he must die in the first alcoves" (97). It's a bracing (and potentially liberating) thought for graduate students approaching (impossibly named) comprehensive exams.

From Seneca onward, writers have invoked the shortness of life to vindicate austere reading practices, and when Emerson in "Books" expresses a preference for his personal library over huge institutional collections, he leans in the direction of deserted island reading. Jonathan Kramnick has shown how eighteenth-century efforts of canonization are linked to the expansion of print culture and reflected in fantasies of textual control.[85] In *Gulliver's Travels* (1735), for instance, the royal Brobdingnag library is limited to a thousand books, while Louis Sébastien Mercier's 1740 novel *The Year 2440* imagines a utopian library containing only four bookcases of essential works, all others being happily burned. Closer to Emerson's time, publishers invested in family and cabinet libraries—from inexpensive series beginning in the 1830s, to collections that included specialized cases for both shipping and display, to influential enterprises such as Charles Norton Eliot's "five-foot shelf" of Harvard Classics.[86] One-stop shopping directed by literary experts is one way to manage textual superabundance. Yet if Emerson's advice in "Books" feels humanist—one's lifespan becomes the measure of all things; men of letters serve as guides to reading—his calculative reasoning exemplifies an informational method of conceptualizing his era's overwhelming profusion of books.

Chapter 3 will take up the subject in more depth, but the quantification of literature can be taken to begin in earnest during the nineteenth century. Printers, publishers, and booksellers had long kept ledger accounts, but with the spread of statistics and the industrialization of print, nineteenth-century businesses and governments increasingly aggregated and published data on books, magazines, and newspapers, some of which provide crucial information for quantitative print histories today. William Hazlitt Jr. boasted that during a three-year period he published 121 works totaling 3,572,400 words and 17,862,000 pieces of movable type that cost readers only thirteen shillings.[87] George Putnam was also a great collector of data, as seen in his *American Book Circular with Notes and Statistics* (1843). In an 1855 toast at a New York Publishers party, Putnam cited the following figures: 1,115 works (including 623 "original" American productions, and 429 foreign reprints) were published in the United States between 1830 and 1842, but in the single year of 1853 the total was 733. Putnam estimated that "the bulk of the book trade advanced ten times faster than the population," and he marveled, "twenty years ago who *imagined* editions of 100,000 or 75,000, or 30,000, or even the now common number of 10,000."⁸⁸ The numbers here and elsewhere matter, not only for the specific amounts they represent, but also because their form of representation subordinates aesthetics to statistics.

Even commentators hostile to industrial print adopted quantitative descriptions of literature. If undiscerning readers at the start of the nineteenth century suffered because they read bad books, critiques of textual excess increasingly focused on numbers as the language of moral and aesthetic degeneracy shared space with statistical anxiety. In "Letters to a Young Man Whose Education Has Been Neglected" (1823), De Quincey complained that the most dedicated reader might cover twenty thousand volumes by the age of eighty and yet read only the equivalent of 5 percent of the books published in any single year. In *Books and Reading* (1860), W. P. Atkinson used the average size of volumes to compute the miles of books on the British Library shelves (forty) and the acreage of printed pages in the Library of Paris (147,760). Other guides to reading invoked Thomas Malthus when describing the "geometrical progression" of print. In a landmark, data-choked 1876 report on libraries for the US Bureau of Education, William Mathews—who later reprinted portions of his report in *Hours with Men and Books* (1876)—quotes De Quincey's calculations, cites Atkinson's figures, plagiarizes Emerson on dying in the first alcoves, estimates that a single scholar might require reference to fifty thousand or even one hundred thousand books in a lifetime, and then wonders: "What reader is not appalled by such statistics? . . . Steel pens and steam-presses have multiplied the power of production, the railways hurry books to one's door as fast as printed; but what has increased the cerebrum and the cerebellum?"⁸⁹

One reaction, as Stephen Arata has shown, is the formulation of systematic reading practices, as when J. J. Wright's *So Many Books! So Little Time! What to Do?* (1891) recommends reading thirty minutes a day, four days a week, for fifty weeks so as to cover two thousand pages every year. Melville satirizes such attitudes in *Moby-Dick* (1851) when Queequeg picks up a "large book," begins "counting the pages with deliberate regularity," and whistles at "every fiftieth page" in "astonishment at the multitude of pages."⁹⁰ Here Melville does not mock the harpooner's illiteracy so much as show that Queequeg's loose reading of what is probably the Bible is not all that different from the practices of serious thinkers who attempt to comprehend an excess of print through skimming and regulated reading habits. Numbers are the most common and perhaps best way to conceptualize superabundance, but even when creatively rendered as acres, miles, pounds, and years in a life, quantitative representations of literature—in Emerson's time and our own—are not equivalent to, and in fact demonstrate the need for, qualitative assessments of texts.

Yet for readers interested in discriminating judgments, "Books" will likely disappoint. Emerson defers the question of aesthetics to what he calls a "method from Nature," under whose auspices "[t]here is always a selection in writers, and then a selection from the selection" (97–98). This logic echoes eighteenth-century views from Hume and Samuel Johnson, who take the cumulative opinion of readers across time to be the best indicator of a book's quality. Emerson's principle of judgment, however, is not directly related to cultivated personal preferences, for Nature's selection in his mind is enacted through print culture: books get into the world because they "utter what tens of thousands feel," a reasonable claim in a transcendentalist universe where every heart vibrates to the poet's iron string. Thus a book becomes a classic when "the wise ear of Time ... out of a million of pages reprints one," after a text "is winnowed by all the winds of opinion, and ... reprinted after twenty years;—and reprinted after a century!" Apparently Emerson never read *Pendennis* (1850), *Pierre*, *Ruth Hall* (1854), Terry Eagleton, or Jane Tompkins, for he naturalizes the machinations of print markets, comparing canon formation to a neutral "filtration" process performed by gasses, plants, winds, and time. Published one year before *On the Origin of Species* (1859), and anticipating Darwinian elaborations on aesthetics from Herbert Spencer and Alexander Bain, "Books" can sound like evolutionary literary history combined with free market idealism. With aesthetic judgment reduced to consequentialist logic, and culture conflated with nature, the fittest books are ultimately those that survive under textual selection.

The deterministic nature of the canon in "Books" becomes explicit when Emerson issues three imperatives: "1. Never read any book that is not a year old. 2. Never read any but famed books. 3. Never read any but what you like" (99). That Emerson focuses on what *not* to read betrays his worries over textual excess. If his final injunction about trusting personal enjoyment sounds more familiarly Emersonian, "Books" never theorizes pleasure or aesthetics and instead spends its time listing famed texts under traditional and idiosyncratic categories. The cataloging that comes to dominate "Books" is both a boon to source study scholars and suggestive of Emerson's disregard for emerging disciplinary classifications. But for lovers of Emerson's quicksilver essays, or for anyone hoping for an intimate account of his reading experiences and sensibilities, "Books" will be a disappointing performance that, despite conceiving of itself as a solution to overwhelming print options, aspires so assiduously to comprehensive advice as to preclude close attention to any single book. It's almost as bad as a library.

Emerson seems to realize as much and so concludes "Books" with a recommendation that, coming from him, is shocking. After "comparing the number of good books with the shortness of life," he advises young men to "read by proxy" (111), by which he means they should form an organization, "divide the whole body [of recommended books] into sections" (112), assign each person a selection to study, and meet periodically to report on their reading, as do members of the Institut de France (founded 1795) and the British Association for the Advancement of Science (founded 1831). Emerson may be thinking of Francis Bacon, who wrote that lesser books could be "read by deputy."[91] But if Emerson elsewhere names compression as a favorite rhetorical virtue, his advice to render books as reports is more about informational efficiency than about *brevitas* or protomodernist aesthetics. Two long decades after "The American Scholar"—years marked by the founding of the American Statistical Association (1839), the beginnings of Antonio Panizzi's innovative catalogue for the British Museum (1839), Charles Coffin Jewett's pioneering cross-referenced catalogue of the Brown University Library (1844), the creation of the Smithsonian Library (1846) and Boston Public Library (1848), the first appearance of William Poole's *Index to Periodical Literature* (1848), the opening of New York's Astor Library to the public (1849), the passage of the British Public Libraries Act (1850), Melville's invention of the Sub-Sub-Librarian (1851), the founding of Reuter's international news service (1851), Dickens's reportage on British bureaucratic processes (mainly in the late 1840s and 1850s), the first edition of *Bartlett's Familiar Quotations, with Complete Indices of Authors and Subjects* (1855), the laying of the transatlantic cable (1858), the ongoing efforts of Charles Babbage to make a calculation machine, the expansion of the census in Britain and America, the formation of data-driven social sciences, the spreading mathematization of the natural sciences, and the continued industrialization of the book trade with its falling prices, expanding reach, and ever-thickening catalogues—Emerson in "Books" asks his readers (not listeners) to acknowledge their limited comprehension capacities. Instead of becoming American Scholars whose creative reading embodies all knowledges, young men facing the trials of too many books should organize, subdivide, read, and report within an organization of specialized knowledge production. It's almost as bad as a university.

"Books" neither advocates nor models anything like close reading—no doubt a function of the article's genre, though also an indication of Emerson's own reading practices, which are not especially literary as the term is generally understood. In 1887, James Elliot Cabot recalled of Emerson's books, "They were pleasant companions, but not counselors,—hardly even intimates." According to another remembrance, Emerson once recommended reading only single chapters of books, for "[t]he glance reveals when the gaze obscures." As Lawrence Buell has put it, Emerson tends toward "alert grazing" more than "assiduous drill," an extensive hermeneutic that accords with his faith in serendipity and intuition.[92] Emerson also lived at a time when the term "rapid reading" became less associated with overhasty elocution and more with extensive reading habits that, while often considered superficial, gradually gained acceptance among educators and intellectuals as a necessary skill in an information age.[93]

An extreme example of the desire for an extensive hermeneutic commensurate with the demands of mass print comes from William Law Symonds—a frequenter of Pfaff's tavern in New York City, and a struggling author who died at the age of twenty-nine, though not before producing (among many other pieces) twenty-six hundred entries for *Appleton's American Cyclopaedia*. Symonds speculates in an 1864 *Atlantic Monthly* article how the outpourings of the press require new reading habits. He calls libraries "a sort of *debris* of the world," notes that the British Museum covers forty full acres and is on average two hundred feet tall, and—after noting that a human on average can write five books in a lifetime—calculates that the holdings of the Imperial Library of Paris represent "ten millions of laborious years." Symonds worries that new writing will become impossible in the future because "letters are capable of only a certain number of combinations." And he predicts that "the green earth will be transformed into a wilderness of books, and man, reduced from the priest and interpreter of Nature to a bookworm, will be like the beasts which perish." Symonds predictably hopes that readers will choose their books wisely, though he also imagines a very different solution:

> [T]ransfer the largest library into a miniature for the pocket.... The contents of vast tomes, bodies of history and of science, may be so reduced that the eye can cover them at a glance, and the process of reading be as rapid as that of thought.... The epoch of the printing-press has run itself nearly through; but a new epoch and a new art shall arise.[94]

Symonds mentions stenography and the condensing of knowledge in encyclopedias as ways to cope with textual excess. His fantasy of reading as rapidly as thought is an outlandish vision, though his dream of carrying the world's largest library in his pocket has come to fruition with the smartphone, and his desire to master superabundant information in a postprint epoch remains alive and well funded today.

Emerson's extensive reading is not entirely different. As powerfully as he can theorize beauty, as poignantly as he sometimes characterizes style, as often as some favorite poem enchants him, and as repeatedly as he returns to his favorite books, he seldom explicates texts. His 1838 address to the Harvard Divinity School scandalously eschewed exegesis. "Art" (1841) and "The Poet" (1844) do not offer sustained discussions of specific aesthetic works. "Shakespeare, or the Poet" (1850) and "Goethe, or the Writer" (1850) quote surprisingly little from their subjects, while "Literature" (1855) and "Thoughts on Modern Literature" (1871; 1893) emphasize authors over passages and generalizations over textual analysis, particularly as Emerson's reading expands across continents and time.[95] Emerson's preface to his poetry anthology *Parnassus* (1874) reiterates the logic of "Books": "Do we read all authors to grope our way to the best? No; but the world selects for us the best, and we select from these our best."[96] As McGill has pointed out, *Parnassus* takes the liberty of reprinting parts of poems, organic unities notwithstanding, as did other poetry anthologies and literary textbooks of the time, an excerpting practice also evident in cheap mass editions that silently truncated and bowdlerized the classics.[97] Compared to Coleridge, Poe, Thoreau, Ruskin, and Matthew Arnold, Emerson's approach to reading remains decidedly desultory. He was happy to read abridgements (a practice Thoreau disdained) and liked to start books in the middle—sometimes putting them down, sometimes focusing on specific passages, sometimes browsing his way forward or back. He borrowed library books that he returned without opening and often misquoted authors in his journals and essays. Emerson was indeed a creative reader, though not the one he describes in "The American Scholar."

Emerson's reading habits—and his thoughts on reading and influence—should be understood within the context of his era's information revolution. He considered Coleridge the best British critic of his time, but while he paraphrased Coleridge's four types of readers in an 1834 journal entry, Emerson is no Great-Mogul's Diamond Sieve, nor does he aspire to be one. In "Quotation and Originality" (1875), he pays Coleridge the dubious compliment of deploying quotations more powerfully than original thoughts, and in his journals, he explicitly criticizes Coleridge for relying too heavily on sources. Nonetheless, Emerson wrote in an 1867 journal entry after complaining of the pressures exerted by books:

And yet—and yet—I hesitate to denounce reading, as aught inferior or mean. When visions of my books come over me, as I sit writing, when the remembrance of some poet comes, I accept it with pure joy, and quit my thinking, as sad lumbering work; and hasten to my little heaven.[98]

Much of the text surrounding this passage condemns overinfluence and is integrated into "Quotation and Originality," but this section praising deserted island reading appears only in Emerson's journal, as if sequestered intimacy with a favorite book is for him a kind of guilty pleasure. Emerson can advise young students to form bureaucratic reading groups, but his personal method of coping with textual excess is to skim and let intuition guide attention. One way to write about such reading is to quote and run—away from overinfluence, toward self-reliant originality, in the impressionistic manner of prophecy, epigram, pastiche, and commonplace books, but always under the knowledge of a superabundance that inevitably extracts some concessions.[99]

The conclusion of Emerson's 1873 Concord Library address can mark a terminus for a uniquely creative writer and reader paying tribute to his era's information revolution. Emerson (given the occasion) praises libraries and (being Emerson) expresses a second thought about books: "I do not for a moment forget that they are secondary, mere means, and only used in the off-hours."[100] The iconoclast of "The American Scholar" has not in this instance forgotten himself, but the declining Emerson in 1873 (whose daughter Ellen had begun to help him during his speeches, handing him pages so he would not stray from—or get lost in—his words) is concerned about his place within literary history, which is also to say mass print.[101] "[R]ead proudly," Emerson exhorts his audience, "put the duty of being read invariably on the author. If he is not read, whose fault is it?" Standing before a superabundant archive of books with his life and lectures passing precipitously into his writings, themselves well on the road to canonization, Emerson empowers his listeners to read selectively as he wonders about not being read or read adequately.[102] His question—"whose fault is it?"—does not seem to me entirely rhetorical. Overwhelming quantities of books, unripe audiences, selection by nature, culture, history, and chance can all account for a book's undeserved neglect. Still, Emerson shoulders the burden and glory of enduring relevance alone, for in his mind an author must rely on himself to distinguish his books from the surfeit around them. This statement of conviction might fittingly end Emerson's public career, though he went on in life and in his library address, which concludes: "there is no end to the praise of books, to the value of a library.... But I am pleading a cause which in the event of this day has already won." The unending accumulation and availability of books can stir unending anxiety and celebration alike, but for an increasing number of nineteenth-century readers and writers, the information revolution was one more fact of modern life.

Emerson's fall into mass print might track other turbulent trajectories across his long career: freedom toward fate, rebellion toward convention, radical individualism toward grudging sociality. As Emerson aged and negotiated between lecturing and print, he wrote increasingly about issues of mediacy, moving (for example) from his speculative "Lecture on the Times" (1841) to a chapter in *English Traits* (1856) titled "The *Times*," which details his visit to Printing House Square in London and describes with a mixture of wonder and worry the centralizing influence of Britain's leading information hub. The *Times* is a recurring prop in *English Traits*, indicating to Emerson both the cosmopolitan reach and self-satisfied provinciality of the British character. Emerson's interactions with Coleridge, Wordsworth, and Carlyle further touch on the ubiquity of the press, often set against—and sometimes perversely set over—the prolix monologues of the aging romantics whose potencies are so reduced that in Emerson's descriptions they fail even to disappoint. Perhaps Emerson turned his attentions toward print because oratory was losing its cultural prominence. Perhaps, too, his ebbing powers of imagination and memory made him self-consciously more reliant on a print culture that seemed all the more inexorable.

But as with other potential arcs in his career, Emerson's views on textual excess are modulated from the beginning. "The American Scholar" derogates bookworms and bibliomaniacs, and yet the lecture assures its listeners and readers:

> I would not be hurried by any love of system, by an exaggeration of instincts, to underrate the Book. We all know, that, as the human body can be nourished on any food, though it were boiled grass and the broth of shoes, so the human mind can be fed by any knowledge.... I only would say, that it needs a strong head to bear that diet. One must be an inventor to read well. As the proverb says, "He that would bring home the wealth of the Indies, must carry out the wealth of the Indies."[103]

The proverb here is fitting, and not simply because it notes that vast textual resources are useless without the power to apprehend them. Being a proverb, the saying has a long history, as if filtered by Emerson's method of nature. As a proverb, its original authorship in obscure, thereby skirting the dangers of influence.

That the source of Emerson's proverb is difficult to identify indicates how the literary and the informational can converge. He probably found the quote in Boswell's *Life of Samuel Johnson* (1791), where Johnson uses it to punctuate a broader complaint about the proliferation of travel writing. But if Emerson in "Quotation and Originality" condemns the reliance on quotation books (whose "jewel[s]" come from the "auctioneer," not the "mine"), he may also have come across Johnson's use of the proverb in *The British Prose Writers: Johnsoniana* (1820) or *Laconics, or The Best Words of the Best Authors* (1827), compendia that selected, compressed, compiled, and organized literary quotations for overwhelmed readers.[104] Emerson may have also heard the line in conversation or come across it in the popular press, though it is surprisingly absent in nineteenth-century databases before Emerson uses it himself. Whatever the case, Emerson slightly alters Johnson's proverb as it appears in all his possible written sources—substituting "carry out" for "carry," and in doing so suggesting his cavalier reading habits and tendency to take ownership of quotes.[105] Thus in a passage that states an aversion to influence, "The American Scholar" slightly misquotes Boswell quoting Johnson, himself a prolific quoter and compiler whose sayings were often quoted and compiled.[106] This is how Emerson, despite the threat of overinfluence, carries out the wealth of his literary researches. Or to put it in a Stanley Cavell–like register to emphasize how broad access to texts can be simultaneously debilitating and inspiring, Emerson's *carrying out* both bears the burden and executes the claims of his reading.

Such carrying out is best represented in Emerson's extensive journals, which in their original forms total 252 volumes and 18.2 linear shelf feet. The proverb about the Indies initially appears in an 1837 entry, which Emerson later strikes through with three lines to indicate its insertion in "The American Scholar." Emerson's multifarious journals are in part a record of a lifetime spent among books, and his indexes, cross-references, and notations show him struggling to manage his superabundant reading—a broader challenge that, as Ellen Gruber Garvey has detailed, prompted a diversity of Americans to take up scrapbooking practices within a longer history of commonplace books.[107] Emerson occasionally repurposed journals first used by his father, crossing out William Emerson's indexes and excising his lists of reading.[108] As Lawrence Rosenwald shows, Emerson's early "Wide World" journals (1820–24) are his most systematically organized, initially following Locke's mechanistic schema for indexing commonplace books: start with a table comprising one hundred empty boxes, and as you transcribe quotations from your reading into your book, label each box with an appropriate subject heading and cite the appropriate page number.[109] As might be expected, Emerson proved unwilling to abide by such disarticulating, taxonomic, regulating structures (not unlike Emily Dickinson, whose herbarium and poetry manuscripts initially follow informational protocols but become increasingly disorganized). Recounting his abandonment of his Wide World journals, which he once called his "Cabinet Cyclopaedia," Emerson wrote in 1839, "I need hardly say to any one acquainted with my thoughts that I have no System."[110]

Such statements accord with views of Emerson as a fluid, moody, intuitive thinker, and yet Emerson's organizational impulses remained. In the mid-1830s, his turn to readymade, prebound journals—as opposed to assemblages of loose pages—both reflected and encouraged a more systematic attitude toward his journaling.[111] He wrote in his notebooks that "Classification is a delight" and expressed a vaguely Kantian wonder in a journal entry from 1841: "Swifter than light the world converts itself into the thing you name, and all things find their right place under this new and capricious classification."[112] Emerson would eventually return to the project of organizing his sprawling journals, creating no fewer than three overlapping indexes between 1843 and 1847 that total over seven hundred pages. As Rosenwald argues, Emerson's hundreds of mature journals constitute a self-standing work, but they also serve (along with his miscellaneous notebooks) as staging areas in which Emerson selects, compresses, sorts, retrieves, and repurposes passages from his promiscuous reading. Among their other alembic transmutations, Emerson's journals and his indexes render literature as information.

The process "works" insofar as some of Emerson's later writings are relatively well organized in structure and more likely to abide by the subjects announced in their titles, though his informational efforts remain bound up with a style (of reading, writing, and thinking) enacted most fully in his more motile, more celebrated essays that tack between glorious and at times dizzying multiplicities as they move toward unconsummated unity. Put differently, Emerson's rhetorical and intellectual capriciousness does not foreclose the possibilities of order but rather can be taken to reflect and even dramatize his generative struggles with information overload. Conceived as such, Emerson's style is about subjectivity and also subject headings, Kant and also cutting and pasting, the postmetaphysical unfolding of being and also the endless reconfiguring of information. Given Emerson's reading, record keeping, and compositional practices—all shaped by his era's information revolution, including the spread of readymade journals, ledgers, and indexes—the dialectic of multiplicity and unity becomes a struggle between excess and order that involve diurnal efforts of dealing with literary materials too numerous to keep in mind all at once.

One hopes this is not to diminish Emerson by turning away from epistemology. As Cary Wolfe has shown, we can think of Emerson's relations with multiplicity through Niklas Luhmann's systems theory in which the limits of knowledge are understood, not as skepticism, but as complexity conceived through information theory.[113] Wolfe's point is vindicated by historical context, for Emerson and others in his time had motive, opportunity, and available technologies and concepts to think about informational complexity. Because Emerson is so keenly aware of textual superabundance, the transcendental subject (if one can still call it such) achieves no feeling of commensurability or closure but may recognize that extensive experiences of reading require the untranscendental work of managing information. It may be strange to conceive of Emerson in this way, particularly if we place him in genealogies with Nietzsche, William James, Heidegger, Wittgenstein, and Cavell—thinkers who in various ways set literary aesthetics and epistemologies over and against positivist models of science, factuality, and philosophical naturalism.[114] Still, we might think of Emerson's encounter with information, not as a fall into nominalism, but as a print culture correlative to more philosophical unfoldings—Richard Poirier's transitions, Barbara Packer's abandonment, Cavell's moods and becoming, Branka Arsić's leaving, Paul Grimstad's claim that for Emerson "composition is not so much a matter of arriving at a fixed or final order but of carrying out an open-ended search."[115] Emerson would surely be open to the possibility that his philosophy coheres with his broad experience, including his experiences in print culture.

That the management of information is never comprehensive or complete seems a vital provocation for Emerson. In *Nature* (1836), his most organized speculative essay, he begins austerely by insisting that to find clarifying solitude one must retire from society and the study alike. Famously crossing a "bare common," he fantasizes immediacy and austerity, imagining himself a transparent eyeball standing on "bare ground."[116] The focus of this section has not been on Emerson's subjectivity but rather on his grounds, which—far from barren—are strewn with a profusion of texts. Scholars have learned not to figure America as a blank slate, virgin territory, or New World, and we have increasingly recognized how mediacy matters, even for American Adams. Nor does Emerson himself long indulge the fantasy of a world stripped bare of books. One year after *Nature* in "The American Scholar" and repeatedly over his career, Emerson acknowledges the textual excess around him and practices reading, record-keeping, and compositional strategies that made peace with—and literature under—the pressures of his era's information revolution.

It worked for Emerson until his house burned in 1872. Fast-acting neighbors rescued most of his library, though Louisa May Alcott reported that the entryway of her family's home was "full of [Emerson's] half burnt papers and books."[117] Some of Emerson's biographers take the fire to mark the end of his creative career, a tragic irony in light of a poem from the late 1840s in which Emerson exulted, "Burn up the libraries!"[118] For Robinson Crusoe, carrying out the wealth of the West Indies proves manageable enough. Careful accounting, business letters, and the beginnings of a modern finance system all help him enjoy his riches. Yet as far as we know, Crusoe never carries his salvaged books off the island, and even the presence of the Bible fades (a fact Defoe belatedly tries to correct in his 1719 sequel to *Crusoe*).[119] Howsoever presciently Defoe embraces information management, he does not envision Crusoe's books moving within informational networks. Such possibilities are more imaginable for Emerson, for as extensive archives and bibliographic resources became more accessible than ever in the nineteenth century, books and their reading—Coleridge notwithstanding—proved increasingly fungible, compressible, and reconfigurable.

The rendering of literature as information helps explain why Emerson's sentences are so exceptionally quotable. They can, and even want to, be unmoored from linear narratives and unified texts. Emerson writes of "the lords of life" in "Experience" (1844), "I dare not assume to give their order, but I name them as I find them in my way."[120] The double meaning here is that reconfigurability—the absence of assumed or fundamental order—is both liberating (one serendipitously happens upon aspects of experience) and constraining (the clutter of disorder can get in one's way). Emerson's aesthetics of reconfiguration can make the contexts of his quotes particularly difficult to recall. Does that chilling line come from "Experience," "Fate" (1860), or "Illusions" (1860)? Is that uplifting maxim from "Self-Reliance" (1841) or "Circles" (1841) or "The Poet" (1844)? Thank heavens for indexes and now searchable texts. The portability of Emerson's sentences is also one reason why divergent views of his work are so hard to adjudicate. As we invoke the quotes that speak to our commitments, Emerson scholarship—more than most literary criticism I know—can resemble something like a commonplace book, which is true even of close readings of specific Emerson essays, whose jagged paths are inevitably smoothed by our thesis-driven assemblages. This is only a problem if one hopes to find in Emerson something essential, systematic, or consistent, a goal that philosophically inflected Emerson criticism has shown to be optional and even counterproductive. Emerson's motility can be explained not only as epistemological skepticism but also by looking at how textual excess treated as information shapes Emerson's distinctive aesthetic. It may be sacrilegious to treat Emerson in this way, though to think of him as an information manager is to assert that information seldom has it so good.

Literature remains difficult to regard as information—especially if we conceptualize texts as organic wholes; if we understand reading as intensive, intimate, and subjective; if we take literature to be unaccountably beautiful; and if books are (quoting a French government memoranda in the case of *Google Books vs. the Authors' Guild*) "a product unlike other products."[121] How such beliefs may or may not be justified are questions of increasing moment as information technologies become more central to the everyday life of literary criticism and as the twenty-first century continues to ask a question that the nineteenth century also broached: What is not subsumed—economically, socially, epistemologically, and aesthetically—under what Hayles has called the "great dream" of disembodied information and John Plotz describes as the "ruthless liquidity" of modernity?[122]

When asking such questions, technology matters well before digitization. Back in Concord in 1872, Emerson's neighbors and friends collected enough money to help him rebuild his underinsured library and home. Among the improvements were stackable, reconfigurable bookshelves with rope handles for quick removal in case of another fire. Today we have more sophisticated tools for carrying out the wealth of our literary resources, but if literary studies is a cluster of postdisciplinary practices that samples omnivorously from other fields, it has traditionally resisted the methods and systems with which most disciplines manage overwhelming information. Such resistance may or may not be waning in our age of extensive reading, though the larger argument of this book is that the relationship between literature and information was formed in the nineteenth century. After *Robinson Crusoe*, commentators imagined deserted island reading as a response to superabundant print, including Coleridge, who helped to formulate a theory of close reading fundamental to modern concepts of the literary. Emerson offers a more accommodating, more dialectical, and in some ways more realistic example for literary scholars today—one that admits the power, attractions, and necessities of extensive reading and information management, even while keeping faith with intuition, immersion, aesthetics, and intensive hermeneutics.

Emerson may not be a representative reader, but he can provoke a way of thinking about and even absolving one's reading in an information age.

We have for centuries browsed, dipped, and wandered in our desultory attentions. We have long taken impressions from other readers and quoted out of context. What serious reader has not in some moments hated books as objects and even as a category? Maybe the ire that a literary critic can feel toward distant reading, or the superficial skimming of students, or reading by committee, or borrowing even unto plagiarism is not only because such practices violate the traditional values of our field but also because they are not as different as we might like from our everyday reading, writing, and thinking. Overwhelmed, we have long treated literature as information, whether our scholarship and pedagogy admit it or not.

But also abiding among our habits is deserted island reading, which will probably stay at the center of literary studies and aesthetic experience for the foreseeable future. For all the efficiencies of extensive hermeneutics and pleasures at the surfaces of texts, we will continue to hasten to our little heavens and dwell on our favorite passages. As in most things, Emerson is too ecumenical to choose between literary and informational reading, nor do I think he offers a synthesis or program for arranging dynamics between the two. Instead, he articulates a set of moods toward reading under conditions of textual excess that, as it tends to be with Emerson, will compel readers to the extent that his experiences speak to their own. Most optimistically, which for Emerson often means most tautologically, he might teach us to acknowledge and thereby accept the inconsistent reading practices that are already our own. He typically does not take his relationship with books as a function of the history that shapes it, but his writings show that how we read and regard our reading these days depends on how the nineteenth century has taught us to handle—and perhaps even save—some portion of our many, many books.

CHAPTER TWO

Searching

On all the floors were piles of books, to the amount perhaps of some thousands of volumes: these still in bales: those wrapped in paper, as they had been purchased: others scattered singly or in heaps: not one upon the shelves which lined the walls. To these, Mr. Fips called Tom's attention.

"Before anything else can be done, we must have them put in order, catalogued, and ranged upon the book-shelves, Mr. Pinch. That will do to begin with."

—CHARLES DICKENS, *MARTIN CHUZZLEWIT* (1844)

To know where you can find anything is, after all, the greatest part of erudition.

—JOHN BARTLETT, EPIGRAPH TO "LIST: OF BOOKS READ" (1900)

IN AN 1850 series of sketches titled "The Doom of English Wills," Dickens (with his collaborator William Henry Wills) recounts the trials of a certain William Wallace, a gentleman from the Royal Society of Antiquaries searching for a historic testament in four ecclesiastical registries. A lyrical introduction extols cathedral towns for charming the imagination of visitors, but when Wallace enters the church archives themselves, textual excess precludes aesthetic pleasure. He finds "parallel rows of shelves laden with wills: not tied up in bundles, not docketed, not protected in any way. . . . [H]e may as well try to find a lost shell on a sea-shore, or a needle in a haystack, as attempt to discover what he is desirous of picking out of this documentary chaos." Dickens laments confusion in the stacks— "testamentary agglomerations, soddened into pulp," old wills cannibalized to bind up newer ones—but he soon shifts his attention from such "hideous disorder" to the "Searching Office[s]" that administer the archives.[1]

The first three offices that Wallace visits are scandalously mismanaged by obstructive bureaucrats guarding their incomplete indexes, and even the best of the dockets categorizes its wills by the first letter of first names so that it takes days just to sort through the centuries of Jameses and Johns. Wallace's search for a text thus becomes a critique of the systems that organize texts, as if Dickens anticipates *The Order of Things* (1966) more than *Discipline and Punish* (1975). In the earlier book, Foucault takes Borges and literature more generally to "[break] up all the ordered surfaces and all the planes with which we are accustomed to tame the wild profusion of existing things."[2] The literary is thus aligned against the informational, a dynamic that the cluttered chaos of Dickens's novels might be taken to exemplify.

However, "The Doom of English Wills" finds no wonder in disorder and champions the rational organization of information. For Dickens, it is remediable chaos, not epistemic overdeterminism, that threatens the truth seeking of Wallace's historicist researches. Dickens even provides a happy ending of sorts in that the final searching office that Wallace visits efficiently indexes its wills, files them in uniform boxes, and guides patrons through its logical and transparent system. The irony is that we never find out what particular will Wallace is after or whether he finds it or not, as if Dickens is previewing *Bleak House* (1853) by refusing to cater to readers expecting the unexpected revelation of a will. "The Doom of English Wills" begins in an aesthetic mode when Wallace, described as a "literary man," enters the archive for "the gratification of a taste." Yet information management ultimately supersedes close reading in the sketch, which is more about what we now call databases and search engines than the scrutiny of any single text. As the information theorist Claude Shannon wrote in 1948 when prioritizing information over meaning, "semantic aspects of communication are irrelevant to the engineering problem."[3]

Dickens's subordination of reading to searching technology, of what we might call the literary to the informational, is very much a theoretical and practical imperative when confronting documentary chaos. As the nineteenth century witnessed the proliferation of texts, the storage, indexing, and retrieval of information became a crisis of unprecedented intensity and scope as information overload became quite literal. Following N. Katherine Hayles and Alan Liu, Mark Gobles has discussed how digital desires for transcendence cannot entirely efface the physicality of information, and so even modernist and postmodernist archival imaginations bear at some level the weight of texts.[4] Leah Price has shown that this was even more true during the nineteenth century as Dickens and his contemporaries alternately foreground and disavow the massive materiality of books and paper.[5] One literary fantasy they have about managing textual excess involves, not transcendence, but targeting—of using aesthetic sensibilities to preternaturally master the chaotic surfeit of print. Some Victorian antiquarians and bibliographers took a different approach by turning to indexing and algorithmic protocols, but whether invoking aesthetic intuition or information technology, nineteenth-century readers and writers encountered a similar challenge: before one can even engage in close reading, one must first find a text worthy to read.

This is also true of modern literary critics who find homologies between our own information revolution and that of the nineteenth century, if only because (in Andrew Piper's words) "the basic concepts we use today to understand the digital can be traced back to origins that reside in bibliographic culture."[6] The production and accessibility of information have of course skyrocketed since Dickens's time, but textual excess to literary critics may be like nuclear warfare or all-you-can-eat buffets: at some scale of magnitude it ceases to matter how many millions of texts are available, how many times over humanity can destroy itself, or how many popcorn shrimp are in the chafing dish. The nineteenth century recognized the informational problem of what Benjamin would figure as the debris of history piling ever skyward, and for Benjamin the rise of information as a form of communication is particularly problematic for narrative literature insofar as the seeming transparency of information counters the spirit of storytelling.[7] Nineteenth-century and modern readers alike may feel overwhelmed by the progress of textual production, but searching technology makes a potential difference as scholars today pluck needles from archival haystacks with a facility that earlier researchers like William Wallace could only dream about.

Perhaps because imaginative leaps require more theoretical awareness than the use of everyday tools, scholars have been slow to follow Dickens and his contemporaries in asking how searching technologies shape literary practices under information overload. The strongest words exchanged over the digital humanities today have involved distant reading and related statistical methods that chapter 3 will discuss at length. But more mundane and thus more broadly influential is the searching technology that literary critics regularly use when gathering information, pursuing hunches, and sorting through potential sources and evidence. Search engines as a technology and epistemology function practically like ideology in that they structure our everyday relationship to texts but are almost never analyzed themselves. Whether or not one follows Lev Manovich in regarding digital databases as a new genre founded on endlessly reconfigurable information instead of linear narratives, few scholars have discussed in sustained ways how search engines influence the interpretive methods of literary critics who do not work—or at least do not self-identify as working—within the digital humanities.[8] Ted Underwood has recently worried that humanists are "using search algorithms we have never theorized."[9] It seems also to me that our practices and theories of searching have yet to be sufficiently historicized.

How search engines are shaping literary studies is an immense, dynamic topic that might be pursued in any number of ways. What follows focuses on how digital searching methods have come to mediate literary texts and their historical contexts, a key question given the continued prominence of historicist criticism and the expansion of digital archives. Whereas the previous chapter explores how textual and informational excess exert pressure on close reading practices, this chapter dramatizes how documentary chaos can be allayed (and disavowed) through an aesthetic mode of searching that includes distinctively literary capacities. If searching is a precondition for explication, it also threatens to preempt literary reading when the claims of the informational seem to be without end.

The New New Historicism

It should be no surprise that literary critics tend to gravitate toward hermeneutics more than informatics, but another reason why database practices are seldom discussed in print may have something to do with anxiety. Faced with an unprecedented wealth of archival resources, critics trained in close reading and engaged in historical research might find themselves turning into what Melville dismissed as a "superficial skimmer of pages."[10] Or a critic, with more teleological drive, might become a data miner guided by key search terms. Like those who worry that the internet makes users intellectually shallow or disinclined to scrutinize individual texts, scholars who value archival discoveries that ground literary interpretation in history may find search engines simultaneously empowering and unnerving, particularly if the rhetorical effect of targeted evidence threatens to exceed its rightful explanatory force.[11] As Liu suggests when discussing the "structural convergence between historicism and informationalism," the uses of historical databases in nineteenth-century literary studies are conditioned for better and for worse by evidentiary techniques once associated with the New Historicism and now normalized in critical practice.[12] One unintended consequence of the New Historicism in our information age is that it simultaneously unleashes and problematizes the power of interpretation—a possibility acknowledged by nineteenth-century writers exploring fears and fantasies of textual excess, and one that can sharpen critical database practices while alleviating some amount of anxiety.

For a literary critic coming of intellectual age during the height of the New Historicism, the World Wide Web could be plenty thrilling but still feel like a different world. Going online was something I did when taking a break from my dissertation. In retrospect, and without intention or coordination, the New Historicism and the internet by the end of the twentieth century were together moving literary studies toward a critical point in which the targeted searching of immense databases could support a myriad of interpretive possibilities by making available all manner of evidence. In general terms, the New Historicism emerged somewhat earlier but rose roughly in parallel with the internet. Both entered broader consciousness in their respective spheres in the mid-1980s and were well established by the early 1990s. If by 2000 both booms appeared to have busted, in actuality they had been integrated into everyday habits that continue to this day. Scholars of nineteenth-century Anglo-American literature were among the pioneers of the New Historicism—from D. A. Miller and Dominick LaCapra arguing over Dickens in a 1984 volume of *Representations*, to a rising generation of critics dubbed "New Americanists" by Frederick Crews in 1988. Two titles from the time indicate how quickly the New Historicism grew from insurgency to incumbency—Carolyn Porter's 1990 essay, "'After the New Historicism,'" and Brook Thomas's 1991 book, *The New Historicism and Other Old-Fashioned Topics*. References to "New Historicism" in nineteenth-century literary journals peaked in the mid-1990s, and by 2000 the movement was less a source of provocation than a subject for retrospection, not because its approaches had been invalidated or abandoned, but because they had been naturalized in a process described by William James: new ideas are first called absurd, then dismissed as trivial, and finally admitted as something already known.[13]

The most controversial aspect of the New Historicism in its heyday was its subordination of aesthetics to ideology, but even if critique in literary scholarship has not run out of steam, the study of nineteenth-century literature today seems generally less committed to theories of ideology and more interested in the messy realities of history as the hermeneutics of suspicion are increasingly tempered by empirical work, New Materialists, and historians of print. That the New Historicism would lead toward a more traditional historicism should not be entirely surprising. Michael Warner noted in 1987 that New Historicists were more hostile to literary formalism than to conventional historical methods, and Fredric Jameson argued in 1991 that the New Historicist affinity for disarticulated homologies constituted, not so much a dissatisfaction with old historicism, so much as a "'resistance to theory.'"[14]

Historians who entered English department frays often found that the New Historicism as a historicism was not so new after all, even if it privileged the thick descriptions of cultural studies and anthropology over the more comprehensive and at times quantitative methods preferred by some social historians.[15] The complaints that historians tended to lodge were more about the New Historicism's evidentiary standards, especially its tendency to use historical anecdotes to represent broadly circulating and causally unspecified discourses.[16] The difference (sometimes only politely implied) was that historians practiced a more rigorous method based in systematic archival and historiographical research instead of idiosyncratic, elaborately interpreted, rhetorically compelling, and potentially subversive pieces of evidence. Some scholars wondered how one could evaluate the significance of a small sampling of evidence without asking how representative it was and thus engaging in a more comprehensive historicism. Put differently, to proceed under the auspices of anecdotes is to prefer nimbler, more speculative acts of interpretation over the aggregative force of informational arguments drawing on larger bodies of evidence.[17]

New Historicists defended their anecdotal methods by advocating hermeneutics over masses of facts, a path smoothed by postmodern and constructivist attacks on recoverable history and scientific positivism. Leveraged for maximum rhetorical effect, singular examples instantiate New Historicist theory: all artifacts require interpretation; micropolitics operate at the level of detail; brushing history against the grain requires close attention to teleology-disrupting anomalies; discourse circulates promiscuously so that evidence appears in odd places, regardless of cultural prominence or authorial intent.[18] Such thinking led to stunning explications based on uncanny connections—homologies of economics and procreation in the Victorian period; links between *Moby-Dick* (1851) and Theodore Parker's abolitionist sermons on King Ahab; sentimental fiction and the "topsy-turvy" dolls that flip the identities of black and white figures; literary naturalism's anxieties over mimesis and monetary policy.[19] The oft-noted danger was that one could mount sweeping arguments on relatively scant proof and that, given the unbounded flowing of discourse, virtually any homology between context and text (if such a distinction was even viable) could become a key to meaning, especially with poststructuralism rendering texts more porous and multiculturalism expanding the canon. Freed from the shackles of narrow curricula, hermetic formalism, exhaustive historicism, and exacting source study, the New Historicism expanded the range of potential evidence to include virtually any cultural expression while simultaneously shrinking the quantity of evidence required to justify interpretive claims. Of course, the most convincing New Historicist scholarship never relied solely on a handful of anecdotes, and the basic recovery of uncanny examples involved, particularly in the absence of electronic databases, a serious commitment to archival work. Yet suspicions remained that the New Historicism had no way to control for what some critics called "arbitrary connectedness."[20] At some point, the boldest literary interpretation starts to sound like conspiracy theory.

The goal here is not to reenact old battles that ended more with fatigue than resolution but rather to explore some new consequences of the New Historicism at a time in which databases render anecdotal logic simultaneously more powerful and more specious. For literary critics, especially those working in the nineteenth century where mass print meets the public domain, unimaginable quantities of historical documents not only theoretically qualify as evidence; they are practically and efficiently accessible as such, whether retrieved from public databases or subscription services. Literary scholars are among other things knowledge workers who have an immense appetite for texts and information, and yet the risk for historically minded literary critics enjoying the fruits of the digital age in the long summer of the New Historicism is that, given the vast and potentially arbitrary connections made available by searchable electronic archives, targeted research can unearth anecdotal evidence to support seemingly any claim. Under such conditions, interpretation can feel like playing tennis with the net down or confirming a bias on the internet. How can a text *not* be about global capitalism? *Literally everyone* knows that game 6 of the 2002 NBA Western Conference Finals was fixed. One can celebrate the creative possibilities of criticism and still harbor some skeptical questions. Are historicist claims sufficiently falsifiable given textual excess, searching technology, and evidentiary inclusiveness? What happens when the arbitrary connectedness of the New Historicism is supercharged by what Patrick Leary called in a prescient 2005 article the "[f]ortuitous electronic connections" of digital searching?[21] Do we have—or do we need—theories and practices for constraining interpretation? How does one answer disbelieving students (usually, in my experience, nonmajors) who complain that

English professors with their cherry-picked and subjectively interpreted evidence can make a text say whatever they please?

Despite much general commentary on information overload and confirmation bias, and despite debates raging in the social sciences over reproducibility and methodological legitimacy, I know of no sustained work in literary studies on the issue of evidentiary excess in the digital age. Though Jonathan Gottschall wants critics to adopt scientific methods so as to make their work falsifiable, and though some scholars in the digital humanities seek in data more objective, testable proof, no one seems to be specifically concerned with superabundant evidence.[22] Scholars of literature and law tend to treat evidence as a historical and narrative practice but seldom as a metacritical issue, while epistemological work in philosophy and literature typically approaches the topic of evidence as a matter of subjectivity, not searching and sampling. Sianne Ngai has shown how the proliferation of possible evidence makes literary judgments hard to adjudicate, a concern that impels Stephanie Burt toward close reading and Franco Moretti in the opposite direction.[23] As Stanley Cavell writes about the refusal to privilege certain aesthetic productions over others when making critical arguments, "The danger is not so much that evidence will be lacking as that there will be evidence for everything and nothing, that theory will not warrant enough confidence to repudiate ill-gathered evidence to test what tests it."[24] Cavell is no fan of scientific methods, but he worries here about falsifiability, for interpretive claims require not only evidentiary support but also a theory for gathering and evaluating it.

Literary critics may be habituated to a sense that there is no arguing about taste, but those of us who use historical contexts to ground interpretation in something that feels firmer than personal impression can find the possibilities of superabundant evidence discomfiting in our search for ostensibly harder truths. Most conventionally threatening are long-standing poststructural challenges to what Barbara Herrnstein Smith has dismissed as "the supposedly autonomous corrective force of brute facts."[25] Such theorizing counters naive empiricism: "It is what it is" is a line for realtors, not critics. But to dispense with the possibility of factual accuracy entirely is to deny the very premises of falsifiability and evidence, which remain vital concepts under any empiricism aware of its own limitations. Literary critics as yet are under no mandate to meet scientific standards of proof, but we might do well to follow Bruno Latour's turn by questioning both scientific objectivity and radical skepticism alike. Symptomatic criticism has long been subject to charges of unfalsifiability (psychoanalysis sees a lack of evidence as evidence; deconstruction takes all evidence to contain its refutation; ideology critique is—to quote Latour—"always right!").[26] Yet given that today's databases and searching technologies so often help critics find the evidence they seek, historicist scholars might reconsider questions of method in an age of information overload.

Slavery and The Scarlet Letter

For New Historicists studying nineteenth-century American literature, no topic proved more popular than slavery and race and no text more compelling than *The Scarlet Letter* (1850), whose dense critical history exemplifies the proliferation of interpretation under New Historicist evidentiary standards. Traditional historicists such as Jean Fagan Yellin took *The Scarlet Letter* to be largely unrelated to chattel bondage, a position shared by influential scholars such as F. O. Matthiessen and Michael Colacurcio.[27] Under the New Historicism, however, slavery becomes an almost unavoidable theme in *The Scarlet Letter*. Jonathan Arac argued in 1986 that while *The Scarlet Letter* lacks an explicit engagement with slavery, this only makes more poignant the book's "adjacency" to the subject, a view compatible with that of Sacvan Bercovitch, who took Hawthorne's novel to be less about slavery itself and more about how conflict in the United States is rhetorically and symbolically managed.[28] More aggressively applying New Historicist theory to *The Scarlet Letter*, Jay Grossman found in 1993 "the simple, untranslated presence of a black man." Dimmesdale is associated with "the Black Man"; Hester is described as a "bond-slave"; Pearl can be taken as a mixed-race character; slavery was of course in the antebellum air. But while Grossman's essay cites secondary sources to establish contexts of African enslavement in America, the one archival artifact he analyzes at length is an 1851 review comparing *The Scarlet Letter* to "patent blacking" that will "*Ethiopize the snowiest conscience.*"[29] The review does not explicitly refer to slavery, but it constitutes by New Historicist logic and Grossman's analytic power a revealing historical anecdote implicating Hawthorne's novel and its cultural resonances in discourses of chattel bondage. Hawthorne's politics regarding slavery and race remain difficult to locate, but as the New Historicism ascended in the 1980s and 1990s, *The Scarlet Letter*'s relation to slavery moved from irrelevancy to adjacency to immediacy.

With the help of nineteenth-century print culture databases, immediacy can become ubiquity, at least as suggested by a day I spent in the digital archives experimenting with key search terms. Using the *Accessible Archives* and *American Periodical Series*, a Boolean search for "scarlet" and variances of "slave" between 1830 and 1850 garnered 247 hits, some of them potentially meaningful. In ethnographic and fictional pieces from the time, slaves in Africa, Cuba, and the Middle East are frequently described as wearing exotic scarlet clothing. In antislavery texts, chattel bondage is linked with the scarlet Whore of Babylon and the scarlet beast from *Revelations*, while defenders of slavery are depicted as turning scarlet-faced with intemperance, passion, and shame. More uncannily, an article in the *Colored American* from 1837 reported that African Americans in Delaware convicted of stealing or receiving stolen goods were whipped, imprisoned, and afterward required to wear "a Roman R in red scarlet, 4 inches long an[d] 1 wide" on their clothing, dimensions nearly identical to Hester's scarlet badge, which Hawthorne (to further the homology of slave punishment) repeatedly describes as a "brand."[30]

My favorite find is a *Liberator* article, "Ministers of the Gospel" (1839), that attacks the anti-abolitionism of northern elites and prophesies the end of American slavery:

> Let anti-slavery ministers preach to the people, not to the doctors, the judges, the generals and the honorables.... We have faithfully done what we could—we have hid the messengers with the stalks of flax, and have nothing more that we can do but bind the scarlet thread in the windows of our houses and wait the coming of the avenging Joshua.[31]

In the book of Joshua, the harlot Rahab of Jericho hides Israelite spies under stalks of flax on her property, lies to authorities about her actions, and her reward is that she will be spared in the coming fall of the city, provided she hangs a scarlet thread from her window. Rahab's scarlet sign looks back to the blood atonement of Passover and forward to the martyrdom of Christ, and when she eventually marries into the tribe of Israel, her story suggests that a fallen woman can be redeemed as one of the chosen people, integrated into providential nationhood, and even become an ancestor of Christ. The typology of the *Liberator* article is more or less clear. Though regarded as outcasts, abolitionists (including those hiding fugitive slaves) will be saved from the impending sin-cleansing apocalypse because they have allied themselves with the cause of righteousness. More critically, if Hester's carefully stitched scarlet letter recalls the scarlet thread of Rahab, then Hawthorne's novel can contain a subtle antislavery parable in which Hester, a fallen-woman-and-liar-turned-heroine-of-grace, becomes the redeemer of God's chosen nation and, through Christ, of the whole world despite—or more accurately, because—of her marginalized position on the verge of political upheaval. Like Rahab and fugitive-harboring abolitionists, Hester is doing God's work.

That she does so in opposition to her Puritan persecutors shows Hawthorne brushing American history against the grain. Cotton Mather's *Magnalia Christi Americana* (1702) does not mention Rahab, but one potential office of *The Scarlet Letter* projects an abolitionist Hester onto the Puritan origins of America—a move that many an antebellum abolitionist made when they contrasted the *Mayflower* and its freedom-loving pilgrims to the contemporaneous ships bearing African slaves to colonial Virginia (a story eliding the slaveholding history of Puritan New England, which Hawthorne either does not know or seems unwilling to broach). Hawthorne's slavery politics remain to some degree blinkered, but if Rahab's scarlet thread ties Hester to abolitionism, he is more radical on the issue of slavery than his correspondence and "Chiefly about War Matters" (1862) suggest. Whatever the case, a Rahab-based reading of *The Scarlet Letter* can be inferred from an anecdotal *Liberator* article and backed by half a dozen other antislavery texts from the period that, as further targeted searches reveal, also associate abolitionism with Rahab. Thus a mere six hours of database research (with occasional checking of email and Yahoo Sports) renders a powerful historical anecdote and supporting examples of a larger discursive formation linking the most canonical of American literary texts with the most notorious of national sins.

This schematic reading of *The Scarlet Letter* is more or less defensible under New Historical methods, but as a whole the database evidence connecting slavery and scarlet may risk an interpretive excess verging on arbitrary connectedness. The keyword searches described above render texts that associate the color of Hester's letter with slaves and slaveholders, black people and white, anti- and proslavery positions, while according to interpretations of Psalm 87, including a Peter Tosh song (thank you, Google), Rahab can also figure Ethiopia and Egypt, thereby connecting Hester to African slavery or, through another typological relay, the Puritan exodus into the New World, a homology that nineteenth-century African American thinkers were not slow to note.[32] As suggested by Hester's scarlet letter (and *The Scarlet Letter* itself), the point may be that anything can figure anything under the indeterminacy of signs and overdetermining sway of ideology, hermeneutics, cognitive dissonance, and historical entanglement. But surely everything does not figure everything equally, at least if historical specificity is to make any difference.

The problem is that the New Historicism and its legacy do not offer much guidance for weighing the significance of competing anecdotal interpretations, especially since New Historicists were often satisfied exposing ideological turbulence rather than attempting to render it coherent. To insist too strongly on stable dynamics, some felt, is to silence counterhistories and textual multivalence, a point Liu makes when comparing the relational configurations of database information with the New Historicism's "random," antihierarchical anecdotes.[33] Liu is brilliant on database theory, but historical anecdotes generated by electronic searches and deployed in interpretive arguments seem to me hardly random insofar as they reflect quite determinately the intentions of a literary critic. Given that we often find what we seek when utilizing search engines, and considering the multitudinous interpretive possibilities unleashed by teleological errands in the digital wilderness, the targeting power of database searches should impel critics to more carefully evaluate anecdotal links between literature and history, returning us to the unresolved question of what differentiates a meaningful connection from an arbitrary one.

One intriguing though ultimately inadequate response involves broader counterfactual search methods. Like Derrida regarding archives and emails, Jerome McGann, N. Katherine Hayles, and Meredith McGill point out that databases do not transparently represent information, for decisions regarding inclusion, classification, and algorithm impose narratives onto masses of facts. In Derrida's words, "The archive *pre-occupies* the future."[34] As painful experience continues to show, the internet is no Habermasian coffeehouse, and for a fuller perspective on how powerfully scarlet correlates with slavery in antebellum print culture, one might perform comparable searches using alternative keywords as controls. In the *Accessible Archives* and *American Periodical Series* from 1830 to 1850, whenever the word "scarlet" appears in an article, there is a 2.2 percent chance that some variation of "slavery" will accompany it. This figure is higher than the correlations of "burgundy" and "vermillion" with "slavery" (1.3 percent and 1.1 percent, respectively), but lower when compared to "crimson" and "red" (.3 percent and 2.8 percent). Among other colors, "Black" has the highest correlation with "slavery" (10%), followed by "white" (9.3 percent), while "scarlet" is about as likely to be appear with "slavery" as "blue" (2.1 percent) and less likely than "yellow" (3.8 percent). It might also help to know that "scarlet" appears with variations of "slavery" about as often as it does with variations of "bank," "clock," and "Indian" (excluding "Indiana"). Thus according to basic quantitative analysis that can be sharpened with historical anecdotes, a blue or yellow letter at least as ably conjures slavery as Hester's scarlet badge, while *The Scarlet Letter* may be no more about chattel bondage than it is about banks or clocks.

This is not to say that Hester's scarlet letter is only arbitrarily connected with slavery or that historical anecdotes mobilized by theories of circulating discourse should bear no critical weight. Rather, seemingly uncanny evidence—Delaware slave laws, a review comparing *The Scarlet Letter* to patent blacking, the scarlet thread of Rahab—may be as much a function of probabilistic coincidence as the political unconscious, as much about the sheer quantity of available information as specific ideological formations. Statistics can help constrain interpretive indulgence, and Moretti is right to argue that in some matters of literary study data can exist "independent of interpretations."[35] Nonetheless, even the most committed digital humanists are not claiming—at least not yet—that literary criticism can be executed solely using data analysis, for interpretation involves (among other things) intuitions informed by contextual knowledge that algorithmic searching has yet to replace.[36] Of the 247 links between slavery and scarlet that a database user might explore, the Rahab connection seemed to me particularly promising because of the long acknowledged typological inclinations of the Puritans, abolitionism, and Hawthorne, as well as *The Scarlet Letter*'s recognized interests in questions of American oppression and liberty. Potential readings of *The Scarlet Letter* and clocks or banks are imaginable but not as viable at this juncture in critical history, though why this is so is as difficult to determine as it is fundamental to interpretive enterprises. Can we dismiss what Roger Chillingworth says to the suffering exegete Dimmesdale? "Aha! See now, how they trouble the brain,—these books!—these books! You should study less, good sir, and take a little pastime, or these night whimsies will grow upon you."[37]

The New Historicism made a strong case for choosing the interpretation of anecdotes over more comprehensive, more informational modes of analysis, though it did so under a logic that in some theory and practice subordinated aesthetic judgment to ideology. Whether or not such disenchantment is necessary or preferable remains an open question. It is also worth noting that the New Historicist emphasis on freely circulating discourse tends to preclude critiques of digital archives as ideologically constructed, overdetermined enterprises often run by governments and for-profit corporations. Be that as it may, writing retrospectively of the New Historicism in 2000, Catherine Gallagher and Stephen Greenblatt argued that anecdotal methods need not devalue and actually depend on aesthetic sensibilities: "new historicism invokes the vastness of the textual archive, and with that vastness an aesthetic appreciation of the individual instance." When pressing themselves to explain which anecdotal instances to honor—which needles to pluck from the vast haystacks of the archive—Gallagher and Greenblatt surprisingly bracket theory and, in what feels like a spirit of reconciliation, turn to poets well loved by literary formalists, quoting Ezra Pound on "the method of Luminous Detail" and William Carlos Williams on "the strange phosphorous of life."[38] I think I know what they mean—or perhaps more accurately, I feel them—but I'm never quite sure how to talk about such things in a methods course, for aesthetics in many ways remains beyond evidence and analysis for critics after the New Historicism. What has changed in recent years is that immense databases with incredibly powerful interfaces oblige scholars to more self-consciously divide their attentions—and in doing so seek the relations—between close reading and data analysis, between the literary and the informational, between texts as objects of aesthetic judgment and searching technologies that shape our interpretations based on what we seek and therefore find in history.

Under such conditions, relations between the literary and the informational can be regarded as productively dialectical. What we search for, where we search, which interpretations we formulate and test are certainly shaped by archival architectures, search interfaces, and their algorithms, but literary critics also exercise less structurally determined kinds of judgment when encountering textual excess. As Charles Peirce would argue in his work on abduction—including an unpublished piece titled, "On the Logic of Drawing History from Ancient Documents, Especially from Testimonies" (1906)—probabilistic methods are ill-suited for deciding historical questions, and so instead we rely on "hope," "guessing," and "feeling" to judge how evidence points toward certain hypotheses that may or may not be testable. Because such judgments, if we can call them such, are hard to justify logically or through what Peirce calls "direct verification," they often seem like intuitions and can be understood as such.[39] That extrarational sensibilities are useful and even necessary for navigating superabundant archives is a supposition that—as the next two sections will argue—helps Hawthorne and Dickens vindicate the literary in their information age.

The Office of Hawthorne and Company

As an allegory of interpretation, *The Scarlet Letter* seems to figure the opposite of information overload. By so intensely focusing the attention of characters and readers onto Hester's letter A, and by setting his novel at least a century before the rise of mass print culture, Hawthorne presents a centripetal hermeneutic challenge centered on a single, absurdly short text—a challenge that generations of literary critics have profitably accepted. The scarlet letter in this sense stands for Anecdote more than

Archive. As described in "The Custom-House" introduction, the historical basis for Hester's tale is an idiosyncratic, elaborately interpreted, rhetorically compelling, and potentially subversive piece of evidence that, as a lost key to the Puritan past, exposes the ideological tensions beneath a monolithic national mythology, so much that a scholar guided by Colacurcio and James Chandler might exclaim: My God—Hawthorne *is* a New Historicist![40] Or at least the narrator of "The Custom-House" is, for Hawthorne's ironic self-presentation invites the literary minded to ask what it means to write history without systematic research and rely instead on anecdotal evidence plucked intuitively from an unmanageable archive. Patricia Crain has argued that Hester's scarlet letter functions as a kind of alphabetizing index that attempts to order the world.[41] More metacritically aware of how a historical romancer might search, and attuned to how documentary chaos both constitutes and complicates historicist projects, *The Scarlet Letter* also dramatizes how an aesthetic mode of searching might engage in information management prior to indexical structures.

Like a scarlet letter guling on a field sable, the centripetal symbol that dominates the story of Hester is defined against Hawthorne's prefatory description of textual superabundance. At the start of *The Scarlet Letter*, the narrator of "The Custom-House" appreciates the facts collected by the "local antiquarian" Pue, whose manuscript (which accompanies the faded scarlet letter) he considers sending to a historical archive (31). The narrator also refers familiarly to Joseph Felt's *Annals of Salem* (1827), an exhaustive history that contrasts the scant printing of colonial Massachusetts to the nineteenth century's "vast" production of texts that "now abound to excess."[42] Not unlike the antiquarian Wallace from "The Doom of English Wills," the "Custom-House" narrator has spent enough time in the archives to feel anxious about information overload, particularly when he visits an unfinished storage space on the top floor of the office:

> At one end of the room, in a recess, were a number of barrels, piled one upon another, containing bundles of official documents. Large quantities of similar rubbish lay lumbering the floor. It was sorrowful to think how many days, and weeks, and months, and years of toil, had been wasted on these musty papers, which were now only an encumbrance on earth, and were hidden away in this forgotten corner, never more to be glanced at by human eyes. (28–29)

Palpable here is Hawthorne's oft-noted unease in the literary marketplace—not so much as "the most obscure man of letters in America" marginalized by economic forces he resents (an older narrative promulgated by

Hawthorne himself), but rather as a savvy, networked careerist navigating the shifting tides of transatlantic publishing (a revisionist account elaborated by McGill, Richard Brodhead, and Joseph Rezek).[43] With commas and clauses lumbering his sentences, the narrator of "The Custom-House" seems to worry that his labors only swell the office's excess of scribbling. He also objects to the commercial nature of the records, thereby linking the nineteenth century's information explosion with the period's industrial revolution. Further troubling is the diaspora of texts that even a custom-house officer cannot regulate, for while the "heaped-up paper" in the office is daunting, "earlier documents and archives" were reportedly shipped to Halifax during the Revolutionary War (29). How in such a wide world of texts can one's historicism not be to some degree anecdotal?

As Henry James would have it, Hawthorne suffered from a thinness of literary culture that James traced to colonial New England, but "The Custom-House" sketches an opposite conundrum—the empirical difficulty and artistic opportunity of reconstructing history from documentary chaos. Hawthorne seems to both acknowledge and evade this challenge in his preface to *Mosses from an Old Manse* (1846) when he dallies with a "dusty heap of literature" in a garret, ruminates on the ephemerality of books, fails to find anything worthy of close reading, and finally flees from the "dreary trash" for pleasant landscapes unencumbered by print.[44] There is a transcendentalist impulse here, as if something in the Concord water makes one desirous of the textual austerity Thoreau extolled at Walden Pond. Hawthorne (or the narrator of the preface, if one prefers) makes clear that he is no comprehensive historian, and yet some of the stories collected in *Mosses from an Old Manse* corroborate the preface's claim that our author, for all his dissatisfactions with textual excess, also discovered in the dusty garret "bits of magic looking-glass among the books."[45] As we will see, antiquarians like Pue need only collect their artifacts and information, whereas interpretive critics and historical romancers must find thicker descriptions and more meaningful order amid the surfeit of ages past.

Informational methods do not answer these imperatives in "The Custom-House," for not only does the narrator never attempt to organize the records he finds; he depicts information management as a narrowly positivist exercise. He writes of an experienced colleague who had mastered the office bureaucracy:

> [T]he many intricacies of business, so harassing to the interloper, presented themselves before him with the regularity of a perfectly comprehended system. . . . A stain on his conscience, as to any thing that

came within the range of his vocation, would trouble such a man very much in the same way, though to a far greater degree, than an error in the balance of an account, or an ink-blot on the fair page of a book of record. (25–26)

Whether or not Hawthorne has in mind Hume's self-interested accountings, Benjamin Franklin's project of moral perfection, or James Mill's hedonic calculus, the "Custom-House" narrator suggests that comprehending a vast bureaucratic system requires a reductive informational mindset untroubled by ethical, affective, and aesthetic sensibilities. It is a deficiency that the instrumental customhouse bureaucrat shares with Roger Chillingworth, a scholar of "many ponderous books" who remains a gatherer and analyzer of information unfazed by textual excess (54). But if Chillingworth's empirical researches can pluck the father of Pearl from the multitudes of colonial Boston, the deeper truths of Dimmesdale finally escape him, as Chillingworth's perceptiveness is merely "almost intuitive" (116). Whereas he feels only a twisted sort of wonder when finding his needle in a haystack, Hester remains a more discerning observer, not only because of her embodied, feminine-coded sympathy, but also because of the aesthetic sensibilities evinced by her embroidered badge, whose mystical power reaches through the centuries to touch the narrator of "The Custom-House." Just as *Moby-Dick* (1851) does not begin with Ishmael, *The Scarlet Letter* does not start at Hester's prison door. As if rebuking teachers who try to alleviate crowded syllabi by omitting Hawthorne's preface, "The Custom-House" foregrounds a larger design that sets the literary over and against the informational.

And yet as is often the case with Hawthorne, seeming dualisms prove difficult to maintain. As an artist and bureaucrat working with documentary chaos, the "Custom-House" narrator does not (like the outraged Wallace) simply insist on better protocols. Instead, he exemplifies a way of making sense of information overload by intuitively discriminating between texts. "Poking and burrowing into the heaped-up rubbish in the corner; unfolding one and another document," the narrator is an extensive, unsystematic reader until drawn to Pue's envelope with "an instinctive curiosity" that cannot be logically explained or replicated by searching technologies (29–30). He is partly charmed by physical attractions lacking in mass print productions—the envelope's "ancient yellow parchment" made of "more substantial materials than at present," the patiently embroidered, fine-but-faded cloth of the scarlet letter itself. When placing the letter on his breast, he feels a burning "sensation not altogether physical"—as if Hawthorne supplements the etymological root of aesthetics in sensation with romantic notions of the artist's supersensible intuition. Like a New Historicist or flaneur of the archives, the customhouse narrator browses superabundance until his imagination is unaccountably piqued by a text he calls "most worthy of interpretation" (31–32). As professors of literature are inclined to notice, the explication of the scarlet anecdote requires interpretive capacities. And as a professor of literature with an administrative appointment might hope, "The Custom-House" suggests that bureaucratic work need not preclude critical practices or aesthetic pleasures. One might even press the limits of cognitive dissonance and convince oneself that dealing with deans and data might lead to some insights about the status of the literary.

Whatever the case, the discovery of Pue's envelope shifts *The Scarlet Letter* from anxieties over textual excess toward fantasies of hermeneutic mastery, though in doing so Hawthorne does not simply recoil from superabundance and bureaucracy so much as acknowledge that individual texts are embedded within broader informational contexts—that selection precedes explication, that scenes of close reading unfold against backdrops of information overload, and that what allows the narrator to find a text most worthy of interpretation is not an index or docket but a purposeless and ultimately purposive mode of searching governed by intuitions described as "sensibilities" beyond "the analysis of my mind" (33). The narrator's encounter with textual excess does not conjure Kant's mathematical sublime and its unaccountable infinitude of numbers, but the "Custom-House" narrator does display an extrarational, spontaneous, and intuitive capacity that thinkers from Kant and Schelling to Coleridge and Emerson associated with artistic genius. Hawthorne's relationship with philosophy and aesthetics may finally be more vernacular than scholarly, more shaped by familiarities with Concord transcendentalism than with immersions in German or British idealism.[46] Still, "The Custom-House" follows a romantic tendency to define individual genius over and against bibliographic efforts to comprehensively index mass print.[47] Call the heat-seeking sensibilities of the "Custom-House" narrator a romantic aesthetic retooled for the information age.

Thus, *The Scarlet Letter* does not so easily juxtapose the literary and the informational, dramatizing instead an aesthetic mastery of documentary superabundance. Cognizant of but choosing against more comprehensive searching methods, "The Custom-House" justifies its anecdotal historicism but departs from New Historicist logic insofar as aesthetics are not marginal or epiphenomenal but rather institutionally valuable and even epistemologically necessary when encountering information overload.

Whereas Kant would distinguish between the scholar's right to reason and the civil servant's duty to obey, and whereas Weber would ruefully recognize that bureaucracies inevitably centralize power and enforce capitalist ideology, Hawthorne imagines a less structurally determined role for knowledge workers laboring within informational systems.[48] What if aesthetic discrimination were part of one's job description? What if beauty had a role in bureaucracy? As dulling as Hawthorne found his government job, the literal office of the scarlet letter houses a disorganized archive that actually animates the artist's imagination. Before *The House of the Seven Gables* (1851) would reflect ambivalently on Hawthorne's success in antebellum print markets, *The Scarlet Letter* proleptically imagines (not without some optimism) how a mere "'writer of story books!'" might matter in an era overwhelmed with information (13).[49]

Hawthorne felt a need for similar self-justifications earlier in his career, though his efforts were not always so carefully arranged in ironic dialectics. Peter West has shown how Hawthorne's *Story Teller* tales, including "Mr. Higginbotham's Catastrophe" (1834) and "Old News" (1835), satirize insatiable desires for information and the inaccuracies of antebellum press networks.[50] Another early tale, "The Devil in Manuscript" (1835), also offers a critical view of informational excess when the narrator marvels at the document-strewn office of a lawyer and aspiring novelist: "What a voluminous mass the unpublished literature of America must be!" Copyright complaints become evident enough, as does the decentralized state of America's publishing industry. But if "The Devil in Manuscript" initially sympathizes with authors shut out of the literary marketplace, it ends by suggesting that print culture is altogether too successful in its dissemination of texts. When the lawyer throws his mediocre manuscript into the fire, a "heap of black cinders," a "multitude of sparks," and a "mass" of burning scraps fly up the chimney and spread fires throughout the city. Voicing a fantasy of unmediated circulation that often accompanies advances in media technology, the lawyer thinks he has somehow transcended print. "My brain has set the town on fire!" he exults.[51] More accurately, the physicality of his manuscript literalizes an information revolution in which news was often compared to flames and wildfire augmented by the accelerant of mass print. "The Devil in Manuscript" risks conflating novels, news, and legal documents, as well as print and handwritten materials, but the point may be that the rise of textual excess threatens, not only the vocational prospects of writers, but also the distinctiveness of literature.

The first strong indication of Hawthorne's interest in searching technology is "The Intelligence Office" (1844), a tale written after his initial stint in the Boston customhouse between 1839 and 1840. Emerging in major antebellum cities and operating as hubs in information networks, intelligence offices served as rental agencies, pawn shops, advertising centers, and lost-and-found counters, though their primary function was to facilitate job searches: laborers, especially immigrant domestics, waited on site or left information with clerks who connected them with interested employers. Some offices were run by benevolent societies and labor organizations, but most were businesses that collected and sold information in a widely criticized industry. Employers complained about the quality of placements (good help was apparently hard to find for what were often sustenance wages), whereas reformers and journalists focused on the exploitation of workers who lacked symmetrical access to information. George Foster in *New York in Slices* (1849) compared intelligence offices to customhouses for people instead of goods, and others likened the hiring of immigrants and African Americans at such establishments to the buying of horses and pigs.[52] Even Emerson's "The Young American" (1844), a lecture largely extolling America's free market system, worried that "[trade] converts Government into an Intelligence-Office, where every man may find what he wishes to buy, and expose what he has to sell, not only produce and manufactures, but art, skill, and intellectual and moral values."[53] At a time when the Associated Press (founded in 1846) and Reuters (established in 1851) commodified information on an unprecedented scale, antebellum critiques of intelligence offices registered how the collecting, searching, and selling of information had become a necessary evil that threatened to reify humans and humanistic values in impersonal information economies.

Hawthorne's "Intelligence Office" follows this pattern, at least in its opening pages. In an urban office echoing the cries of newspaper boys and with advertisements plastered over its windows (as if print literally encompasses the world), a spectacled clerk with a pen behind his ear pores over a "folio volume of leger-like size and aspect." With the impersonal clerk described as "the soul of his own great volume," Hawthorne invites readers to note discordant conflations of information and higher-order truths. A customer seeking a "place" comes looking not for a job but rather for his place in the world. Another man hopes to trade his heart for one that will not torture him with yearnings, while a third patron seeks his lost soul.[54] And on it goes, as if the goal of "The Intelligence Office" is to hammer the fairly predictable point that the most important things in life cannot be registered in ledgers, no more than the mysteries of nature are revealed by "A Visit to the Clerk of the Weather" (1836).

Perhaps "The Intelligence Office" is a minor production indulging a familiar Hawthornian swerve from social conundrums toward fanciful allegories. But if the story prefers symbolism to verisimilitude and variations on a theme to dramatic plotting, it also possesses some subversive energies that so often complicate Hawthorne's seemingly moralistic tales. Rather than setting information against humanistic values, "The Intelligence Office" actually challenges the dualism. When an authorial voice notes that the clerk's "great folio . . . would be curious reading, were it possible to obtain it for publication," and when the voice calls it a "Book of Wishes" that "would be an instructive employment [pun intended] for a student of mankind," and when the voice concludes that "this volume is probably truer, as a representation of the human heart, than is the living drama of action," a critic who prefers his Hawthorne ironic might suspect that it is no coincidence that the volume at the center of the story is described as both a literary "folio" and an informational "leger." Nor should we ignore the possibility that the clerk of the story suspiciously resembles a certain obscure writer who presents himself as an observer of the human heart and not an active participant in the world. What does it mean to conflate the work of a literary writer and that of an intelligence office clerk? Can an author of imaginative folios be regarded as a knowledge worker who organizes information and sells it in the marketplace? One possible difference is that authors have a higher calling, and indeed the final visitor to the intelligence office is a man looking for "Truth" ("Oh weary search!"). Now would be the moment for Hawthorne to clarify relations between the literary and the informational, though the authorial voice abruptly truncates the story: "whether they stood talking in the Moon, or in Vanity Fair, or in a city of this actual world, is more than I can say."[55] Allegory or realism? Artist or clerk? The literary or the informational? "The Intelligence Office" invites such questions but evades determined distinctions.

At the end of his career, Hawthorne would continue to address the rise of information from the wary perspective of an imaginative writer. Hsuan Hsu has shown how quantitative discourse fails to account for religious and aesthetic enchantments in *The Marble Faun* (1860), while Reed Gochberg discusses how informational excess remains a generative problem in Hawthorne's British notebooks and *American Claimant* manuscript.[56] In my account, *The Scarlet Letter* gets the final word. Having spent significant time as a government employee in Salem between 1846 and 1849, Hawthorne in "The Custom-House" reminds his neighbors and fellow citizens how seriously he performed his paperwork, and he does so not only by casting himself as a competent, nonpartisan civil servant in an era increasingly dissatisfied with the spoils system.[57] In addition to being an adequate bureaucrat who serves his country through mundane informational labors, the narrator of "The Custom-House" presents himself as the only office worker capable of recovering the scarlet letter's lost history and recording the spirit of Hester's human heart. Scholars of literature may feel similarly defensive and self-important when justifying their work to their skeptical townsfolk. We teach reading, writing, research, and critical-thinking skills necessary in a modern information economy. Look at the longitudinal data on the salaries of humanities majors (they're not as bad as everyone thinks)! Witness CEOs calling for the creativity of the humanities and arts (but seldom earmarking donations for English departments)! Democracy needs sympathetic, pluralistic citizens aware of history and trained in rational deliberation (how Donald Trump can make one miss the Enlightenment)! Oh, and by the way, people who take literature seriously may have access to certain human values and truths, some of which seem to be irreducibly aesthetic and beyond the reach of ledgers and assessments. It's pretty to think so, and sometimes I do, but like Hawthorne, we should probably also admit that the wonderful things we seek and find in literature are never free from informational contexts. There are barrels of documents to search before we find *The Scarlet Letter*.

Dickens's Dream

A sympathetic reviewer of *Our Mutual Friend* (1865) once noted that "Mr. Dickens's eye is greater than the weight of his brain."[58] George Henry Lewes similarly remarked after Dickens's death that he possessed "merely an *animal* intelligence."[59] Strains of such judgments echo today, for if Dickens more than any other nineteenth-century author occasions discussions about literature in the digital age, he often stands as a prophet who anticipates our moment not so much because of intellectual acuity as through a sheer, even feral, intuitive power evinced by his popular success. No one would describe Dickens as an obscure man of letters, least of all scholars of Victorian literature and media who see him as a kind of "Internet pioneer" (Jay Clayton), a practitioner of "Victorian informatics" (Richard Menke), a witness to the "psychic and social disintegration" threatened by media technology (Kevin McLaughlin), and "the first self-made global media star of the age of mass culture" (Juliet Johns).[60] Dickens has also been vital for scholarship combining literary criticism and print culture studies. He is an exemplar of "the meaningful materiality of texts" (Daniel Hack), an observer of the surfeit of unread paper overloading Victorian readers (Price), and an advocate for intellectual property rights in a transatlantic culture of reprinting (McGill).[61] A former law clerk turned journalist, novelist, editor, and publishing entrepreneur, Dickens worked at the leading edge of his era's information revolution, offering (as many of the aforementioned scholars emphasize) sustained attention to textual excess while also exploring (as has been largely unacknowledged) the possibilities of information management.

Ranging from comedy to reportage to outrage, Dickens critiques the Victorian production of bureaucracy, paperwork, red tape, and facts, though his frustrations are premised on a belief, or at the very least a hope, that social and epistemological benefits accrue from well-regulated information systems—be they scientific undertakings, mercantile enterprises, archival projects, or even government offices. Some of Dickens's harshest detractors were allied with the British administrative class.[62] They sometimes dismissed Dickens as insufficiently gentlemanly to opine on matters of governance, but Dickens's animus and optimism on the topic of information are part of a widespread Victorian dialectic in which dystopian visions exist alongside faith in a better-organized society. We see this in Dickens's journalistic pieces such as "The Doom of English Wills," "Valentine's Day at the Post-Office" (1850), "The Metropolitan Protectives" (1851), "Bottled Information" (1854), and "The Short-Timers" (1863), as well as in novels that dramatize ways in which information is—and is not—handled properly. Amid sprawling plots overrun with cartloads of textual waste, superabundance for Dickens is often a conundrum that, as in *The Scarlet Letter*, requires an artist's touch. But whereas Hawthorne typically discusses the subject in antiquarian and allegorical registers, Dickens speaks more insistently to the cultural work of the literary in a disorienting information age.

From as early as *The Pickwick Papers* (1837), Dickens's fiction is both a product of and a commentary on textual excess, particularly when the book broaches the question of what it means to treat narrative as information. *The Pickwick Papers* is inundated by "multifarious documents," including rambling transactions, overlong pamphlets, and screeds in a scurrilous newspaper war, while the prolix Pickwick and garrulous Sam Weller further saturate the book with verbiage.[63] As if in reaction to information overload, the "stenography" of the aptly named Alfred Jingle ("stopping at Crown—Crown at Muggleton—met a party—flannel jackets—white trowsers—anchovy sandwiches—devilled kidneys—splendid fellows—glorious") suggests how narrative reduced to disarticulated facts is both more efficient and less explanatory than more expansive literary forms, a trade-off Dickens understood personally given his expertise in shorthand (82). Such informational compression proves insufficient when the Pickwickians meet a travel writer known appropriately as "the Count," who organizes his ongoing experiences in a notebook, for instance rendering his meeting with the poet Snodgrass: "Head, potry [*sic*]—chapter, literary friends—name, Snowgrass [*sic*]" (184). The compression and reconfigurability of information is further ridiculed when a journalist assembles an article on Chinese metaphysics using the *Encyclopedia Britannica*: "'he read for metaphysics under the letter M, and for China under the letter C; and combined his information'" (646). As with its inset tale of a haunted filing cabinet, *The Pickwick Papers* anticipates "The Doom of English Wills" by focusing less on individual documents than on the physical, inscriptive, and conceptual indexes designed to order overwhelming information.

This holds true through the end of the book when episodic sprawl gives way to a unified ending in which Pickwick is left "arranging the memoranda" that the Pickwick Society has produced, thus making good on the editor's introductory promise that the contents of the book are all "carefully collated from letters and other MS. Authorities" (781, 6). Pickwick may be vaguely described as a naturalist searching the countryside for scientific facts, but he is also a writer working to organize a chaos of notes, not unlike Dickens himself, who struggled to make his books "harmonious whole[s]" under the pressures of serialization (xxxiv). As Richard Altick has argued, *The Pickwick Papers* was second only to Walter Scott's writings in moving the Victorian publishing industry toward the mass production of cheap editions and serialized novels. Following Pickwick and Dickens, Victorian readers increasingly encountered the boons and burdens of superabundance.[64]

How to manage excessive texts and information becomes a question of deepening complexity for Dickens. Tom Pinch of *Martin Chuzzlewit* not only offers a model for efficiently organizing books; he gestures toward an informational ethic and aesthetic largely absent from the more consistently comic *Pickwick Papers*. In a novel rife with unscrupulous manipulators of information and digressions on America's chaotic print culture (which Dickens witnessed firsthand during his 1842 visit to the country), Pinch constitutes a moral center associated with the artistic ordering of texts. Directed by Mr. Fips, he assiduously catalogues and shelves the elder Chuzzlewit's masses of books—all unnamed, most presumably unread, and some of them still in their wrappers (see figure 2.1). Pinch registers the economic value of the commodities and appreciates his wages as an amateur librarian, but he nonetheless (and perhaps all the more) vindicates the need for aesthetic sensibilities in a world where information is mercilessly monetized and books go largely unread. It turns out that Pinch plays the organ wonderfully at church without charging for his services, and he is enchanted by the physical and imaginative beauties of books—both as a

FIGURE 2.1. "Mysterious Installation of Mr. Pinch," Hablot Browne ("Phiz"), *The Life and Adventures of Martin Chuzzlewit* (London: Chapman and Hall, 1844).

reader and when viewing the "rows on rows of volumes, neatly ranged" in the window of a shop.[65] Like broader complaints about unmanageable library resources, particularly the books at the British Museum, *Martin Chuzzlewit* reflects fears of documentary chaos while holding out hope for informational and moral order combined with and achieved through aesthetic appreciation. It is as if the narrator of Hawthorne's "Custom-House," after intuitively rifling through his barrels of documents, decided to put all the papers in order and found real pleasure in the work.[66]

Dickens most famously confronts textual excess in *Bleak House*, a book that can serve as a kind of limit case in which the literary is almost but not entirely effaced by information overload. In an influential introduction,

J. Hillis Miller takes Dickens's novel to be "about the interpretation of documents."[67] But while the piles of papers that dominate *Bleak House* practically cry out for the extraction of meaning, Dickens chooses instead to set hermeneutic possibilities and even acts of reading aside. In this sense, D. A. Miller's equally influential reading seems right—"Dickens's bureaucracy works positively to elude the project of interpretation"—though I would add that in addition to being about the organization of power, *Bleak House* is also about the organization of information.[68] As with the "heap of paper fragments, print, and manuscript" hoarded by the illiterate Krook, texts in *Bleak House* ultimately have more of a physical than semiotic presence. This is certainly true in the case of Jarndyce and Jarndyce, which generates "immense masses of papers of all shapes and no shapes" but about which we learn next to nothing.[69] Whereas many Victorian novels turn on the revelations of a discovered will, John Jarndyce in *Bleak House* refuses to read a recovered codicil, the contents of which are never specified, as if the actual words of specific documents are less important than the textual superabundance that surrounds them. More extravagantly than anything in Hawthorne's oeuvre, *Bleak House* shows how informational contexts not only frame objects of potential interpretation; they become subjects of obsession themselves. Deconstruction can figure unread documents under a logic of aporia, but scenes of nonreading in which interpretation is invited but finally unattempted suggest how superabundance historically understood can precondition explication to a point of preemption.

It's almost enough to make one doubt the relevance of literary reading. Finding needles in the documentary haystacks of *Bleak House* seems to require only the informational expertise of the utilitarian technocrat Inspector Bucket, aided as he is by the comprehensive browsing and burrowing of the Smallweed clan. The Smallweeds read only legal documents, banish all fairytales and fictions, and algorithmically make their way through Krook's hoard of papers: "regularly, all day, do they all remain there until nine at night . . . rummaging and searching, digging, delving, and diving among the treasures of the late lamented [Krook]."[70] One might even argue that Dickens predicts the victory of Google over Yahoo in that the searches of *Bleak House* are governed less by taxonomic categories than by the analysis of links in a vast network.[71] That is, information is best obtained in the novel, not by assuming stable classifications (e.g., a will is a legal document and therefore should be sought in the Jarndyce papers instead of a rag and bottle shop), but rather by tracing relationships between characters (e.g., who is blackmailing whom). Relationships are the forte of Bucket, whose name may suggest the categorization of information, but who actually serves as a mapper of links.

In this sense and others, *Bleak House* provides a prescient account of informational modernity, though it still holds open the diminishing possibilities of a more aesthetic mode of searching. We see this when Bucket says of the murder of Tulkinghorn: "It is a beautiful case—a beautiful case.... I mean from my point of view. As considered from other points of view, such cases will always involve more or less unpleasantness."[72] Regarded from a New Historicist perspective, Bucket's invocation of beauty can be taken to mask a wholly disciplinary function in that his ruminations on the fine art of murder allow him to surveil the reactions of his suspects, just as he elsewhere ingratiates himself with informants by leveraging his musical talents and taste for gardens and statuary. Yet given the opacity of his character and the mystery of his black-box methods, it seems precipitous to conclude that Dickens denies the power of aesthetics in matters of searching, especially considering how he sometimes compares crimes and crime solving to "schools of Art"—a conflation of the detective and artist figure also evident in Balzac, Poe, and Wilkie Collins.[73] As dramatically as *Bleak House* elaborates on the self-consuming horrors of textual excess, and as brilliantly as Bucket can represent the rise of state informational control, Bucket also points toward the potential of intuitively, artistically, and even miraculously managing superabundance, of returning—like Esther at the end of the novel, or like some oddly insistent teacher of literature—to the reclamation of beauty and wonder in an information age.

Of course, Esther in *Bleak House* is largely excluded from the novel's informational plots, and it is not until *Our Mutual Friend* that Dickens takes up the management of information as a fully elaborated, formally integrated, and richly gendered theme. From Moretti's (quantitative) analysis of character interactions, to Jonathan Grossman's (historicist) discussion of transportation technology, to Anna Gibson's (New Materialist) account of Victorian biology, to Caroline Levine's (more theoretical) focus on the formal and political affordances of distributed systems, scholars have examined how Dickens in general and *Our Mutual Friend* in particular both reflect and reflect on the complexities of Victorian networks.[74] Levine is especially insightful on how Dickens dramatizes the impossibility of curtailing relations, and one further implication of applying network theory to Dickens is the question of how informational webs carrying immense amounts of data challenge the capacities of characters, writers, and readers to find meaning under conditions of excess.

Our Mutual Friend is full of scenes of overwhelming superabundance and searching. Boatmen fish for bodies in the foggy vastness of the Thames. Inspectors seek John Harmon, and suitors track Lizzie through the mazes of London and watercourses beyond. Characters search for everything from books to missing limbs to the perfect orphan for adoption. Excavating a central symbol of the novel, Wegg and Venus dig for treasure in Boffin's dust heaps, a process described in an 1850 *Household Words* article: "We cannot better describe [the dust heaps of London], than by presenting a brief sketch of the different departments of the Searchers and Sorters, who . . . busy themselves upon the mass of original matters which are shot out from the carts of the dustmen."[75] Just as efforts to search and sort material excess are crucial to *Our Mutual Friend*, attempts to find, collect, organize, and monetize information are pervasive in Dickens's novel—at schools, dinner parties, and legal offices; in blackmail schemes and financial conspiracies.

More metacritically, reading itself occurs in *Our Mutual Friend* under conditions of surfeit. Boffin attests that he has no time for "shoveling and sifting at alphabeds [*sic*]" and so hires the somewhat literate Wegg because "all Print is open to him!"[76] Boffin's hyperbole overlooks myriad complications—physical (the finding and retrieving of books), economic (the cost of owning and borrowing reading materials), social (unskilled laborers such as Wegg were discouraged from using public libraries), and epistemological (the thought of anyone comprehending "all Print" is as absurd as Dorothea Brooke imagining, "I should learn everything then").[77] Boffin's misplaced faith in a transparent print sphere subverts a strain of Victorian optimism about the power of texts to promote Christian knowledge and circulate useful information. It can also puncture fantasies of a ubiquitous Dickens who transcended differences of region and class. As Johns, following Altick, has suggested, visions of transatlantic readers tracking together Little Nell's demise may say more about desires for imagined communities than actual historical conditions.[78] Just as print historians are increasingly emphasizing how media ecologies develop in uneven, asymmetrical ways, and just as digital utopians have learned that information is not so easily freed or put in the service of freedom, any hope that Wegg is an enlightened purveyor of information proves false when the villain is overwhelmed by masses of books. Readers know immediately not to trust Wegg, but they may find themselves strangely familiar with his plight as *Our Mutual Friend* taxes capacities for comprehension. Victorian readers on both sides of the Atlantic complained of the novel's mazy plot and legion of characters. Even Dickens struggled to control his information during composition—overwriting installments, changing directions, and straying from his working outline and notes.[79]

One complexity of *Our Mutual Friend* is that the management of information in the novel is not in itself a good or bad thing but depends on the standing of the manager. The murderous Headstone and manipulative financier Fledgeby are miserable conversationalists with no eloquence or wit, and so—by a kind of corollary logic—their treatment of information is systematic to a fault. Headstone's docketing of facts in strict disciplinary categories is compared to "mechanical stowage" in a "mental warehouse," while Fledgeby keeps track of his many accounts through a complex protocol of ledgers, keys, and drawers (217). Yet informational practices in *Our Mutual Friend* are not always insidious or incompatible with the literary. The sympathetic Sloppy pledges to build a bureau with drawers to organize Jenny Wren's fabric scraps, while John Rokesmith (aka John Harmon) serves as Boffin's "secretary," bringing "perfect comprehension" to his "disordered papers" (193):

> Mr. Rokesmith sat down quietly at the table, arranged the open papers into an orderly heap, cast his eyes over each in succession, folded it, docketed it on the outside, laid it in a second heap, and, when the second heap was complete and the first gone, took from his pocket a piece of string and tied it together with a remarkably dexterous hand. . . . All compact and methodical. "Apple pie order!" said Mr. Boffin. (179–80)

Information management in the nineteenth century was often associated with male-coded public spheres, especially when calculating businessmen, scientists, and suitors are set at odds with feminine domesticity. In Dickens's work, Esther Summerson, Sissy Jupe, Florence Dombey, and Dora Spenlow generally participate in this dualism, though Wemmick of *Great Expectations* (1861) exposes the absurdity of too cleanly separating spheres, and *Our Mutual Friend* through Rokesmith and others envisions a domestication of information.

Here aesthetics and ethics again prove decisive. That Fledgeby does business while lying in bed indicates how his manipulation of information corrupts the most personal areas of his life. A happier model is Eugene Wrayburn's bedroom, where he files documents in the alphabetized pigeonholes of a secretary desk, which he associates with the "domestic virtues" of his kitchenette, which shares the same feminized space (284). Similarly, in Rokesmith's domicile, the sitting room contains "sheets upon sheets of memoranda and calculations in figures," but it is also "tastefully" furnished with shelves of literature and an "elegantly framed" print of a "pretty woman" who resembles Bella Wilfer (451). The point is not simply that the "male domestic" Rokesmith handles data and documents as neatly as a reader of *The Complete British Family Housewife* might arrange a room or meal (450). Against the masculine backdrop of ledgers and appointment books, pigeonholed desks and secretaries, mercantile counting houses and bureaucratic police stations with their "methodical book-keeping" and "administrative genius" (762–63), Rokesmith—and to a lesser degree, Wrayburn and Reginald Wilfer—bring to *Our Mutual Friend* a capacity for information management figured positively in domestic registers.

Thus, Rokesmith proves a suitable match for the newly disciplined but still aesthetically sensitive Bella, who brings domestic bliss into her father's counting house and as a wife "store[s] up the City Intelligence" with her "mastering of the newspaper" (682). Bella's facility can indicate how Victorian women were not wholly excluded from informational domains. Conduct manuals on female reading from the early nineteenth century recommended that imaginative books be supplemented with the systematic acquisition of information. Hannah More's *Strictures on the Modern System of Female Education* (1799) actually preferred the acquisition of "accurate and simple facts" over the reading of fiction, while Lydia Sigourney's *Letters to Young Ladies* (1833) warned about "habits of excursive fancy" and recommended informational reading practices instead. Sigourney wrote of the ideal student: "Her first effort is to *receive* knowledge; her second, to *retain* it; her last, to *bring it forth*, when it is needed."[80] Household management manuals from the Victorian period provide familiar evidence of narrow gender roles, but such books, along with etiquette and conduct guides, self-consciously ushered Victorian females into informational modernity by instructing them on how to handle printed materials, correspondence, calendars, and household accounts, including in some cases double-entry bookkeeping.[81] Outside the home, Price has shown how during Dickens's later career secretarial work was becoming less of a white-collar male job and more "pink-collar" employment for women.[82] Females were sometimes discouraged from reading newspapers beyond birth and marriage announcements, but they also handled information understood as such in domestic spheres and beyond.[83] For all of Dickens's gender stereotyping, Rokesmith's domestication of textual superabundance and Bella's mastery of the newspaper show that sympathetic characters regardless of sex can temper the instrumental brutality of single-minded information management. Rokesmith and Bella find each other. Wrayburn (not Headstone) finds Lizzie and redemption. The Boffins (not the police or Wegg) find out Rokesmith's real identity. And readers who are able to both manage

FIGURE 2.2. R. W. Buss, *Dickens' Dream* (c. 1872), unfinished watercolor. By permission of Charles Dickens Museum.

the plot and feel for the characters of *Our Mutual Friend* will find fulfilling reading experiences. To find what one seeks in Dickens's last completed novel is to reconcile the informational and the literary.

The recuperation of virtue, beauty, and truth under conditions of textual excess need not be taken as a denial of or capitulation to the rise of information. In an unfinished watercolor by R. W. Buss titled *Dickens' Dream* (c. 1872), Dickens's prodigious literary creativity is anterior to but also framed by information structures of the Victorian age (see figure 2.2).

As a young man, Buss was fired as an illustrator of *The Pickwick Papers* because he lacked the technical expertise to etch the steel plates necessary for a book that had become a mass print sensation. Four decades after being cashiered, two years after Dickens's death, and basing his painting on an 1862 photograph taken in Dickens's personal library, Buss in *Dickens' Dream* depicts the author lost in thought, his chair pulled back from his desk, while around him float a menagerie of characters from his many famous novels. Dickens is neither reading nor writing. His head is bowed in sleep or reverie. Not a scrap of paper can be seen on his well-ordered desk. His hands are empty except for a cigar (not a pen), as if he has left material textuality behind to enter into a purely imaginative state. We may have a desire, at least partially shared by Buss, to see Dickens's relationships with his fictions as intimate to the point of unmediated—a desire Dickens cultivated with his familiar prefaces to his affectionate public, one he gratified on British and American stages by impersonating characters from his books, one reinforced by rumors of his comment to Dostoevsky about his characters being parts of himself, and one reflected by critics (including some print culture scholars) who take Dickens's work in general and Little Nell's death in particular to evince a transatlantic community of readers enjoying aesthetic experiences simultaneously.[84] A fundamental dynamic of Dickens's enchantment is that he encourages us, and we often abet him, in bracketing the informational contexts that his novels never entirely efface.

Yet if Dickens's mastery of print culture helps us imagine his transcendence of it, in the background of *Dickens' Dream*, partially visible through Buss's lightly sketched clouds of characters, are bookshelves reaching up from the floor and extending rightward and upward beyond the frame of the painting. The shelves are filled with books that visually echo the rectilinear order of Dickens's many-drawered desk. Unlike portraits from the eighteenth century in which a single tome is lovingly held or a few volumes are placed within arm's reach, a multitude of books fill the sunlit shelves that loom behind and over Dickens. The well-organized library contains uniform collections that might include Dickens's own sumptuous twenty-two-volume Library Edition of his works (1859). When compared to the foregrounded swirl of characters conjured by Dickens's fancy, the background of Buss's watercolor evokes a dream very different from one of unmediated transcendence—handsome collections neatly ranged on built-in bookshelves in a roomy, sun-filled office unencumbered by the chaos of informational tasks such as the essays, forms, and memos on my real and virtual desktops that I should be dealing with right now.

In conjunction with dreams of unmediated literary creativity is the fantasy of a well-ordered informational life. In addition to managing newspapers, magazines, serial plots, guild associations, charity homes, theatrical performances, excursions, dinner parties, and extramarital intimacies, Dickens had a habit of reorganizing the furniture in any room in which he stayed. He kept a carefully ordered desk, shipping his ornaments (including bronze dogs, dueling frogs, and a china monkey) so that he could duplicate his desk arrangements when living overseas. During his travels through Italy, Dickens requested of his wife, Catherine, back in England: "Keep things in their places. I can't bear to picture them otherwise."[85] Like Dickens's meticulously casual dress and the carefully organized chaos of his novels, the personal library of *Dickens' Dream* reflects the disciplined orderliness of a man who knew the disorderly excesses of life. It matters how one displays one's books, and *Dickens' Dream* bespeaks respectability and order. But as if to remind the dreamy critic of differences between the literary and the informational, in Dickens's beautifully organized shelves none of the books have legible titles. To manage a large number of texts is sometimes to defer more intensive kinds of reading and writing.

Notes, Queries, and Familiar Quotations

When Hawthorne and Dickens justify the capacities of artists to manage information, their narratives ironically focus less on the content of texts and more on systems and processes of retrieval, as if to encounter textual excess, even with a preference for aesthetic sensibilities, is to work at least partially in an informational mode set in tension with close reading. Explication in this sense is not a hermetic exercise so much as a metacritical and metamedial practice, and similar arguments might be made for other mid-nineteenth-century fictions obsessed with methods of interpretation and searching, reading and nonreading, including

1. Poe's "The Purloined Letter" (1844), wherein the poet and mathematician Dupin combines intuition and informational reasoning to recover a singular missive that escapes the protocols of the Parisian police. Dupin's genius reveals that the stolen letter has been purposely misfiled in an organizing rack intended for visiting cards. The story thus insists that in matters of searching, literary sensibilities surpass algorithmic methods, though Poe elides close reading by withholding and rendering irrelevant the contents of the purloined letter itself.
2. Benjamin Disraeli's *Sybil* (1845), wherein the antiquarian Hatton searches overwhelming archives with a combination of intuitive genius and algorithmic rigor. He thinks to himself, "Those infernal papers! . . . [I]t required thousands [of assistant researchers] to work them, and even with thousands they could only be worked by myself." Hatton learns from close reading a singular document that certain papers will restore Sybil to her estate, but they must be retrieved from a fortress-like library during a laborers' riot in

which a mob rifles through the "piles of parchment deeds, bundles of papers arranged and docketed, [and] many boxes of various size and material." A sympathetic editor discovers the crucial box holding the texts that lead to Sybil's restoration, but—as in "The Purloined Letter"—the exact contents of the documents are never disclosed as systems of storage and methods of retrieval take precedent over textual contents.[86]

3. Melville's *Moby-Dick* (1851), wherein the hunt for a singular whale in the boundless ocean can be likened to the search for an extraordinary text in the vastness of the archives. Punctuated by efforts to gather and organize overwhelming amounts of facts, *Moby-Dick* simultaneously participates in and ironizes information management. Ahab abjures the information of logbooks and whale charts, finally locating Moby Dick through supernatural capacities associated with romantic aesthetics. Yet if Ahab's literary methods help him find what he seeks—the whale most worthy of interpretation—that text remains notoriously illegible, as when Ishmael says of the sperm whale's wrinkled brow, "Read it if you can."[87]

4. Wilkie Collins's *Hide and Seek* (1854), *The Woman in White* (1860), and *The Moonstone* (1868), wherein Collins variously manages the disclosure of information through scenes of reading and nonreading, interpretation and the absence thereof. Reviewers of the time complained that Collins subordinated aesthetics to excessive information, thus making his novels mere narrative puzzles that functioned as data delivery systems.[88] But if the ex-clerk Collins was fully enmeshed in the rise of mass print and factual discourse, his novels—perhaps by way of disavowal and compensation—feature artist-protagonists, heightened sensations, exotic myths, and unaccountable intuitions. Facing information overload, Collins's seekers are often most successful when they proceed in literary modes.

5. Eliot's *Middlemarch* (1872), wherein the roar of reality's excessive details means that "interpretations are illimitable." Finding truth is a challenge of subjectivity and hermeneutics, but also one of superabundance, as suggested by Casaubon's struggle to organize his voluminous notes as he seeks the Key to all Mythologies. The Key is a kind of overdetermining index, but Casaubon cannot even index his notes, bequeathing to Dorothea the fruitless task of creating a "Synoptic Tabulation." No stranger to prodigious

antiquarian researches, developments in information technology, and reflections on reading in an age of mass print, Eliot offers Dorothea as a more humane alternative to Casaubon's desiccated information management, which threatens to reduce the interpretation of art to a kind of algorithmic code breaking.[89]

As different as these fictions are, they share a sense that the literary—variously understood as a genre, a hermeneutic, and a set of personal capacities—is compatible with but offers affordances beyond informational methods of searching.

The felt need to mark distinctions between literature and information comes in part from the possibilities of conflation, which in the nineteenth century included bibliographic efforts to organize superabundant literary texts. Such organization has a history stretching well before the nineteenth century. Yuval Noah Harari has argued that information management preconditions the spread of writing through the ancient world: whether one is talking about cuneiform clay tablets, printed books, or digital materials, texts have little practical use if they cannot be efficiently retrieved.[90] As Anne Blair has shown, the history of managing textual excess can begin in earnest with medieval and early modern bibliographic practices whose emergences predate the ascension of print and prefigure modern efforts to order information—from note-taking systems to indexing methods to the compilation of quotations in florilegia.[91] In the later eighteenth and nineteenth centuries, the scope, accessibility, and sophistication of such projects increased alongside mass print, book collecting, book history, library expansion, and the "black-letter" source hunting of scholars. Jon Klancher notes that *bibliographia* first appeared as an English encyclopedia entry in 1797; Robert Darnton dates the beginnings of analytic bibliography in England to the nineteenth century; and Geoffrey Nunberg points out that the first modern usage of "reference work" appeared in 1859.[92] Encyclopedias flourished, of course, in the eighteenth century, and the nineteenth century saw the rise of library science and bibliographic projects such as William Poole's landmark *Index to Periodical Literature* (1853), which presented magazine resources as an immense "labyrinth" while praising learned articles (as opposed to full treatises) for providing "concise and abbreviated information."[93] German romantics resisted comprehensive efforts to master textual excess through bibliography, a dynamic also evident in Britain, where aesthetically minded critics described bibliographers as "inferior retainers of literature" and called bibliography "not among the first, or even second, order of intellectual pursuits."[94] Nineteenth-century efforts to gather and organize literary information remained aesthetically and epistemologically suspect. What is gained and lost when literature is represented in catalogs, encyclopedias, concordances, florilegia, and antiquarian journals? Is it possible to undertake such work without agonizing over the relationship between the literary and the informational?

Beginning in 1849 (and running to this day), the London-based journal *Notes and Queries* indicates one way in which Victorians attempted to handle superabundant literature by turning it into information. Subtitled "A Medium of Inter-Communication for Literary Men, Artists, Antiquaries, Genealogists, Etc.," the weekly was edited by William Thoms, a leading member of London's Society of Antiquaries, who hoped to consolidate the correspondence that circulated among personal and institutional antiquarian networks. In a playful introduction to the inaugural volume of *Notes and Queries*, Thoms simultaneously laments and praises the vastness of his era's archives. They contain a superabundance of information, which exceeds the capacities of memory, which thus requires the making of research notes, which in turn presents the problem of organizing and retrieving the multifarious forms such notes can take—"some unposted in old pocket books—some on whole or half sheets, or mere scraps of paper, and backs of letters—some lost sight of and forgotten, stuffing out old portfolios, or getting smoky edges in bundles tied up with faded tape [in] countless boxes and drawers, and pigeon-holes." A literary critic might sympathize, though Thoms is more concerned with managing information than engaging in aesthetic or interpretive reading. After focusing on the materiality of notes and the systems that fail to order them, he announces his journal as a "methodizing of the chaos," just as subsequent contributors called for a "SYSTEMATIC ARRANGEMENT of *all* the existing literary knowledge in the world that is considered *of value* by those best qualified to judge."[95] A sense of literary value remained, but *Notes and Queries* largely saw itself as an organizer of antiquarian information.

It really tried. Yearly indexes to the journal included over a thousand subject titles, and issues were divided into various sections—"Notes," "Minor Notes," "Queries," "Replies," "Minor Queries," and "Replies to Minor Queries." The journal soon ran to over one thousand densely printed pages a year, and a single weekly volume could include short pieces on prehistoric tree sloths, similarities between Tajik and Scandinavian legends, the use of water clocks by ancient orators, mosaics in medieval churches, data on how much authors earned for famous works, and rumors about the illegitimate son of Queen Elizabeth. Other queries and replies included information on philology in Shakespeare, the provenance of rare books, historical instances of "Hurrah!" as a war cry, and (as in Dickens's "The

Doom of English Wills") the rights of antiquarians working in parish registers. That *Notes and Queries* contains a "Miscellaneous" section feels like something of a joke, for the entire enterprise is wonderfully and woefully miscellaneous, less a reference work than a loosely refereed LISTSERV or an interdisciplinary journal at its worst.

Hyperspecialized modern scholars laboring under professional strictures may admire the sheer rambunctiousness of *Notes and Queries*, whose promiscuous mixing of lay and scholarly contributors and idiosyncratic jags of enthusiasm suggest the unbounded joy a student might feel in the archives before some stern advisor insists that intellectual curiosity and the interesting information it generates must of course lead toward an intervention with stakes that field experts might recognize as such. This is the linear, hierarchical process by which data and facts become disciplined into knowledge. However, as Noah Heringman has shown, antiquarianism in the romantic period was an expansive, predisciplinary domain, and *Notes and Queries* in its early years continued this tradition as antiquarians, genealogists, artists, bibliophiles, and dilettantes shared equal footing with so-called Literary Men—all of them searching for answers in a network of researchers whose interests were often more informational than literary, more concerned with disarticulated, empirical facts than with aesthetics and interpretation.[96]

Whether the game was worth the candle was not entirely clear. Anthony Grafton's work on the rise of the footnote shows how some nineteenth-century thinkers celebrated the learning and pleasures of archival documentation, while novels such as *Sybil*, *The Scarlet Letter*, and Eliot's *Romola* (1863) dramatize the intellectual contributions of antiquarianism, as well as its affective power—what Piper has called the melancholy "lost-and-foundness" of reaching back to an old book.[97] That said, Emerson's condescension in 1850 was fairly representative:

> We have to thank the researches of antiquaries, and the Shakespeare Society.... [T]hey have left no book-stall unsearched, no chest in a garret unopened, no file of old yellow accounts to decompose in damp and worms, so keen was the hope to discover whether the boy Shakspeare poached or not, whether he held horses at the theater door, whether he kept school, and why he left in his will only his second-best bed to Ann Hathaway, his wife.... There is something touching in the madness with which the passing age mischooses the object on which all candles shine.[98]

Similarly, and in line with his conviction that there are no facts and only interpretations, Nietzsche complained in "On the Uses and Disadvantages of History for Life" (1874) that antiquarian fact gathering is too myopic to inspire personal action, critical thought, or the synthesizing capacities of consciousness.[99] As English literary studies took its modern form, some Victorians also lamented dry-as-dust researches that would reduce literature to mere information, a complaint voiced in a diversity of contexts—from aesthetic commentaries by Arnold and Ruskin to conflicts between rigorous philologists and more speculative literary critics, from debates over literary education (classical and modern) to condemnations of bibliographic tools designed for cribbing literary knowledge. Such worries did not rise to the level of Jamesonian critique, but some Victorians had a sense that antiquarian fact gathering was undertheorized and insufficiently motivated.

More specifically, commentators on *Notes and Queries* in the popular press tended gently to satirize its miscellaneous information. In June 1851, New York's *Literary World* described the journal as an enterprise driven, not by beauty or truth, but by a hankering for information under conditions of textual superabundance:

> The mouldy cheese of antiquarian knowledge, the deeper it is penetrated, the fuller of spicy odors it becomes. It is your antiquarian who is your true querist. No intellectually famished Yankee backwoodsman, thirsty for news and ravenous of gossip, can compare with [the antiquarian's] cultivated style of interrogatory.—He has grubbed and wormed and toiled and asked questions of the past, of old libraries and book-stalls, and manuscripts, and peering brother fact seekers, till his frame has become bowed and bent, and he is the living impersonation in himself of a note of interrogation. . . . After all, what is man, . . . but a fact himself, a stupendous fact, a curious, crusty, moth-eaten fact?[100]

Melville probably read this article while finishing the manuscript of *Moby-Dick* in the summer of 1851. He was at the time close friends with Evert Duyckinck, editor of the *Literary World*, and did not cancel his subscription to Duyckinck's magazine until after its lukewarm review of *Moby-Dick* in 1852.[101] Moreover, the Sub-Sub-Librarian of *Moby-Dick*, whose prefatory "Extracts" present a miscellaneous collection of quotations about whales, appears to be modeled on the *Literary World*'s pathetic antiquarian. Just as the later "has grubbed and wormed and toiled and asked questions of the past, of old libraries and book-stalls, and manuscripts," Melville's Sub-Sub is a "painstaking burrower and grub-worm" who has "gone through the long Vaticans and street-stalls of the earth, picking up whatever allusions to whales he could anyways find in any book whatsoever, sacred or profane."[102] It is not simply that *Moby-Dick* and the *Literary World* patronize antiquarians with similar diction and tone, or that the Sub-Sub-Librarian seems precisely the kind of researcher who might contribute to *Notes and Queries*, or even that Thoms, in addition to editing *Notes and Queries*, also held the subordinate title of Deputy Librarian to the House of Lords.

Most importantly for our purposes here, both the *Literary World* and *Moby-Dick* suggest that the compilation of literary information is something less than a full-fledged literary enterprise. Like the school Usher whose philological charts also preface *Moby-Dick*, the Sub-Sub-Librarian manages literary materials but remains a lowly information worker without aesthetic or generic discrimination. Neither character has cultural or economic capital (the Usher is an assistant teacher whose duties include dusting textbooks; the "poor devil" of a Sub-Sub labors in a bureaucracy through which, we are told, he will never rise). Both fail to make full sense of literature as they pursue their informational projects, for while the Usher's reduction of the literary to etymology does not do justice to the wonder of whales, the Sub-Sub's ecumenical antiquarianism results in an undifferentiated mass of citations—from literary masterpieces and scientific texts, to adventure novels and unpublished manuscripts. Just as *Moby-Dick* pities these information gatherers, the *Literary World* discerns in *Notes and Queries* a lack of higher ambition. Calling contributors to the journal "Professors of Facts" and "dust-shakers," and comparing them to cuckolds supporting the offspring of others, the *Literary World* is devastatingly judicious: "Fact hunting . . . is not the worst species of hunting. . . . It is simply a harmless gratification of a dangerous instinct. . . . When we consider what these crusts and cheese-parings of learning are a substitute for, we may respect them—at least negatively." For Melville and the *Literary World*, there is nothing pernicious about antiquarian compulsions, but to hunt for information without regard to quality or deeper meaning is to miss the choicest parts of literature.

Prefaces seek to shape receptions, though *Moby-Dick*'s introductory materials proved more successful in anticipating than preempting complaints. Some reviewers appreciated the book's extensive information about marine life, whaling, and ships, but—indicating emerging divisions between the literary and the informational—others objected to what Henry Chorley called Melville's "ill-compounded mixture of romance and matter-of-fact."[103] For his part, Duyckinck in his review in the *Literary World* admired some of *Moby-Dick*'s copious "information," but he also worried of Melville's writings in general: "In one light they are romantic fictions, in another statements of absolute fact."[104] As with many modern readers, Duyckinck struggled with the heterogeneous superabundance of *Moby-Dick*, failing to recognize Melville's metacritical interest in the dynamics between the literary and the informational. When *Moby-Dick* draws analogies between taxonomies of whales and classifications of books, the white whale becomes figured as a bibliographic anomaly pointing toward the larger question—and, as Samuel Otter has argued, the history—of ordering texts.[105] Switching metaphorical references, George Frederick Holmes in 1844 launched an attack on mass print by comparing desultory readers to whales who live entirely off of plankton:

> [T]he mighty monster of the land—facetious and courteously termed "the public"—but more justly named Leviathan—browze [*sic*] upon such priceless and unsubstantial garbage, as that with which of late years it has been gorging itself.[106]

Many critics called for a more rigorous curating of the chaos, but *Moby-Dick* wonders whether one needs to choose between high and low writing, aesthetics and brute facts, literature and information. The Sub-Sub may be pathetic or deserving of sympathy, but his extracts are so fascinating precisely because his textual obsessiveness is undisciplined by thesis or taste.

Notes and Queries is very different from *Moby-Dick*, but it too was self-conscious about the relationship between the literary and the informational, using allusions to both announce and ironize its antiquarian commitments to overwhelming archives. Thoms and his contributors compared themselves to Jonathan Oldbuck and Dominie Sampson, comical antiquarians from Walter Scott's *Guy Mannering* (1815) and *The Antiquary* (1816). They also invoked the spirit of Diedrich Knickerbocker from Washington Irving's *History of New York* (1809), whose absurd dedication to arcane facts is exceeded only by the speciousness of his information. Most contributors to *Notes and Queries* used full names or initials, but others adopted self-satirizing monikers such as "Mr. Cramp," "Corkscrew," and "Aegrotus (suggesting that antiquarianism is a kind of sickness). Most telling is the epigraph from the title pages of *Notes and Queries*, a celebrated saying from Dickens's Captain Cuttle: "When found, make a note of." In *Dombey and Son* (1848), Captain Cuttle is a supremely disorganized, chuckle-headed, good-hearted character, who winds up working in a ragtag curiosity shop that stands in contrast to the impersonal, rigorously ordered offices of Dombey's mercantile empire. The invocation of Cuttle in *Notes and Queries* indicates Thoms's ambivalence about his informational endeavor, which aspires to the systematic arrangement of notes even as it relishes its inability to organize the wonderfully wide world of literary facts.

Notes and Queries would become increasingly professionalized and inspire the American historical journal the *Historical Magazine, and Notes and Queries* (begun in 1857), whose purpose was to form a network of state historical societies and thereby "furnish a medium . . . by which important but isolated facts may be preserved, and historic and literary doubts be proposed and solved."[107] Thesis statements and critical stakes would eventually win the day as antiquarian interests were increasingly disciplined or, as Nancy Glazener has argued, marginalized.[108] But the roots of *Notes and Queries* indicate how the hunt for isolated literary information was regarded as an unfinished and unfinishable project steering between order and chaos, seriousness and play, facts and aesthetics, disciplinary knowledge and more trivial pursuits.

Now and in the nineteenth century, it is not difficult to diminish antiquarianism, and one imperative of the current crisis in the humanities is to avoid being tarred by that brush. Yet even Nietzsche, as read by Foucault in a founding document of the New Historicism, came to respect the antiquarian hankering for facts as a worthy intellectual pursuit. In the words of Foucault, "a field of entangled and confused parchments" does not necessarily lead to myopia when documentary chaos reveals to the theoretically inclined eye the "heterogeneous systems" that constitute history.[109] Most Victorian contributors to *Notes and Queries* were far from working in such a critical mode. They found meaning and pleasure in searching the archives for disarticulated literary facts that were not objects for anecdotal interpretation or philosophies of history so much as data to be found, noted, shared, indexed, and thereby made into a kind of information reflecting but not equivalent to a passion for the literary.

We might take the partially organized cornucopia of *Notes and Queries* as an opportunity to think about undisciplined pleasure, scholarly irrelevancy, archival affect, and the epistemological modesty demanded by the heterogeneous systems that often accompany textual superabundance. We might also take *Notes and Queries* to mark the incapacity of informational methods to subsume the literary entirely under its logic, indicating both the distinctiveness and the marginalization of humanistic inquiry in an information age. *Notes and Queries* can even afford an occasion to think about the empiricist turn in current literary studies that includes not only traditional archival practices but also the New Materialism, work in science and literature, the digital humanities, and even surface reading. Empirical approaches to literature entail, among other things, a shifting sense of what counts as literary knowledge. The committed fact gathering of some historicist scholarship can be ungenerously reduced by devotees of aesthetics, interpretation, and theory to the thesis statement, "Hey, look what I found!" This is one of the accusations of "The Manifesto of the V21 Collective" (2015), which conflates archival research, naive positivism, and informationalism in its antihistoricist polemic.[110] A counterargument might point out that archival fact gathering both tempers and offers an alternative to the speculative excesses of interpretation and theoretically driven criticism ("Hey, look what I can think!"). It is also worth noting that antihistoricism has a history that it is practically destined to undervalue.

Be that as it may, the broader argument of this chapter is that literary interpretation and aesthetics are entangled with, not opposed to, the searching of archival information. To reiterate, such entanglement does not amount to equivalence. *Notes and Queries* in the Victorian period largely avoided literary criticism and was happy to satirize its antiquarian aims. It acknowledged but finally left untroubled the "so what?" questions of the literary, as if disarticulated literary information was in itself enchanting or at least diverting enough. A pioneer of archival historicist methods, Leopold von Ranke wrote in 1824:

> Consider the strange feelings that would arise in someone who entered a great collection of antiquities, in which genuine and spurious, beautiful and repulsive, spectacular and insignificant objects, from many nations and periods, lay next to one another in complete disorder. This is also how someone would have to feel who found himself all at once within sight of the varied monuments of modern history. They speak to us in a thousand different voices; they reveal the most widely different natures; they are dressed in all the colors.[111]

Before Ranke goes on to recommend more rigorous methods of curation and argumentation, fans of *Notes and Queries* (and some new historicists) might interject: Yes, yes, a thousand times, yes!

In 1900, five years before his death and suffering from declining eyesight, John Bartlett concluded a ninety-two-page manuscript catalogued at Harvard's Houghton Library under the title "List: of Books Read." Bartlett spent his life surrounded by texts at the forefront of America's print revolution. Born in Plymouth, Massachusetts, in 1820, he did not attend college but progressed from a bookbinder and clerk to owner of the Harvard University bookstore. He ran his own printing business, served as a paymaster during the American Civil War, and later became a partner in the Boston publishing house of Little, Brown and Company.[112] Bartlett authored his century's preeminent concordance to Shakespeare, collected and catalogued hundreds of books on fishing, and between 1855 and 1891 produced nine editions of his most enduring work, *Bartlett's Familiar Quotations*. "List: of Books Read" testifies to Bartlett's ongoing efforts to manage his vast quantities of reading. The manuscript begins with a short autobiographical preface tracing Bartlett's ancestors from the days of William the Conqueror to Plymouth Rock to the American Revolutionary War. Yet when Bartlett begins the story of his own life, he starts not with world events but with books: "I had an early taste for reading and before the age of twelve had read most of the juvenile literature of the period."[113] Bartlett's early favorites included adventure novels from Jane Porter, James Fenimore Cooper, and Scott, but whereas he presents his juvenile reading as comfortable and comprehensive, books come to bring more confusion than joy by the time he becomes an adult. Bartlett recalls, "In 1837 I was entered as clerk in a bookstore, and found myself amid a world of books in wandering mazes lost. Without a guide, philosopher, or friend, I plunged in, driving through the sea of books like a vessel without pilot or rudder." As hard a time as it was, the allusions to Pope and Milton testify that Bartlett survived his rough passage from enchanted youth to overwhelmed young adulthood to a kind of literary mastery. It is not unlike the bildungsroman some imagine for graduate students in English.

Bartlett's autobiographical preface presents him as a highly successful autodidact, though with his fortunate fall into textual excess, the escapist pleasures of his early reading give way to an informational impulse exemplified by the trio of epigraphs to "List: of Books Read":

(1) "Knowledge is of two kinds: we know a subject ourselves, or we know where we can find information upon it.—Samuel Johnson."
(2) "To know where you can find anything is, after all, the greatest part of erudition—Anon." [Translated from Latin.]
(3) "A man may *read* at any time, if he will set himself doggedly to it."

Following these epigraphs and Bartlett's four-page autobiography is a neatly written, eighty-six-page inventory of thousands of book titles, authors, and dates of reading that cover the sixty-three years between Bartlett's first job at a bookstore and the decline of his eyesight at the age of eighty. With no opinions proffered about the texts listed and no commentary on Bartlett's adult reading experiences, "List: of Books Read" is a curious document—both a life story and a catalogue of books by a man who defines himself as a reader but says nothing about the beauty, value, or joy of books. This absence of the literary is also evident in Bartlett's publications, including his *Familiar Quotations*.

Bartlett's signature achievement joined a long-standing genre while also registering important departures. Blair has discussed a florilegia tradition stretching back to the medieval period in which intellectual elites managed textual superabundance by plucking the wisest and most eloquent passages for scholarly reference and personal edification. Price has shown how such practices became increasingly formalized with the emergence of anthologies and other compilation genres during the late eighteenth century as the emergence of "a culture of the excerpt" accompanied shifting legal and educational norms. For Altick, aesthetics and pleasure became more central to quotation books in the eighteenth century, particularly with the success of compendia intended to entertain popular audiences; and this tradition continued into the nineteenth century as most prefaces to florilegia take beauty and morality as primary selection criteria.[114] Sarah Josepha Hale called her *Complete Dictionary of Poetical Quotations* (1849) a "precious casket" of "the most perfect gems" chosen for "beauty," "excellence," "taste," and "Genius." Isabella Rushton Preston's *Handbook of Familiar Quotations* (1853), from which Bartlett cribbed some entries, praised the "imagination" of writers whose "beautiful fragments" she selects.[115] J. Hain Friswell's *Familiar Words* (1865), a book that sparked a dispute with Bartlett over plagiarized entries and indexing methods, also paid tribute to beauty, wit, and pleasure as reasons for including passages.[116]

By contrast, the first preface to *Bartlett's Familiar Quotations* announces its aim to be an "accurate" and "convenient book of reference," while the second edition only nods to the trope of "'beautiful fragments,'" which Bartlett puts in quotes.[117] Later prefaces during Bartlett's life omit such gestures entirely and do not mention aesthetics, instead elaborating on utility, accuracy, indexing, and the ever-growing quantity of entries. Bartlett thus presents his *Familiar Quotations*, not as a guide to or expression of interest in taste, but rather as a tool for managing literary information in an era overwhelmed with texts. This goal was foregrounded by a sympathetic review of *Bartlett's* in 1868: "This is not a collection of 'familiar beauties,'"—"familiar beauties" appearing again in quotes—for *Bartlett's* value lies in "its being indexed, double indexed, and cross indexed to a degree of minuteness and fullness that nothing in it can escape search."[118] As searching technologies such as card catalogs, concordances, Poole's *Index*, and schemes such as the Dewey Decimal System (1876) broadened their scope and sophistication, *Bartlett's* was less an occasion for aesthetic experience than a literary reference work.

Accordingly, the book was vulnerable to charges of reducing literature to information. As suggested by its use of familiarity as a main principle of selection, *Bartlett's* was not premised on enchantment or intimacy but rather on conventional literary knowledge, which Bartlett associates with "'household words.'"[119] Such familiarity occupies what Nancy Bentley has shown to be the slippery ground between high literature and mass culture, between cultural capital and popular entertainment.[120] Bartlett does not justify his selection of quotations with some Arnoldian notion of "best" and in fact specifically notes in an 1863 preface that quotations are not admitted "simply on their own merits."[121] Nor does Bartlett imply under the era's evolutionary logic that familiarity correlates with quality. Nor does he deploy the usual disclaimer that his selections reflect his own idiosyncratic tastes (except perhaps for a frontispiece quote from Montaigne that appears in some editions: "I have gathered a posie of other men's flowers, and nothing but the thread that binds them is mine own"). Nor does *Bartlett's* follow the practices of nineteenth-century scrapbook makers who, as Ellen Gruber Garvey has shown, managed textual and informational excess through highly personalized curatorial efforts.[122] The only self-regard in *Bartlett's Familiar Quotations* lies in the title itself.

Like E. D. Hirsch's controversial *Cultural Literacy* (1987), Bartlett's principle of familiarity subordinates sensibilities to convention by situating readers within a mainstream literary heritage that is more or less assumed. Some of Bartlett's prefaces briefly mention the difficulty of determining degrees of familiarity, but unsurprisingly the Bible and Shakespeare dominate selections throughout the nineteenth century. Moreover, just as Hirsch treats literature as "information" and privileges "writings that culturally literate people have read about but haven't read," *Bartlett's* answers the challenge that textual excess poses to canons and cultural homogeneity: even if one has no firsthand experience of Literature, one should at least know what that Literature is.[123] *Bartlett's* also had a further informational purpose in that by identifying passages, assuring accuracy, and rendering its entries so searchable, it served as an authoritative reference work for quotations and their sources. In the mid-nineteenth century, literary magazines such as the *Literary World* and the *Critic* followed *Notes and Queries* by running columns that verified and identified lines submitted by inquiring readers. Toward the end of the century, such magazines increasingly referred such questions to *Bartlett's* while chiding questioners for not consulting *Bartlett's* first.

Compared to the loose networking of *Notes and Queries*, *Bartlett's Familiar Quotations* offered a smaller database and superior searching technology, though it too treated literature, not as organic texts in which sensitive readers immerse themselves, but rather as information to be isolated, indexed, retrieved, reconfigured, recirculated, and repurposed, often—as many detractors complained—as a sort of counterfeit cultural capital. Such critiques were hardly new to the Victorian age or to *Bartlett's Familiar Quotations*. As early as the fifteenth century, scholars charged that florilegia "maketh men idle, and yet opinionative, and well conceited of themselves," while also helping "students show a learning that they do not really have."[124] Hannah More voiced similar concerns in her *Strictures on the Modern System of Female Education* (1799) when complaining about the "swarms of *Abridgements, Beauties*, and *Compendiums*" that are "an infallible receipt for making a superficial mind."[125] Jane Austen's Emma Woodhouse evinces this point insofar as she is a clever dilettante who never finishes her lists of books to read (let alone the books themselves) but is well acquainted with Vicesimus Knox's *Elegant Extracts* (1784), a popular compendium that *Blackwood's* in 1859 designated an "Objectionable Book" favored by the "superficial boarding-school miss."[126] One such miss, though hardly superficial, is Lucy Snowe of Charlotte Brontë's *Villette* (1853), who faces the accusation that one of her essays "had extracted the pith out of books [she] had not so much as heard of."[127] In Price's words, quotation compendia can pose an "ethical embarrassment" when users neither earn nor profit from an ornamental literary knowledge that (to quote Emerson's metaphor) comes from the "auctioneer," not the "mine."[128]

More specifically, critics dismissed *Bartlett's Familiar Quotations* as a tool for philistines in the same way that some intellectuals belittle Wikipedia (no matter how much they actually use it). Writing of a gentleman caller who made reference to *Bartlett's*, the Civil War diarist Sarah Morgan proclaimed, "Human intelligence must be of the lowest order when such an auxiliary is called in."[129] An 1890 satire in *Puck* made a similar point when describing a drunken college student skimming textbook indexes, encyclopedia entries, and a well-worn edition of *Bartlett's* as he desperately churns out a hackneyed essay for his next day's rhetoric class.[130] Michael David Cohen has shown how Little, Brown and Company began marketing *Familiar Quotations* to a middlebrow audience after Bartlett's death, and such readers are the butt of Jeanette Gilder's joke in a 1906 column from the *Critic*: a woman announces that Bartlett is her favorite author because he writes the best epigrams.[131] During a period in which the expansion of reference books made it easier to make a passing acquaintance with literature, failing to distinguish the literary and the informational was becoming all too common.

Which can be particularly threatening to literary writers committed to aesthetic distinctions. In Edith Wharton's *The Custom of the Country* (1913), the unscrupulous Elmer Moffatt draws heavily from *Bartlett's Familiar Quotations* when compiling a grandiloquent July Fourth speech to bedazzle his midwestern audience.[132] Here *Bartlett's* stands not only for superficiality and bombast but also for the fungibility of cultural capital in an age of information. Unlike Henry James's Gilbert Osmond or Lambert Strether, whose antiquarianism and book collecting can be distressingly tasteful, Moffatt is a vulgar political operator who masters the information networks of the novel and whose appetite for beautiful things, including women, has less to do with aesthetic sensibilities than with an instinct for the collection and display of commodities that other consumers desire. The word "familiar" appears thirty-nine times in Wharton's novel; and just as being socially familiar with suspect characters implicates Undine Spragg in social arrangements she does not fully understand, *Bartlett's* helps Moffatt instrumentalize literary knowledge he does not grasp through intimate reading. Because people desire the things with which they are familiar but do not fully possess (economically or epistemologically), familiarity for Moffatt strikes a profitable balance between aesthetics and mass culture, between what Wharton presents as the legitimately personal appreciation of art and the reduction of artistic judgment to cultural and economic capital. Wharton is no Adorno or Horkheimer. She believes in a domain of autonomous aesthetics, howsoever anachronistic and untenable that domain might be. As a result, *The Custom of the Country* is all the more sensitive to how projects like *Bartlett's* turn literary knowledge into portable commodities stripped of humanist value—how (quoting Bentley on Wharton's novel) "[a]ny real distinction between beauty and property has collapsed."[133] Elmer Moffatt thus stands as a rebuke to one of Bartlett's epigraphs from "List: of Books Read": knowing where to find something is *not*, in the age of *Bartlett's* or Google, the greatest part of erudition.

More extreme than *Bartlett's Familiar Quotations* in subordinating literary reading to informational searching is Bartlett's monumental concordance to Shakespeare, published in 1894. Three decades earlier, Bartlett edited *Choice Thoughts from Shakespeare* (1861), selecting passages that would please "fastidious persons" while representing Shakespeare's "most prominent beauties."[134] But by 1894, after laboring intermittently for twenty years on the 1,910-page *New and Complete Concordance, or Verbal Index to Words, Phrases, and Passages in the Dramatic Works of*

Shakespeare, Bartlett introduces his opus on the greatest English author with a half-page note focused entirely on editorial decisions regarding source texts and the exclusion of minor words from the index.[135] There may be some extravagant Yankee reticence here—fain would the self-effacing indexer stand between the Bard and his reader—though Bartlett's restraint more fully accords with the genre of the literary reference book. Saying nothing about the beauty, wit, or wisdom of Shakespeare, and offering no personal reflections on his achievements, Bartlett's preface values accuracy, objectivity, comprehensiveness, and reader interface—traits that impressed but also concerned an 1895 review of the *Concordance*:

> The dictionary is a characteristic volume of this era. Without an enumeration, one can hardly realize to what an extent the labors of later years have made complete the list of dictionaries, glossaries, and concordances most useful to the scholarly reader. . . . It may be that to some of us there seems to be in it all a tendency not quite so hopeful for the Creator in literature as for the Scholar in literature.[136]

This is not to say that Bartlett did not love books and reading in ways that we associate with the literary. It is to suggest that when compared to more aesthetic modes of searching, his commitments are of a decidedly informational order that held for him and others a lasting appeal. At the end of Bartlett's "List: of Books Read" is a handwritten addendum from 1906 followed by an illegible signature. After listing his reading from 1837 to 1900, and despite his failing eyesight, Bartlett apparently continued his bookish habits until his death in 1905, leaving a supplementary list of 214 additional titles, these too without any commentary.

How and why do relationships with literature shift between—and conflate—aesthetics and information? At what point in a life, afternoon, or paragraph does a reader suddenly find, lose, or recover the literariness of literature? Any answers are at the very least conjectural in the case of John Bartlett and his audience. Nineteenth-century readers put *Bartlett's Familiar Quotations* to instrumental, informational purposes, but they also resisted Bartlett's rendering of literature as mere information. Bartlett himself sidesteps questions of literary value and affect, but nineteenth-century commentators on his compilations debated in aesthetic terms the inclusion and exclusion of specific entries and alternative standards that might be better applied. Marginalia in old editions of *Bartlett's Familiar Quotations* intimate a range of individual responses, though of course it is difficult to know what to make of a dog-eared page or check in a margin. An 1856 edition of *Bartlett's* at the American Antiquarian Society was originally donated by Bartlett himself to the Boston Mercantile

Library Association. Was it a class-conscious laborer who made the first penciled "X" in the book next to a line from Psalm 133, "Behold, how good and how pleasant it is for brethren to dwell together in unity"? And who checked Poor Richard's "God helps them that help themselves" and Edward Coke's "Corporations have no souls"? What are the aesthetic tendencies of the person who made their distinctive mark next to both Reginald Heber's "Missionary Hymn" and Charles Sprague's "To My Cigar"? Why is an 1871 edition of *Bartlett's* free from marginalia, except for half a dozen checks on lines from Wordsworth? What does it mean for a literary critic to encounter a copy of *Bartlett's* with a research agenda in mind and, after some instrumental skimming and dipping, become immersed in its wealth of quotations—finding pleasure in familiar beauties, wondering about unexplored texts, feeling chagrined by some forgotten passage from a book he thought he knew well, imagining lines of intertextual influence across the years and scores of years?

In 2012, Little, Brown and Company (now a division of Hachette) published the eighteenth edition of *Bartlett's Familiar Quotations*, which the cover announces as "The Most Substantial Revision Ever—With 2,500 New Quotations." Considering the searchable resources available on the internet, one wonders how *Bartlett's* survives in the twenty-first century. Yet consumers who purchased the eighteenth edition on Amazon also bought other quotation compendia—*The Oxford Dictionary of Quotations*, *The Yale Book of Quotations*, *1001 Smartest Things Ever Said*, and so on. Reviews of *Bartlett's* eighteenth edition on Amazon averaged 4.7 stars out of 5. Fans appreciated the organization and indexing of the book, as well as its instrumental uses for teachers, authors, and speechwriters. Some reviewers were displeased—about the difficulty of using *Bartlett's* index on a Kindle, about modern quotations supplanting older ones, about the supposedly liberal slant of the quotations selected (one post complained that Barack Obama got more entries than Clarence Thomas). One two-word review simply said, "boring book," suggesting not only a *This Is Spinal Tap* (1984) reference but perhaps also a category error. It is tempting to dismiss the bored reviewer of *Bartlett's* for confusing literary and informational genres by expecting a reference book to bring narrative pleasure, but a number of comments, which may or may not come from sock puppets, found in *Bartlett's* something more than information. "Paige Turner" (heh-heh) of Brooklyn offered this modulated assessment:

> Why in the age of Google and an internet flooded with quotation sites would we need a big heavy book of quotations? One word: serendipity. With this great book, you can page through and randomly find amazing

quotations. Or you can read the book in order, which is chronological. What a way to discover great thinkers, writers and statesmen! I love to randomly open a page and just see what interesting quote I can find. Of course the other reason to buy this book is: organization. It is well indexed by key word and also organized by whom is quoted, in chronological order. What a fantastic desk-top resource this is.

More authentic to my ear is "Becky B" of Hot Springs, Arizona, whose 2012 review suggests the resilience of the literary within informational domains:

> One of my childhood memories is the copy of Bartlett's on my parents' desk. I would spend hours browsing the familiar quotes, especially those made by famous, familiar people. Although I purchased this for my college age grandchild, I found myself again browsing its pages. Some of the quotations were the ones of old, but as I read so many that have been added since the ones I loved as a child, I became nostalgic. I would read a quotation and memories would come flooding back. I would think of what was going on in my life at the time, the state of the world when the quote was made. Many quotes made me sad because I know what the future held for the speaker. Others made me smile. Most made me grateful for the life I have lived through these recent historic decades. Bartlett's is not merely a list of memorial quotes, but a commentary of our culture and times.

Posted on December 25, Becky B's review of *Bartlett's Familiar Quotations* and the scene of reading it conjures underscores how informational resources might inspire interpretation and emotion. Literature can be turned into information, but the reverse is also true, and there are always residua.

From a certain perspective, *Notes and Queries* and *Bartlett's* stand in contrast to our fictions from Hawthorne and Dickens. The former subordinate excessive literary materials to informational systems, while the later imagine literary sensibilities mastering archival searches. Yet as much as these bibliographic and aesthetic projects differ, they meet from opposite directions on a middle ground where the informational and the literary are difficult to distinguish. *Notes and Queries* and *Bartlett's*, sometimes despite their intentions, evoke literary pleasures and passions. Hawthorne and Dickens, for all their resistance to informationalism, imagine artistic approaches to searching that are compatible with and even privilege information management.

Literary critics today also cross and occupy a similar middle ground. Along with the pleasures we take in aesthetics and interpretation, we are information workers in an industry shaped by information technology and ideology. Our work, especially when searching digital archives in the wake of the New Historicism, entails the handling of vast amounts of information, whether or not history has conditioned us to regard our critical methods in this way. Historicism is facing increasing challenges as the dominant method in literary studies, but informationalism is a related and equally influential paradigm that we will not turn away from anytime soon. Insofar as methodological awareness matters, it seems to me that we ought to acknowledge our informational commitments and practices, particularly when gathering evidence, even if doing so compromises the force of some claims by acknowledging the inevitable partiality of our research. Aspirationally, we might be more forthright about our searching protocols by reporting parameters, key words, and hits. We might identify archival outliers as such, register failed searches, note negative evidence, and perform controlled experiments. We can even foreground statistics, which is the subject of the next chapter.

CHAPTER THREE

Counting

> "[F]our times five is twelve, and four times six is thirteen, and four times seven is—oh dear!"
>
> —ALICE, LEWIS CARROLL'S *ALICE'S ADVENTURES IN WONDERLAND* (1865)

> "Five against three leaves us four to nine. That's better odds than we had at starting. We were seven to nineteen then."
>
> —CAPTAIN SMOLLETT, ROBERT LOUIS STEVENSON'S *TREASURE ISLAND* (1883)

A LITERATURE PROFESSOR feeling beset by information overload should probably not lecture his class too self-righteously on the glories of a well-laden syllabus. Nor should that professor too glibly invoke Frederick Douglass when his kids are insufficiently enthused by the books they get for their birthdays. It is of course a privilege to complain about a surfeit of reading materials, and yet for all the advantages it evinces and conveys, much can be lost under textual excess—attention, order, comprehensiveness, joy, the dream (or less skeptically, the experience) of an autonomous aesthetic realm. From a critical perspective, superabundance becomes a problem when reading habits prove inadequately capacious, especially in comparison to quantitative methods designed to handle large amounts of information. Numbers are a powerful way of representing, organizing, and analyzing multiplicity, and in sampling some nineteenth-century reading and searching practices that treat literature as information, the previous two chapters have gestured toward the question of how literature might be understood in quantitative terms.

Historical trajectories remain too turbulent for comfortable generalizations, but the statistical rendering of reading and writing—what this chapter will call "the accounting of literature"—can be taken to develop in conjunction with the nineteenth-century development of mass print and quantitative methods. What follows is not about Adolphe Quetelet, Charles Babbage, John Venn, or George Boole, and Johanna Drucker's point that "[c]ounting is not statistics" is an important reminder of differences between the nineteenth century's accounting of literature and more sophisticated distant reading practices today.[1] As Theodore Porter has argued, accounting is less about pure mathematics and its geometrical roots and more about the "social technology" of arithmetic and its accompanying "spirit of rigor."[2] Such a spirit influenced reading and writing across the nineteenth century as thinkers explored the practical application of numbers to literature.

Reflecting the literary/informational divide that this book is both elaborating and challenging, the accounting of literature has proven to be more controversial than the accounting of most things. There is no decisive cultural moment when compensatory fantasies of intensive reading (chapter 1) and intuitive searching (chapter 2) emerge as responses to textual excess, though a sense of belatedness—both personal and historical—is especially strong in nineteenth-century readers at a time when literary domains were increasingly enumerated, bureaucratized, and organized around discipline more than pleasure. Among the things one can lose under the accounting of literature is a feeling of enchantment, an elusive concept that (practically by definition) resists logical explanation.

Against rationalism, instrumentalism, data-driven analysis, and modes of ideology critique that may or may not be running out of steam, Rita Felski—and in different ways, Nancy Bentley and Christopher Castiglia—have called for renewed attention to the enchanting possibilities of literature, not only to deepen critical practices and advance social goals, but also to justify literature itself.[3] Felski associates enchantment with a cluster of privative experiences—from the surrender of selfhood through radical intersubjectivity, to the loss of distinction between fantasy and fact, to negative somatic and affective states such as abandonment, numbness, suspension, and shock. Felski's sense of enchantment can be so manifold as to risk blunting its analytic edge, but what grounds her approach is the assumption that enchantment in all its diversity entails absorptive reading practices in which the work of art (here she quotes Stephen Greenblatt) "draws a circle around itself from which everything but the object is excluded."⁴ Such views, including Philip Fisher's "pure presence" of wonder, are in many ways compatible with what chapter 1 has described as deserted island reading.⁵ Felski's taxonomic argument does not press a historical line of inquiry, but she joins others such as Jane Bennett and Simon During in setting the decline—or at least, displacement—of aesthetic enchantment in the postromantic nineteenth century.⁶

Here Max Weber can be taken as a catalyzing figure in narratives of disenchanted modernity, though he actually exemplifies a crucial ambivalence about the relationship between aesthetic enchantment and information. Weber famously argues in "Science as a Vocation" (1919) that "rationalization and intellectualization" have led to the "'disenchantment of the world,'" and he links this development with the scientific presumption that "one can, in principle, master all things by calculation."⁷ Weber's position may sound like Nietzschean critique or be set within nineteenth-century sociological debates about the limits of positivism, but his views—as influential as they have been—remain hard to stabilize.⁸ With a dialectical energy that ends not with synthesis but with a separation of professional and personal spheres (as in Kant), Weber traces a post-Renaissance split between science and art, fact and value, quantitative method and qualitative experience. He ultimately situates enchantment in the overlapping regions of religion, mysticism, and aesthetics, though his separation is neither equal (in his account, scientific logic comes to dominate) nor total (his dualisms are not absolute). It is not only that Weber predicts a return of reenchanted gods and demons; he also resists binaries that would set "cold calculation" over and against what he calls "'heart and soul.'" Science for Weber remains on the whole a quantitative, disenchanting enterprise, but it also affords unpredictable potentialities of "intuition," "imagination," "inspiration," "frenzy," and "enthusiasm"—a complexity also evident in *The Protestant Ethic and the Spirit of Capitalism* (1905), where Weber mentions "the mystique of figures."⁹

Many thinkers following Weber are less open to reconciling the literary and the informational. Adorno and Horkheimer argue that art is everywhere threatened by "the rule of computation and utility," while Walter Benjamin sets mass print and information against the mythic entertainments of the storyteller.¹⁰ Foucault could write that "the mere act of enumeration" has "a power of enchantment all its own," though he regards such mixing with more suspicion than joy as such enchantments reinforce structures of domination.¹¹ But from Weber's less totalizing nineteenth-century perspective, calculation need not be absolutely disenchanting or entirely disenchanted itself. When scientists talk about beautiful data, elegant formulas, and ecstatic conceptual leaps, they may not be talking about aesthetics per se, but they are speaking in enchanted idioms that were historically constructed alongside computational practices that spread in the nineteenth century. As scholars in a range of fields have shown over the last two decades, modern reenchantment can take a variety of shapes, including what Michael Saler has described as an "antinomial" form in which enchantment and disenchantment coexist in unresolved tension.[12] This is why Bennett appreciates "efforts to remain *scientific* while acknowledging some *incalculability* to things."[13]

Decades before Weber set the terms of debate over enchantment, disenchantment, and reenchantment, some novelists explored potential affiliations between enchantment and the informational, even as the gaps between literature and science, aesthetics and quantification, widened. As chapter 1 has argued of nineteenth-century responses to *Robinson Crusoe*, nostalgia for immersive childhood reading became acute at a time when textual superabundance drove the accounting of literature. Such nostalgia can help explain the swelling popularity of juvenile adventure fiction among Victorian youths and adults as excursions to deserted islands and lost worlds seek a refuge from—and in doing so, mark—the encroachments of information.[14] We know much about how adventure novels engage capitalism, imperialism, gender, and race, and the accounting of literature is another aspect of modernity that the genre simultaneously registers and disavows.[15] Literature for and about young people often take numbers as a sign of adult disenchantment—from Wordsworth's "We Are Seven" (1798), to *Alice's Adventures in Wonderland* (1865), to Kenneth Grahame's *The Golden Age* (1895), in which a boy insists that seven times seven might as well be forty-seven because "[o]ne number was no prettier than the other to look at, and it was evidently only a matter of arbitrary taste."[16] One can certainly define richly imaginative worlds over and against calculative logic, but there is also a counterdiscourse in Victorian juvenile literature that finds information in general and quantification in particular a resource for aesthetic enchantment.

This is especially true of adventure novels that imagine flights from the textual excesses of modernity but do not leave informational modernity behind, making for narratives rife with ideological, aesthetic, and epistemological disjunctions. A hand-sewn account book nicked from a pirate's chest, a ragged sketchbook of dinosaurs with immense scientific value, a mildewed diary marked with fingerprints that require forensic analysis, an out-of-date newspaper with a romantic message and financial accounts scrawled in the margins—such texts figure potential gaps and syntheses between data and enchantment, reminding us that the relationship between information and literature is less determined than sometimes supposed. Mary Poovey has shown how political economy and Literature (with a capital "L") diverge in the eighteenth and early nineteenth centuries as status conscious authors, pressured by social science and mass print, define the value of their art against instrumentalism, information, and quantification.[17] Poovey does not focus on enchantment, but the terms of her argument are correlative; and by turning to nineteenth-century adventure fiction (a subgenre seldom accused of being High Art), we can see how the accounting of literature finds an uneasy home on enchanted desert isles.

Proceeding in a metacritical mode, the argument that follows is multiscalar. Working toward a deep history of statistical literary analysis and its reception, and with an eye toward current distant reading practices, this chapter begins with some Victorian contexts on the accounting of literature, especially books for youth. It then turns toward adventure fiction to examine the relationship between literature and quantification using three differently dilated methods—a close reading of Robert Louis Stevenson's *Treasure Island*, a literary history constructed from canonical Anglo-American adventure fictions, and a modest distant reading of a larger corpus of novels that tracks the frequency of terms associated with quantification and mass print. Commentaries on statistical literary analysis tend to swing between utopian and dystopian views, but deserted island and lost world novels from the long nineteenth century negotiate less polemically than might be supposed between science and art, information and literature, numbers and enchantment. Whether we take them to do so successfully or not may depend as much on their own aesthetic achievements as on the dynamic status of the literary in our post-Weberian age.

Quantity and Quality

Though the early nineteenth century witnessed important developments in statistical science, the growing dominance of quantification is marked less by leaps of scholarly invention than by an accelerating spread across cultural and intellectual domains. A brief history can sound something like this. The earliest known examples of writing involve tallies carved in bone and inscribed on clay tokens, while many inventories, ledgers, and records of births, marriages, and deaths predate the invention of print. Modern forms of statistics in Europe are generally traced to specialized discourses in the seventeenth century as governments and merchants began collecting demographic and financial data for the purposes of taxes, warfare, insurance, and health.[18] More proximate to our period of study, a "Quantifying Spirit" possessed the later eighteenth century, which included the broadening reach of statistics, the improvement of measuring instruments, the mathematization of the sciences beyond astronomy and physics, and the beginnings of what Ian Hacking has called "an avalanche of printed numbers."[19] As both agents and objects of the information revolution, eighteenth-century printers, booksellers, and circulating libraries gathered and disseminated some commercial data, but statistical descriptions of reading and reading materials, let alone analyses of such figures, remained uncommon and decentralized. This begins to change in the nineteenth century as quantitative practices spread to literary areas—from governmental tracking of literacy and literary knowledge, to sociological studies of reading and book ownership, to the systematic collection of data by libraries, schools, and an increasingly industrialized book trade, to protostylometric literary criticism and the thematics of literature itself.

Numbers and writing, counting and reading, are historically and cognitively intertwined, but in the nineteenth century, the accounting of literature met with a range of objections.[20] Friedrich Kittler's history of the antagonism between numerals and language can help explain but seems to me only a subterranean driver of nineteenth-century divisions between quantification and literature.[21] More immediate were struggles between literary values and epistemologies and the burgeoning authority of statistics, as well as the encroachments of a market economy that rendered literature as fungible, quantifiable units. William Dean Howells in "The Man of Letters as a Man of Business" (1893) complained that compensating authors by the word or page was as absurd as paying sculptors by the pound or painters by the square inch.[22] Other practices—from ranking books on enumerated lists, to statistically measuring reading materials and experiences, to organizing books by number as in the Dewey Decimal System (introduced with similar schemes during the 1870s)—also struck some literary commentators as misguided. In "Fenimore Cooper's Literary Offenses" (1895), Mark Twain accuses Cooper of committing "114 offenses against literary art out of a possible 115" and of violating eighteen of the nineteen artistic tenets (though, Twain notes, by some accounts there are actually twenty-two).[23] Twain's humor rests on the absurd notion that aesthetics can be reduced to a quantitative formula, though a deeper irony emerges when he attacks Cooper's *The Deerslayer* (1841) by turning Cooper's own numbers against him. How in the world, Twain fulminates, could five of six Indians fail to drop from a sapling onto a 140-foot ark passing below at one mile per hour when, Twain calculates, the passage would take a minute-and-a-half and the width of the stream is only between eighteen and twenty-five feet? Twain's complaint, as convincing as it is, registers a broader complication, for if it is ridiculous to reduce aesthetics to numbers, quantitative logic retains real force in the domain of aesthetic judgment.

Tensions around the accounting of literature are especially evident in juvenile books that imagine (or appear to imagine) enchanted escapes from informational modernity at a time when some Victorians disputed the invention of childhood as an idealized and discrete developmental stage.[24] Such fantasizing, often self-conscious and thus partial, is reflected in anxieties over textual excess and the burgeoning children's literature industry. Elizabeth Rigby's pioneering 1844 article warned against the "overstock," "legion," and "incalculable number" of pedantic children's books, while the first sentence of Charlotte Yonge's influential essay "Children's Literature of the Last Century" (1869) complains of Victorian books for youth, "the press groans with their multitude."[25] Yonge sketches a history of declension in which the eighteenth century's benign neglect of children's reading allowed for their unmediated experience of adult books, until nineteenth-century moral and educational strictures forced "reason . . . into the nursery."[26] Yonge may underestimate the rise of children's literature in the eighteenth century, but her views were echoed in subsequent commentaries such as Kate Douglas Wiggin's *Children's Rights* (1892), which favorably contrasts adult adventure classics to the "tons of children's books turn[ed] out yearly by parental publishers."[27] If *Huckleberry Finn* (1884) critiques adventure novels from Defoe, Scott, Cooper, and Dumas, Twain was not alone in preferring such old-fashioned fare to the formulaic Sunday-school books and educational texts that were ubiquitous in transatlantic print culture, which included massive efforts from the Society for Promoting Christian Knowledge and the Society for the Diffusion of Useful Knowledge.[28] Such organizations could be downright hostile to the imaginative pleasures of literature, while some educators argued that children's books should not include irrational phenomena such as magic and talking animals. In the supposed golden age of children's books, many feared that youthful reading was becoming less enchanted under the pressures of mass produced piety and facts.[29] As a nostalgic *Blackwood's* article complained of contemporary literature, "What would any veteran of us give to be back again in the days when the whole world of wonders lay before us unexplored."[30]

A related concern was that systematized schooling was ruining the relationship between children and books. Chapter 4 will address the topic in more depth, though for now it is worth noting that students in nineteenth-century Britain and America increasingly encountered reading in institutionalized settings characterized by routinized methods, quantitative assessments, and depersonalizing bureaucracies that (under monitorial pedagogical systems) sometimes identified students by number and rank while teaching reading through group recitation. Such practices were especially prevalent in state-supported schools that provided new educational opportunities—and new informational regimes—for laborers, females, and students of color. Many commentators saw no need, and even positive dangers, in exposing such classes to the enchantments of reading, though others worried that mass education and rote learning at all institutional levels crushed the aesthetic sensibilities of youngsters, who (to use metaphors rampant at the time) drowned in oceans of print, staggered under burdens of books, and swallowed more information than they could digest. Another metaphor was that of the mechanized reader, as when James Russell Lowell in *A Fable for Critics* (1848) describes an overworked student:

> In this way our hero got safely to college,
> Where he bolted alike both his commons and knowledge;
> A reading-machine, always wound up and going,
> He mastered whatever was not worth the knowing.[31]

In general, opponents of standardized education charged that children learned to read too early, that "overpressure" in schools was unhealthy and even fatal (especially for girls), and that highly regulative pedagogies led to anhedonic reading habits that sacrificed quality to quantity, imagination to information, and absorptive reading to extensive skimming. Educational debates in the early nineteenth century should not be rendered in simple terms of reason versus fantasy, but literary figures worried about the institutionalization of literary learning—from attacks on moribund students in Emerson's "American Scholar" (1837) and Thoreau's *Walden* (1854), to critiques of cramming in British novels about school life, to John Stuart Mill's unflattering appraisal of his mechanistic education, to satirical depictions of the children's literature industry in *Alice's Adventures in Wonderland*, Louisa May Alcott's *Little Women* (1869), and George Gissing's *New Grub Street* (1891), to the torn allegiances of Matthew Arnold and Horace Mann, both of whom advocated standardized educational assessments while still praising the ineffable beauties of literature.

Dickens's *Hard Times* (1854) may be the most obvious example of enchantment set against the accounting of literature in the context of children's reading, though an earlier article, "Full Report of the First Meeting of the Mudfog Association for the Advancement of Everything" (1837), is both a precocious satire on emerging statistical efforts to measure literary practices and a prescient exploration of differences between informational and aesthetic conceptualizations of books.[32] Mocking the British Association for the Advancement of Science as well as scientific reportage in the popular press, Dickens's "Mudfog" introduces Mr. Slug, a statistician whose presentation on books owned by London children includes the following table:

Jack the Giant-killer	7,943
Ditto and Bean-stalk	8,621
Ditto and Eleven Brothers	2,845
Ditto and Jill	1,998
Total	21,407

Slug calculates "the proportion of Robinson Crusoes to Philip Quarlls" (4.5 to 1), "Valentine and Orsons" to "Goody Two Shoeses" (3⅛th to one-half), and "Seven Champions" to "Simple Simons" (also 3⅛th to one-half). The Mudfogians then debate the morality of Jack and Jill while lamenting that some children believe in Sinbad the Sailor. Just in case some readers fail to notice the juxtaposition of aesthetics and information, the section concludes with President Woodensconce's call for avoiding imaginative books and instead "stor[ing] the minds of children with nothing but facts and figures."[33]

Slug's work in "Full Report of the First Meeting of the Mudfog Association" reflects a growing tradition of quantitative studies that enumerated overwhelming amounts of print. Such efforts occasioned some unintended irony, as when Charles Henry Timperley's *Dictionary of Printers and Printing, with the Progress of Literature* (1839) cited "[c]yclopedia without measure" and "compilations without number" before offering detailed statistical tables, including the number of newspaper stamps issued in Britain (in 1837 the total was 53,496,207).[34] Dickens's satire in "Mudfog" is heavy-handed enough, and yet the incongruity between Slug's dismal informational science and the imaginative play of children's literature is not as simple as it may initially appear. The children's books themselves betray a lack of creativity in that Jack is a mass-produced protagonist, while the very titles of some books—"Seven Champions," "Goody Two Shoes," "Jack and Eleven Brothers"—hint how children's literature is already embedded in quantitative discourse (a suspicion some twenty-first-century parents might share; there's a whole lot of counting in bedtime books).[35] Dickens thus suggests that under industrialized print, numbers gain authority, aesthetics languish, and books proliferate without bringing variety or joy, as if it is more than a coincidence that sellers of weekly and monthly publications were known as "number-men." David Copperfield offers a more optimistic view of literary pleasure insofar as his fertile imagination survives the rigors of schooling and clerkships, but in "Full Report of the First Meeting of the Mudfog Association," the enchantments of literature cannot be disentangled from heaps of texts and insinuating accountants. The very sort of Victorian statistical studies that print historians now put to good use were, for Dickens, threatening indicators of the dominance of quantification.

By the end of the nineteenth century, the accounting of literature had become more common and sophisticated—not only in the tracking of sales figures, literacy rates, circulation statistics, and library inventories, but also in the way that cultural authorities discussed reading under textual excess. Parents and teachers were the primary directors of reading, but the problem of choosing books under information overload was taken up by influential thinkers and institutional projects—from Emerson's "Books" (1858), Thomas Carlyle's "On the Choice of Books" (1866), and Frederic Perkins's *The Best Reading* (1872), to Charles Francis Richardson's *The Choice of Books* (1883) and Frederic Harrison's (identically titled) *The Choice of Books* (1886), to William Sonnenschein's *The Best Books* (first published in 1887, swelling to six volumes by the 1930s), and the 1891 *Guide to Best Books* (which included contributions from over 150 experts).[36] By the turn of the century, anthologies of reading advice—including *Right Reading* (1902), *Right Reading for Children* (1902), and *Books and Reading* (1908)—indicate not only the flourishing of long-standing practices of recommending books and reading habits; they also show how the sheer excess of such advice required curating and compiling. In these and other venues, Victorians railed against (in the words of Harrison) "aimless, promiscuous, vapid reading," the "poisoning inhalation of mere literary garbage," and the "impotent voracity for desultory 'information'" that make readers "gorged and enfeebled by excess."[37] This all from Harrison's first three pages—before he goes on to compare modern print to an insurmountable mountain, pathless sea, riotous crowd, and cataract of ink, before he likens modern readers to spectators at a carnival (with booksellers as barkers), Ancient Mariners (books everywhere, none to drink), and drunkards who brag of their capacity for imbibing information (before throwing up what they consume). Harrison's overheated prose reflects a general fear of textual pandemonium that brought forth calls for more attentive reading practices and a more careful ordering of reading materials.

The later concern drives John Lubbock's "Hundred Best Books" (1886), a much debated, frequently reprinted, often imitated speech presented to the Working Men's College of London and first published in the *Pall Mall Gazette*. Scholars have recognized Lubbock's list as one marker along the journey of canon formation, though what helps explain the popularity of "Hundred Best Books" is its novel application of quantitative form to the challenge of textual excess at a time when manifold areas of culture were subjected to informational ordering.[38] Lubbock's introductory comments complain that books are now "almost innumerable" but "our hours for reading are, alas!, very few," and he fears that "overwhelmed" readers choose books by "hazard" and "chance," especially at railway stations. Lubbock's canon was by some lights idiosyncratic in his predilection for modern novels and non-Western entries such as the Koran and Confucius's *Analects*, but much of his speech is typical of the period—from its uneasy praise of widening access to texts, to its positing of a "'survival of the fittest'" among books, to its goal of molding less cultivated readers under an Arnoldian ideology.[39]

The outsized influence of Lubbock's list did not stem from his success as a popularizer of science or founder of modern archaeology. Nor did Lubbock simply appeal to a rising liberal meritocracy that relied on measurements and rankings. More crucially, numbered lists presume to order information-rich contexts without requiring prolonged attention or hermeneutic expertise, which makes listicles popular not only in our information age but also, as Ryan Cordell has shown, in nineteenth-century print culture.[40] More specifically, and as we know from the Modern Library's One Hundred Best Novels list (not to mention *People* magazine's fifty most beautiful people), the quantification of aesthetic value is compelling precisely because the informational form of the numbered list actually highlights the impossibility of definitive judgment. Pseudo-information on aesthetic topics can stimulate critical faculties when desires for objectivity are stirred but remain unsatisfied, as in debates over the ten best films. Making what today is an obvious point, and thereby indicating the newness of the genre, one commentator complained of Lubbock's list: "Why not ninety-nine [best books], or a hundred and one? Simply because a hundred is a round number. That fact alone shows the arbitrary and artificial character of the list."[41]

Yes, it does, and the practice spread. Following Lubbock, a slew of articles offered iterations—from the ten or twenty-five best books for businessmen, travelers, and Bible study, to polls in which American periodicals asked readers to vote for their favorite books and authors (a self-consciously democratic method).[42] If nobody was so naive as to proclaim their list definitive, opinions still carried weight. Arnold declined *Pall Mall*'s invitation to comment on Lubbock's choices or submit an alternative list, but many others accepted—from literary luminaries such as Stevenson, Ruskin, Arthur Conan Doyle, Wilkie Collins, Algernon Swinburne, and William Morris, to prominent figures such as the chief justice of England, the American minister to England, Lady Dilke (Emilia Francis Strong), and the prince of Wales (who wished only to add Dryden). Routledge in 1891 began marketing a book series based on Lubbock's list, and the proliferation of best book lists joined a larger great books movement in curricula, publishing, and libraries. Literary critics mounted occasional resistance, as when Edward Dowden argued in "The Interpretation of Literature" (1886) that intensive, cultivated, sensitive reading was more important than working one's way through any list of books.[43] Moreover, as Robert Belknap has shown, lists and catalogues can ironically subordinate hierarchical order to aesthetic and epistemological play—a point suggested by the Sub-Sub-Librarian of *Moby-Dick* (1851), the encyclopedic wildness of Whitman, and Umberto Eco's argument that lists by their nature cannot help but acknowledge the chaotic infinitude they aspire to order.[44] Nonetheless, the proliferation of numbered book lists at the end of the nineteenth century shows how the accounting of literature shared an uneasy symbiosis with aesthetics as thinkers, some of whom remained skeptical of the exercise, sought to order literary qualities using quantitative forms.

Books for youths were not exempted from the transatlantic ranking fervor, in part because such readers were seen as particularly vulnerable to textual promiscuity. Soon after publishing Lubbock's speech, *Pall Mall* brought out "The Best Hundred Books for Boys" (1886) in an effort to order "the ever-swelling volumes of juvenile literature."[45] Other lists for boys and girls soon followed from publishers, booksellers, librarians, and educators (both male and female), including George Hardy's *Five Hundred Books for the Young: A Graded and Annotated List* (1892). Hardy quotes Elizabeth Barrett Browning on the "Sublimest danger" young people face when choosing reading materials, and he frames his project as an effort to manage the "rapid multiplication of books," particularly dime novels.[46] In 1890, the American Library Association objected to the rise of best hundred book lists, though it did so on the grounds that top ten lists within subgenres would be more helpful to librarians and patrons. What overwhelmed readers apparently needed were more lists in finer-grained categories.

During the same period, quantitatively oriented observers followed the example of Dickens's Mr. Slug, including Edward Salmon, a journalist who collected survey data on the reading habits of laborers, women, and children. As in the social sciences today, underprivileged populations were more likely to be subject to statistical examination. Covering literature "from the gutter to the classic," Salmon's *Juvenile Literature as It Is* (1888) begins with statistics on the favorite authors, books, and genres drawn from an 1884 survey of some two thousand British schoolchildren.[47] (Ironically enough, Dickens turned out to be the most popular author for both girls and boys.) A more sophisticated 1897 study in the Illinois-based *Public-School Journal* reported the results of a survey on reading preferences given to three thousand Chicago schoolchildren. The favorite book for nine-year-old boys was *Robinson Crusoe*, which came in at number two for girls. Of all the boys surveyed, 13.2 percent listed adventure novels as their favorite subgenre (compared to 1.7 percent of girls), though 77 percent of girls listed fiction as their most preferred genre (compared to 46 percent of boys). The numbers go on, including demoralizing news for poetry, the favorite genre of only 3.3 percent of girls and 2.6 percent of boys.[48] Whether gathered for business, administrative, or pedagogical purposes, these and similar studies unabashedly quantified the relationship between children and books, even while occasionally admitting that empirical studies could not account for more subjective and enchanting aspects of reading.[49] Leslie Butler has shown how Victorian elites in Britain and America held court on the best thought and known, but when surveys and voting deployed statistics to rank books, they shifted debate from the aesthetic category of "best" to more measurable standards of "popular."[50]

Given the spread of quantitative practices across the nineteenth century, and considering ongoing constructions of the literary as an autonomous aesthetic realm, it should be no surprise that the accounting of literature both flourished and met with resistance. Nicholas Dames has discussed a strand of Victorian aesthetics that sought to measure the responses of readers, though more typical were objections to quantitative practices that would echo across the decades in various forms—from Carlyle (who took science to "destroy Wonder, and in its stead substitute Mensuration and Numeration"), to John Dewey (who contrasted unified aesthetic experiences to the "ledger-entries" of "bookkeeping"), to W. H. Auden (who joked seriously to Harvard's Phi Beta Kappa society, "Thou shalt not sit / With statisticians nor commit / A social science"), to F. R. Leavis (who wrote in response to C. P. Snow, "individual lives cannot be aggregated or equated or dealt with quantitatively in any way").[51] Twenty-first-century jeremiads against distant reading are part of this tradition. When Geoffrey Harpham defines humanistic inquiry against the "mere accumulation of facts or information," or when Stephen Marche calls literature "the opposite of data," or when Caleb Crain writes that "literature will survive if readers declare war on counting," they voice a sense that the literary is losing its sway under a set of dire conditions—the deepening crisis in the humanities; the dominance of STEM fields; the ascendency of Big Tech and Big Data; the emergence of computational literary methods that move beyond statistical accounts of books and reading to enter domains of interpretation and criticism often regarded as literary study's home turf.[52]

It can seem like a newly disenchanting age for lovers of the literary, and yet computational literary criticism has a history that begins before machine learning, the internet, optical character recognition, and Roberto Busa's punch cards from the 1940s.[53] One nineteenth-century example is Lucius Adelno Sherman, professor of English at the University of Nebraska, whose *Analytics of Literature: A Manual for the Objective Study of English Prose and Poetry* (1893) offers a range of protostylometric case studies, often with accompanying graphs (see figure 3.1). Sherman calculates the average sentence lengths of admired prose stylists (Macaulay 22.45 words per sentence, Emerson 20.58, Spenser 49.82, etc.). He determines ratios of

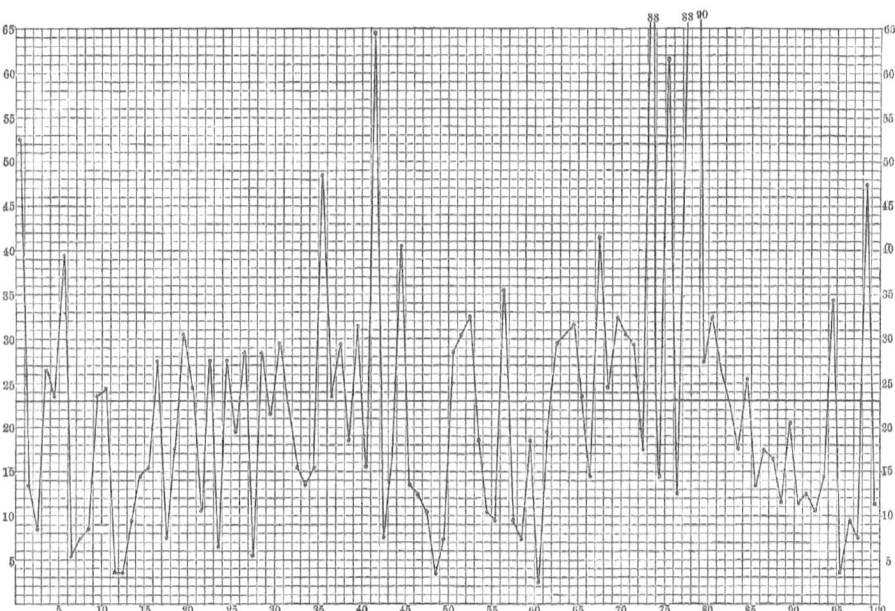

FIGURE 3.1. Lengths of the first one hundred sentences of Macaulay's *Essay on History* (x-axis is the number of the sentence; y-axis is the number of words). From Lucius Adelno Sherman, *Analytics of Literature: A Manual for the Objective Study of English Prose and Poetry* (Boston: Ginn, 1893), 288.

stressed to unstressed syllables as a measure of poetic force (for instance, the three stanzas of Robert Browning's "Count Gismond" move from 23:38 to 24:41 to 30:44). He also demonstrates the superiority of *Hamlet* (1609) to Percy Bysshe Shelley's *Alastor* (1816) by comparing ratios of phrases ranked according to five classes of rhetorical power. Sherman studied philology at Yale and aspired to scientific objectivity, though his *Analytics* also acknowledges the "very natural antipathy to treating aesthetics by scientific methods."[54] Sherman's book, like much early DH scholarship, both insists on the power of computation and strikes a conciliatory tone.

Sherman's concerns about the reception of his work are more personally expressed in an 1893 letter to the poet and anthologist E. C. Stedman (a letter Stedman pasted into his copy of *Analytics of Literature*, now at Harvard's Widener Library). Answering Stedman's "very kind" note, Sherman is both defensive about his quantitative methods and adamant that he shares with his correspondent a love of literary aesthetics. Sherman writes: "I am glad that the aspects of literature treated in the 'book' were not uninteresting to you who have given your life to its aesthetic side. Believe me, if such analyses as the book advises did not enable aesthetic association I could have none of them." Sherman then appends one of his recent stylometric papers with the hope that the "statistics will not unendurably bore you." And with appeals to "inspiration," "refinement," and "taste," he writes: "Pardon my garrulousness. I am anxious to prove myself a worshipper of Apollo in spite of all."[55]

Sherman's anxieties turned out to be well founded and can point to the development of a two cultures divide between literature and quantification. Willa Cather, who once called literary scholars "information vampires," took a course from Sherman at the University of Nebraska and ridiculed his methods in a poem titled "He Took Analytics."[56] Stephen Crane, after speaking with Cather about Sherman's techniques, wrote to her: "Where did you get all that rot? Yarns aren't done by mathematics."[57] Writing in 1896, Frank Norris expressed similar disdain for the quantitative criticism he encountered at the University of California, Berkeley:

> Classification ... is the one thing desirable in the eyes of the professors of "literature" of the University of California. The young sophomore ... is set to work counting the "metaphors" in a given passage. This is actually true—tabulating them, separating them from the "similes," comparing the results. ... The conclusion of the whole matter is that the literary courses of the University of California do not develop literary instincts.[58]

Yet if Cather, Crane, and Norris unequivocally reject quantitative projects such as Sherman's, reviews of *The Analytics of Literature* were surprisingly mixed—ranging from positive assessments ("worthy the attention of teachers and students") to gentle corrections ("over-emphasizes the importance of tabulations and mathematical modes") to harsher objections ("ingenious theories that will not stand examination").[59] Nor was Sherman an anomaly, for his colleagues G. W. Gerwig, Louis Pound, and R. E. Moritz took up similar work, while the physicist and meteorologist T. C. Mendenhall independently developed similar methods for his studies in author attribution. (Mendenhall's 1887 article in *Science* magazine drew on analogies to spectroscopy when comparing word lengths in Dickens and Thackeray, a method that at least three literary commentators called "curious" without explicitly denigrating the project.)[60]

Like an orphan in a Victorian novel, stylometry would remain at the margins of literary studies throughout the twentieth century—often ignored, sometimes abused, but never entirely beyond the reach of recognition and legitimacy. Its tenuous position is suggested by Vernon Lee and I. A. Richards, who, as Benjamin Morgan and Yohei Igarashi have argued, exemplify how aesthetics and close reading prior to the dominance of New Criticism were not hostile to statistical methods.[61] Richards wrote in *Practical Criticism* (1929), a work that included empirical surveys of students' reactions to poetry:

> Statistical inquiries into the "efficiency" of different forms of composition, into types of imagery, into the relative frequency of verbs and adjectives, of liquids, sibilants and fricatives in various authors; classifications of literary "motives," of "drives" that may be employed by writers; inquiries into the propositions of "sex-appeal" present; measurements of "emotional response," of "facility in integration," of "degree of retention of effects"; or gradings of "artistically effective associations"; such things will make any reader of poetry feel curiously uncomfortable.[62]

The scare quotes here suggest some disdain for computational criticism, though importantly Richards adds to his passage (and probably puns) that if literary scholars feel uncomfortable with statistics, "[t]his prejudice must be countered." Nineteenth-century negotiations between quantification and literature can prefigure conflicts over distant reading today, but given the less defined disciplines of earlier eras, battle lines were not so strictly drawn. If some literary figures could not countenance the accounting of literature, others were curiously attracted.

Stirring Enumerations in Treasure Island

Against the backdrop of late nineteenth-century efforts to understand literature quantitatively, Robert Louis Stevenson published *Treasure Island*, an apparent escape from the accounting of literature that actually stages a complex encounter between aesthetic enchantment and numbers. Stevenson liked to describe his best-selling novel as a spur-of-the-moment creation, but he had already confronted modern disenchantment in an 1874 autobiographical essay that defined aesthetics over and against calculation: "After we have reckoned up all that we can see or hear or feel, there still remains to be taken into account some sensibility more delicate than usual." For Stevenson, these finer perceptions and ineffable feelings depart as quickly as they come, leaving us with "the sense of want, and disenchantment of the world"—a loss Stevenson associates, not only with reckoning, but also with the pressures of mass print.[63]

Prior to the success of *Treasure Island*, Stevenson nearly starved in a transatlantic marketplace saturated with writing, and he complained that the popular press degraded the public intellect by pandering to extensive reading habits. Stevenson defended romantic views of authorship, insisting that writers pursue aesthetic ideals before they "calculate the wage" of their labors.[64] And yet elsewhere he subjected literature to calculative logic, complaining that the average writer earns as much as the average clerk while expending ten to twenty times the mental energy.[65] Stephen Arata has argued that Stevenson in *The Wrecker* (1891) draws homologies between ledgers and literature, bookkeeping and the writing of books, though one might add that the novel is highly suspicious of print culture and informational documents—from dishonest advertisements and newspaper articles to falsified shipping logs and navigation manuals (one of which is called "a lying book").[66] Arata sees Stevenson resisting regulated reading in favor of aesthetic pleasure, but if *Treasure Island* thematizes the desire to geographically and temporally distance literature from mass print and modernity, the novel displays—and, it seems to me, deploys—anxieties over textual excess as it traces both the imaginative possibilities and the limitations of information.

Treasure Island shares with *Robinson Crusoe* talking parrots, goat-skinned maroons, and racial anxieties under empire, but Stevenson's novel is also self-conscious about textual superabundance, both marking and bridging differences between deserted island and disenchanted reading.[67] Indicating how robust constructions of childhood alterity only sharpen yearnings for good days gone by, many commentators likened Stevenson to a grownup boy and praised *Treasure Island* as a novel in which "old age and youth combine."[68] Suggesting how many so-called juvenile books attracted adult audiences in the Victorian period, Henry James (no friend to children's literature in general) wrote in 1887:

> *Treasure Island* is a "boy's book" in the sense that it embodies a boy's vision of the extraordinary, but it is unique in this, and calculated to fascinate the weary mind of experience, that what we see in it is not only the ideal fable but, as part and parcel of that, as it were, the young reader himself and his state of mind: we seem to read it over his shoulder, with an arm around his neck.[69]

Such pleasures a weary English teacher might know, and James's nostalgia almost echoes wistful memories of first encountering Defoe. But whereas nineteenth-century recollections of reading *Robinson Crusoe* often mirror the solitude of the castaway himself, James's scene of reading, like Jim Hawkins's adventure in *Treasure Island*, includes adult supervision both intimate and coercive ("an arm around his neck").

Treasure Island was self-consciously written for and marketed with juveniles in mind, and so even first encounters with the book are mediated by a print industry that, as Bill Brown has written of Victorian children's toys, "struggled to efface [its] modernity."[70] A 1901 article in the *Edinburgh Review* indulges the fantasy of exempting children's classics from literary economies of superabundance:

> In these later days, when one publication follows upon the heels of another, and when each work of current fiction, eagerly demanded and received with acclamation, gives place to its successor and passes with ever accelerating speed into the limbo of forgotten books . . . the schoolroom classic—boy and girlhood possessing, it may be, some strain of conservatism lacking in maturity—retains a living vitality.[71]

Intensively read children's classics may ease the vertigo of textual excess, and yet the *Edinburgh Review* article cannot deny their modernity: "The re-read story which stamped itself upon the donor's imagination in his own youth . . . is selected as the gift-book for the new generation, that it in its turn, and generations to come in theirs, will select according to no other rule." The disavowal here resembles Fredric Jameson's "nostalgia for the present" insofar as the desire to stave off historical change—and thus deny historical consciousness itself—drives a burgeoning, nostalgia-based consumerism that threatens the innocent reading it seeks to salvage.[72] When my first child was born, we received no fewer than four copies of *Goodnight Moon* (1947).

Treasure Island knowingly appeals to readerly nostalgia as it simultaneously exposes and effaces its conditions of production. The deserted island setting combined with a breathless present tense makes it easy to forget that the novel presents a retrospective narrative of the eighteenth century. Accordingly, nineteenth-century responses to the book often show how historical forces that might be recognized as such (say, changing constructions of childhood, or the industrialization of print, or the ever-shrinking lands unexplored by Westerners) are often understood psychologically and self-reflexively (Jim figures a universal coming-of-age while his maturation stirs memories of the reader's lost youth). *Treasure Island* can be an escapist book, and yet its disavowal of modernity is partial to the point of irony. In "My First Book—'Treasure Island'" (1894), Stevenson calls the reading public his "paymaster," and even the novel's epigraphic poem, "To the Hesitating Purchaser," admits the power of the book trade.[73] The possibility of an unmediated relationship with *Treasure Island* is thus a tenuous one from the start, for with children's literature becoming increasingly institutionalized at the level of genre, commodity, and social practice, the dream of deserted island reading was more compelling and more fragile, particularly as literature fell under the logic of accounting.

Strong readings of Stevenson have discussed his affinities for information, whether understood as technical knowledge (Cannon Schmitt), transparent style (Ian Duncan), or engineering know-how (Rosalind Williams).[74] Accordingly, his aversion to disenchanted modernity can be taken as a kind of disavowal. Reflecting on Defoe in 1882, Stevenson wrote of Crusoe's salvaged items, "the bare enumeration stirs the blood," and the following year he filled *Treasure Island* with his own stirring enumerations.[75] The absence of quantification matters at the start of the novel when Billy Bones takes up tyrannical residence at the Admiral Benbow Inn. Mr. Hawkins's failure to settle the pirate's account sets the stage for Jim's maturation as numbers come to drive the plot and suffuse the enchantments of the novel. Flint's treasure, the very object of fantasy, is repeatedly referred to as "seven hundred thousand pounds" (247). Numbers even work their way into romantic pirate ballads: "Fifteen men on a dead man's chest" (3); "one man [returned] of her crew alive, / What put to sea with seventy-five" (172). When the pirates first attack the loyalists' stockade, Captain Smollett reckons the proportion of good guys to bad by subtracting casualties and wounded: "Five against three leaves us four to nine. That's better odds than we had at starting. We were seven to nineteen then" (160). With Long John Silver calculating interest rates and Jim enumerating the topography of the isle, *Treasure Island* can be read as an escapist novel that actually furthers the disciplinary purposes, not only of global capitalism and imperial bureaucracy, but of the informational logic fundamental to both.[76]

And yet the numbers that appear throughout *Treasure Island* advertise the limits of their explanatory power as Stevenson displays a tension that Poovey sets at the center of novelistic aesthetics—the urge both to leverage material particulars and to differentiate literature from the information-rich genres of political economy. Jim's measurements and even *Treasure Island*'s famous map cannot compass the full geography of the island. Smollett's calculations on the stockade battle feel fatuous, for he himself has been incapacitated. Surely the stalwart captain counts for more than one feckless, drunken pirate. Jim suggests a similar point when first calculating the loyalists' odds aboard ship: "there were only seven out of the twenty-six on whom we knew we could rely; and out of these seven one was a boy, so that the grown men on our side were six to their nineteen" (94). How one should count—that is, whether one can count on—a boy is a central question that *Treasure Island* resolves not with blunt statistics but through moral decisions and dramatic unfoldings. As physiological and legal discourse in the nineteenth century sought to fix the moment when children become adults, Stevenson suggests that to come of age is not simply to reach a set number of years.

Economic value in *Treasure Island* also escapes quantification, not only by pointing to problems of representation (in the mode of Walter Benn Michaels) or the irreducible presence of play (as Matthew Kaiser has emphasized), but also by showing that aesthetic pleasures are beyond numerical measurement.[77] After Billy Bones dies before settling his account, Mrs. Hawkins tries to take from his sailor's chest the seven guineas he owes. The problem is that she will not be satisfied with "a fraction" more or less than her due, but she can only "make her count" in English money whereas Bones's coins come from all over the world. Lacking a standard metric—and thus unable to put quality under a uniform system of quantity—Jim and his mother finally flee, though not before Jim grabs Bones's oilskin packet to, in his words, "square the count" (32–33). Jim is more calculative than his no-account father, but his coming-of-age will entail a recognition of the limitations of accounting, for English money, foreign coins, and oilskin packets are not wholly transparent or fungible under informationalism.

Nowhere is this lesson more forcefully rendered than when Jim describes Flint's treasure at the end of the book:

> It was a strange collection, like Billy Bones's hoard for the diversity of coinage, but so much larger and so much more varied that I think I never had more pleasure than in sorting them. English, French, Spanish, Portuguese, Georges, and Louises, doubloons and double guineas and moidores and sequins, the pictures of all the kings of Europe for the last hundred years, strange Oriental pieces stamped with what looked like wisps of string or bits of spider's web, round pieces and square pieces, and pieces bored through the middle, as if to wear them round your neck—nearly every variety of money in the world must, I think, have found a place in that collection, and for number, I am sure they were like autumn leaves, so that my back ached with stooping and my fingers with sorting them out. (260–61)

This enchanted passage contains stirring enumerations reminiscent of *Robinson Crusoe* and Poe's "The Gold-Bug" (1843), except that numeracy gives way to an unaccountability in which counts cannot be squared. It is as if Stevenson anticipates John Guillory's argument that aesthetic value defines itself against economics but cannot erase the connection.[78] Flint's treasure is irreducible to a single unit of value as Jim's description grows increasingly lyrical, subjective, affective, and (in a word) literary. Coins conjure romantic histories and faraway lands. They become pieces of jewelry with totemic power. The informational job of sorting is painful but also intensely pleasurable in the manner of the sublime. And as "for number," Jim can only equate the haul to "autumn leaves."

This final metaphor hints at the vexed intersections of numbers and texts in Treasure Island as Stevenson's novel does not quite recapture an innocence free from the accounting of literature. The story appears initially uninterested in books insofar as Jim is no reader and the two texts that do appear seem to offer alternatives to mass print. When a group of rebellious pirates deliver their proverbial "black spot" to Long John Silver, they use for their paper the "last leaf" from a Bible, prompting Silver to argue that once so defaced, the Bible "don't bind no more'n a ballad-book" (225). With a possible pun on binding, Silver exploits differences between literacy and orality, canonical and ephemeral texts, while the Bible page itself displays two kinds of writing in a moment of inscriptional juxtaposition and confusion. On one side is printed the end of Revelations over which the crew has made its black spot in firewood ash. On the other side in ash is "the one word 'Depposed,'" which Silver describes as "[v]ery pretty wrote, to be sure; like print" (221). Silver's ironic comparison highlights differences between modern and premodern writing, and the narrator Jim adds in retrospect: "I have [the page] beside me at this moment; but not a trace of writing now remains beyond a single scratch, such as a man might make with his thumb-nail" (225–26). The point here is not simply that biblical truths, even apocryphal ones, outlast the degenerative scribblings of pirates. More challengingly, though readers may wish to escape modernity by absorbing themselves in a deserted island book, no suspension of disbelief erases in *Treasure Island* the indelible presence of mechanized print. The mass-produced text of the Bible remains, while the atavistic scratchings of the pirates fade away, as if the black spots that punctuate Stevenson's novel express and expose the unsustainable desire to set enchanted, anachronistic literary experiences over and against mass print. As we have seen in chapter 1, the paradox of deserted island reading is that singular texts can be conceived as such only in the context of textual and informational superabundance.

The other book that appears in *Treasure Island* is the one Jim finds in Bones's oilskin packet. Because it is hand-sewn, handwritten, and personalized with codes and a copy of Bones's tattoo, the book can be taken to represent textuality before the onset of mass print. But if Bones's book introduces an adventure beyond the pale of modernity, it is first and foremost an "account-book" containing geographic coordinates, financial data, and a "table for reducing French, English, and Spanish moneys to a common value" (46–47). Like the coded, media-conscious messages of "The Gold-Bug" and Henry James's *In the Cage* (1898), Bones's ledger reduces the stuff of romance to numbers in seeming anticipation of Weberian disenchantment. Yet as with Poe's Legrand and James's telegraph operator, numerical codes open imaginative possibilities to readers of sufficient literary sensibilities. Finding the treasure of "The Gold-Bug" requires interpretive savvy, perspectival sophistication, and knowledge of Captain Kidd's legend, while only James's clever, dreamy, novel-reading protagonist can make sense of numerically coded telegrams. Tellingly in *Treasure Island*, the romantic Squire Trelawney, not the scientific Dr. Livesey, first cracks the code of Bones's book, a scene that displays the two characters' very different senses of what Flint's treasure might "'amount to'" (45).

For Jim and his companions, no less than for readers of *Treasure Island*, the path to enchantment runs through—but does not end with—stirring enumerations, for while Stevenson makes good literary use of numbers, he ultimately does not square the count by rendering quality and quantity commensurate. The numbering of weapons and combatants sets the stage but does not fulfill the drama of Jim's bildungsroman. Seven hundred thousand pounds can fire the imagination, but the figure does not adequately figure the aesthetic pleasures of pirate booty. Stevenson thus limits but does not go so far as to deny the explanatory and aesthetic affordances of informationalism, for even when invoking an enchanted past, the two texts that appear in *Treasure Island*—the ash-marked Bible, and Bones's ledger—are shadowed by mass print and the accounting of literature. So also are the final two sentences of the novel, spoken by a parrot once owned by the legendary Captain Flint. The repeated lines haunt the recurring dreams of Jim's backward-looking and no longer innocent self: "Pieces of eight! pieces of eight!" (266). *Treasure Island* ends with this anxious parroting of *Robinson Crusoe*, but if symbols of enchantment can speak in numbers, Stevenson—unlike Defoe—feels the need to defend the literary in an age of accounting. Like the repeated lines of Poe's raven or Melville's Bartleby, Captain Flint's parrot suggests the limits of meaningful communication, even as the transmission of information conjures the feeling of myth.

A Literary History of Adventure Novels

Treasure Island is hardly the first adventure story to entangle enchantment and information in complicated ways. When Don Quixote is parodically sworn in as a knight, the ritual includes him pledging allegiance on an innkeeper's ledger containing accounts of barley and straw. Nineteenth-century versions of Aladdin and his fantastical lamp from *Arabian Nights* so relentlessly enumerate the treasures of the tale that one veers between wonder and boredom. Yet as a text that draws on Robinsonade traditions and influences subsequent adventure fiction, *Treasure Island* can be taken to represent a shift in which the accounting of literature becomes an increasingly prevalent and self-consciously executed theme, particularly in lost world novels that discover primitive cultures set in primeval locales. Many of these novels are not technically deserted island narratives, but there is much to justify conflating the subgenres—overlapping readerships and distribution channels, common formal features and sources, and (as emphasized by Joseph Bristow and others) shared ideological preoccupations.[79] Adventure fictions are of course historically conditioned, and in addition to recognized and intertwining discourses of Darwinism, the New Imperialism, and the New Woman, the rise of quantification and mass print shape deserted island and lost world novels. At least this is the impression given when chronologically tracking a handful of canonical

Anglo-American texts that do not take stable positions on the accounting of literature but register a curious pattern—an increasing deployment of stirring enumerations accompanied by anxious flights from textual excess.

First published seventy years before *Treasure Island*, Johann David Wyss's *Swiss Family Robinson* (1812) and its English iterations stand as negative examples, for as the Robinsons industriously recreate civilization, including a small library they salvage from their wreck, the narrative shows little interest in numbers and print culture, something that can also be said of Frederick Marryat's popular Robinsonade, *Masterman Ready* (1841). R. M. Ballantyne's *Coral Island* (1858) edges closer to such topics when a protagonist rails against reading, but if the novel plays to juvenile fantasies of school being out forever, it ultimately accedes to institutionalized literacy when the boy-heroes are rescued by Polynesian missionaries who translate the Bible using English spelling books. More committed to mediacy and quantification is Jules Verne, who aspired to a comprehensive mastery of information and was internationally celebrated for combining scientific rigor with literary enchantment.[80] In Verne's *Mysterious Island* (1874), the aptly named Gideon Spillet is a voluble journalist known for telegraphing biblical passages to keep competitors from using the lines, but when forced into austerity after his hot air balloon crashes on a deserted island, he and his friends send concise messages to each other carried by dog, gorilla, and jerry-rigged telegraph. Books eventually wash up on the island, but they have no publishing information and (except for the Bible) are uncut, suggesting in insipient form an ambivalence about modern print.

Closer to the turn of the nineteenth century, escapes from textual superabundance become a structuring theme and metadiscourse in many adventure novels. Inspired by *Robinson Crusoe* and *Treasure Island*, H. Rider Haggard's seminal *King Solomon's Mines* (1885) offers stirring enumerations of supplies, topographies, and battles, though books are willfully exempted from such reckoning when Haggard traces a deep history of textuality: a treasure map originally inscribed on parchment is transferred to linen to loose paper to a standardized pocketbook and finally to industrial print. The narrator Allan Quatermain offers this final line as he leaves southern Africa for London, "I must . . . look after the printing of this history, which is a task that I do not like to trust to anybody else."[81] If *King Solomon's Mines* does not explicitly disavow the mass print culture it distrusts, Haggard's *She* (1887) makes a more concerted effort, elaborately framing its mythic quest with iterations of ancient, unreproducible texts (most centrally, a potsherd engraved with uncial Greek wrapped in linen and then wrapped again in what appears to be papyrus accompanied by a Latin translation on sixteenth-century parchment). Along with its commitment to media archaeology, *She* sets supernaturalism over and against the authority of numbers, as when the introduction of occult artifacts interrupts the narrator's cramming for a mathematics exam, which he abandons in favor of his atavistic mission. Disenchanted modernity in Haggard is marked by quantification and industrial print.

Nowhere is his hostility to the accounting of literature more evident than in *Mr. Meeson's Will* (1888), a novel that is both a deserted island fiction and a satire on the publishing industry. We begin in a world in which the literary is brutally reduced to information:

> [The publishing house of] Meeson and Co. . . . employed more than two thousand hands; and its works, lit throughout with the electric light, cover two acres and a quarter of land. One hundred commercial travellers, at three pounds a week and a commission, went forth east and west, and north and south, to sell the books of Meeson; . . . and five-and-twenty tame authors (who were illustrated by thirteen tame artists) sat—at salaries ranging from one to five hundred a year. . . . Then there were editors and vice-editors, and heads of the various departments, and sub-heads, and financial secretaries, and readers, and many managers; but what their names were no man knew, because at Meeson's all the employés of the great house were known by numbers; personalities and personal responsibility being the abomination of the firm.[82]

After being shipwrecked, Meeson dies from a fever while raving about the ghost of author "Number 25," though not before writing a will, which in the absence of paper he has tattooed on the back of one of his female authors whose body then becomes a piece of evidence in a sensational chancery case.[83] *Mr. Meeson's Will* is an awful book that (as Garrett Stewart has argued) literalizes the process of constructing a reader, though it also highlights how Haggard's early novels recoil from—and are thus shaped by—the accounting of literature.[84] That Haggard's escapes from modern print sold well in mass markets is just one of their many disavowals.

As a belated example of the subgenre it retrospectively names, Arthur Conan Doyle's *Lost World* (1912) simultaneously deploys and parodies adventure novel tropes.[85] The narrator Edward Malone is a London journalist struggling to compete in saturated print markets until he is shown a battered sketchbook of dinosaurs that is compared to Shakespeare's First Folio. The singular text entices Malone to leave the "'ink-pots of civilization'" for the Amazon, a seeming rejection of industrial print that eventually involves a map drawn with charcoal on bark by a preliterate early human. Yet if *Lost World* yearns for a premodern textuality and is mainly told through handwritten dispatches trekked across uncharted wilds, Malone's narrative remains mediated by the *Daily Gazette* ("And now my patient readers, I can address you directly no longer" but only "through the paper which I represent").[86] Nor does *Lost World*, for all its atavistic urges, abandon informational discourse. Malone's notes include the naturalist data of professors Summerlee and Challenger, while Doyle entertains a synthesis of enchantment and science when a *Gazette* reporter gushes about Malone's narrative: "Apparently the age of romance was not dead, and there was common ground upon which the wildest imaginings of the novelists could meet . . . actual scientific investigations."[87] It seems unlikely that Edward Malone is meant to conjure Edmond Malone, the eighteenth-century editor who used quantitative methods to discern the authorship of plays attributed to Shakespeare, but *Lost World*—like many a Sherlock Holmes story—seeks to reconcile information and enchantment.

Doyle, however, complicates this project when Malone returns to London and finds his love interest married to a fussy clerk. From the ink-stained office workers of Dickens, Melville, and Trollope, to John De Forest's military bureaucrats, Gissing's Edwin Reardon, and Edith Wharton's Lily Bart, nineteenth-century writers feared that the accounting of literature threatened to conflate aesthetically sensitive writers with instrumental secretaries and clerks.[88] It is not only that many Victorian authors worked in offices during the rapid expansion of governmental and business bureaucracies. As Thomas Augst demonstrates in America, and as Ceri Sullivan shows in Britain, white-collar workers engaged in literary pursuits, including the accounting of their lives in diaries.[89] Ronald Zboray has shown how bookkeeping in the nineteenth century linked numeracy and literacy for young men on the rise.[90] Even the mathematical calculations that appear in the margins of Emerson and Thoreau's journals, or the algebra problems worked out on the title page of Dickens's *American Notes* (1842) in Emily Dickinson's family library suggest how the literary and the informational are not so easily divorced. The New York minister Henry W. Bellows made this point in his Phi Beta Kappa address "The Leger and the Lexicon" (1853):

> Might you penetrate that inner counting-room, the merchant's brain, you find at work there an Imagination, whose familiar sweep circumnavigates the globe, penetrates the policies of distant cabinets, and anticipates the prospects of remote kingdoms; studies the play of social

caprices, and calculates the orbit of feminine fancies; predicts the yield of fields he never saw, and the fertility of seasons yet to roll; weighs in his letter-scale the chances of peace and war. . . . He lives half a poet's life.[91]

At a time when literary authorship became increasingly associated with paperwork and bureaucracy, Bellows combines aesthetics and calculative business with none of the critical reservations later expressed by Weber and his Frankfurtian heirs. In *Lost World*, Malone and his clerk-rival are distressingly interchangeable, but Doyle's hero retains sufficient imagination to leave his London office for another expedition. As Malone prepares for his next adventure and Doyle sets the stage for a sequel, *Lost World* works hard to regain at its end a sense of premodern wonder.

As if to embody the obverse relationship between numbers and enchantment, the most popular, most prolific lost world novelist of all time wrote his most famous book while working as a manager for the business magazine *System*, a publication extolling the informational ideologies of Henry Ford and Frederick Winslow Taylor.[92] Edgar Rice Burroughs hated his emasculating office job but still described himself as an "expert accountant" and internalized the profession's quantitative ethos. He graphed his literary productivity on a day-to-day basis, calculating that his top year was 1913 when he logged a total of 413,000 words. Burroughs continues a pattern that Mark Seltzer and Martha Banta have studied in the later nineteenth century where human bodies and social practices were organized by managerial systems dedicated to mensuration, statistics, bureaucracy, and other forms of informational control.[93] Not unlike Jack London, who also carefully recorded his words written per day, Burroughs's feverish fantasies of escape from civilization pay tribute to the quantitative modernity they resent.[94] In his 1913 novel *A Man without a Soul* (originally titled *Number Thirteen* and later called *The Monster Men*), characters are—for better and worse—identified by numbers. A mad eugenicist has populated a deserted island with abominable humanoids labeled only by numerals, while the sole clue to the identity of the amnesiac hero is "Nine ninety nine Priscilla," which turns out to be his home address.[95] Burroughs's *Efficiency Expert* (1921) is similarly torn, for while it satirizes scientific management systems and celebrates untamed masculinity, the swaggering hero of the novel—a former college athlete and boxer—ultimately defeats his embezzling antagonist, not by punching out his lights, but by posing as an efficiency consultant and reconstructing payroll accounts.[96] It's an odd inversion: the superhero triumphs over villainy by transforming into a mild-mannered information worker.

Even *Tarzan of the Apes* (1912), despite its popular reputation for utterly rejecting modernity, draws on contemporary developments in biology and anthropology to naturalize the accounting of literature. Scholars have taken Tarzan's seemingly instinctual literacy as a sign of Burroughs's white supremacy, but when writing that the young Tarzan "could not count as we understand it, yet he had an idea of quantity," Burroughs also broaches long-standing questions about the biological origins and cultural meanings of numeracy.[97] Philosophers from Aristotle and Locke to Kant and William Whewell regarded quantity as a fundamental metaphysical category, and the capacity to conceptualize numbers and mathematics was often taken to separate animals and humans, infants and adults, the savage and the civilized. In a somewhat muddled chapter of his *Essay concerning Human Understanding* (1689), Locke calls numbers "the most universal idea we have," before explaining that children cannot initially count because they lack the proper experience. Locke's thinking then takes a proto-ethnological turn when he notes that the "Tououpinambos" of Brazil do not reckon above the number five and that the Native Americans he has met in Britain do not count much above twenty, perhaps (he surmises) because their "simple life" does not require the use of large numbers.[98] Explorers, naturalists, and ethnographers after Locke also reported on the diverse numerical practices of so-called primitive peoples, offering a predictable range of explanations—from charges of immutable inferiority to claims of civilizing potential to appreciation of their innocent natural state. Stereotypical idioms attributed to indigenous characters in fiction can thus be taken to signal intellectual differences, whether *many moons*, *heap big*, or *more people than the trees of the forest* are meant to be romantically eloquent, invidiously innumerate, or both.

Speculations on numeracy became a topic for social scientists with the emergence of evolutionary anthropology and Edward Tylor's *Primitive Cultures* (1871), whose chapter "The Art of Counting" defined the state of the question by synthesizing scholarship from naturalists (especially Alexander von Humboldt), philologists (most notably, William Jones), and ethnological studies from around the globe (including work on the Dakota Sioux by the anti-Tom novelist Mary Eastman). Siding with John Stuart Mill against Whewell, Tylor argued that numeracy and mathematics are not universal intellectual capacities but rather are acquired through experience and education. He then posited continuity between human races by comparing the base-ten system of Western mathematics to the quinary, decimal, and (in rarer cases) vigesimal systems that some peoples employed when counting on fingers and toes. Tylor's work on numeracy was widely circulated—in children's magazines, popular and high-minded journals, and scholarly works such as Lubbock's *On the Origin of Civilization* (1870), Darwin's *Descent of Man* (1871), and James Frazer's fieldwork.[99] However, consensus proved elusive, as suggested by Levi Conant's *The Number Concept* (1896), which not only catalogued a host of anthropological exceptions to Tylor's generalizations but also resisted Tylor's gestures toward racial equality. For Conant, "It is only when the savage ceases to be wholly an animal, and becomes a thinking human being, that number in the abstract can come within the grasp of his mind."[100] That Conant does not say whether such grasping comes through evolution, education, or not at all points to continued uncertainties about quantitative thinking as a marker of racial and cultural difference.

While anthropologists took numeracy and numerical systems as a basis for comparing human beings, biologists looked to quantitative capacities when studying speciation. Arguing against Alfred Russell Wallace, and claiming evolutionary connections between humans and animals, George Romanes in *The Mental Evolution of Man* (1888) joined other naturalists and popular articles in speculating on the numerate capacities of insects, birds, dogs, and horses.[101] A section in Lubbock's *On the Senses, Instincts, and Intelligence of Animals* (1894) summed the ongoing discussion. After crediting examples of basic counting in animals—crows tracking how many hunters enter and exit a blind; wasps allotting specific quantities of grubs to larval cells—Lubbock proceeds to more challenging cases of mammals that seemingly answer arithmetical problems, such as the dog that supposedly calculated square roots by barking at the correct answer. Lubbock correctly suspects that such animals respond to unconscious cues from their handlers (what he calls "thought-reading"), but he also refuses to preclude the possibility that animals possess mathematical capacities.[102] As notions of human exceptionalism weakened under Darwinism, who could say for sure that animals can't count?

Burroughs followed his era's evolutionary debates, once calling *Tarzan of the Apes* "a contest between heredity and environment," and so it matters that neither the apes nor the Africans of the novel seem capable of quantitative reasoning, whereas we are told of Tarzan's arithmetical thinking, "the base of his calculations [was] the number of fingers upon one of his hands."[103] Burroughs's dispositions on biology and race can be unstable to the point of incoherence, but Tarzan's quinary numeracy—which seems a feature of his Anglo-Saxon heredity—lifts him above other races and species well before he is tutored by the Frenchman D'Arnot. Tarzan's remarkable potentiality is on full display in the book's climactic scene in Wisconsin when he saves Jane Porter from a disastrous marriage by returning a pirate treasure discovered by her father and subsequently lost in the African jungle. Or rather, Tarzan presents Professor Porter with a "letter of credit" and announces: "two hundred and forty-one thousand dollars. The treasure was most carefully appraised by experts, but lest there should be any question in your mind, D'Arnot himself bought it and is holding it for you, should you prefer the treasure to the credit" (394–95). Here we see in condensed form Burroughs's negotiation of accounting and enchantment. By offering a choice between a fungible, enumerated, informational document and a chest full of "pieces of eight" heroically lugged from the wild, Burroughs suggests that, despite their asserted equivalence, potential differences and preferences might remain. As with Stevenson, the aesthetic pleasures of pirate treasure are comparable to but not fully captured by numerical representation.

A related complication with Tarzan's letter of credit is that the novel is ambivalent about informational genres, for (as with Haggard) the authority of texts in *Tarzan of the Apes* is inversely related to their modernity. The frame narrative of the novel cites the bureaucratic "records of the Colonial Office" as evidence of the story's authenticity, though more telling are the "yellow, mildewed pages" of the elder Greystoke's diary, which contain even better proofs of Tarzan's identity—not only in the father's handwritten narrative but most convincingly in the five inky fingerprints accidentally left by the infant Tarzan (2). One of Burroughs's fantasies is to trace numbers and writing to their purest, most primitive state—from bureaucratic documents, to a handwritten journal, to preliterate expressions of the body on the page. And yet the power of modern accounting endures. Tarzan's quinary fingerprints must be validated by scientific techniques pioneered by the statistician and eugenicist Francis Galton, and even when Tarzan educates himself, he does so using the mass-produced primers left behind by his parents. Burroughs describes the print of the primers as "bugs" that teach Tarzan to read and write, adding in a gesture toward quantification, "Copying the bugs taught him another thing—their number" (82).

This moment is a concession to the accounting of literature insofar as literacy and numeracy are entangled at their origins, but it also offers the potential for reenchantment under the logic of social Darwinism and masculine adventure. If in the beginning there are words and numbers—that is, if literacy and numeracy are inherent capacities, at least for whites—then counting words at a writing desk or working as a bookkeeper can be as natural and manly as fighting beasts in the jungle. This was a particularly attractive possibility to someone like Burroughs, who labored in an informational profession that was becoming increasingly feminized.[104] If the nineteenth century (as Andrew Piper has argued) begins to regard numeracy and literacy as largely commensurate sign systems, and if (as Burroughs imagines) the expansion of information management has roots in primitive masculinity, then one need not choose between quantification and literature, accounting and heroic fantasy.[105] Statistical literary studies might even be natural: Tarzan, Lord of DH.

Less compromising in its resistance to modernity, and kaleidoscopically self-conscious in its escape into fantasy, J. M. Barrie's *Peter and Wendy* (1911) can stand as a limit case that rejects the accounting of literature so emphatically as to render its erasure conspicuous. The only book appearing in *Peter and Wendy* is Mr. Darling's personal ledger in which he crunches the family's budgetary numbers when learning of his wife's pregnancy:

> I have one pound seventeen here, and two and six at the office; I can cut off my coffee at the office, say ten shillings, making two nine and six, with your eighteen and three makes three nine seven, with five naught naught in my cheque-book makes eight nine seven,—who is that moving?—eight nine seven, dot and carry seven— . . . eighth nine seven, dot and carry child—there, you've done it!—did I say nine nine seven?[106]

Neverland is not only a refuge from such abortive calculations; it also offers a respite from print. The illiterate Peter Pan summons Wendy to tell stories, not read them, to the Lost Boys, and the written examinations in Wendy's short-lived school expose how out of place such informational efforts are on Barrie's fantastical island. Numbers and literacy mark the boundary between Neverland and the adult world of information, and so before joining the Darling household and entering modernity, the Lost Boys must first count to five hundred, after which they enter school. The conclusion to the novel looks back wistfully to Neverland, no longer accessible to the grownup Wendy: "Years rolled on again, and Wendy had a daughter. This ought not to be written in ink but in a golden splash."[107] Just as adventure novels offer alternatives to mass print by conjuring texts written in blood, chalk, and ash on bark, skin, and stone with bones, sticks, and fingers, Barrie imagines writing in a kind of fairy dust beyond the reckoning of intermediating print and ledgers, a starry wish that the Disney Corporation maintains in logos for its films and books. *Peter and Wendy* is especially vigilant in policing the border between enchantment and accounting. Yet the boundary is so stubbornly enforced that, following Jacqueline Rose's line of argument, the novel remains too self-aware of its binary distinctions to be considered a children's book at all.[108] Like Mr. and Mrs. Darling and ultimately Wendy, adult readers of Barrie's novel cannot forget their lost numbers and texts. *Peter and Wendy* can thus serve as a culmination to a literary history of adventure fictions that finds the accounting of literature both threatening and stirring as the tense interplay between enchantment and information becomes increasingly difficult to escape. Or so it would seem.

Lost Worlds, Found Words

From novels by Wyss, Ballantyne, Verne, and Stevenson to those of Haggard, Doyle, Burroughs, and Barrie, the accounting of literature appears to become more prevalent in adventure fictions across the long nineteenth century as mass print anxieties and stirring enumerations increasingly characterize the subgenre. Given the proliferation of print and spread of quantification in the period, this literary-historical narrative makes sense, though one might wonder if we can take it to be true. The nine books schematically treated in the previous section constitute an influential but relatively narrow sample of deserted island and lost world novels published in the long nineteenth century. The trick is that an alternative subset from the subgenre might tell an opposite story in which preoccupations with textuality and quantification instead decline over time. Such an argument could start with Poe's obsessions with enumerations and mediacy in *The Narrative of Arthur Gordon Pym* (1838), move through Cooper's *The Crater* (1847), in which a census and printing press help destroy a Robinsonade utopia, continue with the localized treatment of textual excess in Edward Bulwer-Lytton's *Vril* (1871), and end with the largely negative examples of Stevenson's *Kidnapped* (1886) and Abraham Merritt's *The Moon Pool* (1919), neither of which is much interested in the accounting of literature. Literary histories based on handfuls of books depend heavily on selection, which as these two competing narratives suggest can lead to sampling errors and confirmation biases that (as some scientifically minded literary scholars have worried) are not subject to falsification.[109]

To what extent such possibilities are problematic is so fundamental a question that literary critics seldom ask it, and perhaps rightfully so. It may not be troubling, and may be theoretically inevitable, that literary criticism is subjective. Interpretation (to paraphrase Gerald Graff) is what a lot of people do around English departments, and one need not embrace a hermeneutic of suspicion to note that other disciplines do something similar, whether they care to acknowledge it or not.[110] Less aggressively, literary histories made up of canonical texts can simply beggar questions of sampling error: one just takes what one believes to be the texts most worthy of attention according to whatever criteria one prefers and arranges constellations as critical intelligence directs. To challenge selection in such cases is to complain about objects of study, not the validity of claims. But when a handful of texts, howsoever respected or supposedly representative, is used to stand in for a larger genre or track broader cultural and intellectual trajectories, then the method of stringing close readings together becomes vulnerable to charges of teleology—both in the selection of texts and in how one chooses or is inclined to interpret them.

One obvious solution is to analyze more texts more objectively, though here a number of challenges emerge. Rhetorically, readers of literary criticism have limited (and what seems to be diminishing) patience for the kind of serial explications that more representative literary histories require. Epistemologically (and perversely), the more texts that one closely reads, the harder it can be to draw conclusions about a corpus, for the dialectics and contingencies of multitudinous interpretation can overwhelm synthetic capacities, and one risk of gathering an abundance of evidence without a systematic method is that it enhances opportunities for cherry-picking, whether one does so consciously or not. Of course, some corpuses are simply too large for any one person to attentively read, and even a relatively limited project—say, a study of quantification and mass print in adventure novels between 1816 and 1920—can be unmanageable enough. Speaking personally, my life feels too short to read more than a few Burroughs's novels, let alone William Russell's *The Frozen Pirate* (1887), James Cobban's *The Tyrants of Kool-Sim* (1896), or Victor Appleton's *Tom Swift and His Big Tunnel* (1916). Books should not be judged by their covers or titles, but even if one did set aside one's prejudices and read these and many other texts, how could generalizations about their attitudes toward the accounting of literature across time move from highly educated impressions toward falsifiable claims?

Data-driven digital humanities scholars are attempting to answer these sorts of questions, though the possible relationships between close and distant reading remain not only controversial but unclear. In an oft-cited quote from two decades ago, Jerome McGann predicted, "*the general field of humanities education and scholarship will not take the use of digital technology seriously until one demonstrates how its tools improve the ways we explore and explain aesthetic works—until, that is, they expand our interpretational procedures.*"[111] Even Franco Moretti has recently written that "any new approach—quantitative, digital, evolutionary, whatever— must ... do formal analysis better than we already do."[112] Digital humanities scholars continue to pursue such goals, but a reminder from N. Katherine Hayles also remains accurate: the digital humanities with its broad interdisciplinary mandate and technical commitments to database and tool construction has only recently begun to move toward field- and method-specific interpretations of artistic objects of study.[113] This is not a problem for some DH scholars who have turned away from explication. Matthew Jockers polemicizes, "Close reading is not only impractical as a means of evidence gathering in the digital library, but big data render it totally inappropriate as a method of studying literary history."[114] Jockers's genre-based distant reading goes well beyond the experiment described below, but if he ultimately sees statistical analysis and traditional explication as complementary methods, he does not significantly engage in close reading or take up a multiscalar, mixed-method approach. Something similar can be said of Frederick Gibbs and Daniel Cohen, who provide excellent reasons for resisting "the false dichotomy of close and distant reading" but end up doing the latter almost exclusively.[115] And while Stephen Ramsay's "algorithmic criticism" conjoins computational methods and close reading by quantifying word frequencies, collocations, and linguistic patterns in individual texts, his analysis does not focus on literary history or take up large numbers of texts.[116]

A few reasons make it easier to theorize syntheses of close and quantitative reading than to practically integrate such practices. In the ever-shifting confederacy of literary studies, New Critics and New Historicists, poststructural and cultural theorists, multicultural and canonical literary critics all rely to some degree on explication. Distant reading not only operates at a different scale; it requires significant investments in informational methods against which literary criticism has defined itself. Moreover, innovative quantitative methods often occupy discussions to a point where the method becomes the argument. As is often the case with emerging technologies, scholars outside DH often require an instruction manual to understand various quantitative reading practices (in contrast to close reading, which as a method naturalized in high school is more or less plug and play).

In the spirit of comparative methodology, and doing some DIY DH on the DL, the following experiment performs a statistical analysis of 105 deserted island and lost world novels between 1816 and 1920. At the risk of attempting to make mediocrity a virtue, the limited corpus size and basic statistical methods employed should make the experiment both testable by close reading and accessible to non-DH specialists. Just as one need not be Helen Vendler or explicate a text line-by-line to engage in meaningful close reading, it seems to me that modest distant reading experiments can contribute to multimodal arguments. By tracking keyword strings that reference quantitative and textual discourses across a hand-selected adventure novel corpus, the following experiment hopes to (1) gather additional evidence as to whether the accounting of literature becomes a more prevalent theme in the subgenre between 1816 and 1920; (2) compare in a specific analytic context the capabilities of close reading, literary history, and distant reading; and (3) more metacritically, see how DH in general and distant reading in particular might begin to tell its own history insofar as the nineteenth-century relationship between information and literature both anticipates and conditions attitudes toward quantitative literary criticism today.

One way to think about the scale of analysis employed in what follows is to place it, using Lev Manovich's terms, between "deep data" (detailed information on a few objects of study) and "surface data" (small amounts of information drawn from a huge number).[117] According to Manovich, deep data is what literary critics gather when explicating individual texts, while surface data (not to be conflated with surface reading) figures in the quantitative social sciences and DH projects involving thousands of texts. The number of available nineteenth-century deserted island and lost world novels encourages an intermediate approach in part because the scale and status of the adventure subgenre complicates corpus formation. Large-scale statistical analyses of literary texts are usually premised on widely used metadata (author, date, place of publication, broad generic categories such as poetry or the novel), thus making most distant readings a function of long-standing bibliographic categories. Classification is relatively easy in such cases, and it is no coincidence that traditional metadata accord with established methods in literary studies: authorial, geographic, historical, and generic concepts continue to structure the discipline, even (and sometimes especially) when such organizational principles are challenged.

More complicated are content-based distinctions, including subgeneric categories such as deserted island and lost world novels that overlap with related subgenres (exploration narratives, nautical adventures, pirate stories, frontier novels, science fiction, etc.).[118] Even if such subgenres were a historically stable category (which they are not) and can be identified through machine learning (which they can to some degree, as Jockers shows), there is still the problem of what Ted Underwood calls "internal heterogeneity"—the mixing of subgenres within novels so that a single novel can be labeled in multiple ways, thus creating problems for classificatory models.[119] A more specific challenge in corpus formation for the experiment at hand is that many nineteenth-century adventure narratives are subcanonical dime novels, penny dreadfuls, and serialized pulp fiction that are not currently digitized or even extant. If quantitative reading is radical in method, the clarity of existing metadata and the convenience of already digitized texts incline many distant reading projects, for better or worse, toward conventional categories and canons.

All this said, from a list of nearly two hundred deserted island and lost world novels published between 1816 and 1920, my research assistant Carl Weitkamp and I formed a digital corpus of 105 novels that we data-mined for two keyword strings using Voyant, an open source tool created by Stéfan Sinclair and Geoffrey Rockwell. The first string included words associated with quantification (Arabic numerals, numbers in word form above ten, terms associated with numeracy, mathematics, and calculation). The second string included words associated with textuality (types of texts and documents, writing paraphernalia, acts of reading and writing). The creation of these strings involved intuitions and judgments ("count" and "novel" were included though they might refer to a nobleman or something new; "account" and "news" were excluded because they often do not refer to informational and media discourses; after much debate, we included "countless" as a term associated with quantitative thinking). The cleaning of texts was done by hand and involved removing page numbers, tables of contents, numerical chapter titles, and editorial (though not authorial) footnotes.[120]

Using Voyant, frequencies of keyword strings in each novel were calculated as percentages of each novel's total words, and these percentages were then graphed along a chronological axis. One hypothesis was that as the nineteenth century progressed, the frequencies of references to quantification and textuality would increase with the rise of information and mass print. A related hypothesis was that our keyword frequencies would rise together, suggesting that the accounting of literature increases as writing and reading across the long nineteenth century become increasingly entangled with quantitative discourses. Finally, and using a different function of Voyant, we tracked keyword frequencies within individual texts by deciles (the first tenth of the novel, the second tenth, etc.), so that references to quantification and textuality could be graphed across single narratives. Many deserted island and lost world novels begin and end in modernized locales with long middle sections taking place in premodern settings. By aggregating decile counts across the corpus as a whole, we could see if keywords on average had higher frequencies in early and later sections of novels. We also created an archetypal graph of the adventure novel subgenre that could help generalize about thematic structures and against which individual novels could be compared. A fundamental assumption of the experiment was that keyword frequencies indicate, not specific attitudes toward quantification and textuality, but levels of thematic engagement—a supposition shared by Gibbs and Cohen when dealing with titles, and one that we hoped would be borne out at the level of entire texts.

The results of the experiment were mixed though often useful as both positive and negative evidence. Compared to a small control corpus of fifty-three nonadventure novels between 1816 and 1920, the 105 deserted island and lost world novels had on average higher frequencies of quantitative keywords (22.4 per 10,000 words as compared to 14.4 in the control corpus) and lower frequencies of textual terms (14.1 for the adventure novels as compared to 24.3 for the control). Such data support a main argument of this chapter—that adventure novels often stage escapes from textuality while retaining a commitment to stirring enumerations, suggesting in their anxious relationships to modernity more consistent evasions of print culture than of quantitative discourse. In terms of literary history, and counter to expectations, keyword frequencies tracked by decade across both the adventure and the control corpuses did not rise or fall in a discernible pattern (see figure 3.2). Moreover, the correlation between the two

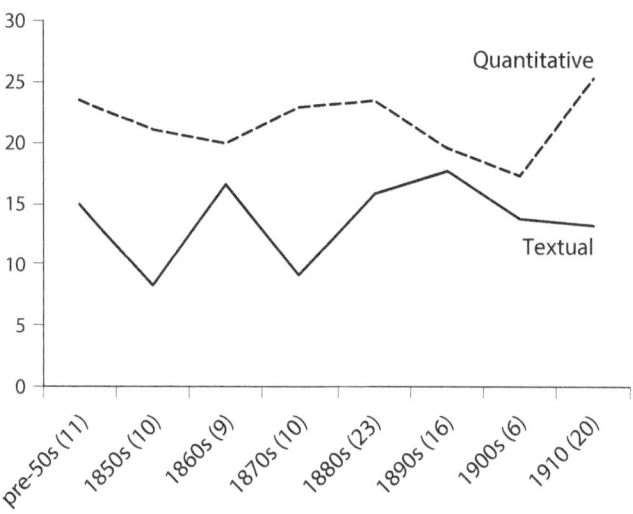

FIGURE 3.2. Keyword frequencies for adventure novel corpus, 1820–1920 (frequencies per 10,000 words).

keyword frequencies across the adventure corpus was a negligible .138, practically equal to the control corpus's .139 (figures based on a scale from −1 to 1 with zero indicating no correlation). These data suggest that the accounting of literature—that is, the entanglement of quantitative and textual thematics—did not significantly rise in the corpus over time, at least not in ways visible to our study.

These negative results do not invalidate the two literary histories previously traced by close reading. As figures 3.3 and 3.4 indicate, the nine novels taken to track a historical rise in quantification and textuality (*Swiss Family Robinson, Masterman Ready, Coral Island, Mysterious Island, Treasure Island, King Solomon's Mines, She, The Lost World,* and *Tarzan*—call them Group A) roughly show increasing keyword frequencies across the century, especially in regards to references to textuality. The five novels briefly hypothesized to narrate a decline in the accounting of literature (*Pym, The Crater, Vril, Kidnapped,* and *The Moon Pool*—call them Group B) roughly indicate a decrease, though again predictions about textual frequency were better supported by data than those regarding quantification.

As shown by figures 3.3 and 3.4, statistical methods and close reading generally yield concurring results for both Group A and Group B, which is also true at the scale of many individual texts. *Tarzan*, for instance, is indeed committed to textuality (31.7 textual words per 10,000, the fifth highest frequency of the corpus), and *King Solomon's Mines* does indulge in stirring enumerations (41.0 quantitative words, the sixth highest frequency). Such concurrences help to vindicate the legitimacy of taking keyword frequencies as indicators of thematic commitments, no small relief to a traditionally trained literary critic (that is, me) uncertain about the design of his experiment. Such a critic, especially if he has been worrying about confirmation bias, might also confess (and confess the urge to confess) that the data made him feel better about his close readings. When quantitative and close reading point to similar conclusions, mixed methods can inspire mutual confidence under a logic of consilience.

Less affirming are discrepancies that give some pause in both worrisome and productive ways. The keyword trajectories for neither Group A nor Group B correlate strongly with trajectories in the entire corpus, indicating that close reading these particular samplings of canonical adventure novels is an inadequate basis for generalizing about the evolution of the subgenre as a whole. Data on individual texts also contradict some claims based on close reading. For example, measured by keyword frequency and compared to corpus averages, quantification does not figure heavily in *Treasure Island* (19.4), nor is textuality especially weighty in *Pym* (13.9)

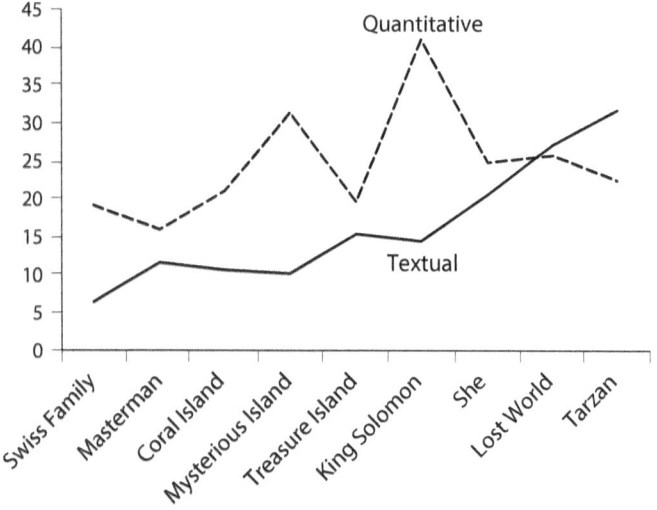

FIGURE 3.3. Keyword frequencies for adventure novels, Group A (frequencies per 10,000 words).

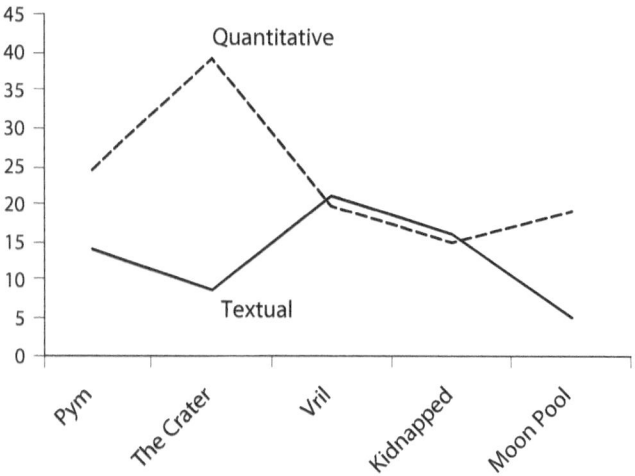

FIGURE 3.4. Keyword frequencies for adventure novels, Group B (frequencies per 10,000 words).

or *King Solomon's Mines* (14.3). In these instances, I find my confidence in close reading stronger than my belief in computational analysis, though the purpose here is not to accord explication or statistics absolute authority at various levels of scale. Rather, it is to take Ramsay's point that quantitative methods can provide "constraint" rather than "falsification." And, of course, close reading constrains statistical analysis, not only because (as

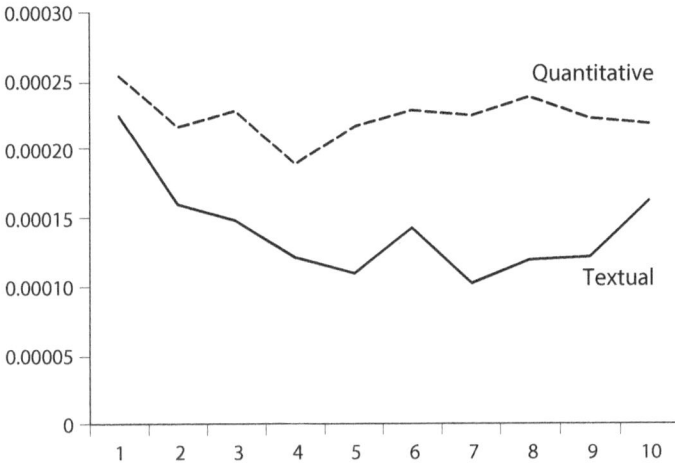

FIGURE 3.5. Average adventure novel by decile (frequencies per 1,000 words): x-axis is deciles of the novels; y-axis is frequency.

Lisa Gitelman and Theodore Porter have emphasized) the categorization necessary for data analysis involves all sorts of rhetorical impositions and cultural valuations that are not objective, but also because quantitative methods struggle to measure semantic contingencies (what Warren Weaver called, the "difficult aspects of meaning, namely the influence of context").[121] How does one measure, for instance, connotation, irony, repression, and dramatic tension? How does a person love a text?—we cannot, at this point, count the ways. The frequency of quantitative terms may be low in *Treasure Island*, but I still hold that quantification is crucial to the book, the number of numbers be damned.

More striking than keyword frequencies measured across the long nineteenth century are data on individual novels broken down by decile and aggregated from across the corpus. As expected, quantitative and textual keywords are on average more frequent at the start and (to a lesser degree) at the end of adventure novels, creating a loose U-curve for each keyword string in contrast to the less patterned graphs of the nonadventure corpus (figure 3.5). The more pronounced U-curve for textuality suggests how protagonists, often impelled by discovered manuscripts and engraved artifacts, leave a modernity saturated with texts for primitive and often preliterate cultures, until the adventure ends, civilization is rejoined, and stories are rendered in written form. The flatter shape of the archetypal quantitative U-curve indicates that numbers tend to appear more consistently across any given adventure novel, suggesting that flights from modernity leave texts behind more readily than they do enumerations, additional

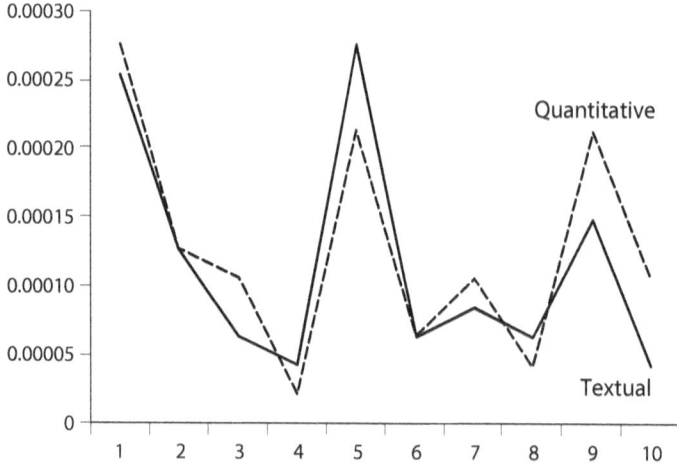

FIGURE 3.6. Quantitative and textual terms by decile in *Peter and Wendy* (frequencies per 1,000 words): x-axis is deciles of the novel; y-axis is frequency.

evidence that textuality more than quantification is a source of anxiety in the subgenre. Moreover, the average internal correlation between quantitative and textual terms by decile is a modest .53 (compared to .47 in the control corpus), showing at the level of individual text only limited entanglement between the two keyword strings. Simply put, references to numbers and texts do not dramatically rise and fall together.

That said, because each decile involves a large amount of prose, correlations between quantitative and textual terms are not in themselves convincing, as indicated by three novels with the highest internal correlations of the corpus. Close reading shows that in *Peter and Wendy*, reading, writing, and arithmetic are tightly entangled, a dynamic reflected by the novel's high correlation of quantitative and textual terms (.89). Figure 3.6 demonstrates that as *Peter and Wendy* moves between modernity and Neverland, Barrie consistently restricts quantification and textuality to London, except in a clearly demarcated instance when Wendy attempts to start a school for the Lost Boys (decile five). By contrast, Melville's *Typee* (.92) and Frank Atkins's *The Devil-Tree of El Dorado* (.92) have the highest internal correlations of the corpus, but close reading does not reveal strong associations between quantification and textuality in either novel. A narrower parameter for collocations (not possible in Voyant) might render more reliable results. Topic modeling is another possibility, but this too proved unsuccessful in establishing a strong correlation between quantitative and textual discourses in Melville's or Atkins's books.

Using a different strategy, correlating the decile curves of individual novels with the average U-curves of the entire adventure corpus can help identify novels that significantly conform and depart from the subgenre's archetypal trajectories. In accordance with judgments based on close reading, *Pym*'s textual correlation (.70) with the archetypal U-curve is the strongest of any text before 1862, while *King Solomon's Mines* has the highest textual correlation (.91) of any novel in the corpus. Such data can indicate a novel's influence and imitativeness, particularly in a subgenre known for being formulaic. Conversely, Charlotte Perkins Gilman's *Herland* (1915) has a lower-than-average textual correlation (.29) and the strongest inverse correlation for quantitative terms in the corpus (−.53), which makes sense given that the novel is a feminist satire of the male-dominated adventure subgenre. Instead of the usual patriarchal plot (white men discover and dominate a primitive society, whose women promptly fall in love with them), the male adventurers of *Herland* are humbled by a pastoral female utopia characterized by a commitment to education and autonomy. As our corpus and nineteenth-century reader surveys suggest, adventure novels were typically written for and by males (though not exclusively so), a dynamic that may be intensified by selecting available digital texts (for instance, at the time of the experiment we found no digital version of Pauline Hopkins's *Of One Blood* [1902–3]).[122] Yet if *Herland*'s gendered critique of the adventure subgenre is reflected in its atypical decile data, the six female-authored novels of the corpus taken together actually have a slightly higher than average correlation with both archetypal U-curves.

Overall, statistical analysis problematized some of my literary-historical assumptions about the development of adventure novels across the long nineteenth century. Given the inconclusive correlation data between keyword frequencies at the level of corpus, and considering the unreliability of internal correlations at the level of individual novels, the above experiment proved to be of limited help in tracking the interrelations of quantitative and textual discourse—whether across time or within individual texts. More positively, the data do support some claims initially based on close reading. The average deserted island and lost world novel leverages quantification and evades textuality more than the average nonadventure novel, and these dynamics across individual narratives tend to wax and wane in patterns that reflect the subgenre's vexed relationship with modernity, especially textuality. That is, based on both close reading and data analysis, adventure novels from 1816 to 1920 are likely to deploy stirring enumerations and fantasize departures from textual excess.

In theory, assessments of different methodologies should proceed according to rational protocols, though one need not cite *Descartes' Error* (1994), affect theory, or the pragmatists to point out that our standards for and choices of compelling argumentation are entangled with personal experience. My own introductory experience with distant reading unfolded in surprising ways. As the organization of this chapter suggests, close reading for the most part preceded statistical analysis in my thinking about adventure novels, though in addition to countervailing, constraining, and confirming initial claims based on intensive reading practices, frequency data also proved generative within a dialectical process. For instance, the high internal correlation data of *The Devil-Tree of El Dorado* prompted me to read the novel, which turned out to be instructive, not because quantification and textuality are meaningfully entangled (they are not), but because its gender politics and setting in Roraima make it a plausible source text for *Herland*. On a larger scale, close reading a portion of the corpus made it possible to make an accurate prediction of the archetypal U-curve for textuality, but statistical analysis was necessary to detect the spike in the sixth decile that disrupts the general pattern (see figure 3.5 again). The spike may be a statistical anomaly, though in retrospect it seems to highlight specific narrative moments such as the creation of the library in *Swiss Family Robinson*, the discussion of alien books in *Vril*, and the appearance of an ancient parchment in *The Devil-Tree of El Dorado*. That these and other high-frequency moments tend to occur in the sixth decile may speak to the formulaic structures of the adventure subgenre and can further suggest how deserted island and lost world fantasies are defined against but never break free from textual superabundance. Even in the middle of escapist adventures, writing and reading assert a presence that cannot be consistently bracketed.

To conclude in a more impressionistic mode, the dialectical movement between close reading and statistical analysis in this experiment proved useful and did not feel unnatural or unwarranted. Historians and sociologists, anthropologists and business people, journalists, sports fans, and cagey consumers often shift between quantitative and qualitative analysis. Distant and close reading can share common goals, and their methods are often comparable insofar as explication involves the recognition of patterns (frequency), the tracing of connections (correlation), the weighing of evidence (calculation), and the plausibility of speculations (probability). It is tempting to follow Gibbs and Cohen when they write that literary critics can "move seamlessly between traditional and computational methods," or to agree with Ramsay, who sees his algorithmic criticism as "fully compatible" with close reading.[123] Yet "seamlessly" and "fully" may be as overstated as claims that traditional literary criticism is fundamentally at odds with quantitative approaches. As in Robert Frost's "Range-Finding" (1920), the movement between scaled epistemologies is seldom smooth or without some epistemological sacrifice, and it is the tensions inherent in a mixed methodology—the shooting of the gulf between anecdotal interpretation and more comprehensive data analysis—that may best yield sharper judgments and alternative possibilities.[124]

All this said, critical affect suggests another axis of affiliation between distant and close reading, especially if one finds one's data intoxicating and again confesses a sense of wonder at the distillations of distant reading. There can be an anticipatory thrill when, after the repetitive work of corpus formation, cleaning, and data gathering, one nears the results of an experiment. The satisfaction of a hypothesis supported (or even debunked) is as real as the disappointment of inconclusive results. One can also lose oneself in the play of numbers as data analysis opens up interpretive possibilities. Neuroscience has even generally linked mathematical and artistic pleasure (the magic happens in the A1 field of the medial orbito-frontal cortex, for those keeping score at home).[125] But if the joys of enumeration are of a different order than literary or literary-critical enchantment, they do not seem to me unrelated or reducible to the satisfactions of rational mastery. Aspiring to consilience may betray a fantasy of reconciliation for humanists in an age of ascendant informationalism, and it can be regarded as capitulation to the point of treachery (if you can't beat the positivists, join them, or at least apply for their funding). Yet if certain questions come from a position of weakness, they may be all the more worth posing. Can close reading, aesthetics, and enchantment be saved when there are too many texts *not* to count? Can the literary find a way to not only coexist but collaborate with the informational? Adventure fictions of the long nineteenth century try (sometimes desperately) to answer "yes," even if enchantment remains a final frontier in the empire of accounting.

How we respond in the twenty-first century is a momentous question. My sense is that mainstream literary studies will increasingly—and should—answer in the affirmative when facing the question of whether to integrate data analysis into more traditional critical practices. It is not only that quantitative methods offer epistemological advantages that do not oppose familiar goals of literary interpretation. Nor is it only that, as the authority of information rises, literary critics will continue to be influenced by inducements from administrators, funding entities, colleagues in other disciplines, and students. Nor is it only that broadening access to DH tools and corpuses will make it easier to execute quantitative projects, or that coming generations of literary critics will on the whole have better computational skills. All this seems to me likely, though the thrust of this chapter has been to trace a history that shows that the boundary between the informational and the literary has always been porous and negotiable. Just as literary studies has accommodated other supposed insurgents—New Historicism, new canons, high theory, other disciplines—it will integrate the quantitative approaches of DH and indeed already has.

Too Many Codas: Dark Continents, Repulsive Figures, Six Shooters, and Lost Arks

One limit of data-driven literary analysis is that it requires brightly lined categories, no matter if the texts in question are omnivorous hybrids and baggy monsters that do not conform to rigorous generic definitions. The foregoing section has argued that the accounting of literature can be empirically studied in a bounded corpus of deserted island and lost world novels, and yet something in literature and literary criticism does not love categorical walls. With a more catholic attitude toward intertextuality, and with an eye toward projecting interpretive possibilities beyond the adventure novel subgenre narrowly construed, what follows offers a series of codas that press the contingencies of literary history beyond a clearly demarcated group of books. If Robinsonade and lost world novels are especially stirred by numbers and anxious about textuality, they are not alone in acknowledging how the merging of literature and information bears on the prospects of enchantment. The dangers of confirmation bias and teleological reading should not be underestimated, but one measure of the generative, self-reinforcing power of any literary-critical argument is that obsessive scholars start to see their thesis refracted everywhere—in this case, in Henry Morton Stanley's *Through the Dark Continent* (1878), Joseph Conrad's *Heart of Darkness* (1899), Owen Wister's *The Virginian* (1902), and Steven Spielberg's *Raiders of the Lost Ark* (1981).

In 1886, the *Pall Mall Gazette* capitalized on the success of Lubbock's "Hundred Best Books" by publishing a special issue on the topic that included diverse commentaries and alternative lists. Among the contributors was Henry Morton Stanley (of "Dr. Livingstone, I presume?" fame), who listed the books he brought on his second expedition to central Africa, a massive undertaking that took three years to finish (1874–77) and at one point included a caravan of 2,290 people. Stanley begins his *Pall Mall* piece by quantifying the books his porters carried on the expedition ("three loads, or about 180 lbs."). He then provides an inventory of seventy titles—from philological and scientific works, to Greek and Roman classics, to canonical British literature and modern novels. Stanley's selections are not particularly surprising, but what he calls his "portable library" is uniquely compelling because of the attrition it suffers on his trek. He writes in *Pall Mall*, "as my men lessened in numbers, stricken by famine, fighting, and sickness, one by one they [the books] were reluctantly thrown away." After the deaths and desertions of most of his party, Stanley is left with one book—the Bible, of course—his volume of Shakespeare having "been burned by demand of the foolish people of Zinga."[126] As if facing a very real deserted island scenario—if you could have only one book, which would you choose?—Stanley experiences textual excess as a physical reality in which empty spaces on the map are no place for backbreaking loads of print.

Stanley's recollection in *Pall Mall* presents him as a lover of literature, in part by eliding important details about the abandoning of his books in central Africa. More expansive is his exploration narrative, *Through the Dark Continent*, an influential account of his expedition that maps, along with the Congo River, relations between information and literature. Drawing on the talking-book trope, *Dark Continent* recounts at various points how his books awed African natives, including the Zinga, who see Stanley writing in his notebook and insist that the fetish be burned. Stanley's notebook included important geographic, commercial, and military data that he would later pass on to Leopold II. But because the people of Zinga fear touching the volume, Stanley manages to burn in its stead an edition of Shakespeare of similar size and color. Stephen Greenblatt ends *Shakespearian Negotiations* (1988) with a discussion of *The Tempest* and Stanley's switching of texts, which for Greenblatt points both to Shakespeare's implication in colonialism and to differences between literary and factual discourses.[127] For Greenblatt, *The Tempest* is entangled in imperial projects, but Stanley's writings—unlike Shakespeare's play—directly informed Leopold II's devastation of the Congo. Greenblatt concludes his prophetic interpretation with New Historicist self-recrimination, emphasizing how Stanley exchanges a mass-produced aesthetic object (Shakespeare) for a homologous notebook that is more complicit in imperialist violence but is not as different as some literary critics might like to think. On Prospero's island and in Stanley's Congo, art negotiates with—and thus participates in—ideological structures of domination.

Or in the terms of this chapter, *Dark Continent* sacrifices literature to numbers, indicating both their difference and their fungibility while reflecting the tense interplay between the literary and the informational that appears throughout Stanley's narrative. Juxtapositions can be stark and brutal, such as the thrilling description of a hunter's single shot versus inventories of killed game, or the poignant eulogizing of a fallen British comrade versus cold statistics on Zanzibarian casualties. Yet aesthetics and calculation prove difficult to separate as struggles against topography, hunger, and hostile tribes are rendered in stirring enumerations. (By way of comparison, only three of the 105 adventure novels treated in the previous section have a higher frequency of quantitative terms than *Dark Continent*.) For anyone interested in the dramatic unfoldings, moral implications, and ideological inclinations of Stanley's enterprise, it matters how many miles must be walked, how many yards of cloth can be traded for food, how many warriors are in how many canoes, and how many lashes Stanley assigns his subordinates. The substitution of Shakespeare for Stanley's notebook can point to how literary and quantitative discourses can be brought into a kind of equivalency, though Stanley remains discomfited by this possibility—bemoaning the loss of Shakespeare's intimacy, paying homage to literature's special affective power, and a decade later in the pages of *Pall Mall* omitting the fact that he, and not the Zinga people, was directly responsible for sacrificing the Bard. Stanley writes of burning Shakespeare in *Dark Continent*:

> We walked to the nearest fire. I breathed a regretful farewell to my genial companion, which during many weary hours of night had assisted to relieve my mind when oppressed by almost intolerable woes, and then gravely consigned the innocent Shakespeare to the flames, heaping the brush-fuel over it with ceremonious care.[128]

Here Stanley conjures a mythic pyre for a fetishized Shakespeare volume, but informational modernity, not primitive superstition, is what kills Shakespeare in the Congo.

Stanley's switching of texts is just one instance in which he complicates distinctions between literature and information. Stanley was inspired by David Livingstone's widely read *Missionary Travels and Researches in South Africa* (1857), a book that makes reference to *Robinson Crusoe* as well as Scott's Waverly novels. Stanley's writings in turn influenced lost world novelists such as Haggard, Doyle, and Burroughs, and *Dark Continent* itself refers to *Crusoe* and Charles Kingsley's *Westward Ho!* (1855), draws heavily on adventure fiction tropes, and roughly correlates with the quantitative U-shape of the adventure novel corpus (.61).[129] Stanley's porters carry novels from Scott, Kingsley, and Bulwer-Lytton, and in *Pall*

Mall he faults Lubbock for not including on his list (of all authors!) Frederick Marryat and James Fenimore Cooper. Clearly adventure novels and exploration narratives share formal features and (let's just say) imperial entanglements. As Daniel Bivona has emphasized, both genres seek to reconcile incompatible liberal fantasies: the triumph of heroic Western individualism, and the efficacy of what Stanley calls in *Dark Continent* his "proper method of organization," which includes the bureaucratic and informational control of overwhelming peoples, supplies, and topographies.[130] Stanley thus appeals to the Victorian desire for what the historian of science and technology Jon Agar calls the "super-statistician possessing an interpretative gaze over the British Empire," a legacy stretching back to *Crusoe*.[131]

Yet as we have seen, adventure narratives are often uncomfortable with informational modernity, an anxiety evident in Stanley's relationship with superabundant print. Like a hero who happens upon a long-lost document, Stanley at the start of *Dark Continent* decides to return to Africa after discovering in an out-of-the-way bookshop a dusty volume titled *How to Observe*. Indicating the nineteenth century's passion for empiricism, a number of titles can fit this description, including *How to Observe: Geology* (1835)—a book by the founder of the Geological Survey of Great Britain, Henry De la Beche, who champions quantitative methods, cites Charles Babbage on data-driven efficiency, and quotes John Herschel when instructing readers how to record and organize "an immense mass of valuable information."[132] Inspired, Stanley immediately purchases "over one hundred and thirty books upon Africa," but on finding their information on the Congo region lacking, he begins mapping his own routes and making lists of supplies.[133] Stanley thus appears to leave print behind. His imagination and expedition begin where book knowledge of Africa leaves off, though as Hester Blum and Adriana Craciun have shown, eighteenth- and nineteenth-century journeys of discovery were intensely committed to documenting and disseminating their information through print.[134] Such is the case with Stanley's second African expedition, for his project is enmeshed in a transatlantic print industry hungry for exploration narratives.[135] London's *Daily Telegraph* and the *New York Herald* jointly sponsored what Stanley calls his "Anglo-American Expedition," and because both papers immediately published the dispatches that Stanley managed to send home, some detractors accused him of grandstanding for the public and even seeking armed conflicts to boost circulation.[136] Excessive books are abandoned and burned, but Stanley's travels remain shadowed by mass print.

Stanley's imperial explorations thus bring into relief—and also fantasize relief from—textual excess. Like deserted island and lost world novelists, he seems aware of the potential but is not quite able to imagine print culture existing beyond the metropole, a limitation that Pascale Casanova and modern historians of print are beginning to rectify.[137] Speculating in *Pall Mall* on the fate of the books he discarded during his expedition, Stanley writes, "[They] will be kept as fetishes until some African antiquarian will pick some of them up a century hence, and wonder how on earth 'Jane Eyre,' printed in 1870, came to be in Ituru, or Thackeray's 'Esmond,' Dickens and Scott, came to be preserved among the Lubari of Gambaragara."[138] It is not entirely clear from this syntax whether Stanley's African collector is an indigenous or European antiquarian. Either way, and despite the Whig history of *Dark Continent*, Stanley believes that the Congo region will be for the foreseeable future impenetrable to print culture, and that any discovery of reading materials will be an unlikely occasion for wonder. Books can be brought to and even preserved in central Africa but only as fetishes whose power depends precisely on their not being read. That many Westerners also fetishize without reading their great books is an irony Stanley does not register, nor does he recognize that colonized peoples across the world were not only bearing the burdens of white literary fantasies but were also engaging in global print markets themselves.

Stanley's *Pall Mall* piece is ultimately most concerned with the books, not the bodies or cultures, he leaves behind. For Victorian adventure narratives that imagine colonial subjects more actively negotiating between the literary and the informational, one might look to the Indian cram boys and bureaucratic spies of Rudyard Kipling's *Kim* (1901), or to Bram Stoker's immigrant Dracula, who (as Friedrich Kittler has argued) is unable to control telegraphic technology but does manage to master railway schedules, blue books, and reports on commercial statistics.[139] Perhaps such informational reading explains why the aptly titled count falls asleep during the workday, though even to attempt a joke of this sort is to ignore the stirring, chilling enumerations that are everywhere in Stoker's novel. (It is also to neglect the folklore that vampires suffer from arithmomania—compulsive counting—as suggested by the count of *Sesame Street*.)[140] In contrast to Stanley, colonial subjects in Kipling and Stoker enter into modernity when they manage information. They may not be allowed to speak, but some subalterns can count, though whether they can or should appreciate literature—that is, whether racial others possess or have a need for aesthetics—is an insidious question taken up in chapter 4.

As postcolonial scholars following Said have detailed, British imperialism in the nineteenth century was characterized by devastating combinations of racism, science, bureaucracy, and print.[141] An early critic of Stanley, Joseph Conrad dramatizes such alliances in *Heart of Darkness*, a novella that acknowledges but does not quite abjure the brutalizing conflation of literature and information. Most obviously, the Company managers in Conrad's Congo make a mockery of Stanley's "proper method of organization" (not to mention the bureaucratic ideology that Arnold White would soon champion in his histrionic 1901 book, *Efficiency and Empire*).[142] Along with the Stanley-like enumerations of Marlow's overland trip—sixty men carrying sixty pounds each for two hundred miles—the violence of forced marching becomes painfully clear as dead porters begin littering the roadside. Particularly damning is the Company's "chief accountant" who complains that the immeasurable suffering around him makes accurate "book-keeping" a trial.[143] When Marlow later discovers in an upriver hut a decomposing navigation manual containing "repulsive tables of figures," *Heart of Darkness* shows that quantitative modernity has already penetrated the Congo (39). At the same time, the manual also recalls the premodern texts that launch so many adventure fictions: Marlow first takes the manual's marginalia to be written in code, and the hand restitching of the decrepit volume suggests a regression from industrialized print. When the poetry-mad Russian who owns the manual returns to the jungle like some atavistic character from the pages of Rider, Doyle, or Burroughs, he carries with him the tables of figures in one pocket and rifle cartridges in the other. *Heart of Darkness* thus links imperial violence and the pervasive enumerations of adventure fiction, even if Conrad remains more concerned with European souls than African interiors.

In acknowledging, howsoever partially, the complicity of literature and information in nineteenth-century imperialism, *Heart of Darkness* resists escapist fantasies and easy reconciliations alike. Conrad's critique of the adventure novel subgenre is not a satirical inversion like *Herland* or *Of One Blood*, but he does depict a Congo already invaded by Western writings, as suggested by the negative correlation (−.28) between textual keywords in *Heart of Darkness* and the standard U-curve of the adventure novel corpus. Not unlike Conrad's recollection of Stanley Falls, in which he calls Stanley's *Dark Continent* a "prosaic newspaper 'stunt,'" the end of *Heart of Darkness* associates imperial oppression with the production of superabundant documents—informational and literary alike.[144] After Kurtz dies amid textual excess ("a lot of torn envelopes and open letters littered his bed. His hand roamed feebly amongst these papers"), Marlow takes charge of Kurtz's textual estate, which includes a range of genres (59). "[F]amily letters and memoranda" go to a clueless cousin with almost no commentary, and a journalist gets Kurtz's handwritten report on the Suppression of Savage Customs with the genocidal postscript removed (71). But whereas Marlow placates these parties with false ideals, he rebuffs the litigious Company lawyer who demands with insinuated threats that he hand over "certain 'documents'" and "information" (70). Such documents reflect the corporate production of informational texts that accompanied centuries of British exploration and are reminiscent of the notebook that Stanley switched with Shakespeare and eventually delivered to Leopold II.

Marlow refuses to participate directly in the Company's imperial accounting, but as much as *Heart of Darkness* distances itself from Stanley's brutal bookkeeping and bookmaking, Conrad is too canny about the empire of information to offer up literature as an uncomplicated alternative. It is not only that the chief accountant is a kind of writer ("he wrote, he wrote") or that the murderous Kurtz is also a poet and prose stylist whose report is "a beautiful piece of writing" (22, 50). More metacritically, Marlow conflates the connotations of accounting (information, moral responsibility, and storytelling) when he stammers during the novella's frame narrative, "I am trying to account to myself for—for—Mr. Kurtz" (50). The shadow of the informational looms from the start of *Heart of Darkness*, as Marlow's listeners—the Director of Companies, the Lawyer, and the Accountant—mirror the Company men of the intradiegetic tale. The novella's unnamed narrator can fantasize about romantic explorers, whom he dubs "the great knights-errants of the sea," but Marlow corrects him by commencing a deeper, disenchanting history by invoking Roman merchants, prefects, and tax gatherers who perform the informational work of empire at the origins of Albion (8). Marlow is not entirely ironic when he remarks, "What saves us is efficiency—the devotion to efficiency," for *Heart of Darkness* recognizes the power, horror, and also appeal of an informational imperialism in which literature plays a part (10). In this way, Marlow's synchronic historicism suggests that accounting is less a nineteenth-century phenomenon than a founding episteme of the West. In "Geography and Some Explorers" (1924), Conrad would insist on distinctions between imperial exploitation and the "blameless" maps of "imaginative" adventurers, but in *Heart of Darkness* the documents of civilization are the documents of barbarism, including "certain 'documents'"—ledgers, company reports, navigation manuals, and adventure fictions—in which enumerations are more repulsive than stirring.[145]

Meanwhile back at the ranch, US authors also explored the relationship between the literary and the informational. If Robinsonade and lost world novels found fewer explicit practitioners in America, adventure fiction flourished in a similar register on the vanishing frontier.[146] The Americas had of course long inspired European dreams of an Edenic, premodern New World, but the late nineteenth century witnessed an acceleration of US expansionism from an ex-colony that continued to imagine itself bearing westward the star of empire. Older narratives of American studies has it that US transoceanic aggression rose only after continental conquest: before Hawaii, Cuba, Puerto Rico, Guam, the Philippines, Panama, and Haiti could be coveted, the expanding nation first needed to vanquish Santa Anna, slavery, and the Sioux. Such narratives overlook much—extracontinental exploration and filibustering before the Treaty of Guadalupe Hidalgo; conflicts in the American West and South that continued beyond the nineteenth century; advances by scholars such as Amy Kaplan, John Carlos Rowe, and Jennifer Greeson that challenge distinctions between domestic and foreign imperialism; European anxieties about the "*fin du globe*" that make American fears of the closing frontier less unique than sometimes supposed.[147] And yet the image of Teddy Roosevelt reaching the end of the western trail and wheeling his horse toward San Juan Hill had imaginative force at the end of the nineteenth century and still retains some hold today. Owen Wister's *The Virginian*, dedicated to Roosevelt, both reflects and extends the myth of the American frontier forever on the verge of its end. It can also be read as a lost world narrative aspiring to reconcile enchantment and accounting.

From a historiographical and sociological perspective, the frontier's days were literally numbered at the end of the nineteenth century. Frederick Jackson Turner's "The Significance of the Frontier in American History" (1893) has provided some wonderfully elegiac quotes for scholars of the myth and symbol school, and Turner's thesis comports with eighteenth-century stadialist models most famously represented in America by Cooper: the frontiersman gives way to the surveyor, businessman, government official, and schoolmarm who bear with them, not the restless spirit of adventure, but measurements, ledgers, bureaucracy, and books.[148] The irony is that Turner participates in the disenchantment he describes, for as much as he laments the lost world of the frontier and mythologizes a romantic American character, he helped establish statistical analysis in the increasingly professionalized field of history, pioneering the use of census data to define the frontier and calculate its demise. As if hoping to synthesize new quantitative methods with the narrative forms that traditionally dominated his discipline, Turner would later insist that in the American West "bare statistics become eloquent."[149]

A homologous tension can be found in Weber's "The Protestant Ethic and the Spirit of Capitalism" (1905), which came out of research Weber did in preparation for a 1904 visit to the United States that included frontier travels through Missouri, Arkansas, Oklahoma, and Muskogee Indian Territory. Weber was well versed in the American frontier mythos. He read Cooper's Leatherstocking novels and as a child heard stories of how his father met Sitting Bull during Buffalo Bill's Wild West European tour.[150] Weber's firsthand experience in the American West largely confirmed his sociological theories insofar as his writings in "The Protestant Ethic" and beyond argue that the individualistic agrarianism of the frontier inevitably gives way to the bureaucratic, quantitative, disenchanting forces of capitalist modernity. As we have seen in "Science as a Vocation," Weber predicts a concomitant formation of extrarational beliefs, while also acknowledging that quantitative science can involve enchanting experiences. Yet Weber does not embrace a reconciliation of wonder and accounting, no more than popular images of Roosevelt reflect his dedication to standardizing the civil service and expanding federal bureaucracies. Big sticks, big game, Rough Riders, and Yosemite feel inconsistent with informational management.

The Virginian, however, finds accounting at home on the frontier as Wister offers a series of stirring enumerations. The book begins with jokes about Uncle Huey's incorrect calculations of his age and the precise number of women he has tried to marry. The heroic Virginian is later called suitor "Number—six" until he charms his way up to "number one," and he counts off reconfigurable babies at a dance ("Nine, ten, eleven, beautiful sleepin' strangers") before switching them around as a prank.[151] Suspenseful scenes in *The Virginian* are paced by numbers—when Molly Wood counts off the miles she and the injured Virginian must travel; on the train headed toward a conflict with the villain Trampas ("Portland 1279. . . . Portland 1266. . . . Portland 1256"); and when the Virginian calculates the time before his marriage to Molly ("Twenty [hours] by sixty [minutes] is twelve hundred. Put that into seconds, and yu' get seventy-two thousand seconds") (135, 357). On Wister's frontier, numbers do not signal epistemological authority or institutional power. Rather they serve the purposes of drama, humor, and heroism in the manner of some earlier frontier fiction—from the enumerated tall tales of Davy Crockett (who reported killing three bears in a day, fifteen in a week, fifty-eight during a fall and winter, and 105 in a year) to Huck Finn confusing Aunt Sally's domestic economy (after he playfully steals and replaces her spoons, she pledges to "kill anybody that wanted her to ever count [spoons] any more").[152] Even the accounting of literature proves harmless in *The Virginian*. The protagonist's masculinity is undiminished when he takes up secretarial duties on the ranch; and though Molly is described as someone who might have been a "women typewriter" in another era, the schoolmarm retains traditional feminine charms (71). When Molly imports boxes of books ("Cheap editions, of course"), she not only fails to domesticate the Virginian (he cannot get through Jane Austen); she actually bolsters his rugged individualism (among his favorite authors are Scott).[153]

Most centrally, the climax of *The Virginian* reconciles enchantment with numbers and mass print in a kind of wishful, symbolic synthesis. The Virginian is distraught when his ex-friend Steve does not speak to him before being lynched for cattle rustling. But later when searching the body of another rustler, the Virginian finds a newspaper on which Steve has written a masculine farewell and from which we first learn the Virginian's real name. "Good-by, Jeff," it reads, "I could not have spoke to you without playing the baby" (329). Here is the intimate reticence of the American West as imagined in the cowboy literature and films that Wister helped to codify, and yet Steve's note, which the Virginian later uses to start a campfire, bears imprints of the informational. The citified narrator of *The Virginian* first gives Steve the newspaper—"brought from the railroad and on which I had pencilled a few expenses" (298). And so the novel's fullest expression of its frontier mythos is an intensely personal note written by hand on what amounts to a repurposed account book made from a mass print artifact brought by train from the metropole, circulated by rustlers, and used finally to start a fire on the desolate plains of Wyoming—a not quite lost world suffused with numbers and shadowed by mass print. This synthesis of past and future, West and East, enchantment and information is recapitulated when the Virginian, after reading Steve's note, dreams of Steve handing him a newspaper that then changes into a "six-shooter" (324). The dream seems less a revelation of the Virginian's interiority than an anxious conflation of domains. Combining mass print and information with the totemic six-shooter, itself also an enumerated, mass-produced commodity, *The Virginian*—like a deserted island or lost world novel—cannot escape the accounting of literature. In Wister's western, the genre-defining phrase "I reckon" appears sixty-eight times.

Finally, here are the last words of Indiana Jones, played by Harrison Ford, in *Raiders of the Lost Ark*. After the US military takes possession of the Ark of the Covenant, Indy growls, "Fools, bureaucratic fools! They don't know what they have." Steven Spielberg's blockbuster borrows heavily from adventure fiction tropes while also reenacting the genre's negotiation of enchantment and information under mass media. Representing alternatives to industrial print are familiar ancient texts—parchment maps, hand-illustrated tomes, hieroglyphics carved in stone. Of special interest is the golden headpiece to the Staff of Ra with its engraved directions for finding the Ark. The information on one side is accidentally burned onto the hand of a Nazi agent, a brutally ironic media considering the impending horrors of the Holocaust. *Raiders*, however, presses an informational twist. The agent's hand is branded with the data that the Staff of Ra is "six kaddams" long, but because the Nazis lack a copy of the headpiece's obverse side, they do not know to "take back one kaddam to honor the Hebrew God." They end up digging in the wrong place because numbers— correct numbers—mark the path to enchantment. This is also evident when Indy recounts the story of the Ark in a university library, for if the scene is heavy on Christian mythos, calculative logic asserts its presence as Indy combines a passion for ancient mystery with an archaeologist's scientific knowledge. Oddly prominent in the background of the library scene is a blackboard with algebra problems written in chalk, and when Indy flips the board to its obverse side, he does so to diagram how the Staff of Ra reveals the placement of the Ark according to astronomical and geometrical principles, thus suggesting that enchantment and accounting are two sides of the same coin. Cracking the ancient code will lead to the Ark, rumored to contain the pieces of the Ten Commandments—a literal touchstone for Western literature that is also an enumerated list, as if embodying a lost numerological synthesis of wonder and information.

And yet synthesis proves elusive in *Raiders of the Lost Ark*, especially as the climax unfolds. Representing bureaucratic evil in an Arendtian mode, the Nazis—with banners vaguely reminiscent of Leni Riefenstahl— attempt to film the opening of the Ark on their deserted island base. But instead of (or in addition to) the Ten Commandments, the Ark contains wraithlike spirits (first angelic, then demonic) that short-circuit the filming equipment and kill the assembled Nazis, in one instance blasting a soldier through the lens of his camera. The corpses are ultimately sucked into the Ark, leaving nothing behind but Indy, Marion Ravenwood, and the remnants of broken technology. It seems a triumph of myth over modernity foreshadowed throughout the film, particularly when the Ark supernaturally burns off a swastika on the crate in which it is packed. The instrumental Indy initially mocks what he calls "superstitious hocus-pocus," but one pleasure of the film, if one can hold in abeyance its Orientalism and artifact theft, is watching its cocksure hero discover his fallibility, as when he learns that the unworldly power of the Ark exceeds his rationalist calculations. In this way, *Raiders* appears to operate according to a literary/informational dualism, lifting myth and wonder beyond the imperial reach of mass media, Nazi bureaucracy, science, and accounting.

Except for the denouement of the film, which almost stands as a synopsis of Adorno and Horkheimer's claim in the "Culture Industry" (1944) that, despite "the blindness and muteness of the data to which positivism reduces the world," informational forms can take on a power "which makes them like their extreme opposite, incantations."[154] After the US government takes final possession of the Ark, it is packed in another crate stenciled, "ARMY INTEL 9906753." This time there is no burning of labels, no liberation from classificatory boxes. One might recall at this moment that Indy stands for Indiana (not Independent), that he is funded by the US military, and that the Ark itself is a glorified storage unit—as if to demonstrate that under the dialectic of Enlightenment, myth and institutional rationalism are inseparable; as if angels, demons, and biblical injunctions are not the only primary objects of interest in a world in which informational, classificatory structures such as arks take on titular importance. The US National Security Agency would have us believe that metadata, not content, is its business—that what matters is how communications are categorized and analyzed after messages are disarticulated from senders and broken into smaller units, not unlike the tablets of Moses.

Whatever the case, and whatever the physical cases, the credits of *Raiders of the Lost Ark* roll as the crate with the Ark (that is, the container of the Container) is wheeled down a dimly lit aisle that, as the camera pans back, is seen to run through an immense warehouse of shelves (other containers of containers) stacked ever higher with innumerable crates extending beyond our field of vision. The moment might feel to a literary critic like a library simultaneously rich and foreboding in its superabundance of enumerated objects of enchantment. More likely, the warehouse seems intended to echo the conclusion to *Citizen Kane* (1941), in which the object of wonder is destined to be lost in unknowable, overwhelming excess. The uncertainty that leaves the audience suspended at the end of *Raiders of the Lost Ark* is marked not by the ambiguities of close reading but by the problem of information overload. Retrieving God's word does not require the prayerful exegesis of tablets but an index to master the archive. I find the ending strangely pleasurable, suggesting as Jane Bennett has argued in the context of Kafka that bureaucracy has its own power to enchant.[155]

The long argument of this chapter has been that adventure novels of the long nineteenth century are haunted by the accounting of literature, even (and especially) when they flee toward the textual austerity of deserted islands and blank spaces on a map. Under a strain of postmodernism, wonderful lost worlds more explicitly lurk within systems overwhelmed by information—the sprawling libraries of Borges and Eco; the oversaturated semiotic conspiracies of Pynchon; the swamped bureaucracies of DeLillo, Saramago, and Foster Wallace; the unmappable networks of cyberfiction. *Raiders of the Lost Ark* displays a postmodern commitment to the wonders of information overload as Indy's last line about bureaucrats not knowing what they have indicates both the incorporated reach and the epistemological limits of efforts to classify, enumerate, organize, and contain a kind of enchantment that we still might associate with the literary, thus setting in productive competition and potential conflation calculation and myth, numbers and art, the sciences and the humanities. Like literature in an information age, the bearer of enchantment in *Raiders of the Lost Ark* is simultaneously found and lost. It abides somewhere contained within mediated excess, its fate still unresolved, waiting for some future discovery or at least an adequate sequel.

CHAPTER FOUR

Testing

They would not let me go: I must sit down and write before them. As I dipped my pen in the ink with a shaking hand, and surveyed the white paper with eyes half-blinded and overflowing, one of my judges began mincingly to apologize for the pain he caused.

—CHARLOTTE BRONTË, *VILLETTE* (1853)

How can we raise the question of accountability without always already giving in to the logic of accounting? In some sense, we cannot.... The exponential growth in the commodification of information itself, thanks to new technologies, renders the current situation even more acute.

—BILL READINGS, *THE UNIVERSITY IN RUINS* (1996)

WHAT COUNTS AS LITERARY KNOWLEDGE, and is it information? Can the fruits of literary study be measured? How might capacities for aesthetics, interpretation, and judgment be recognized across large populations? Such questions pivot from challenges of mass print toward those of mass assessment, though they retain a focus on methods and systems that would render the literary as information. The assessment of literary attainments feels especially pressing today with the broad ascendancy of data analysis and the penetration of the accountability movement into the humanities. Memos from the dean about measurable outcomes may threaten teachers suspicious of informational regimes, but long before Bill Readings identified quantitative assessment as a feature of the corporate university, and long before AP, SAT, GRE, A-level, and Common Core tests sought to measure literary knowledge, standardized literature examinations emerged in Britain and America in the middle of the nineteenth century.[1]

Scholarship on the production of literary knowledge and the formation of literary studies as a discipline has tended to focus on institutional histories, critical methods, and cultural capital. Also crucial but undiscussed are nineteenth-century controversies over standardized literature tests that foreground the fraught relationship between metrics and aesthetics during a period in which concepts of the literary took shape alongside developing informational discourses—statistics and sociology, utilitarianism and mass pedagogy, bureaucracy and liberal meritocracy. The study of literature in English can be taken to rise under a welter of ideological forces committed to what Foucault called "complete enumeration."[2] Yet aesthetics and interpretation proved difficult for Victorians to measure as literature exams and the objections they engendered helped to produce the literary as such and impelled writers to consider the status of literature in their information age.

Victorian reactions to standardized exams in general and literature tests in particular uncannily anticipate twenty-first-century debates over the accountability movement, the corporatization of education, and the vocational relevance of literary study. The ossified state of discussion might be discouraging (for all the current furor over standardized testing, the conversation has not radically changed in 150 years). But it can also offer cold comfort to literary critics in the lengthening shadow of the humanities crisis (the four horsemen of assessment are not suddenly upon us; they were in the saddle at the beginnings of the discipline). There are, of course, important distinctions to be made between nineteenth- and twenty-first-century literary testing, but we should still look to history to understand the conditions in which literary knowledge is adjudicated today. We may even find some guidance for navigating our era of data-driven accountability in which the learning of literary content is increasingly subordinated to more generalizable, more explicitly instrumental skills. A range of authors—from Dickens, Trollope, Mathew Arnold, Thomas Hughes, and Charlotte Brontë, to Fanny Fern, Louisa May Alcott, and Frank Webb—reflect on tensions between standardized literary knowledge and unaccountable aspects of art. In various ways, these writers resist the reduction of literary knowledge to information, but if they thereby participate in a growing divide, their views are surprisingly modulated, suggesting that differences between the literary and the informational are not as great as they sometimes appear.

Subjects for Examination

To be a modern discipline is to encounter the demands of standardized testing. Most explicitly in *Discipline and Punish* (1975) but as early as *The Order of Things* (1966), Foucault conceives of institutional examinations as a fundamental technology in knowledge production, identity formation, and power distribution. Foucault begins his history in the seventeenth century before moving quickly to the end of the eighteenth, where examinations come to function less as overt forces of homogenization and more as measures that coercively define individuals against aggregative norms.³ Foucault is not primarily concerned with educational assessments, nor is *Discipline and Punish*, for all its influence in literary studies, much interested in the history of the field. When *The Order of Things* does touch on literary studies as a discipline, Foucault describes it as a "twin figure" of philology that attempts to repudiate the genealogical link by asserting an autonomous aesthetic realm (literature "folded back upon the enigma of its own origin and existing wholly in reference to the pure act of writing").⁴ However, literature examinations of the Victorian period tell a less hermetic story as they attempt to translate generally understood but loosely defined aesthetic qualities into classifiable, quantifiable, socially useful forms of knowledge. Whether literary attainments can be measured with standardized tests was a question for many Victorians, so much so that the history of literary studies can be approached as a history of the limits of informationalism.

An oft-noted moment in the emergence of English literary studies occurred in 1887 when Oxford University, after an acrimonious debate, appointed a philologist instead of a literary critic to its first professorship of English literature. Leading the short-lived conservative victory was the historian E. A. Freeman, who charged that literary study not centered on facts indulged merely in "the reading of books, the criticism of books, the finding out everything about the writers of the books ... but all essentially as a matter of taste." Cunningly turning literature's aesthetic self-image against its pretensions as a field of knowledge, Freeman argued that philology can be taught and tested but literary sensibilities cannot. He wrote:

> As subjects for the examination ... we do not want, we will not say frivolous subjects, but subjects which are merely light, elegant, interesting. As subjects for examination we must have subjects in which it is possible to examine, ... possible to say of two answers to a question that one is right and the other is wrong. ... Facts may be taught, but surely the delicacies and elegances of literature cannot be driven into any man.⁵

One might think that knowledge production precedes assessment standards. First come objects of study, then methods, and thereby knowledge on which exams are then based. But Freeman unfolded an opposite logic in which what counted as scholarly knowledge needed to be something that could somehow be counted in exams—a premise that made literary knowledge unteachable to the point of oxymoronic. How can seemingly unfalsifiable learning based on (or at least closely associated with) untestable capacities of taste, feeling, interpretation, and imagination be incorporated within educational systems increasingly committed to standardized knowledge? Freeman's answer was simple: it can't.

The most searching response to Freeman's polemic came from the literary critic John Churton Collins, who—in addition to hoping to secure the Oxford appointment for himself—joined other Victorian men of letters in arguing that the systematizing of literary study need not be a wholly positivist enterprise. Collins acceded to Freeman's formulation of knowledge but insisted on a higher, more liberal set of goals: "the foundations of taste must be laid with the foundations for knowledge, for literary knowledge without literary taste can have no literary value."[6] Invoking rhetoricians from Aristotle to Quintilian, and risking references to Schiller and Coleridge, Collins lamented fact-based literature exams before describing his own alternative pedagogy. Instead of quizzing his students on sources, interpolations, and Elizabethan grammar in *Macbeth* (1606), Collins preferred more open-ended questions: "Is Macbeth to be regarded as a responsible agent? . . . Through what phases did the style of Shakespeare pass? . . . [W]hat strike you as being particularly subtle dramatic touches. Explain your reasons for thinking them so."[7] Such questions feel recognizably modern in that they require interpretive and aesthetic capacities, and yet the shadow of Freeman's accountability loomed, for to protect themselves from charges of "shallow unsystematic dilettantism," literary critics (Collins included) standardized knowledge in their developing field by designating a canon, formalizing literary history, and retaining connections to philological methods already institutionally entrenched.[8] Concessions, perhaps, but literary critics today may still find themselves on the defensive when facing the charge—and occasional forehanded compliment—that what we do is more or less about personal preferences that are neither right nor wrong but nonetheless form the basis for professional expertise and power over grade point averages. I'm not entirely sure why, but when I've mentioned in talks that Collins did not get the Oxford job and later committed suicide, there's usually some dark chuckling.

The Oxford controversy is a telling moment in the institutionalization of English literature, but the opposing positions of Freeman and Collins are so exemplary because debates over the standardization and assessment of literary knowledge had been maturing for half a century. Scholarship on the rise of English literary studies is extensive—from early historical descriptions from D. J. Palmer and Thomas Heyck, to Gerald Graff's foundational work on literary studies in America, to more critical scholarship by Terry Eagleton, Ian Hunter, Gauri Viswanathan, John Guillory, and David Shumway.[9] This last group, with its various deployments of Marx, Foucault, Said, and Bourdieu, are skeptical of the humanist logic under which literary studies initially justified itself in the nineteenth century. If Victorian proponents of liberal education set the moral and aesthetic benefits of literature over and against commodification, positivism, and cultural disintegration, histories of the discipline from the 1980s and 1990s took literary studies from its beginnings to be complicit in regnant power structures. In Eagleton's aggressive line of argument, not long after romanticism fantasized an autotelic realm of aesthetics, literary critics secured institutional gains by asserting a "*pacifying* influence," exchanging (as it were) a walk-on part in the war for a lead role in an academic cage.[10] Even scholars such as Graff who are less committed to ideology critique tend to emphasize tradeoffs and sellouts as literary critics became specialized, self-regulating professionals paying uneasy tribute to the sciences. In many ways, it makes sense that histories of the discipline have not focused on standardized literature exams. For liberal humanists in the tradition of Palmer, the Victorian rage for examination is simply "one of the least attractive aspects of nineteenth-century education," while for scholars exposing literary studies as a discourse of control, standardized tests are too obviously coercive to even bother unmasking.[11]

But there are other ways to track the disciplinary rise of literary studies in the nineteenth century. Jon Klancher, Elizabeth Renker, and Nancy Glazener have shown how literary studies emerged, not in elite institutions, but through cultural organizations and schools for women and laborers.[12] More specific to questions of assessment, Cathy Shuman and Jennifer Ruth discuss how standardized testing converted cultural capital to marketable knowledge, a transformation that enticed and worried Victorian authors in the throes of professionalization.[13] Shuman and Ruth helpfully connect standardized testing to the British liberal state, but curiously their discussions treat assessments in general without addressing literature examinations, nor do they explore the influence of standardized testing on American literature of the time. Overall, a metahistorical narrative can help explain the ways in which scholars have described the formation of literary studies: early historians of the discipline accepted the premises of liberal humanism; scholars in the age of theory and critique interrogated such claims; literary critics at the turn of the twentieth century found Victorian anxieties over professionalism coordinate with the vocational crises of their time; and this chapter reflects, not only recent moves toward transatlanticism and the relations of science and literature, but also the dominance of educational policies that require literary scholars and teachers to quantify, standardize, and thereby justify their work in an information age.

Standardized examinations in the Victorian period are seldom acknowledged as a background for today's accountability movement, which typically locates its origins in more rigorous assessments from the early twentieth century—America's College Entrance Examination Board, the invention of multiple choice questions, Alfred Binet's IQ tests, and military exams during World War I.[14] Yet as early as the late seventeenth and eighteenth centuries, professional examinations in Britain regulated areas of medicine, law, the military, and church leadership.[15] Standardized testing then rose in the 1840s at state-supported schools, teacher credentialing programs, extension lectures, and the civil and military service (the later spurred in part by perceived mismanagement during the Irish famine, Crimean War, and administration of India).[16] Less studied are nineteenth-century American contexts, for standardized testing in the less centralized United States emerged later and less evenly, though (as we will see) some tests in antebellum schools paralleled British examination practices, while civil service reformers aspired to institute British assessment policies in America.[17]

There is no standard definition of standardized testing in the nineteenth century, but the emergence of what were often called "competitive examinations" entailed a series of shifts.[18] Instead of ad hoc invigilators orally and often randomly quizzing subjects before relating their impressions to local authorities, assessments increasingly involved written answers to uniform questions that could be graded right or wrong and were administered simultaneously to large bodies of test takers by professionals who reported data to centralized institutions. Standardized testing in the period seldom distinguished between achievement and aptitude, accomplishment and potential. It also served a range of purposes—qualification (meeting minimum standards for accreditation or to enter an applicant pool), ranking (awarding school admissions, academic prizes, and professional appointments and promotions), and resource allocation (including school funding and teacher compensation). Standardized exams were a fundamental tool of liberal meritocracy with supporters arguing that testing improved efficiency by rewarding deserving candidates and excluding stereotypical free riders (in Britain, idiot-gentlemen serving as military officers and sinecured bureaucrats; in the United States, the parasites of the spoils system, often depicted as ethnic and racial others). Accountability proponents in Britain and America drew on Continental models, as well as real and imagined Chinese history. They also aligned standardized testing with informational modernity—quantitative analysis, mass production, scientific objectivity, and bureaucratic impersonality. As described by a test preparation book from 1859, "Examinations, as tests of competency or fitness for posts of trust and usefulness, are amongst the distinguishing marks of progress of the present age."[19] More broadly, standardized tests embodied a spirit of procedural reform that Elaine Hadley sets at the center of Victorian liberalism.[20]

Needless to say, they were well hated by some. Victorian critics focused on problems that remain with us today—the disjunction between scores and actual capabilities, cramming and teaching to the test, the depersonalizing of the teacher-pupil relationship, the distortion of learning under market competition, and the unhealthy pressures of high-stakes tests that led to breakdowns and, by some accounts, death. Observers complained that standardized exams gave undue advantage to those with elite educations (training in the classics and mathematics were often emphasized). Others charged that exams were too much of a leveling force, rewarding crass ambition and mechanical learning over refinement, character, and blood.[21] Opponents from all sides railed against "the examination octopus" and "the boa-constrictor system of competitive examination," which one detractor in 1861 called "a mental police."[22] Such concerns may sound familiar enough today, though a powerful Victorian counterpoint also survives. As one commentator acknowledged in a collection titled *The Sacrifice of Education to Examination* (1889): "competitive examination is a very imperfect test, but it is better than none."[23]

Neglected by historians of testing but of special interest here are emerging disciplinary distinctions. Whereas standardized exams were often seen as appropriate for subjects such as geography, arithmetic, and history, efforts to test literary accomplishments were more suspect, exemplifying what Guillory and Mary Poovey have identified as a growing divergence at the end of the eighteenth century between factuality and aesthetics, positivist and post-Kantian epistemologies, informational and literary genres.[24] Just as Victorians came to worry that standardized poetry recitations emphasized informational skills such as memory at the expense of aesthetic training, many argued that standardized literary testing missed or violated something special about literature.[25] Tests destroyed the love of reading, stunted artistic capacities, and encouraged students to skim primary texts or memorize the summaries provided by a burgeoning test preparation industry that included literary tutors and cram guides. If Freeman later took the untestability of literary criticism as evidence of its illegitimacy, others regarded the unaccountability of literature as an indictment of standardized testing. John Henry Newman in *The Idea of a University* (1858) charged that standardized exams subordinated unified cultivation to disarticulated facts, so much that he preferred an unstructured gathering of young men to schools such as the University of London that awarded degrees solely by examination. For Newman, who had suffered a mental breakdown during his examinations at Oxford, standardized testing threatened to turn education into "a foundry, or a mint, or a treadmill" that churned out mere "men of information."[26] By the time of the Taunton Commission on endowed grammar schools (1864–67), some educators pushed back against prevailing assessment practices, arguing that English literature should be taught not simply to inculcate grammar, religion, and patriotism but also to foster a sense of beauty and pleasure.[27]

Under such pressures—and in a spirit of pluralism, compromise, and incoherence that still characterizes literary studies today—standardized literature examinations from the Victorian period were methodologically mixed. In tests available in government reports, educational treatises, and reprintings in Victorian study guides, most questions involved philological facts, historical contexts, biographical backgrounds, argument summaries, and passage identifications. Such is standardized literary information: answers are right or wrong; interpretation is not required; results can be quantitatively rendered and ranked; knowledge and ignorance are so starkly distinguished that an English professor encountering such tests 150 years later might find himself feeling a sense of inadequacy not felt since he took the GRE Literature in English subject exam (more on which at the end of this chapter).

Yet if the informational dominated standardized literature exams, the literary was not wholly excluded. In 1855, candidates for the Royal Artillery and Engineers Corps encountered the following query: "Mention the most illustrious authors who flourished in the first thirty years of the present century; and estimate the influence of the French Revolution upon them."[28] This question was written by the poet Arthur Hugh Clough, who also served as examiner for the Education Office, and who insisted in 1852, "Examinations, I repeat, are essential; but no examinations will do much good unless there be, independent and irrespective of them, a real inward taste, and liking, and passion."[29] The 1859 Indian Civil Service exam also included a question that emphasized the literary: "Whom do you reckon the greatest English poet of the nineteenth century? Justify your preference by argument and quotations."[30] I have not found graded answers or rubrics to such questions, but even if there were surely correct and incorrect answers (Wordsworth and Tennyson yes, Keats and Hemans no), test takers appear to have enjoyed (or suffered) some critical latitude as the literary retained a tenuous hold in information-based standardized tests.

For a more holistic, more proportional sense of the diverse knowledges measured in English examinations, consider three sections from the 1858 Indian Civil Service test (each section to be finished in three hours; each worth 500 points out of a total of 8,375, or about 6 percent total).[31] The eleven questions on the "English Language" section are decidedly informational, covering etymology, spelling, vocabulary, and the history of English. The thirteen questions on the "English Literature" section are somewhat more varied and are included here nearly in full:

1. Give an account of Brut of Layamon, *or* of the Ormulum, *or* of the Chronicle of Robert of Gloucester, *or* of the Chronicle of Robert de Brunne, *or* of the Visions of Piers Plowman; noticing the date, authorship, language, form of verse, and subject.

2. Give a similar account of Chaucer's Canterbury Tales, or of Gower's Confessio Amantis.

3. Sketch the origin and growth of the English drama to the appearance of Shakespeare.

4. Estimate the influence exercised by popular poetry on the character and spirit of a nation, and quote any striking passages that you may remember from English or Scottish ballads.

5. Compare Chaucer, Spenser, Dryden, Pope, and Wordsworth; first, in respect of the general spirit and manner of their poetry; and, secondly, in respect of their versification.

6. Sketch the biography of Pope, or of Swift, or of Johnson, or of Burke, or of Scott.

7. Give a short account of the principal English works of Francis Bacon; arranging them either in the order of time, or according to the departments to which they belong; and noticing generally the subject of each, and the manner in which it is treated.

8. State the argument of Milton's Monody of Lycidas, and explain the expressions printed in *Italics* in the following passage. . . .

9. Describe the course of the action either in Milton's Comus, or in his Samson Agonistes.

10. Compare Bacon and Burke, first as thinkers, and secondly as writers.

11. Characterize succinctly any six of the most distinguished English poetical writers of the present century, and any six of the most distinguished English writers in prose during the same period.

12. Enumerate and characterize briefly the principal English Parliamentary orators of the last and the present century.

13. From which of Shakespeare's plays is each of the following passages taken? Mention the character who utters them, and the context in which they occur, and explain the peculiarities of idiom and the allusions contained in them. . . . [twenty passages from Shakespeare follow].

The majority of these questions are dedicated to informational forms of knowledge (summaries, identifications, formal classifications, literary-historical facts), but they also offer limited possibilities for more critical demonstrations (comparisons, characterizations, aesthetic judgments). Implicit is the sense that English literary study should inculcate mainly informational competency but also some interpretive habits of mind.

Interestingly, some questions in the third and final section, "English Composition," sound most like questions that a literature teacher might ask today:

1. Write a short but careful exposition of what appears to you to be the true conception of any of the following characters of the Shakespearian Drama:—Hamlet, Macbeth, Lady Macbeth, Lear, Falstaff.

2. Compare, or contrast, the Poetical Genius of Shakespeare with that of Milton.

3. Describe an Earthquake, a Volcanic Eruption, or a Shipwreck.

4. Write a narrative of the Indian Mutiny . . . with as little expression of opinion as possible.

5. [Discuss] the influence of public schools on English life.

Questions 1 and 2 require aesthetic and interpretive capacities but also indicate the uncertain status of literary criticism at the time, for if such questions represent a kind of knowledge worth testing, that knowledge was not considered literary enough to be included in the English Literature section. Instead, it appears under English Composition, as if anticipating present-day debates about the special role (or lack thereof) that literature should play in composition and rhetoric courses as we write in and across the disciplines. Further indicating ambivalence about literary sensibilities, question 3 (the description of various disasters) invites artistic expression, which question 4 then balances by requiring informational objectivity (write "with as little expression of opinion as possible"). Question 5, while turning to the kind of nonliterary content currently preferred in standardized writing exams, is obviously biased toward the gentlemanly classes. Asking about the influence of British public schools such as Eton and Rugby is not unlike the vilified SAT question that required knowing the definition of "regatta."

Also negotiating between the informational and the literary were Victorian study guides to English literature tests, which paid tribute to aesthetics while still justifying their provision of excerpts, summaries, lists, and mnemonic aids. Robert Demaus's 1866 primer to English literature denied the efficacy of "'ingenious cramming,'" insisting instead that a student must read great texts in full to "form for himself some definite principles of literary taste." However, Demaus then praises standardized tests, quotes Pliny and Bacon on the value of skimming, and opines that "older writers are characterized by a tediousness that is too great a trial for modern patience."[32] In his popular 1873 study guide to literature exams, the Oxford philologist William Skeat also derided the "mere gorging of undigested information" while defending the memorization of facts as a necessary basis for literary taste.[33] Arguing from defensive postures, cram books typically acknowledged the aesthetic claims of the literary before focusing their energies on testable facts and extensive reading for an information age.

Even Matthew Arnold illustrates the tense relation of information and literature during the standardization of Victorian education. While advocating for the liberal arts under a homogenizing ideal of Culture, Arnold supported "a uniform standard of examination," admired standardized testing in Germany and France, and by his own account was responsible as a school inspector for assessing twenty-five thousand students a year.[34] Yet Arnold admitted the dangers of standardized testing when detailing how cramming could leave students "bewildered and oppressed by a mass of information hastily heaped together."[35] He fought against the 1862 Revised Code, a controversial accountability measure that tied teacher compensation and school funding to student scores on national tests. The main driver of the policy was MP Robert Lowe, who wrote, "I do not deny that quality is a very important thing, but when I come to a final system I cannot but think that quantity is, perhaps, more important."[36] Arnold's objections in "The Twice-Revised Code" (1862) are typical of his time and ours: "absolute standards" are difficult to define and administer, ignore unequal social and institutional contexts, encourage teaching to the test by rote methods, and mimic imperial China, which Arnold associates with rigid hierarchy and narrow-minded competition.[37] Arnold acknowledges the value of examination "data" but worries that standardized exams cannot account for "real attainments," by which he means "moral tone," "inventiveness," *"free play,"* "feeling and taste," and "animation of mind."[38] Arnold ultimately sets his real attainments against systems in which the student becomes "a mere ladder of 'information' " taught to "acquire a number of 'knowledges.' "[39] The scare quotes here sum the critique: acquiring *information* is not serious learning, nor are multitudinous *knowledges* truths.

What is unclear is how Arnold hopes to reconcile the real attainments of literary study with his desire for national standards. His inspector reports complain that students lack aesthetic judgment in part because they are assigned "dry scientific disquisition[s]" and "jejune encyclopaedia of positive information."[40] Yet Arnold also privileged grammar over literary reading, admitted the difficulty of teaching literary taste, and brought what Poovey has called a "procedural objectivity" to literary criticism.[41] As with German intellectuals who hoped that cultivated individuals could unify the fragmented knowledges of mass print, Arnoldian *bildung* imagines liberally educated citizens gaining the ethical, epistemological, and aesthetic capacities to incorporate information into higher-order thinking. Arnold the inspector and Arnold the humanist are never in full accord, for the former regards standardized exams as legitimate and necessary, while the later insists that such testing cannot measure the choicest qualities of the literary. Similar ambivalence is more fully, more dramatically elaborated in Anglo-American novels from the Victorian period, for unlike etymological roots, logarithms, tributaries, and trilobites, literary texts are objects of study that aspire to teach themselves and thus address their cultural and epistemological status under the pressures of informationalism.

Impersonality and Impersonation in Our Mutual Friend

Given his mixed experiences as a pupil, and considering the rapid modernization of pedagogy during his lifetime, it makes sense that Charles Dickens was both interested in and unsettled by his era's educational reforms. As if in reaction to what John Forster called Dickens's "haphazard" education, Dickens was a frequent visitor at schools, funded scholarships for disadvantaged children, supported improved education for the masses, and favored a "comprehensive, liberal education," particularly but not exclusively for boys.[42] Intentionally or not, his depiction of abusive Yorkshire schools in *Nicholas Nickleby* (1839) spurred regulatory action, and *Dombey and Son* (1848) attacks the standardization of charity schools (where Robin Tootle is pupil "one hundred and forty-seven"), as well as the philological cramming in more privileged institutions (under Dr. Blimber and Mr. Feeder, "all the fancies of the poets, and lessons of the sages, were a mere collection of words and grammar").[43] *David Copperfield* (1850) and Dickens's famous autobiographical fragment show that shoddy schooling remained for Dickens a deeply emotional concern.[44] But if Dickens has been lauded as "England's greatest educational reformer," he was not (as Phillip Collins has argued) a consistent worker in the cause, nor do his novels (as Amanda Claybaugh has shown) support reforms that subordinate sentiments to systems.[45] This is certainly true of Dickens's attitude toward uniform curricula and national exams. On the strength of *Hard Times* (1854) alone, Dickens can seem a savage opponent of standardized education, and yet he remains a nuanced observer of its claims and implications.

One measure of Dickens's thinking on standardized education is his friendship with James Kay-Shuttleworth, the statistician turned reformer who became a founding figure of the Victorian accountability movement. The two men agreed on the desperate need to train teachers and better educate the poor, so much that Dickens proposed in 1851 that they collaborate on a model school. But after reading Kay-Shuttleworth's *Public Education* (1853), Dickens complained of the book's "supernatural dreariness" and later wrote in a letter to Angela Burdett Coutts that "much Boredom, and Red Tape, and what I may call Kayshuttleworry are associated with the word 'Education.'"[46] To a novelist's eye, *Public Education* is indeed a dreary book full of bureaucratic reports, statistical tables, and a complete copy of a teacher credentialing exam requiring fifty hours of written answers on subjects ranging from arithmetic, geography, and bookkeeping to scripture and English history. The section "English Grammar and the History of English Literature" consists of four equally weighted parts—three on philology, and one asking test takers to paraphrase a passage and parse selected words from either Wordsworth's *Excursion* (1814), Edward Young's *Night-Thoughts* (1745), or Milton's *Areopagitica* (1644). Similarly weighted is the 1854 national examination for teachers, which Dickens requested to see while writing *Hard Times*. While one section asks candidates to "analyze" a passage from *Henry V* (c. 1599) or *Paradise Lost* (1667), most questions follow the informational model of emphasizing historical and philological facts.[47] Dickens surely has such standardized testing in mind when *Hard Times* introduces the Gradgrind School and the brutally ineffective M'Choakumchild, a mass-produced teacher trained and credentialed in the kind of utilitarian normal school championed by Kay-Shuttleworth. When Sissy Jupe is introduced as "Girl number twenty," Dickens links his critique of standardized education to the novel's broader attack on statistical thinking and institutional impersonality.[48] If standardization for Kay-Shuttleworth was necessary to ensure educational quality, the informationalism of the Gradgrind School shows it to be painfully reductive.

However, setting the metric-minded Kay-Shuttleworth against a more aesthetic, more sentimental Dickens obscures how both men reckoned simultaneously with the need for and limitations of standardized education. In *Four Periods of Public Education* (1862), Kay-Shuttleworth retains a commitment to accountability, using the word "examination" 147 times, as compared to "knowledge" (164), "pupils" (164), "teacher" (146), "character" (132), "arithmetic" (89), "art" (65), "taste" (18) and "literature" (3). The book advocates in exhaustive detail a method for measuring student outcomes:

> The sum of the numbers thus attached to each answer is entered in the examination-book opposite to the name of each pupil. These numbers are added up at the end of the week, and reduced to an average by dividing them by the number of days of examination which have occurred in the week. In a similar manner, at the end of the month, the sum of the weekly average is, for the sake of convenience, reduced by dividing them by four; and a convenient number is thus obtained, expressing the intellectual progress of each boy.[49]

Who needs *Hard Times* when educational reformers practically satirize themselves? But as much as Kay-Shuttleworth can sound like a Dickensian bureaucrat, *Four Periods of Public Education* actually objects to the excesses of the 1862 Revised Code—from its overreliance on exams that fail to account for migratory students and dysfunctional homes, to high-stakes tests that tie teacher compensation to student scores and threaten their social status so that only the lower classes will seek to enter the profession. Kay-Shuttleworth pioneered accountability in education, but in a remark reminiscent of Arnold, he also warned against administrators and political leaders "trusting merely to the result of examination."[50]

For his part, Dickens comes to modulate his attacks on standardized schooling, especially the juxtaposition in *Our Mutual Friend* (1865) of two educational models that together indicate the difficulty of disentangling the literary and the informational. On the one hand is Eugene Wrayburn, an Oxbridge dilettante who appreciates aesthetics, literary allusions, and well-turned Latin jibes. On the other is the unbrilliant Bradley Headstone, the product of a utilitarian education who has worked his way up to headmaster of a national school. When the men compete for the affections of Lizzie Hexam, one might expect Dickens to begrudge the arrogant Wrayburn and favor the self-reliant Headstone who, as Lauren Goodlad has emphasized, struggles under a marginal social status as predicted by Kay-Shuttleworth.[51] But while Dickens recognizes the plight of Victorian teachers, Headstone is no sympathetic figure. Under his lifelong regimen of testing, "the habit of questioning and being questioned had given him a suspicious manner," and his standardized education has partitioned his intellect into a "wholesale warehouse": "history here, geography there, astronomy to the right, political economy to the left—natural history, the physical sciences, figures, music, the lower mathematics, and what not, all in their several places."[52]

Drawing and music gesture toward a liberal education, but literature is conspicuously absent from Headstone's training during a period in which proponents of literary study fought for its place in curricula. Headstone has a mastery over factual knowledge but lacks Arnold's real attainments of feeling, character, and taste, which becomes brutally clear when he dons a plebian disguise and attempts to murder Wrayburn. The trick is that the despicable canal worker Roger Riderhood sees Headstone dispose of his incriminating clothes by sinking them in the river. When Riderhood blackmails Headstone in front of his students, he does so by giving them an extemporaneous exam:

"Wot's the diwisions of water, my lambs? Wot sorts of water is there on the land?"

Shrill chorus: "Seas, rivers, lakes, and ponds."

"Seas, rivers, lakes, and ponds," said Riderhood. "They've got all the lot, Master! . . . Wot is it, lambs, as they ketches in seas, rivers, lakes, and ponds?"

Shrill chorus (with some contempt for the ease of the question): "Fish!"

"Good agin!" said Riderhood. "But what else is it, my lambs, as they sometimes ketches in rivers?"

Chorus at a loss. One shrill voice: "Weed!" . . .

"You'll never guess, my dears. Wot is it, besides fish, as they sometimes ketches in rivers? Well! I'll tell you. It's suits o' clothes." (794–95)

This menacing parody of student assessment is not professionally administered in written form, but it represents a move toward standardized testing marked by taxonomic factuality, informational parroting, and the aggregation of pupils into an impersonal mass. The scene can embody in grotesque form Kay-Shuttleworth's fear that under the Revised Code teachers will be drawn from the inferior classes and examinations will threaten instructors with fiscal punishment and professional ruin.[53] Riderhood's exam also exposes the epistemological limits of standardized testing, for if Headstone and his students are crammed with facts, they fail to account for an imaginative truth at the heart of *Our Mutual Friend*: waterways contain all sorts of surprises, particularly in murky areas where taxonomic order gives way to interpretation and judgment.

In contrast to Headstone's standardized schooling, Wrayburn's liberal education and literary sensibilities show his social, intellectual, and aesthetic superiority. We do not hear much about Wrayburn's education beyond the fact that he was lazy, though as Elisa Tamarkin has argued of nineteenth-century Anglophiles at Harvard, and as Oxbridge novels from the Victorian era dramatize, a practiced disregard for official curricula could be a badge of refinement at prestigious institutions, particularly at a time when the ideology of accounting was associated with scholarship students and government-supported schools.[54] Then as now, some blue bloods and cool kids identify themselves by not trying too hard on exams, a posture that Dickens seems to have internalized to some degree despite his resentments of aristocratic privilege. Be that as it may, Wrayburn increasingly stands as a nobler suitor than Headstone, especially as Lizzie's gendered influence augments his genteel attainments with the kind of moral and emotional improvements that cannot be measured with standardized tests.

In this sense, *Our Mutual Friend* sits comfortably in the polemic tradition of *Hard Times*. Lizzie stands opposite her cram-boy brother, Charley, whose training under Headstone stunts his character and imagination, thus fulfilling a mission of standardized education (the reproduction of knowledge and knowers), as well as a more pernicious goal for some (the reproduction of social organization insofar as Charley's education only marginally increases his cultural capital and economic opportunities). The literary/informational dualism that divides the Hexam siblings is contained within Headstone's colleague, Miss Peecher. Her capacity for love "had never been examined or certificated out of her," though she has been trained to be a "methodical" thinker who can "write a little essay on any subject, exactly a slate long" (332). Miss Peecher keeps at hand a "set of tables and weights and measures," but upon realizing that Headstone is attracted to Lizzy, she learns a hard lesson that some of us encountered in high school and that twenty-first-century neuroscience has yet to disprove: "'There is no accounting,' said good Miss Peecher with a little sad sigh which she repressed by laying her hand on her neat methodical bodice, 'there is no accounting for tastes'" (219, 710).

The limits of standardized metrics appear repeatedly in *Our Mutual Friend*. Noddy Boffin's dust heaps are beyond calculation. Headstone's lies are "carefully weighed and measured" but spin beyond his control. When we first meet Silas Wegg vending his wares, he is fraudulently measuring out nuts (291). The Six Jolly Fellowship Porters tavern, a major setting in the novel, further points to problems of standardization and mensuration. The Union of Fellowship Porters represented London's official measurers of incoming goods at the docks, and it figured centrally in parliamentary debates over the 1864 Weighing of Grain Bill. The policy proposed to measure grain more accurately by switching from volume to weight, though deliberations revealed that weight-based metrics could be manipulated by adding moisture and sand, just as volume-based metrics could be gamed by pouring grain from different heights and unevenly leveling the contents of barrels.[55] If corn cannot be objectively measured, how does one account for literary learning or love?

Readers familiar with Dickens will not be surprised by the antipositivist animus of *Our Mutual Friend*, but what differentiates the novel from *Hard Times* is a tonal and ideological ambivalence about the possibilities of information in general and standardized assessments in particular. The disorder of Charley's early, ragged schooling ("jumbled jumbled jumbled jumbled jumbled") can vindicate Headstone's standardized methods. Wrayburn, too, must overcome the desultory habits of his own disorganized and unaccountable education (215). When the barely literate Wegg becomes a kind of tutor to Boffin, one might wish for a teacher credentialing program replete with standardized exams (a measure Dickens explicitly supported in his 1848 preface to *Nicholas Nickleby*). *Our Mutual Friend* also offers an effective model of information management in its depiction of the London police, whose notes and ledgers indicate a competent bureaucracy, and whose methodical interrogations of witnesses recall other scenes of examination in the book. In a novel sometimes criticized for unintegrated plotlines, one question that binds together *Our Mutual Friend* is how best to assess somebody.

This challenge drives the main twist of the book—John Harmon's testing of Bella Wilfer under his assumed identity, a plot device that seems poorly disguised to some readers, though the obviousness of which suggests that Dickens's purpose has less to do with narrative surprise than with thematic interest. Harmon's testing of Bella is hardly a standardized exam insofar as his methods cannot be scaled and Bella's character, not her knowledge, is at issue. Harmon's assessment stratagem can thus serve as a foil to Headstone's pedagogical practices, setting domesticity over bureaucracy, emotion over utility, individuation over uniformity, the literary over the informational. Except that, as we have seen in chapter 2, the Harmon-Bella romance does not escape the logic of information as the lovers become managers of textual excess and consumers of mass print facts. Harmon's ruse actually shares with standardized education and the larger designs of liberal meritocracy a desire for objective mensuration that can (to use a word that appears frequently in the novel) "prove" the merits of a person through an impersonal process—here and elsewhere, one involving impersonation. From Harmon's stratagems, to the Boffins' dissembling, to Mr. Inspector's character work (the police do themselves in different voices), the most accurate assessments in *Our Mutual Friend* pursue information through performance. In this sense, the identity crises of the novel are less about philosophical sources of selfhood, scientific desires for the death of the subject, or a carefully cultivated detachment.[56] Instead, they involve anxieties about measuring the real attainments of people within a liberal state, which is to say that Dickens's thinking about selfhood emerges from his era's social and informational practices.

By combining the impersonal with impersonation, *Our Mutual Friend* envisions a mode of assessment centered around aesthetic performance, a pedagogy evident in "The Short-Timers" (1863) where Dickens, writing in his Uncommercial Traveler persona, visits a working-class school in Limehouse. Dickens begins with the failure of mass education, recalling his own classroom struggles as one of seventy boys. But at the Limehouse school, standardization is wonderfully humanizing as one hundred happy boys pretend to be soldiers, marching the yard in "perfect uniformity" but without "a monotonous or mechanical character."[57] Next comes vocational training on a model ship in which a raucous "Skipper" (the teacher) and his jolly "crew" (the students) imaginatively practice sailing the vessel, a performance that Dickens cannot resist ("A man overboard!" he cries to thicken their plot). Lively lessons in music and singing ensue before Dickens turns to the harder cases of mathematics, history, and geography.

Here is a potentially Gradgrinding scenario of informational recitation and recall, except that the students retain their enthusiasm, even during an extemporaneous examination that Dickens himself performs. His testing initially tends toward standardization as hands and voices are raised in unison to answer his factual inquiries. But Dickens also includes a clever question: How many birthdays would a fifty-year-old man celebrate who was born on February 29? Dickens admires how quickly the boys see through his trick, thereby demonstrating a creative intelligence that leaps beyond routinized cramming. He then ends the article by defending the school's scalability and robust return on investment, noting its low costs and successful record in placing pupils in respectable laboring jobs. Written in a hopeful mood, and oddly silent on whether literature is included in the curriculum, "The Short-Timers" advocates a system of liberal education in which informational and artistic training are methodically and creatively taught and tested, not under utilitarian or sentimental auspices, but in a spirit of dramatic performance. At a time when romantic educational theories held that play rendered a child's character transparent, Dickens asserts in "The Short-Timers" and *Our Mutual Friend* that playacting has pedagogical and epistemological value—no small concern for a writer who spent significant time on stage performances and who himself was a talented impersonator.[58] Dickens's insistence on the utility of playacting may risk capitulating to instrumentalism. Think of improvisational acting exercises at corporate retreats, or design-mindset consultants using rhetorics of play, or for that matter humanities departments touting the vocational relevance of studying imaginative art. *Hard Times* and Bradley Headstone show the dangers of informational education, but Dickens—for better or worse—envisions a role for the literary in assessment regimes.

What seems to bother Dickens most in *Our Mutual Friend* is that the narrowest, most informational forms of standardization are imposed on the most vulnerable students, a hypocrisy in that supposedly uniform methods are applied unevenly across social classes. Then as now, accountability measures tend to fall hardest on the poorest of schools. Headstone's bad end does not condemn state-sponsored education, competitive examinations, or teacher credentialing in total so much as the aggressive standardization of education in which students, disciplined under informational policies, do not taste the best fruits of literature and art. Unlike "The Short-Timers," *Our Mutual Friend* does not offer a working educational model, but it does evince a tense desire to reconcile ideals of standardized testing with the real attainments of a liberal education—no easy thing given the rise of Victorian examinations that did not invent but powerfully revealed differences between the informational and the literary, between positivist knowledge and less measurable merits of aesthetics and interpretation.

Dickens opposed Lowe's Revised Code, yet he had no qualms about his son Henry taking the Indian Civil Service exam, and he chastised his prodigal son Plorn for not acquiring the knowledge needed to pass a national test.[59] Like many of my students, most of whom have done quite well on their boards, Dickens recognizes and resents the factitiousness of standardized testing while still according it a measure of legitimacy. The SAT and ACT are of course limited and demonstrably biased tools, but many a student still believes they deserve their acceptance letter in part because of their scores. Educational metrics do not merely gauge the aptitudes and achievements of test takers; they shape how subjects understand their places and selves as members in a self-styled meritocracy. Dickens anticipates this Foucauldian point while seeking a purchase for social reform that includes but is not limited to informational methods. One reason for Headstone's bitter end—drowned with Riderhood in a system of locks that imposes distinct levels on the natural flow of a river—is that in his world of standardized tests, he has no better measure of himself.

Fictions of Examination

Nineteenth-century novels do not simply reflect the rise of standardized education; they drive public debates as indicated by the high frequency of educational terms in novels that precede important educational legislation.[60] Around the time that Dickens explores forms of examination that are both factual and imaginative, systematic and playful, other novelists struggle with competing desires to exempt literature from the standardization of knowledge while still justifying literary attainments under the informational assessments of liberal meritocracy. Part of the turbulence involves tensions between genteel decorum and market competition, an ambivalence that scholars following Bourdieu have traced to the period's uneasy disavowals of the capitalization of literature.[61] To shift the focus onto literary testing is to see how Victorian writers struggled to determine, not just the market value of aesthetics, but what it means to render literary attainments as information to be measured, ranked, and rewarded. British novels from the 1850s and 1860s by Frederic Farrar, Thomas Hughes, Charlotte Yonge, Charlotte Brontë, Anthony Trollope, and George Trevelyan quarrel to varying degrees with standardized exams but still manage to present literary sensibilities as compatible with informational meritocracy. The relatively large sampling of texts in this section show the prevalence and range of literary responses to competitive examinations. That many of the novels trace the rise of middle-class protagonists suggests how dramatically standardized testing comes to govern professional prospects and how, in Friedrich Kittler's formulation, the nineteenth century merged the formerly distinct discourses of bureaucracy and bildungsroman.[62] Rather than simply reflecting such developments as a matter of sociological effect, some Victorian scholastic novels self-consciously explore how standardized testing comports, and does not comport, with the literary. Examination scenes themselves are often elided—perhaps because detailed questioning and answering is hard to dramatize, perhaps because the uncertain status of literary knowledge invites a kind of anxious evasiveness. Whatever the case, standardized exams exert a palpable pressure that is both epistemological (how can one measure literary attainments?) and political (what is the proper role of literary studies in meritocracies inflected by class, gender, and race?).

With the broadening of educational opportunities in Britain, and with liberalism's concomitant emphasis on accountability and fair play, standardized assessments became increasingly important in state-sponsored and, to a lesser degree, elite schools. Helping constitute what *Blackwood's* described in 1861 as a burgeoning subgenre of "scholastic novels," Frederic Farrar's bildungsromans are conventional examples that treat standardized testing as a positive good, even for devotees of literature.[63] This is certainly true of *Julian Home* (1859), Farrar's most popular novel. The story opens on speech day at Harton, a thinly fictionalized version of Harrow, where Farrar was a teacher and headmaster.[64] Most of the spectators at the unstandardized demonstration take the bombastic Bruce to be a future top boy, but one discerning father instead favors the middle-class Julian, whose "musical" recitations of Shakespeare and Tennyson show him to be "entirely absorbed in the subject."[65] Julian has a passion for Wordsworth, Byron, and Coleridge, and—as if in rebuke to tests and study guides that would reduce literature to mere information—he does not "content himself with eviscerating the general meaning of a passage, without any attempt to feel the finer pulses of emotion, or discriminate the nicer shades of thought" (95). *Julian Home* believes in unparaphrasable beauty, though the standing of aesthetics in educational institutions is not initially guaranteed. When a sympathetic tutor tells Julian, "at the universities, more than anywhere, the aristocracy of intellect and character are almost solely recognized" (19), the careful qualifiers and silence on aesthetics point toward a lurking concern: Are examinations, like the judicious father at Harton, capable of recognizing Julian's finer qualities?

Happily, the answer is "yes" as high-stakes exams structure Farrar's plot. Julian wins a scholarship to attend Cambridge, then a fellowship that lifts him above servitor, then medals in Latin and English verse (despite being locked in his room by a jealous competitor just before one of the novel's testing scenes). Examinations not only mark Julian's rise; they organize the book's moral universe. One wayward student is plucked after failing his exams and returns a soberer and wiser young man, while the bullying Bruce mocks examinations before being expelled, falling into poverty, and ending the novel in pathetic regret. More centrally, Julian's poetic friend Kennedy is tempted into glancing at a question on Aeschylus prior to an exam. He afterward tries to read *Agamemnon* closely, but with his foreknowledge of the test, he "skips involuntarily every topic which he knew had not been touched" (190). Here the cramming encouraged by competitive examinations violates aesthetic unity and intensive reading practices, though Kennedy (after some romantic soul searching in the Alps) regains his moral footing and—as a measure of his redemption—gets the top mark on a civil service exam. Kennedy's trajectory makes two points on which *Julian Home* is consistent: cheating, the violation of informational protocols, is the problem (not standardized testing itself); and an artistic temperament correlates with success on competitive exams. That a romantic poet can ace a civil service test reconciles aesthetics and informationalism.

Farrar's support of accountability measures is also evident in his edited collection *Essays on Liberal Education* (1867). One contributor does complain, "There are some subjects upon which it is hardly possible to gauge a man's real knowledge by any set of questions that can be devised," and he worries that "[s]ubjects in which attainments can be accurately tested come to take precedence of subjects in which they cannot."[66] However, most of Farrar's contributors vindicate standardized exams, including the classicist and poet William Johnson Cory:

> Any one, they say, can get up an English book just for an examination; it is no test of power or of taste.... But let the questions be in some measure of the nature of "problems" as opposed to "book-work," let them vary from minute particulars to broad generalities, ... let the manuscripts be to some extent treated critically, ... and then an examination in a book will be an intellectual process.[67]

Julian Home dramatizes how literary knowledge and sensibilities can in fact be measured insofar as aesthetic attainments are recognized and rewarded in Farrar's narrative of standards upheld. Small wonder that some commentators mocked Farrar's novels for their priggish, milquetoast, self-righteous conventionality. Then as now, proclaiming the justice of exams is seldom endearing to one's peers.

A friendly amendment to Farrar's easy faith in accountability is Thomas Hughes's *Tom Brown at Oxford* (1861), a novel that harbors lingering doubts about measuring literary merit. In *Tom Brown's School Days* (1857), the young Tom's occasional cribbing at Rugby is of little consequence, but at Oxford his social negotiations and adolescent peccadilloes are punctuated by dramas of studying and examination that, along with other contests of muscular Christianity, form the basis of Hughes's meritocracy. The second sentence of *Tom Brown at Oxford* offhandedly mentions that Tom is "examined" before entering his college, but as we follow the progress of various students, sharper patterns of commentary emerge.[68] Tom himself is a middling student who is "fairly placed at the college examinations," and when the grinding but mediocre Grey fails to win honors, the outcome is painful but does not feel unfair (183). Most readers root for the hardworking servitor Hardy, who papers his room with indexes and charts but is at heart a serious intellectual who can joke about his cramming. "Why, you irreverent beggar," he tells a friend fiddling with a chart, "those pins are the famous statesmen and warriors of Greece and Rome" (51). It is clearly a case of virtue rewarded when Hardy wins honors and a fellowship, suggesting that Hughes takes Oxford's increasingly standardized exams as both an accurate measure of learning and a legitimate means of advancement.

Except for the anomalous example of Blake—the brilliant, eloquent, undisciplined student whose debts oblige him to win honors to placate his family. Blake begins to study in earnest, wins a Latin prize, and does well on a "taste-paper" (123), but he remains impatient with factual knowledge and is plucked after arguing with a hostile examiner. Vowing to return to Oxford, Blake takes up private lessons with Hardy, who reports by letter to Tom:

> [Blake] reads fiercely by fits and starts. A feeling of personal hatred against the examiners seems to urge him on more than any other motive.... The philosophy of Greece and the history of Rome are matters of perfect indifference to him—to be got up by catch-words and dates for examination and nothing more.... The greatest names and deeds of the old world are just so many dead counters to him. (153–54)

Before Oxford included English literature in its curriculum, and dramatizing long-standing complaints about the reduction of classical literature to philological and historical information, Blake's aesthetic relationship to literature is warped by a positivist examination system that treats most students fairly enough but cannot account for the romantic genius suggested by Blake's name.

Blake's fall into cramming certainly acknowledges the dangers of standardized testing, though in another sense, his mistreatment by the biased examiner simply indicates the need for better-regulated exams. Hughes's overall support of standardized testing resurfaces near the end of *Tom Brown at Oxford* when Hardy, now a College Fellow, commences flunking wealthy students who are not "'quite up to the commoner standard.'" He writes to Tom of the ensuing scandal:

> Luckily, as you know, it has always been given out here that all undergraduates, gentlemen-commoners and commoners, have to pass the same college examinations, and to attend the same courses of lectures. You know also what a mere sham and pretense the rule had become. Well, we simply made a reality of it, and in answer to all objectors said, "Is it our rule or not?" (231)

Such sympathies accord with long-standing meritocratic sentiments inched forward by Oxford's controversial 1850 Commission, which recommended more scholarships for students with high exam scores, finer-grained distinctions for academic honors, and more frequent examinations (increasingly written instead of oral) on a broader range of subjects.[69] Less historically accurate is Hardy's claim that rigorous standards uniformly applied were always the rule and, in earlier days, the practice at Oxford. Set some time in the 1840s and filtered through the soft lens of nostalgia, *Tom Brown at Oxford* imagines that a more standardized examination system will return Oxford to some mythic meritocratic past.[70]

In the Victorian era and today, proponents of accountability tend to align themselves with technocratic, forward-looking informationalism, while their opponents, then and now, are more likely to dwell on fond memories of school days gone by. In *Tom Brown at Oxford*, Hughes tries to have it both ways as both a reformer and an old boy, which requires not only that he misrepresent Oxford's history but also that he bracket the example of Blake, who is entirely absent from the last third of the novel until his fate is finally, briefly related through secondhand reports. Blake, we hear, is reading for the bar, angling to enter London society, and writing political articles "devilish[ly] well" (246). With no word on whether he returned to Oxford or ever passed his exams, and with nothing like the just rewards and narrative closure granted Tom's other university mates, the most literary character of *Tom Brown at Oxford* escapes the novel's meritocratic logic. Blake remains unaccounted for—an aesthetic exception that proves the rule of exams.

Hughes and Farrar wrote their novels primarily for boys (young and old), and competitive examinations of the Victorian period most often regulated masculine pursuits, but efforts to measure literary knowledge also implicated female readers and writers. When Frances Trollope wrote to her fiancé in 1809, "I sometimes fear you may be disappointed in me, that you will find me less informed, less capable of being a companion to you, than you expect," she used a traditional definition of information synonymous with general knowledge and current events.[71] There are no synoptic histories of gender and emerging concepts of information during the nineteenth century, though information was typically coded as masculine, especially as it took modern forms associated with data, finance, and science. Yet there are prominent exceptions to this rule—including mathematicians and astronomers such as Ada Lovelace, Caroline Herschel, Maria Mitchell, and Mary Somerville—and the nineteenth century's pervasive information revolution also took place more generally in feminine domains. Along with the rise of female education and domestic science, the Victorian period witnessed the entry of women into informational vocations—as teachers in Britain's newly regulated schools, in the British Civil Service (first as telegraph operators in 1869), and as secretaries and later typists working white-collar jobs no longer reserved for male clerks.[72] As Kate Flint has documented, middle-class women of the era took standardized tests in secondary schools, college courses, and teacher credentialing programs, on average outperforming their male peers on language and composition exams.[73] Some commentators complained about females taking standardized tests, not only because it involved competition in the public sphere, but also because women were seen as guardians of beauty, emotion, intuition, and other qualities defined against the informational. As the roles of women shifted under Victorian liberalism, the relation of females to examinations in general and literary tests in particular came under careful, divergent critiques from Charlotte Yonge and Charlotte Brontë.

Yonge's *Daisy Chain, or Aspirations* (1856) finds no fundamental conflict between literary aesthetics and assessment, but it exposes and reinforces gendered distinctions in meritocratic testing. The novel focuses on the middle-class May family, opening with the news that the oldest brother, Richard, has suffered a nervous breakdown during his Oxford exams.[74] Against this backdrop, we follow Ethel and her older brother Norman, who together share a tutor, respond passionately to literature, but encounter disparate challenges in their comings of age. Norman must win a scholarship in order to attend Oxford, which he does by acing his examination's section on poetry ("It was the verses that did it," he says of his victory).[75] He goes on to excel at Oxford, win a poetry prize, and earn a reputation as an orator, further indicating correlations between literary prowess and examination success. Before *Julian Home* and *Tom Brown at Oxford*, *The Daisy Chain* vindicates competitive testing, while Yonge later supported credentialing teachers through standardized exams.[76] What troubles her in *The Daisy Chain* are the moral pitfalls of competition, voiced by Norman's mother, who worries that he lives "a life of emulation, . . . caring for what he is compared with others, rather than what he is himself" (45). Yonge shows through Norman how examinations enforce conscripted identities and liberal norms (pun intended), though he ultimately triumphs by mastering his competitiveness and recognizing his true aspirations, turning down prestigious political opportunities to become a missionary in New Zealand. While his literary merits are richly recognized through exams, Norman learns to look beyond such standards—not because they are inaccurate, but because he reclaims better measures of himself. This is not the case with Bradley Headstone, who has no women in his life to balance the ideology of accounting, though Fred Vincy of *Middlemarch* (1872) is more fortunate, for if Eliot trusts that his examination failures accurately reflect his idleness, Fred finds with the help of Mary Garth less normative ways to assess his worth.

If Norman's experience in *The Daisy Chain* supports the legitimacy but limits the reach of competitive exams, Yonge does not extend such thinking into feminine domains. Ethel's coming of age runs parallel to Norman's, though her circumscribed opportunities disrupt the analogy almost to the point of social complaint. Having no prospects of a formal education, Ethel founds a charity school but is enraged when a town committee presumes to examine her pupils, a problem that recurs when she and teachers from the town's national school compete so fiercely during a Sunday school examination as to judge each other's students unfairly. Ethel fits the model of the sentimental heroine who must learn to conquer her desires—in this case, the desire to triumph through competitive testing, which she finally overcomes through a process of "self-examination" in which she measures herself against "her own standard" (458, 45). We might take this as a liberating revelation akin to that of Norman, though as scholars have generally noted, Yonge is no radical.[77] The fiery Ethel is adept in classical languages and has a greater aptitude for literature than even Norman. But if as a youth she imagines herself competing for college prizes, she ultimately conforms to a traditional role as the self-sacrificing caretaker of her father. Nowhere in *The Daisy Chain* does Yonge mention that Victorian women had increasing opportunities to test their scholarly mettle at institutions such as King's College, the University of London, and dozens of normal schools. Whereas Norman agonistically transcends examinations, Ethel in the end opts out—not because literary sensibilities are beyond informational metrics but because, for Yonge, women are not proper subjects for exams.

In theory, standardized tests are meritocratic because they are impersonal, though as Foucault argues, as *The Daisy Chain* intimates, and as many an applicant and student has felt, measuring people against standardized norms can produce concepts of selfhood at odds with autotelic identity, thus setting a main tool of liberal meritocracy against notions of liberal individualism. Put differently, standardized examinations aspire to align individual merit with commensurate responsibilities and rewards, but in doing so, they neglect central aspects of individuality such as subjectivity, interiority, and autonomous concepts of self. Charlotte Brontë's *Villette* (1853) interrogates this disjunction, especially in regards to how aesthetic capacities may or may not be assessed.

As reported by Elizabeth Gaskell, Brontë experienced the injustice of testing at the age of sixteen:

> [T]owards the end of the two years that she remained as a pupil at Roe Head, she received her first bad mark for an imperfect lesson. She had had a great quantity of Blair's "Lectures on Belles Lettres" to read; and she could not answer some of the questions upon it: Charlotte Brontë had a bad mark. Miss Wooler was sorry, and regretted that she had overtasked so willing a pupil. Charlotte cried bitterly. But her school-fellows were more than sorry—they were indignant.... until Miss Wooler, who was in reality only too willing to pass over her good pupil's first fault, withdrew the bad mark.[78]

Brontë did not fail a standardized test, nor do her novels explicitly discuss competitive examinations, nor is *Villette* (at least as Brontë described it to Gaskell) much interested in "topics of the day."[79] However, Brontë had access to debates over standardized testing through her extensive visits with James Kay-Shuttleworth and her reading of Arthur Stanley's *Life and Correspondence of Thomas Arnold* (1844), a book that includes careful discussions of examination practices (and was also read by Matthew Arnold, Dickens, and Hughes). It may not matter that Brontë's first failure as a pupil involved her inability to answer questions about the rule-bound aesthetic standards of Blair, but *Villette* is attuned to how imaginative powers fare in highly regulated educational environments as Lucy endures systematic attempts to render her elusive interiority visible.

Particularly important are literary examinations that seem inimical to female artistic expression and that complicate Lucy's relationship with Paul Emanuel, the belles-lettres professor who is initially hostile to "learned women."[80] At their first meeting, Emanuel examines Lucy's physiognomy, thereby reducing her character and intelligence to bodily measurements. Later, literary testing marks the fitful development of their intimacy when Lucy criticizes the school's "examination-day" and declines to display her attainments in English (173). Lucy's refusal occasions some friction with Emanuel, but when he is accused of writing an essay in her name, she resolves to face the "torture" of a "forced examination" given by two chauvinistic invigilators in a chapter titled "Fraternity" (455).

Lucy's performance on the compulsive exam is both an indictment of and a triumph over literary testing. At first the examination does not do justice to her knowledge when her mind goes blank on subjects she knows well. The process also throws her agency into tumult: "I either *could* not, or *would* not speak" (452). Here we might recall Brontë's general aversion to informational assessments, as when Helen Burns of *Jane Eyre* (1847)—an original thinker, absorptive reader, and unsuccessful student at Lowood—confesses to (and also diagnoses) Jane, "like you, I cannot *bear* to be subjected to systematic arrangements."[81] Brontë's *Shirley* (1849) makes a similar point when characters best learn French, not with "'analyses logiques'" focused on grammatical rules, but rather by immersing themselves in poems that correspond with their emotional states. In a climactic scene in which Shirley rejects her uncle's choice for a husband, she proclaims, "We do not view things in the same light; we do not measure them by the same standard."[82] For a writer who admired the humanism of Ruskin and Newman, and who accordingly denounced what she called the "hard, dry, dismal world" of utilitarianism, Brontë takes standardized assessments as affronts to individual autonomy and creative sensibilities alike.[83]

Lucy's "forced examination" in *Villette* seems to sum Brontë's case against literary testing, but just when Lucy appears destined to fail her belles-lettres exam and in doing so fail Emanuel, she finds furious inspiration in the realization that her invigilators cannot possibly account for her writing. In a lengthy passage, she vindicates her creative process:

> I got books, read up the facts, laboriously constructed a skeleton out of the dry bones of the real, and then clothed them, and tried to breathe

into them life, and in this last aim I had pleasure. With me it was a difficult and anxious time till my facts were found, selected, and properly [j]ointed; nor could I rest from research and effort till I was satisfied of correct anatomy; the strength of my inward repugnance to the idea of flaw or falsity sometimes enabled me to shun egregious blunders; but the knowledge was not there in my head, ready and mellow; it had not been sown in Spring, grown in Summer, harvested in Autumn, and garnered through Winter; whatever I wanted I must go out and gather fresh, glean of wild herbs my lap full, and shred them green into the pot. Messieurs Boissec and Rochemorte did not perceive this. They mistook my work for the work of a ripe scholar.

They would not let me go: I must sit down and write before them. As I dipped my pen in the ink with a shaking hand, and surveyed the white paper with eyes half-blinded and overflowing, one of my judges began mincingly to apologize for the pain he caused. (453)

Here we see untestable literary potential defined over and against an examination regime in which positivism and patriarchy combine. Yet the passage does not deny the necessity of "facts" as a basis for literary achievement, nor does it dismiss "research" in reference books that differentiate "correct" and "fals[e]" views. Lucy's writing is not reducible to factual knowledge that is fixed in the mind and then displayed on the page. Rather, it emerges from an organic process that begins with and then exceeds information. In a novel that so often withholds joy from its narrator, Lucy finds "pleasure" in her writing, which her increasingly lyrical description associates with clothing, cooking, and the giving of life. Examinations provide no insight into her art, and Lucy's invigilators are brutes, but *Villette* presents her feminine aesthetics, not in opposition to masculine-coded information, but rather as an improvement on it, as a step beyond.

Whether Lucy possesses artistic potential is a question that haunts *Villette*—a book with powerful autobiographical elements, and one in which a more experienced Brontë revisits her first effort at a novel, *The Professor* (1857), which an array of publishers initially rejected and that would appear only after Brontë's death. How does one recognize artistic potential? How does one measure originality and talent? In her forced examination, Lucy's invigilators compel her to write an essay on "Human Justice," which she spontaneously allegorizes as a callous woman abusing the weak and placating the strong (454). Given the reticence of so much of *Villette*, Lucy's flight of fancy may be intentionally overwrought, as if to show not only that her art is immature but also that impromptu examinations are poor indicators of literary merit. (Consider the discredited SAT writing test or Miss Peecher's penchant for churning out essays "exactly a slate long.") More ironically, we never see the results of Lucy's composition—never see her examiners embarrassed by her manifest literary powers, unripe though they may be. But manifest they are because of Lucy's outrage at the unfairness of her exam, which awakens her demonic "Creative Impulse" that earlier she finds impossible to summon on demand (403).

Precisely because of its failure to register her real attainments, Lucy's literary test fulfills its office by making her aesthetic power legible to readers of *Villette*. That is, the inadequacy of Lucy's examination induces her most impassioned prose, arousing our suspicion that she has literary talent and that *Villette* can be read as a kunstlerroman. The pressures of being publicly judged as a writer weighed heavily on Brontë throughout her life, and *Villette* works through problems of aesthetic standards in the context of a patriarchal exam. Lucy never becomes the figure of the artist whose genius transcends the standards of her time, but in a novel that everywhere invites readerly speculation, it seems likely that Lucy will someday pass the test that *The Professor* initially failed. One dynamic of the literary/informational divide, particularly under a romanticism still in force today, is that the writer of genius *should* do poorly when measured by conventional standards. In this sense, literary assessments correlate negatively with a literary potential that shows itself only belatedly, as if Brontë had some inkling of her own deferred literary-historical fame. Be that as it may, Lucy joins a host of literary women who overcome male examiners overcommitted to informationalism—not only Jane Eyre, but also Elizabeth Barrett Browning's Aurora Leigh, George Eliot's Maggie Tulliver, some of Emily Dickinson's speakers, and (as we will see) Fanny Fern's Ruth Hall.[84]

The successful failure of Lucy's exam might even reach forward toward Bill Readings's concern: "how we can raise the question of accountability as something that *exceeds* the logic of accounting?" Readings hopes for pedagogical and assessment practices that are neither naively empirical nor corrosively postfactual:

> Doing justice to Thought, listening to our interlocutors, means trying to hear that which cannot be said but that which tries to make itself heard. And this is a process incompatible with the production of (even relatively) stable and exchangeable knowledge. Exploring the question of value means recognizing that there exists no homogeneous standard of value that might unite all poles of the pedagogical scene so as to produce a single scale of evaluation.[85]

Villette concurs insofar as it acknowledges the explanatory power of information without ceding a fundamental skepticism that respects the demon of creativity, the opacity of interiority, and the concomitant difficulty of knowing other minds through systematic examinations that smack of surveillance, patriarchy, and reductive positivism. Sympathetic, partial, personal assessments seem a better hope, even if they remain a slim one.

Whereas Farrar, Hughes, and Yonge for the most part align literary attainments with testing success, and whereas *Villette* perversely inverts the relationship, Anthony Trollope in his account of the British Civil Service questions whether any connection exists at all. Trollope was a notoriously irregular young man—sloppy in manners, schoolwork, and his duties as a low-level postal clerk. In his early twenties, he wrote in his commonplace book under the entry "Order—Method": "I am myself in all the pursuits (God help them) and practices of my life most disorderly and unmethodical."[86] It is tempting to picture Trollope misaligning his buttons and trailing breadcrumbs from an unkempt beard, but his confessions about his shambolic youth attest to an abiding desire for informational mastery. Like his barrister father, who for decades labored over a massive and unfinished ecclesiastical encyclopedia, Trollope aspired to organize vast stretches of humanistic knowledge, including a "History of World Literature" that would treat the subject in its entirety.[87] He eventually won high positions in the British postal service, a crucial institution in the Victorian information revolution. More controversially, his posthumously published *Autobiography* (1883) includes a ledger sheet of his earnings from his books. Trollope's accounting of his literary production damaged his reputation with generations of commentators who set literature and information in opposition. What his detractors failed to notice was that Trollope posited a similar separation of spheres in a novel committed to maintaining distinctions between the literary and the informational.

For scholars of Victorian standardized testing, no literary text is more compelling than *Three Clerks* (1857). Most readers find in the novel a robust resistance to civil service examinations, though Ceri Sullivan sees Trollope defending institutions in which standardized testing plays a role.[88] *Three Clerks* seems to me oddly evasive in debates over civil service exams. If a successful author and bureaucrat like Trollope might be expected to assert correlations between literary and informational capacities, as an ironist with a jeweler's eye for self-serving justifications (his own included), Trollope seems most interested in denying significant links. *Three Clerks* certainly satirizes the Victorian rage for information management and standardized testing, most explicitly in the character Gregory Hardlines—a stand-in for

Sir Charles Trevelyan, whose influential Northcote-Trevelyan Report (1854) advocated for competitive examinations across the British Civil Service. Much of Trollope's novel concerns two clerks who work (fittingly enough) at Hardlines's Department of Weights and Measures, an office symbolizing the ascension of standardization and reflecting, as Richard Menke has emphasized, the centrality of mensuration in the Victorian information revolution.[89] The first clerk we meet is Harry Norman, a fastidious gentleman nominated for his position and appointed after a laughably nonchalant interview given prior to Hardlines's reforms. The second clerk is Norman's coworker and friend Alaric Tudor, whose nomination is arranged by family connections and who passes his own unstandardized interview with cleverness and charisma after flubbing some mathematical questions. Trollope presents such casual assessments as arbitrary but is harder on Hardlines's newly instituted exams, which Harry and Alaric take with other clerks in the office when competing for a promotion. The examination is absurdly informational ("how would you calculate the distance in inches, say from London Bridge to the nearest portion of Jupiter's disc, at twelve o'clock on the first of April"). It is administered by Mr. Jobbles, a Hardlines underling who dreams of perfectly standardized testing ("55,000 printed papers, containing 555,000 questions, answered at the same time").[90] After Harry decides to quit the exam, Alaric wins the promotion and marries Harry's love interest before being disgraced for financial malfeasance as the trustee of an estate. Trollope thus seems to register a common opinion of the time: competitive testing may measure cleverness, cramming, and ambition but not moral character or dedication to duty.

And yet *Three Clerks*, as its title suggests, does not simply pick one side in the controversy over civil service examinations. Less discussed by Victorian reviewers and modern scholars is the third clerk, Alaric's cousin Charley, who falls into debt and shirks his work at the seedy Internal Navigation Office before improving his behavior, publishing some light fiction, moving into a better position at Weights and Measures, and making an appropriate match. Charley may be a didactic convenience, but he adds a twist to Trollope's apparent attack on standardized examinations. Because he is hired at Weights and Measures through the personal influence of Harry, scandal erupts when a parliamentary committee learns that he has been appointed "without any examination" (536). It seems patronage will again give way to competitive testing and liberal meritocracy, until a supporter vindicates Charley's hiring by bringing to the committee's attention a favorable review of his novel. The modest literary attainments suggested by the review fall beyond the purview of Hardlines's positivist exams, though in truth some civil service tests of the time included sections on English literature—too lightly weighted for champions of social refinement and liberal education, too heavily for proponents of practicality and leveling who saw literary knowledge as an ornament of privilege. Charley's happy ending can appear to represent a victory of aesthetics over informationalism, except that Trollope makes no claims for the quality of Charley's novel (which sounds rather hackneyed), nor does he follow Hawthorne and Dickens (as chapter 2 has argued) in suggesting that artistic sensibilities are useful for bureaucratic work. Instead, Parliament's linking of literary and civil service merit in *Three Clerks* appears specious to the point of risibility. As MP George Cornewall Lewis argued in 1856, quizzing low-level clerks on Chaucer and Shakespeare is easily subjected to "ridicule," a point that Trollope later made under parliamentary questioning from none other than Stafford Northcote of the Northcote-Trevelyan Report.[91]

Such is the skepticism of *Three Clerks*, a novel driven by questions of meritocracy, but one in which neither social station nor factual knowledge nor literary attainments consistently indicate professional capacities, which themselves do not seem of much importance. Merit, that is, is strangely emptied of meaning by the conclusion of the novel. Charlie's literary talents, such as they are, have no relation to his clerking abilities. The genteel Harry quits his promotion exam, not because of some moral superiority, but because he knows he will not win. (And once he comes into his inheritance, he quits Weights and Measures without compunction, indicating how little he thinks of his duties.) Even Alaric does not present a clear case on how meritocracies should function, for the fallen man is neither an unalloyed villain nor a positivist crammer who games the examination system. Neither the absence nor the presence of standardized exams makes much difference in the performance of the Office, whose operations are either vaguely described or lampooned as irrelevant paper pushing. Why not have Alaric's fall occasioned by a dereliction of duty at Weights and Measures, or have the projects of the office bear on the outcome of the plot? Why not explore, as do so many authors of the period, homologies between authorship and white-collar work? Why not draw bright lines between clerks appointed by patronage and those who win their positions through exams?

By ecumenically undercutting measures of merit, and by diminishing the work of the civil service itself, *Three Clerks*—for all of Trollope's satire—never rises to the level of an anti-examination polemic. In contrast to sharper post-Crimean critiques, most famously Dickens's Circumlocution Office, Trollope in *Three Clerks* does not get much exercised in his descriptions of governmental ineptitude, as if ironic fatalism in the face of inefficiency and irrelevance is one lesson that time in a bureaucracy can teach (just ask your friendly neighborhood administrator). Trollope was proud of his postal service contributions and had little sympathy for incompetent colleagues, but he was far from thinking of his job as a calling. As he wrote in "The Civil Service as a Profession" (1861), one should simply do one's contracted labor and "not care a straw for any man," an attitude reflecting what Elaine Hadley has called Trollope's "committed mediocrity."[92] It is a comportment I have found at the Department of Motor Vehicles and, on some days, practiced in my own professional life.

The impersonal detachment that *Three Clerks* sometimes exhibits can border on existential emptiness. For Nicholas Dames, Trollope's novels reflect an emergent professionalism marked less by value-based deliberations and more by "a linear narrative of technical, means-oriented, rule-bound activity whose sole desideratum is upward progression in a correct sequence."[93] A softer version of such instrumentalism might be attributed to the novels of Farrar, Hughes, and Yonge insofar as they accept without seriously interrogating the protocols of liberal meritocracy. *Three Clerks* does trace professional trajectories in the manner that Dames describes, though what I take to be the self-conscious arbitrariness of systems that govern advancements in the novel indicates how assessments of vocational capacity lack, not only value content, but also procedural and predictive force. Moral merits and flaws are to some degree rewarded and punished in Trollope's novel, and Shuman is correct in pointing out that *Three Clerks* is a highly predictable narrative. Yet this is so because an omniscient authorial voice flaunts a foreknowledge that can exist only in fiction, as if the evasive fantasy of Trollope's novel is that justice will be served despite our incapacity to weigh and measure merit.

In real life, Trollope argued that seniority and job performance, not exams, should determine civil service advancements. The problem he does not consider is that any legitimate meritocracy should adjudicate not only promotions but also appointments, thus raising the questions: How does one fairly and effectively determine who receives an opportunity? Who gets the chance to perform on the job and thereby demonstrate one's merit? *Three Clerks* does not address such issues except to suggest that one should be born a gentleman (like Harry) or have connections (like Alaric and Charley). That the only economic distress in the novel is caused by excusable moral indiscretion, as opposed to structural inequality, indicates how, for Trollope and many Victorian commentators, meritocracy was a middle-class topic.

Trollope is certainly aware in *Three Clerks* that his fictional world is not precisely fair, but—unlike Dickens and (as we will see) Fern and Frank Webb—he lacks a sense of rage or even righteous indignation. Another lesson that time in a bureaucracy can teach is that one need not mistake one's profession for one's life, as if to work within informational systems is to regard a portion of one's self impersonally. In 1860, Trollope congratulated George Henry Lewes after his son scored well on his civil service examination, though the advice Trollope offered from his position of experience was not about honor, duty, or advancement. He noted instead that one can be both a civil servant and a writer precisely because of the lack of relation between the two: "Do not therefore let [your son] think that six hours a day at the shop is to be the Be all and End all of his life."[94] Sullivan goes further in arguing that Trollope sees literary writing and government service as "*mutually beneficial*," and she demonstrates how many Victorian men of letters found their bureaucratic posts quite congenial, thank you very much.[95] This differs, however, from what I take to be a carefully maintained pose of *Three Clerks*—that (to quote Samuel Smiles on the subject) government service and literary achievement ought to be described, not as mutually beneficial, but rather as "not incompatible."[96] Trollope's separation of the literary and the informational thus tempers the satire of *Three Clerks*. If neither testing nor station nor connections nor aesthetic sensibilities prove to be a reliable measure of professional aptitude, the novel offers a hope embodied in Trollope's dual careers: authorship can exist alongside information work, not through compromise or congruence, but because they do not overlap. Or as Trollope advised aspiring artists in his *Autobiography*: "Take the stool in the office as recommended to you by the hard man; and then, in such leisure hours as may belong to you, . . . persevere in your literary attempts."[97]

Of course, compartmentalization is a fundamental aspect of professional identity and bureaucratic management, and Trollope's *Autobiography* cannot help but reflect how tenuous aesthetic autonomy can be. Trollope infamously wrote of his literary habits:

> [I]t still is my custom . . . to write with my watch before me, and to require from myself 250 words every quarter of an hour. I have found that the 250 words have been forthcoming as regularly as my watch went. . . . This division of time allowed me to produce over ten pages of an ordinary novel volume a day, and if kept up through ten months, would have given as its results three novels of three volumes each in the year.[98]

Just as critics of textual excess complained about mechanical reading, they also worried about mechanical writing—from Coleridge's image of "language, mechanized as it were into a barrel-organ," to an 1854 article imagining that masses of print were authored by a "steam-engine at work somewhere in the British Museum," to Melville's Bartleby, who does "an extraordinary quantity of writing.... silently, palely, mechanically."[99] Trollope in his *Autobiography* does not shy away from the informational protocols of his authorship, and so for all the irony of *Three Clerks*, the novel's disarticulation of the literary and the informational can be taken as a kind of disavowal.

Well before Trollope's *Autobiography* cemented his reputation as a machine-like writer and author-accountant, most reviews of *Three Clerks* were quick to conflate Trollope the novelist and Trollope the civil servant. One American review moved immediately past the book itself to praise Britain's superior civil service system, arguing not only that standardized meritocracy leads to better efficiency, but that it also protects society from "sarcastic" men such as Trollope who, if removed during changes in administration, might become "troublesome" as political satirists.[100] Perhaps the review has Hawthorne's "Custom-House" in mind. Perhaps it misses Trollope's point that civil service need hardly keep writers from writing. And yet the review is correct in a larger sense, for despite his novel's sarcastic attacks on standardized examinations, Trollope—who measured his aesthetic efforts by number, time, page, and pound—does not separate the literary and the informational. Even when three sisters marry his three clerks, the urge for ranking and competition is inescapable. Linda considers Harry the best of the bunch. Katie thinks Charley the most handsome. His dishonor notwithstanding, Gertrude believes that Alaric's manhood "outweighs" that of the others (456). Trollope can insist that one's informational vocation has no relation to one's literary pursuits, but to imagine even a portion of life to be independent of weights and measures is, in the final accounting, a dream that *Three Clerks* does not work hard enough to maintain.

As well chosen as the Weights and Measures Office is for the setting of *Three Clerks*, of all the agencies in the British government, none adopted standardized examinations earlier and none emphasized literary testing more heavily than the Indian Civil Service. As might be expected from the son of a coauthor of the Northcote-Trevelyan Report, George Trevelyan in *The Competition Wallah* (1864) vindicates standardized examinations in the Indian Civil Service, even as he indulges in some Trollope-like irony. The lightly fictionalized missives that make up *The Competition Wallah* come from the less-than-studious Broughton, who sends a series of personal and expository letters from India to his intellectual Cambridge friend Simpkins. Both men took the civil service exam, but surprisingly only Broughton passed (coming in third, behind one candidate who spent three weeks at university and seven years cramming with a tutor). Simpkins demurs in his preface to Broughton's letters, "For the result of that examination I do not pretend to account."[101] Broughton, too, is ambivalent, for while he admires the camaraderie of the East Indian Company's Haileybury College (which had trained civil servants under a patronage model), and while he concedes that standardized testing favors grinders who lack manners and sporting skills, he concludes that civil service examination reforms are on the whole an improvement. Good work, Dad! But still *The Competition Wallah* pokes fun. A civil servant loses his beloved to a rival because he is too busy studying for a promotion test. An English gentleman hires a "crammer" to "turn his son into a walking encyclopaedia against the next Indian competitive examination" (92). In a scene anticipating the education of Rudyard Kipling's Kim, Bengalese students in "mongrel costumes" study for their own standardized civil service tests by reciting passages from Samuel Johnson and Oliver Goldsmith, grandiloquent efforts portrayed with racist humor but also equated with ridiculous pedagogies at home (50). For Trevelyan, examinations are dubious enough, but literary testing is especially absurd.

Trevelyan thus complicates the project of his father, as well as his uncle, Thomas Macaulay, who as a member of the Council of India worked to create a class of indigenous civil servants trained in English literature and culture.[102] As Gauri Viswanathan has shown, the enterprise helped to standardize British literary knowledge in the colonies and at home, thereby implicating main goals of literary study—character building, critical thinking, and aesthetic development—in imperialist designs. Viswanathan describes how literature tests for Indian students were actually less factual than those of their Anglo counterparts, for the internalization of British culture was taken to require, not simply the memorization of facts, but also higher-order judgments and values (assuming of course that they accorded with prescribed norms).[103] As argued by proponents of literature exams in the Indian Civil Service, literary attainments had distinctive civilizing power, even if, as *The Competition Wallah* indicates, testing for such attainments was suspect. As Trevelyan's letters increasingly take up the momentous challenges of administrating an empire—including vexed discussions of the Great Mutiny, home rule, miscegenation, and racism—the satirizing of standardized testing and meritocratic sorting does not seem so lighthearted after all.

From the earnest approbation of Farrar, to the qualified support of Hughes, Yonge, and Trevelyan, to the equivocal critiques of Brontë and Trollope, there is no single explanation for why a range of Victorian novelists accommodate standardized literature tests. They share with their culture diverse reservations about meritocracy and the metrics it requires, but they often endorse accountability measures in British schools and the civil service. Many of the novelists treated in this section temper claims for aesthetic autonomy, not only by writing in realist modes, but more specifically by acknowledging how literature operates within informational contexts. The literary may escape the purview of standardized exams, but to insist on this position too emphatically is to risk the implication that literary attainments carry no weight in liberal meritocracies. Memos from the dean about measurable outcomes can indicate the extent to which the humanities have been marginalized in modern universities, but railing about bureaucracy, technocracy, and positivism, as cathartic as it may be, is at this moment as easy as it is unproductive.

One point of this chapter is that "this moment" has an extensive history. Philip Hartog, an influential turn-of-the-century educator and champion of standardized testing, wrote in *Examinations and Their Relation to Culture and Efficiency* (1918):

> It may be held, and I should agree, . . . that culture may be killed, that it cannot be caught, by examinations. Yet teachers who realize all this, who think examinations in their subjects mischievous rather than helpful, implore the authorities to include it in every possible examination syllabus. Why? Because, under the present *regime*, a subject that is not examined in is likely to disappear speedily from our teaching curricula.[104]

Perhaps it helps, if only a little, to recognize that the discipline of English literary studies from its nineteenth-century beginnings struggled to define and defend its work under informational ideologies of accountability. Perhaps, too, literature from the period can remind those of us who read it that, despite the many compromises a lover of literature might make, information management was not and need not become the be all and end all of life. It is not courageous or principled advice. Even if you doubt that standardized assessments can say anything about aesthetic or interpretive attainments, and even if you are confident that supposedly objective measures can tell you nothing about literary knowledge and pedagogy, give unto the dean the data required, regard metrics as a necessary eval, and—knowing that you join a rich tradition of realists (or is it trimmers?)—get on with your literature. And may God have mercy on our souls.

US Correlations

This chapter might very well end here, if only because competitive examinations and their standardization of literary knowledge emerged earlier and more comprehensively in Britain than in the United States. William Huntting Howell has shown how Americans of the Early Republic and even romantic era valued emulation, imitation, uniformity, and other discourses of standardization.[105] Relative to Britain, however, mid-nineteenth-century America had smaller government bureaucracies, less centralized institutions, weaker credentialing bodies, and—notwithstanding the obvious and powerful exceptions of racial and gender exclusions—an image of itself as a nation in which opportunity is shaped less by formal regulative mechanisms than by expansion and entrepreneurialism. Nineteenth-century America had no national educational tests, while widespread competitive testing in the US Civil Service did not begin until the Pendleton Act of 1883 (following the assassination of President James Garfield by a frustrated office seeker in 1881). Keyword searches associated with standardized examinations have lower yields in American print culture databases than in their British counterparts, and hits often point to articles reprinted from British sources or that refer to practices overseas.

Literary examples also point to a lag in US standardized testing. In his travelogue *North America* (1862), Trollope is pleasantly surprised by Harvard's dearth of competitive exams, and the titular character of his *American Senator* (1875) visits England in part to study its civil service system as a model for reforms at home. Whereas examinations are critical to British scholastic novels, often marking the rise and fall of characters' fates, they seldom figure in American college fictions that emerged in the postbellum period. When they do, they are often occasions for satire or invidious comparisons between ethnic grinders and more genteel, less studious WASPs.[106] In a Burt Standish dime novel from 1903, the hero, Frank Merriwell, helps a fellow applicant cheat during their entrance exam to Yale, but the act is not presented as a moral failure or even quandary so much as a token of Merriwell's chumminess.[107] Horatio Alger also makes light of competitive testing in *Strive and Succeed* (1872) and *The New Schoolma'am* (1877) when invigilators blunder their way through poorly improvised exams in which the test takers know more than they do.[108] Luck and pluck, not cramming and testing, are for Alger and others the best means of advancement in America.

That said, some Anglo-American parallels suggest that the rise of standardized testing was a transatlantic phenomenon. Well versed in European pedagogical theory and practice, Horace Mann and Henry Barnard established state educational systems in antebellum New England, sparking regional debates over standardization that resembled those in Britain. Appointed the first secretary of the Massachusetts Board of Education in 1837, Mann instituted uniform curricula and quantitative assessments, sometimes marginalizing literary study by associating it with feminine pursuits.[109] American opponents of standardized education were most concerned with the autonomy of local schools, though some also worried that competitive testing failed to account for humanistic values. The same year Mann was appointed to his post, Ralph Waldo Emerson—who was serving on the Concord school board and met with Mann in that capacity—wrote in "The American Scholar" (1837) that "Nature" and not the standards of bookworms should be "the measure of [a student's] attainments."[110] Other objections are exemplified by an 1863 comment from a Massachusetts high school teacher, who supported standardized testing in arithmetic, spelling, and geography but complained that "formal examination[s] in English literature" touch only "the shell without reaching the kernel," treat "facts" but not "ideas," are "superficial" instead of "deep," and require "only memory and milk-teeth" rather than "judgment and wisdom teeth."[111] Professors at Harvard voiced similar concerns after the college in 1874 made impromptu essays on English literature part of its application process. So too did leading American university presidents in the essay collection *Examination and Education* (1889), as did Thorstein Veblen more generally in 1918 when complaining about the informational ethos of the modern, business-oriented, positivistic university.[112]

Indicating the mixed feelings of many educators toward the standardization of literary knowledge, Jeannette Marks, an English professor at Mount Holyoke College, published a 1905 article in the *Critic* titled "The American College Girl's Ignorance of Literature." Marks laments, "We are reading nowadays to arrest thought and not to excite it; of this the very quantity of books read is sufficient proof." She then reports what she calls "depressing" data on sophomores who had been assigned a list of literary works. Of the 186 students tested, 54 did not know who wrote *Don Quixote*, 127 could not name Samuel Johnson's biographer, 167 did not know the author of "Christabel," 59 did not know Maggie Tulliver, 58 could not identify the century in which Hawthorne lived, and the dispiriting results go on. ("Of spelling I will not speak," Marks writes. "It was essentially modern.") Marks was hardly the first or last teacher to lament that her students lacked what she called "general information" about literature. And "information" seems the appropriate word given the positivist questions of Marks's exam. What is unexpected is that she attributes her students' shortcomings, not to insufficiently rigorous training or the distraction of trashy reading, but rather to literature courses in which "appreciation with all its shades of discrimination, delicacy, sympathy, and finally imagination [is] lacking." Marks ends by advocating the unregulated pleasures of Pater's "'truant reading'" instead of what she calls "the mechanical, multiplication-table teaching of English literature in the elementary schools." Defining the literary against the informational is by now familiar, though Marks is an especially turbulent case in that her positivist assessments and quantitative reporting sit uneasily with her aesthetic commitments.[113]

Nineteenth-century American novelists express a similar ambivalence as they reject and reflect the rise of information. Cathy Davidson has shown how novels in the Early Republic share features with other pedagogical forms, but whereas didactic textbooks and moral philosophies focused on protocols and abstract rules, literature could provide affective and aesthetic instruction in more dramatic, more memorable forms.[114] In reaction to the mid-nineteenth-century standardization of education, novels by Fanny Fern and Louisa May Alcott take a somewhat different approach, serving less as supplements to and more as critiques of informationalism. Both authors explore how standardized assessments operate in America's flawed meritocracy at a time when information penetrated domestic domains and women became professionalized as teachers and authors. Compared to most of the British novelists treated in this chapter, Fern and Alcott more aggressively resist the standardization of literature, though even in doing so their writings indicate the entanglement of information and aesthetics.

As agonistically as any romantic, and after hard experience in antebellum print markets, the eponymous protagonist of Fern's *Ruth Hall* (1854) learns to deploy her artistic talents in a surplus information economy. The status of the literary is under duress from the very start of the novel. While the young Ruth loses herself in poetry amid the flora of her pastoral home, her juvenile writings are commandeered by plagiarizing fellow students and a local editor who gives her neither compensation nor attribution, suggesting that notions of aesthetic autonomy and professional honor are naive.

This becomes abundantly clear when poverty forces Ruth to monetize her writings, allowing Fern (as Lara Langer Cohen has emphasized) to demonstrate the workings of print culture, which she presents as a complex information system in which literature is reprinted, reconfigured, and capitalized within a media ecology of editors, booksellers, reviewers, and readers all operating under textual excess.[115] Fern valorizes her autobiographical heroine for mastering networks of print, and she depicts an unforgiving but meritocratic industry that ultimately rewards aesthetic talent when combined with entrepreneurialism. In many ways, Ruth's fall into informational modernity feels like a fortunate one.

Yet Fern is never entirely comfortable treating literature as information. Her first known composition—"Suggestions on Arithmetic" (1829), written at the age of eighteen at Catherine Beecher's Hartford seminary— describes a young woman who crams so intensely for a math test that she spoils her budding relationship with a beau.[116] Beecher's school taught higher mathematics to young women, and Beecher wrote popular books on domestic economy, suggesting how women in antebellum America, as in Britain, participated in the spread of information and its management. Nonetheless, *Ruth Hall* initially contrasts feminine aesthetics and masculine information. Ruth's unfeeling father-in-law is an almanac-reading utilitarian with a touch of arithmomania, while the hard-dealing editor of the aptly named *Standard* values Ruth's writing solely by "[t]he law of supply and demand."[117] The cruel bookseller Tom Develin and ledger-toting Mr. Millet work in "[c]ounting houses ... beyond the pale of female jurisdiction," and when they serve as invigilators during Ruth's examination for a teaching post, Fern offers up an unholy alliance of patriarchy and standardized testing (89).

Combining the absurd informationalism of *Three Clerks* with the gender dynamics of *Villette*, Ruth's examination is particularly attuned to the untestability of literary merit. Summoned in alphabetical order, the female candidates are first interrogated viva voce. They then take their written exams as a group, calculating "[l]ittle armies of figures" and answering ridiculously factual questions such as "Was Christopher Columbus standing up, or sitting down, when he discovered America?" (128). The candidates do recite some verse, which in theory should assess their literary attainments, but the passage is excerpted from an epic poem, making it impossible for the very literary Ruth to "gather up the author's connecting thread." That the passage is marked by a cut from a penknife underscores Fern's complaint: not only do literature exams violate formal unity and aesthetic sensibilities; they operate in a violent information system associated with male supervision. Fern actually passed the Boston teacher's examination that she took in 1847, but when Ruth fails to land a teaching position under the harsh standards of Develin and Millet, the disjunction between literary merit and test performance is on full display.[118]

And so Ruth becomes a professional writer who learns to anticipate the movements of the marketplace, out-negotiates grasping editors, cannily retains her copyrights and pen name, and becomes rich and influential. Her transformation can be taken to show how Fern regards literature as an informational commodity, and yet an odd reticence remains in *Ruth Hall*. The novel reports the prices of a coral pin ($10), velvet jacket ($40), cough medicine (three shillings), and wet-nurse ($6 per week), but the most consequential economic data in the novel—Ruth's scandalously low rates of remuneration, the raises she receives after asserting herself, the profits from her best-selling book—are either evaded or conspicuously elided with dashes. No Trollope-like ledgers for Fern. It is not simply a case of genteel refinement as in Henry James's "Greville Fane" (1892), a story in which a fading authoress accepts ever-diminishing payments for her books but is too ashamed to name the amounts. *Ruth Hall* indecorously displays a copy of Ruth's $10,000 in bank shares, but Fern cannot quite bring herself to render literature as quantitative data. She prefers instead to emphasize literary qualities—the frequently cited "genius" of Ruth's work, the sympathetic bonds she forms with readers, her power not simply to make money as a professional author but to support herself and her daughter (195). Ruth's victory lies in her ability to balance beauty and business, aesthetics and calculation, suggesting that literature can survive but not escape nineteenth-century economies of information.

Louisa May Alcott's *Little Men* (1871) also arrives at a compromise, though with less attention to gender and, perhaps not coincidentally, less dialectical struggle. Alcott was aware of British developments in standardized education. She refers to Charlotte Yonge in *Little Women* (1869) and to Dr. Blimber and Tom Brown in *Little Men*, and her father, Bronson Alcott, was an educational reformer who rejected Victorian standardization in favor of the pedagogies of Johann Pestalozzi and the *naturkunde* tradition.[119] The Plumfield School of *Little Men* can be taken to exemplify many of Bronson's views, as when we meet a formerly bright boy rendered an idiot by his father, who was "keeping him at his books six hours a day, and expecting him to absorb knowledge as a Strasburg goose does the food crammed down its throat" (25). Plumfield by contrast offers so much imaginative play and Socratic discussion that a reader might forget it is actually a school. The only tests in the novel are the students' self-examinations that Jo records in her "conscience book" so as to "keep a little account" (31–32)—a practice reminiscent of Benjamin Franklin and easily interpreted as Foucauldian discipline, though *Little Men* remains committed to mediating conflicts between the literary and the informational.

Most crucial to this goal is Demi Brooke, the son of John and Meg from *Little Women*. He is a creative lad who loves his music and books, but when the crisis of the novel comes with his father's sudden death, Demi sets aside his aesthetic pleasures, commits himself to "the hated arithmetic," and resolves, "I am going to be a bookkeeper when I grow up, like papa, and I must know about figures and things, else I can't have nice, neat ledgers like his" (330). Some innocence is lost in Demi's coming-of-age, and yet it is less a tragic fall into accounting and more a manly rise to duty that recalls the kind of informational aesthetic John Harmon exemplifies in *Our Mutual Friend*. Demi envisions his ledgers "nice" and "neat," not accurate, though for Alcott such qualities go hand in hand. In the final installment of the March family trilogy, *Jo's Boys* (1886), Demi—who continues to appreciate books and demonstrates "some literary taste and judgment"—takes a job as an accountant in a publishing house where he eventually makes partner.[120] Like Fern in *Ruth Hall*, and as with Jo March's negotiations between literary ideals and market calculations in *Little Women*, Demi's happy vocational end reconciles the literary and the informational. Bridging the gap requires some work, for Alcott and Fern find standardized pedagogies at odds with aesthetic values. Still, they join other Victorian authors by imagining worlds in which one need not choose between the love and the keeping of books. If only we could as successfully manage the vocational anxieties of potential English majors.

More than in educational contexts, standardized examinations in the US Civil Service subordinated the literary to the informational during the nineteenth century. Some local, state, and military appointments required standardized exams before the Civil War. In the 1860s, Emerson, George William Curtis, Charles Eliot Norton, and Henry Adams supported the unsuccessful Jenckes Bill, which aspired to follow the British example of extensive civil service testing. Most US reformers hoped that standardized exams, rather than broadening opportunities, would restrict appointments to better educated candidates and thereby raise the status of government work.[121] Even so, literary knowledge was largely ignored when civil service testing was finally instituted. Dorman Eaton, a leading proponent who helped draft the Pendleton Civil Service Act, argued in 1881 that standardized exams should not bother with "literary or ornamental attainments" and instead should focus on a candidate's "practical information and capacity needed for the public work."[122] Given such instrumentalism, and considering the fledging status of the field, it makes sense that American literature was almost never a subject in US Civil Service exams.

However, a telling exception is literary testing in the Bureau of Indian Affairs (BIA) at the turn of the nineteenth century—a period in which, as Shumway has argued, American literature became increasingly institutionalized under a homogenizing nationalism.[123] In *How to Prepare for a Civil Service Examination* (1898), Francis Leupp—who would later head the BIA—supported the "practical character" of exams, but because American literature was taken to be useful in assimilating native peoples, BIA educators tested in the subject.[124] Some evidence from the Chilocco Indian Agricultural School indicates that BIA teachers at the turn of the century paid occasional attention to aesthetics, though for the most part they focused on practical literacy.[125] Or as Leslie Marmon Silko has written of her later experiences, there was "damn little" literature taught in reservation schools.[126] The weighting of nineteenth-century BIA educator tests further suggests how information ruled the day:

American Literature:	5%	Geometry	10%
Penmanship	5%	Physiology and Hygiene	10%
Spelling and Copying	5%	US History and Civics	10%
Geography	5%	School Management	15%
Natural history	5%	Industrial Economics	15%
Bookkeeping and Arithmetic	15%		

The emphasis on information is also apparent in the contents of BIA American literature exams, which reflect both empirical and imperial commitments. The majority of questions ask for positivist facts about periods, genres, authors, and titles, while William Prescott's celebratory histories of European conquest figure heavily, sometimes serving as the sole text for one of four essay questions. In 1895, BIA American literature examinations began treating topics in more depth to discourage "recent text-book coaching."[127] But the informational orientation remained, as seen in this complete list of questions from the 1901 test:

1. (a) Name the two divisions or classes into which Literature may be divided as to its form. (b) Name five of the divisions as to subject. (c) Name three divisions of poetry.

2. Who wrote Thanatopsis? Evangeline? Snow Bound? Kathrina? The Conquest of Mexico? Knickerbocker's History of New York? The Spy? Uncle Tom's Cabin? The Biglow Papers? The American Flag?

3. American literature is frequently divided into the colonial period, the revolutionary period, and the national period. To which of these periods does Nathaniel Hawthorne belong? Cotton Mather? James Otis? John Eliot? Edgar A. Poe?

4. Name a well-known poem written by Oliver Wendell Holmes; by Will Carleton; by John G. Saxe; by Julia Ward Howe; by Francis Scott Key. Name a well-known work written by Lew Wallace; by James G. Blaine; by Louise [sic] M. Alcott; by Nathaniel Hawthorne; by John Lothrop Motley.

5. State briefly (150 to 175 words) how you would cultivate a taste for good reading in your pupils.[128]

Many of these texts and authors explicitly or implicitly support assimilation under the intertwined ideologies of manifest destiny and American exceptionalism—including patriotic paeans to American unity from Key, Howe, and Joseph Rodman Drake, as well as Eurocentric narratives of national origin and Providence from Mather, Otis, Prescott, Motley, Hawthorne, and Washington Irving. Even the less obviously nationalistic writings of Stowe, Wallace, Alcott, and Carleton valorize Christian piety and the Protestant work ethic enforced by BIA schools. Some choices are curious—the satirist Saxe (perhaps best known for his 1861 poem, "The Puzzled Census-Taker"); Poe (hardly a democratic icon and, as usual, on the margins of a Yankee-dominated canon); and Josiah Holland (family friend of Emily Dickinson, editor of *Scribner's Monthly*, and author of *Kathrina*, a 287-page poem that I plan to never finish).[129] Given the impetus of the Pendleton Act, the diplomat Blaine (who also spearheaded the Chinese Exclusion Act) was probably added for his eulogy for the assassinated Garfield. And just as the inclusion of Eliot, the so-called Apostle to the Indians, accords with BIA ideology, so too does the selection of Cooper's Revolutionary War novel *The Spy* (1821), instead of his better-known *Leatherstocking Tales* (1823–41), which famously depicts Native Americans as unassimilable and doomed to extinction.

Bureau of Indian Affairs American literature exams do gesture toward aesthetics (150 words on "good reading"), but as in Britain's Indian Civil Service, they combine imperialist goals and positivist standards under a broader logic of informational meritocracy. Assimilation is at its core a kind of standardization, and to pursue assimilationist goals through bureaucratic systems is to render cultural values as information. It is unsurprising that the production of American literary knowledge during this time participates in cultural hegemony, but the specific mechanisms of such production in the case of standardized testing show how literary knowledge in an information age struggles to account for the literary. Nineteenth-century Americans may have been less committed than their British peers to standardized literature tests, but they had transatlantic coordinates and some proximate reasons for thinking about what constitutes literary knowledge and whether it can be systematically measured. Some Americans also had especially compelling reasons to at once both support and fear objective assessments.

"By What Standard Shall We Measure Men?": Testing African Americans

A familiar argument against standardized testing is that the uniform conditions required for its legitimacy are practically unattainable in the face of social inequality, a point recognized to some degree in the Victorian age. A more fundamental critique is that in a pluralistic society in which knowledge production is shaped by preference and prejudice, objective standards of knowledge simply do not exist, particularly in the humanities.[130] The prospects of assessing literary attainments are complicated by, among others things, race—a fact modern critics have long debated in regards to canonicity, but one that has yet to be situated in histories of information and standardized testing. More specifically, the measurement of African American aesthetic capacities was at issue during the nineteenth century—a period in which, as Kenneth Warren has argued, African American literature emerged as a self-consciously distinctive tradition subject to its own criteria.[131] A line of inquiry that black writers of the postbellum era pursue, and one that Frank Webb anticipates in *The Garies and Their Friends* (1857), is not only how African Americans might measure up to dominant aesthetic standards but whether they should even try.

The American struggle over racial equality has long been waged in informational and aesthetic registers. Thomas Jefferson supervised the first US Census as secretary of state in 1790, and as a naturalist, he collected and analyzed data on flora, fauna, land forms, and human beings. His writings on race in *Notes on the State of Virginia* (1785) are deservedly notorious, though as powerfully as they reflect and project scientific racism in the Age of Enlightenment, they are punctuated by moments of epistemological circumspection that acknowledge the limits of assessment. Jefferson observes that one must be cautious when evaluating the "reason and imagination" of Africans, for unlike bodies that can be measured, dissected, and otherwise rendered as information, intellectual and artistic capacities remain elusive because "it is a faculty, not a substance, we are examining."[132] Such qualms did not stop Jefferson from denying the aesthetic sensibilities and thus full humanity of blacks, including those of Phillis Wheatley, who in 1772 had endured a literary examination by Boston's leading citizens so as to prove herself the author of her poems.

Neither Jefferson nor Wheatley participated in what might be considered standardized testing, but they suggest how African American artists had much to gain and lose under nineteenth-century informational assessments. Efforts to measure African Americans take many pernicious forms in the period—from craniology, phrenology, ethnology, and eugenics to the commercial valuation of slaves. Even reformers could impose prejudicial assessments. Eli Cook notes that wealthy white men "dominated the realm of social measurement since its early beginnings," while Oz Frankel has shown how progressive projects after the Civil War adopted the statistical methods of slaveholders and formalized invidious categories of race.[133] The history of American racism is also a history of information, which is why Frederick Douglass complained in 1862 that black Americans "have been weighed, measured, marked and prized—in detail and in the aggregate."[134] This is why the slave master Schoolteacher in Toni Morrison's *Beloved* (1987) wields, not a whip, but a measuring string.[135]

Small wonder that African American responses to early standardized testing registered theoretical and practical objections, though reactions also included hopes for an informational meritocracy that might mitigate the era's pervasive racism. From as early as the 1830s, the antislavery and black press celebrated the successes of African American students in public school demonstrations, a tradition that continued under more standardized exams, as indicated by an 1854 article from the *Provincial Freeman* celebrating a competition in which black pupils were identified "not by names, but by numbers affixed to the breast."[136] Strong performances by black students on formal exams supported claims for equality throughout the mid-nineteenth century, including the school desegregation argument in *Roberts vs. the City of Boston* (1850), in which Charles Sumner insisted that African American children should not be judged inferior without objective testing.[137] During a period in which scientific racism reduced black capacities to bodily attributes, some antiracists focused on intellectual abilities as demonstrated by standardized exams. In this way, information became contested signs of interiority.

A particularly concentrated discussion about race and standardized testing took place in the black press during and after the passage of the Pendleton Act (1883). Between the Fourteenth Amendment and Woodrow Wilson's resegregation of the US Civil Service in the 1910s, Republican administrations offered African Americans career opportunities often unavailable in the private sector, a path to upward mobility increasingly regulated by standardized exams. Like other black periodicals of the era, the *Christian Recorder* announced the times and places of civil service tests, reported on African Americans who scored well, and praised standardized testing as a method in which "prejudice is largely disarmed and the man in question has for once a fair chance."[138] "[L]argely" and "for once" suggest the limits of standardization and the ubiquity of racism in the United States. Indeed, the *Christian Recorder* also printed multiple articles on civil service candidates who earned top scores but were not appointed because of prejudice, while an 1897 article titled "Merit vs. Favoritism" expressed a deeper concern: "Favoritism must yield to merit however stubborn the fight may appear.... [But] who shall be the judge of the meritorious?... By what standard shall we measure men?"[139] Such concerns reflect a tangle of factors—the ongoing scientific mismeasurement of blacks, post-Reconstruction disenfranchisement efforts that included literacy and civics exams, the benefits that some African Americans received from unregulated Republican patronage, and a keen awareness that educational discrimination disadvantaged black people under testing policies. More fundamentally, to ask who judges and what constitutes merit is to challenge not only the execution of exams but the validity of standardization. It is to doubt the informational foundations of liberal meritocracy.

In questioning the legitimacy of standardized testing and knowledge, some African American thinkers at the turn of the nineteenth century paid special attention to aesthetics, though rather than reject meritocratic assessments in total, they tended to advocate for more catholic, more pluralistic measures. In *A Voice from the South* (1892), the educator Anna Julia Cooper vindicates the achievements of a former black pupil by reporting how she won honors at the University of Chicago by excelling in competitive exams. Yet in a chapter titled "What Are We Worth?," Cooper worries how African Americans and others are judged by narrow informational standards. According to Cooper, the world asks of all peoples:

> Show us your cash account and your balance sheet. In the final reckoning do you belong on the debit or the credit side of the account? according to a fair and square, an impartial and practical reckoning. It is by

this standard that society estimates individuals; and by this standard
finally and inevitably the world will measure and judge nations and
races.

Cooper's extended accounting metaphor is only partially ironic. She cites
statistics regarding the material conditions of African Americans before
arguing that evaluations should be premised, not only on sociological
data, but also on "the *measure of the stature of the fullness of a man.*"
Faith, resilience, and sympathetic capacities should figure in what Cooper
calls "the final test by which the colored man in America will one day be
judged."[140] Aesthetics also matter in this fuller accounting, a point Cooper
makes when reporting how a black woman was accepted into an art school
based on her drawings but was then denied admission because of her race.
Invoking Michelangelo, Shakespeare, and Beethoven, Cooper calls for the
objective application of universal standards of beauty.

Also valuing aesthetic merits but, unlike Cooper, championing the distinctive contributions of black art, W.E.B. Du Bois had complicated views
on standardized examinations.[141] In 1901, he described civil service testing as "a great boon" to young African American men; and when he later
denied that data from intelligence tests proved the mental inferiority
of Africans, he did not argue that measuring intellect was illegitimate or
impossible but rather that the biases of the test in question led to faulty
results.[142] Du Bois's hopes for standardized testing are evident in *The Quest
of the Silver Fleece* (1911) when the novel's hero, Bles Alwyn, demonstrates
his merits by scoring ninety-three on his civil service exam. That Bles still
requires a senator's patronage to overcome racism and land a clerkship
in Washington is not an attack on standardized testing itself so much as
a reminder that American meritocracy remains an unrealized ideal. Such
reminders appeared regularly in the pages of the *Crisis* during Du Bois's
tenure as editor in the 1910s. While some articles detailed civil service testing policies and listed the scores and salaries of black civil servants, others
described instances of discrimination, including the practice of officials
simply cancelling job searches when African Americans achieved the best
marks.

Du Bois's profoundest concerns about standardization and testing appear in *The Souls of Black Folk* (1903), which moves dialectically
between quantitative sociology and more aesthetic, more spiritual commitments. Du Bois introduces a liberal view of merit when describing how as
a child "the sky was bluest when I could beat my mates at examination-
time, or beat them at a foot-race, or even beat their stringy heads." Du Bois

competed well in educational contexts increasingly regulated by standardized exams, but because for him a pitfall of "double-consciousness" includes "measuring one's soul by the tape of the world," he holds that African Americans in general and black artisans and artists in particular should look instead to "self-examination." Rather than joining the "cold statistician[s]" who reduce black experiences to blunt information, Du Bois reverses the power dynamic, writing in appropriately inverted syntax, "Merely a concrete test of the underlying principles of the great republic is the Negro Problem."[143] Du Bois insists that for America to pass the test imposed by its self-proclaimed ideals, it must recognize (among other things) achievements such as slave spirituals that may not meet—or may not initially appear to meet—European aesthetic standards. The question of how to measure black artistic attainments would continue to occupy New Negro thinkers such as Alain Locke, William Pickens, Martha Gruening, and Allison Davis, all of whom followed Du Bois in using the language and logic of testing when discussing the possibilities of combating racism through art and resisting the temptations of assimilating to prejudicial norms.[144] Langston Hughes described the danger in 1926 as "the desire to pour racial individuality into the mold of American standardization."[145]

A unique feature of Frank Webb's *The Garies and Their Friends* (1857) is its early attention to the racial dynamics of aesthetic testing under liberal meritocracy. Webb finished the book while living in England in 1856 and 1857, years marked by debates over standardized exams and the publication of Trollope's *Three Clerks*. Harriet Beecher Stowe, who wrote a prefatory letter for Webb's novel, is an important interlocutor, but at least as powerful is the influence of Dickens, who once declined a letter of introduction from Webb's wife, sending his own wife to meet her instead.[146] Like some Dickens novels, *The Garies and Their Friends* alternates between sentimental domesticity and bureaucratic institutions—Philadelphia's school boards, government offices, hospitals, and court proceedings with documents sealed by red tape. Webb's characters must navigate such information systems, including aesthetic assessments, as they seek to rise in an American meritocracy while carrying the burden of racism.

Much nineteenth-century African American literature attempts to vindicate racial equality through exhibitions of intellectual attainments, though Webb's depictions of formal and informal examinations reveal the limits of this strategy. In *The Garies and Their Friends*, Charlie Ellis, the son of a respectable black carpenter, initially works as a servant for a white woman who opposes the liberal education of blacks. When a party guest remarks that salad is not mentioned by any of the old British poets, Charlie quotes a passage from Chaucer's "The Flower and the Leaf," convincing Webb's readers—though not Charlie's employer—that he possesses some literary talent. Later at a common school examination, Charlie recites his exercises so well as to gain the favor of a white patroness, who awards him a volume of *Robinson Crusoe* and tries to enroll him in a prestigious academy. Charlie is barred because of his race and instead attends a segregated Sunday school where he is selected, after another sterling test performance, to be catechized in front of the largely white church. *The Garies and Their Friends* admires these achievements as Charlie comes of age, but his mastery of recitation causes the illiterate Aunt Comfort to marvel, "[He] talks jis' de same as if he was white."[147] This is hardly an offhand comment in a novel suspicious of assimilation and profoundly opposed to racial passing. Aunt Comfort is a figure of piety and wisdom, but her aesthetic sensibilities and vernacular knowledge are beyond the reach of standardized—which is to say, white—exams.

Intensifying his focus on social mobility, and conflating artistic and artisanal talent, Webb further critiques meritocratic assessments when Charlie looks for a job. After applying by letter to an advertisement for a law clerk, his excellent handwriting and compositional abilities elevate him to the top of the list until racism trumps talent in an interview. This happens again when his skillful drawings win him a job engraving bank certificates until fellow workers object to his color and again he loses out. No matter how many tests he passes, discrimination blocks Charlie's rise. There is no question about his aesthetic attainments, no concern on Webb's part that his writing and drawing abilities go unrecognized or do not align with dominant aesthetic standards. In fact, Charlie ultimately earns a spot at another engraving business where he works on illustrations suitable for novels, thereby offering a relatively optimistic portrait of the artist and artisan as a young black man. Charlie is no Bartleby the scrivener. He is happy to recite verses, memorize facts, copy documents in a law office, engrave instrumental bank certificates, and create images for commercial reproduction. Artistically gifted but uninterested in romantic originality, autonomous beauty, or a black aesthetic, Charlie blurs distinctions between the literary and the informational as Webb seemingly accepts prevailing aesthetic standards and assessments as the basis for a flawed but ultimately functioning meritocracy.

And yet *The Garies and Their Friends* is not nearly so stable, formally or ideologically. When Charlie studies for a geography exam, Webb suggests that positivist knowledge fails to capture the wonders of the natural world. As Samuel Otter has shown, the book revels in superabundant details that escape taxonomic order.[148] Rule-bound systems are constantly violated in Webb's racist Philadelphia, and even when the second engraver hires Charlie, it is because of the prodding of his sympathetic wife, not because of some fidelity to bureaucratic impersonality. All this suggests how informationalism in *The Garies and Their Friends* is epistemologically and politically limited, including the dangers of standardization, best exemplified by Clarence Garie, Charlie's peer who passes for white before being exposed and dying of a broken heart. Whereas Charlie aces his exams without denying his heritage, Clarence—who becomes an aesthete obsessed with European standards of beauty—loses his identity in two ways: he severs his ties with the black community, and he becomes a literary trope part tragic mulatto, part Wertherian romantic. Webb may or may not have intended to cast Clarence as a stereotypical character in a conventional subplot, but Clarence's fate warns against pouring black individuality into the mold of American standardization.

Nowhere is this risk more curious and conflicted than in the hospital where Charlie's father is taken after being critically injured by a white mob. The brutal riot is the climax of *The Garies and Their Friends*, and yet the hospital itself is a colorless eye at the center of the racial storm. Its rules are enforced by a nameless doorkeeper who knows Charlie's father only as patient "number sixty": "Never know names here—go by numbers. . . . I see so much of these things, that I can't feel them as others do" (242–43). This Dickensian character, extraneous to the plot, indicates the pitfalls but does not explicitly reject bureaucratic impersonality. Nothing indicates the color of the doorkeeper, as if the informational effaces, not only feelings, but race. Nothing suggests whether the hospital is segregated or not—this in a novel that takes extraordinary pains to track the color lines running through workplaces, schools, churches, graveyards, and city grids. Only the hospital appears to operate beyond race in *The Garies and Their Friends*, diverging from the novel's general realism and America's history of segregated health care.[149]

Whether this is a good thing or not is unclear. Charlie's father receives adequate care during his extended stay at the hospital, but he returns home disabled in body and mind, a reminder of racism's ongoing trauma that no amount of procedural impersonality can cure. Webb's hospital points to how the informational is both a boon and a horror, thereby undermining the faith in standardization suggested by Charlie's impressive testing and eventual success. If Charlie dramatizes how aesthetic standards impersonally applied are a salutatory ideal for an imperfect America, and if Clarence shows how assimilation too fully pursued leads to tragic results,

Webb's hospital suggests that standardization might successfully leave race and racism behind and yet remain a humanistic failure. Abolitionists of Webb's time frequently proclaimed that God is no respecter of persons, and many African Americans hoped that standardized tests could provide some protection from prejudice. But if bureaucratic, rule-bound, impersonal color blindness is an informational answer to discrimination, Webb suggests that even if such a comportment were possible, too much of life would be lost.

As a text that worries about the racial implications of aesthetic standards, *The Garies and Their Friends* both countervails and supports Kenneth Warren's thesis in *What Was African American Literature?* (2011)— that a distinctive African American literary tradition existed only under the conditions of Jim Crow. Contra Warren, Webb seems to recognize— before the Fourteenth Amendment and well before *Plessy vs. Ferguson* (1896)—that bureaucratic impersonality, standardized assessments, and other forms of informational objectivity that might transcend race are not only unworkable but unwise. That is, the basis for a black aesthetic can be found in *The Garies and Their Friends*, whose critique of standardization can mark a turn toward African American literary distinctiveness earlier than Warren allows. That said, any black aesthetic in *The Garies and Their Friends* is thematically and formally incipient, which can help explain why the novel feels at times derivative and at others brilliantly weird. Its publication date notwithstanding, the book focuses on segregation and assimilation in the manner of a postbellum race novel, and so if it violates the law of Warren's chronology, it still abides by the spirit of his argument.

More to the broader point of this chapter, *The Garies and Their Friends* is unsure how artists might be measured. Like other Victorian novels we have seen, but with an attention to race that challenges liberal meritocracy, Webb simultaneously hopes and fears that aesthetics might be standardized, tested, and rewarded under informational systems. Matthew Arnold never found a synthesis of the informational and the literary. Dickens imagined a reconciliation of impersonality and artistic play. Farrar, Yonge, and (for the most part) Hughes believed that literary attainments can be measured, usually for the better. Brontë, Trollope, Fern, and Alcott are more skeptical, though they do not polemicize against informationalism, and Trollope found ways to not care. At the heart of *The Garies and Their Friends* is a conviction we have seen throughout this book: the literary operates and sometimes thrives in informational contexts, and yet vital aspects of aesthetics remain unassimilated and unassimilable. Charlie makes his artistic merits matter in an information economy. How happy an ending this is, is a question Webb leaves unresolved.

Coda: Retaking the GRE

Whether one can measure literary sensibilities—conceived as knowledge or skill, attainment or aptitude, instrument or ornament—remains a crucial question today as policy makers, ranking entities, accreditation institutions, administrators, parents, and even some teachers and students increasingly call for quantitative assessments of academic and pedagogical qualities. Like Gerald Graff and Cathy Birkenstein, we might see standardization bringing increased transparency and equal opportunities to the academy in general and to literary studies in particular. Or like Kathleen Woodward, we might worry that our work cannot be captured by measurable outcomes, a response that John Guillory takes to originate in a post-Kantian antipositivism fundamental to the profession of English and increasingly marginalized in broader educational debates.[150] With backgrounds in literary criticism, Cathy Davidson and Christopher Newfield have recently lodged far-reaching objections to standardized testing, though literary studies, at least in the near future, will continue to be shaped by the accountability movement, even as discussions of measurable outcomes still tend to overlook disciplinary differences and histories of knowledge production.[151]

For example, sociologists Richard Arum and Josipa Roksa in their widely cited book *Academically Adrift* (2011) quantify the inadequacies of American higher education with a large-scale longitudinal study based on the College Learning Assessment test (CLA), a "state-of-the-art" tool for assessing critical thinking, analytic reasoning, problem solving, and writing skills.[152] The CLA consists of three written assignments: (1) a ninety-minute "performance task" (e.g., write a memo recommending which aircraft to purchase based on newspaper articles, safety reports, and emails); (2) a thirty-minute critique of an argument (couples should avoid June weddings because they are statistically more likely to end in divorce); and (3) a forty-five-minute essay that argues a position (do you agree with the following statement: "In our time, specialists of all kinds are highly overrated?").[153] It seems clear how proponents of the CLA would answer this final question. Designed to measure learning across institutions and disciplines, the CLA does not test for specific content knowledge, even as it purports to measure college learning. Literature instructors might feel that their courses have little relation to an exam that deals in airplane procurement, rewards polemic argumentation, and is sometimes scored by natural language processing software. Like the recently discontinued SAT writing exam, the CLA faces a number of challenges: higher-order critical thinking is difficult to assess using standardized rubrics; the time and energy required to meaningfully evaluate essays makes large-scale testing impractical; impromptu timed assignments do not adequately assess the kind of reflective, recursive, dialectical writing and thinking that humanities disciplines tend to value.

It is easy, of course, to be irritated by administrative reaching after data and facts, and it is easier to quarrel with general tests such as the CLA than to offer viable alternatives. To repeat a quote from *The Sacrifice of Education to Examination* (1889), "competitive examination is a very imperfect test, but it is better than none."[154] The closest thing that the field of literary studies in English has to a discipline-specific standardized exam is the GRE subject test in English literature, which allows two hours and fifty minutes for 230 multiple-choice questions, roughly split between those requiring factual recall and those involving the explication of passages provided on the test. The Educational Testing Service, which runs the GREs, claims in its materials that subject scores in general are good predictors of graduate school outcomes, but it makes no such claims in the specific case of the English literature subject exam and even acknowledges "the limitations of the multiple-choice format . . . for testing competence in literary studies."[155] It has proven difficult to show that the GRE English literature subject test offers much in the way of predictive value, as if the gap between the literary and the informational remains too wide to bridge.[156]

As a director of graduate admissions, I never knew what to make of GRE subject scores, and there was wide disagreement among my colleagues, as there is in the field at large. So in 2013, having worked as an English professor for over a decade, and following the example of Michael Bérubé, I retook the GRE subject exam in English literature—paid the $150 fee, sharpened my pencils, and soaked up the ambient unease.[157] As it had two decades before, many of the factual questions I encountered on the GRE test felt unrelated to what I take to be literary studies, and even the explication questions about given passages could be frustrating. On the practice exam that I received with my admissions ticket, I missed a question on a paragraph from Emerson's "Experience" (1844), an essay I teach on a regular basis and have analyzed at length in print. Maybe I have read *too much* Stanley Cavell, Sharon Cameron, Barbara Packer, and Branka Arsić to identify the meaning of grief in "Experience." Maybe the essay is *not really* about Emerson's self-denial of the tempting comforts of grief, a comfort that remains epistemologically impossible to hold if a knowledge based on skepticism would recognize its own limits. Apparently, Emerson *doesn't actually* show that the experience of grief cannot be stabilized or reduced to multiple-choice options. Perhaps the question was a *brilliant* metacritical exercise intended to demonstrate Emerson's point that we can never know for certain the minds of others, in this case the people who wrote the test. I'm still angry about missing that Emerson question. I still can't help feeling that my literary attainments were not reflected in my score on the actual GRE exam.[158] Of the four fellow test takers I interviewed before and after the session, all seemed resigned to standardized assessments and were quick to offer their study tips, none of which involved intensive reading. At the same time, none of them felt that the GRE subject test in English literature had much to do with their educational attainments, scholarly potential, or relationship to literature. As a senior English major from Boston College put it, "I don't think you can test this stuff."

The sense that literary attainments cannot be measured—that the literary and the informational are incommensurate—remains a powerful intuition in our age of data-driven accountability. Whether or not one believes that literature cannot or should not be rendered as information, this final chapter's turn to standardized examinations in the context of discipline formation and liberal meritocracy highlights a claim that has become increasingly prevalent in writings on the crisis in the humanities: the relationship between the literary and the informational is vital to the future of literary studies. This has been historically true, and it seems to me that negotiations between the literary and the informational are as necessary as ever at this time. Compromise, accommodation, entanglement, and pluralism can lack the sharp satisfactions of polemic critique and the consistency of theoretical bright lines. But as this book has aspired to show, differences between the literary and the informational have not been as great nor as fixed as is often thought. There are good reasons for humanists to resist the rise of information, but an imagined history of unequivocal antagonism between literature and information is not one of them.

It is tempting, and I have sometimes been tempted, to appeal to instrumental considerations. The ubiquitous authority of data analysis, the corporatization of higher education, the relentless rankings of liberal meritocracy, the everyday practices of digital natives—resistance can feel futile in our information age, so we should salvage what we can of the literary. But the stronger, and not necessarily happier, position is that modern conceptions of literature have been since at least the nineteenth century bound up with the informational and that historically conditioned dynamics between the domains have helped constitute the literary as such. It is not an argument, but I like the literature treated in this book all the more after exploring its informational commitments. Some wonderful literary stuff cannot be tested or counted. Literary sensibilities will seek and find meanings unavailable to algorithmic methods. Readers will surf, dip, skim, and harvest data, but they will still be enchanted by their favorite passages. All this has happened and, I think, will continue to happen in our long information revolution. New contingencies will shift literary theories and practices, and such shifting may disadvantage literary studies in its current vulnerable form, but what we have learned to call the literary will still flourish in a wide world.

NOTES

Introduction

1. Herman Melville, *Moby-Dick* (1851), in *Redburn, White-Jacket, Moby-Dick* (New York: Library of America, 1983), 782.

2. Evert A. Duyckinck, "Melville's Moby Dick; or, The Whale: Second Notice," *Literary World*, November 22, 1851, 403-4.

3. Stephen Marche, "Literature Is Not Data: Against Digital Humanities," *Los Angeles Review of Books*, October 28, 2012, https://lareviewofbooks.org/article/literature-is-not-data-against-digital-humanities/#!. See also the controversy touched off by Nan Z. Da's "The Computational Case against Computational Literary Studies," *Critical Inquiry* 45:3 (Spring 2019), 601-39. Da's article and the ensuing forum discussion were published while this book was in press.

4. See, for instance, Jonathan Gottschall, *Literature, Science, and a New Humanities* (New York: Palgrave Macmillan, 2008) (scientific methods). Stephen Ramsay, *Reading Machines: Toward an Algorithmic Criticism* (Champaign: University of Illinois Press, 2011); Franco Moretti, *Distant Reading* (New York: Verso, 2013); Matthew Jockers, *Macroanalysis: Digital Methods and Literary History* (Chicago: University of Illinois Press, 2013); and Andrew Piper, *Enumerations: Data and Literary Study* (Chicago: University of Chicago Press, 2018) (statistical analysis). Bruno Latour, "Why Has Critique Run Out of Steam? From Matters of Fact to Matters of Concern," *Critical Inquiry* 30 (Winter 2004), 225-48 (empiricism and facts). Stephen Best and Sharon Marcus, "Surface Reading: An Introduction," *Representations* 108:1 (2009), 1-21; Elaine Freedgood and Cannon Schmitt, "Denotatively, Technically, Literally," *Representations* 125:1 (2014), 1-14; and Heather Love, "Close Reading and Thin Description," *Public Culture* 25:3 (2013), 401-34 (approaches that constrain interpretive license).

5. Yuval Noah Harari, *Sapiens: A Brief History of Humankind* (London: Harvill Secker, 2014), 119-32; Robert Darnton, *The Case for Books: Past, Present, and Future* (New York: PublicAffairs, 2010), 23. As early as 1853, the London *Times* referred to the period as "an age of information" (Toni Weller, *The Victorians and Information: A Social and Cultural History* [Saarbrücken, Germany: VDM Verlag Dr. Müller, 2009], 9).

6. For the exclusionary influence of masculinist information on literature, see Margaret Cohen, *The Sentimental Education of the Novel* (Princeton, NJ: Princeton University Press, 1999).

7. Michel Foucault, "What Is an Author?" (1969), in *The Foucault Reader*, ed. Paul Rabinow (New York: Vintage, 1984), 101-20.

8. Lisa Gitelman, *Paper Knowledge: Toward a Media History of Documents* (Durham, NC: Duke University Press, 2014), 5.

9. "Current Educational Topics," *Public-School Journal*, May 1897, 517-19.

10. Darnton, *Case for Books*; Roger Chartier, *The Order of Books* (Stanford, CA: Stanford University Press, 1992); David McKitterick, *Print, Manuscript, and*

the Search for Order, 1450–1830 (Cambridge: Cambridge University Press, 2003); Ann Blair, *Too Much to Know: Managing Scholarly Information before the Modern Age* (New Haven, CT: Yale University Press, 2011); Chad Wellmon, *Organizing Enlightenment: Information Overload and the Invention of the Modern Research University* (Baltimore: Johns Hopkins University Press, 2015).

11. Nineteenth-century book and print culture histories include Richard Altick, *The English Common Reader: A Social History of the Mass Reading Public, 1800–1900* (Chicago: University of Chicago Press, 1957); William St. Clair, *The Reading Nation in the Romantic Period* (Cambridge: Cambridge University Press, 2004); William Charvat, *The Profession of Authorship in America, 1800–1870* (Columbus: Ohio State University Press, 1968); Ronald J. Zboray, *A Fictive People: Antebellum Economic Development and the American Reading Public* (New York: Oxford University Press, 1993); Trish Loughran, *The Republic in Print: Print Culture in the Age of U.S. Nation Building, 1770–1870* (New York: Columbia University Press, 2007).

12. See, for instance, Friedrich Kittler, *Gramophone, Film, Typewriter*, trans. Geoffrey Winthrop-Young and Michael Wutz (1986; Stanford, CA: Stanford University Press, 1999).

13. Friedrich Kittler, *Discourse Networks 1800/1900*, trans. Michael Metteer, with Chris Cullens (1985; Stanford, CA: Stanford University Press, 1990); Lisa Gitelman, *Paper Knowledge*, and *Always Already New: Media, History, and the Data of Culture* (Cambridge, MA: MIT Press, 2006). See also *Comparative Textual Media: Transforming the Humanities in the Postprint Era*, ed. N. Katherine Hayles and Jessica Pressman (Minneapolis: University of Minnesota Press, 2013).

14. Histories of nineteenth-century information include Richard Brown, *Knowledge Is Power: The Diffusion of Information in Early America, 1700–1865* (Oxford: Oxford University Press, 1989); Daniel R. Headrick, *When Information Came of Age: Technologies of Knowledge in the Age of Reason and Revolution, 1700–1850* (New York: Oxford University Press, 2000); Oz Frankel, *States of Inquiry: Social Investigations and Print Culture in Nineteenth-Century Britain and the United States* (Baltimore: Johns Hopkins University Press, 2006); Weller, *Victorians and Information*; James W. Cortada, *All the Facts: A History of Information in the United States since 1870* (Oxford: Oxford University Press, 2016).

15. Lorraine Daston and Peter Galison, *Objectivity* (Brooklyn, NY: Zone Books, 2010); Ian Hacking, *The Taming of Chance* (Cambridge: Cambridge University Press, 1990); Theodore Porter, *The Rise of Statistical Thinking, 1820–1900* (Princeton, NJ: Princeton University Press, 1986), and *Trust in Numbers: The Pursuit of Objectivity in Science and Public Life* (Princeton, NJ: Princeton University Press, 1995). For a more cultural approach to statistics and numeracy, see Patricia Cline Cohen, *A Calculating People: The Spread of Numeracy in Early America* (Chicago: University of Chicago Press, 1982).

16. Jerome McGann, *A New Republic of Letters: Memory and Scholarship in the Age of Digital Reproduction* (Cambridge, MA: Harvard University Press, 2014), 14; Piper, *Enumerations*, 3.

17. Mary Poovey, *A History of the Modern Fact: Problems of Knowledge in the Sciences of Wealth and Society* (Chicago: University of Chicago Press, 1998); Richard Menke, *Telegraphic Realism: Victorian Fiction and Other Information Systems*

(Stanford, CA: Stanford University Press, 2008); John Guillory, "The Memo and Modernity," *Critical Inquiry* 31:1 (2004), 108–32; Mark Gobles, *Beautiful Circuits: Modernism and the Mediated Life* (New York: Columbia University Press, 2010); Jessica Pressman, *Digital Modernism: Making It New in New Media* (New York: Oxford University Press, 2014); James Purdon, *Modernist Informatics: Literature, Information, and the State* (New York: Oxford University Press, 2015). See also portions of Caroline Levine's *Forms: Whole, Rhythm, Hierarchy, Network* (Princeton, NJ: Princeton University Press, 2015), esp. 112–31.

18. Meredith McGill, *American Literature and the Culture of Reprinting, 1834–1853* (Philadelphia: University of Pennsylvania Press, 2003); Leah Price, *How to Do Things with Books in Victorian Britain* (Princeton, NJ: Princeton University Press, 2012); Ellen Gruber Garvey, *Writing with Scissors: American Scrapbooks from the Civil War to the Harlem Renaissance* (New York: Oxford University Press, 2012); Andrew Piper, *Dreaming in Books: The Making of the Bibliographic Imagination in the Romantic Age* (Chicago: University of Chicago Press, 2009), and *Book Was There: Reading in Electronic Times* (Chicago: University of Chicago Press, 2012). See also Peter West, *The Arbiters of Reality: Hawthorne, Melville, and the Rise of Mass Information Culture* (Columbus: Ohio State University Press, 2008), which is primarily interested in epistemology and the literary marketplace.

19. See, for instance, a recent forum on distant reading, which shows the uneven ways in which data-driven literary analysis can be situated within and against other modes of literary criticism: Nancy Armstrong, Warren Montag, Alison Booth, et al., "On Franco Moretti's Distance Reading," *PMLA* 132:3 (2017), 613–89.

20. For a sense of the multiple definitions of information, see Luciano Floridi, *Information: A Very Short Introduction* (Oxford: Oxford University Press, 2010); Geoffrey Nunberg, "Farewell to the Information Age," in *The Future of the Book*, ed. Geoffrey Nunberg (Berkeley: University of California Press, 1996), esp. 108–15; Cortada, *All the Facts*, 5–10.

21. T. S. Eliot, "The Rock" (1934), in *Collected Poems, 1909–1962* (1934; New York: Harcourt, 1963), 147.

22. Floridi, *Information*, 39.

23. Herman Melville, "Bartleby, the Scrivener," in *Pierre, Israel Potter, The Piazza Tales, The Confidence-Man, Uncollected Prose, Billy Budd, Sailor* (New York: Library of America, 1984), 647.

24. Claude E. Shannon, "The Mathematical Theory of Communication" (1948), in Claude E. Shannon and Warren Weaver, *The Mathematical Theory of Communication* (1949; Urbana: University of Illinois Press, 1963), 3.

25. Edgar Allan Poe, *Poetry and Tales* (New York: Library of America, 1984), 83.

26. Warren Weaver, "Recent Contributions to the Mathematical Theory of Communication" (1949), in Shannon and Weaver, *Mathematical Theory of Communication*, 116–17. See also Gobles, *Beautiful Circuits*, 5.

27. Gregory Bateson, *Steps to an Ecology of Mind: Collected Essays in Anthropology, Psychiatry, Evolution, and Epistemology* (Chicago: University of Chicago Press, 1972), 271–72; 230.

28. Niklas Luhmann, *Introduction to Systems Theory*, ed. Dirk Baecker, trans. Peter Gilgen (Cambridge, MA: Polity, 2013), 28.

29. Kittler, *Discourse Networks 1800/1900*; Stuart Hall, "Encoding/Decoding" (1973), in *The Cultural Studies Reader*, ed. Simon During (London: Routledge, 1993), 97.

30. *Cybernetics: The Macy Conferences 1946–1953; The Complete Transactions*, ed. Claus Pias (Chicago: University of Chicago Press, 2016), 266, 256, 269. A version of Shannon's paper would later be published as "Prediction and Entropy of Printed English," *Bell System Technical Journal* 30 (1951), 50–64.

31. N. Katherine Hayles, *How We Became Posthuman: Virtual Bodies in Cybernetics, Literature, and Informatics* (Chicago: University of Chicago Press, 1999), esp. 1–20.

32. Nunberg, "Farewell to the Information Age," 114–15. See also Alistair Black's germane question: "If information itself defies precise definition, what chance is there that its definition might be historicized?" ("Information History," *Annual Review of Information Science and Technology* 40 [2006], 442). My answer: information must be historicized precisely because it defies precise definition.

Chapter One. Reading

1. Franco Moretti, "Conjectures in World Literature," *New Left Review* 1 (2000), 55. For nonreading, see Pierre Bayard, *How to Talk about Books You Haven't Read* (New York: Bloomsbury, 2007); and Leah Price, *How to Do Things with Books in Victorian Britain* (Princeton, NJ: Princeton University Press, 2012).

2. For the persistence of close reading, see Andrew DuBois, "Introduction," in *Close Reading: The Reader*, ed. Frank Lentricchia and Andrew DuBois (Durham, NC: Duke University Press, 2003), 1–42; and Heather Love, "Close but Not Deep: Literary Ethics and the Descriptive Turn," *New Literary History* 41 (2010), esp. 371–75.

3. Alan Jacobs, *The Pleasures of Reading in an Age of Distraction* (Oxford: Oxford University Press, 2011); Andrew Piper, *Book Was There: Reading in Electronic Times* (Chicago: University of Chicago Press, 2012).

4. N. Katherine Hayles, *How We Think: Digital Media and Contemporary Technogenesis* (Chicago: University of Chicago Press, 2012), 55–80.

5. Stephen Best and Sharon Marcus, "Surface Reading: An Introduction," *Representations* 108 (2009), 1–21.

6. See, for instance, the debate touched off by Stephen Marche's "Literature Is Not Data: Against Digital Humanities," *Los Angeles Review of Books*, October 28, 2012, https://lareviewofbooks.org/article/literature-is-not-data-against-digital-humanities/#!.

7. Robert Darnton, *The Case for Books: Past, Present, and Future* (New York: PublicAffairs, 2010), 23; Roger Chartier, *The Order of Books* (Stanford, CA: Stanford University Press, 1992), vii; Ann Blair, *Too Much to Know: Managing Scholarly Information before the Modern Age* (New Haven, CT: Yale University Press, 2011); Chad Wellmon, *Organizing Enlightenment: Information Overload and the Invention of the Modern Research University* (Baltimore: Johns Hopkins University Press, 2015).

8. Lennard J. Davis, *Factual Fictions: The Origins of the English Novel* (Philadelphia: University of Pennsylvania Press, 1983); Michael McKeon, *The Origins of the English Novel, 1600–1740* (Baltimore: Johns Hopkins University Press, 1987); and

Mary Poovey, *A History of the Modern Fact: Problems of Knowledge in the Sciences of Wealth and Society* (Chicago: University of Chicago Press, 1998), and *Genres of the Credit Economy: Mediating Value in Eighteenth- and Nineteenth-Century Britain* (Chicago: University of Chicago Press, 2008). See also the influential collection *This Is Enlightenment*, ed. Clifford Siskin and William Warner (Chicago: University of Chicago Press, 2010).

9. Friedrich Kittler, *Gramophone, Film, Typewriter*, trans. Geoffrey Winthrop-Young and Michael Wutz (1986; Stanford, CA: Stanford University Press, 1999); Geoffrey Nunberg, "Farewell to the Information Age," in *The Future of the Book*, ed. Geoffrey Nunberg (Berkeley: University of California Press, 1996), 103–38; Lisa Gitelman, *Always Already New: Media, History, and the Data of Culture* (Cambridge: MIT Press, 2006); Piper, *Book Was There*, esp. vii–xiii.

10. Ian Watt, *The Rise of the Novel* (London: Chatto and Windus, 1957); Maximillian Novak, *Economics and the Fiction of Daniel Defoe* (Berkeley: University of California Press, 1962); Sandra Sherman, *Finance and Fictionality in the Early Eighteenth Century: Accounting for Defoe* (Cambridge: Cambridge University Press, 1996); Wolfram Schmidgen, "*Robinson Crusoe*, Enumeration, and the Mercantile Fetish," *Eighteenth-Century Studies* 35:1 (2001), 19–39.

11. Daniel Defoe, *Robinson Crusoe* (New York: Modern Library, 2001), 16. Subsequent references to this volume cited parenthetically. For *Crusoe* and science, see John Bender, "Novel Knowledge: Judgment, Experience, Experiment," in *This Is Enlightenment*, 284–300. For Defoe as Baconian empiricist, see Ilse Vickers, *Defoe and the New Sciences* (Cambridge: Cambridge University Press, 1996).

12. McKeon, *Origins of the English Novel*, 316.

13. Alberto Manguel, "The Library of Robinson Crusoe," *American Scholar* 70:1 (2001), 61.

14. One exception is James Hervey, who selects Walter Marshall's *The Gospel-Mystery of Sanctification* (1692) as the one book "besides my Bible" that he would take to a "desolate island" (*Theron and Aspasio*, vol. 2 [1755; London: Hamilton, Adams, 1824], 473). Hervey's passage is quoted occasionally in the nineteenth century, though always to make the point that the Bible is the only real choice. Also, James Russell Lowell in *A Fable for Critics* (1848) mentions "*Literature suited to desolate islands*," though by this he means books that are so bad that one would read them only if one were stranded on an island (*Poems*, vol. 3 [Boston: Houghton, Mifflin, 1891], 36). In short, deserted island reading was an available concept but does not seem to be a cultural trope prior to the twentieth century.

15. Prospero twice refers to his "book" (III.i.113; V.i.66), but Gonzalo initially furnishes him with "books" and "volumes" (I.ii.198–99), and Caliban thrice refers to Prospero's multiple "books" (III.ii.98–104).

16. For *Journal of the Plague Year*, see Katherine Ellison, *Fatal News: Reading and Information Overload in Early Eighteenth-Century Literature* (New York: Routledge, 2006); Paula McDowell, "Defoe's *Essay upon Literature* and Eighteenth-Century Histories of Mediation," *PMLA* 130:3 (2015), 568; Poovey, *Genres of the Credit Economy*, 93; Friedrich Kittler, *Discourse Networks 1800/1900*, trans. Michael Metteer, with Chris Cullens (1985; Stanford, CA: Stanford University Press, 1990), 15 (see also 115 on *Robinson Crusoe*).

17. Jean-Jacques Rousseau, *Emile*, trans. Allan Bloom (New York: Basic Books, 1979), 267.

18. *Monthly Review*, March 1775, 274, rpt. in *Defoe: The Critical Heritage*, ed. Pat Rogers (London: Routledge, 1972), 54.

19. For a reappraisal of Rolf Engelsing's classic formulation, see Reinhard Wittmann, "Was There a Reading Revolution at the End of the Eighteenth Century?," in *A History of Reading in the West*, ed. Guglielmo Cavallo and Roger Chartier, trans. Lydia Cochrane (Amherst: University of Massachusetts Press, 2003), 284–312. It is difficult to generalize about reading habits, not only because evidence can be hard to find and interpret, but also because official and everyday practices differ across demographic categories and—as emphasized here—individual lives and memories. For an overview of the challenges involved, see Leah Price, "Reading: The State of the Discipline," *Book History* 7 (2004), 303–20.

20. George Crabbe, *The Library: A Poem* (London: J. Dodsley, 1783), 7–8.

21. James Boswell, *The Life of Samuel Johnson* (1791; London: J. Richardson, 1823), 40. The other two books were *Don Quixote* (1605, 1615) and *Pilgrim's Progress* (1678).

22. Sir Walter Scott rpt. in *Defoe: The Critical Heritage*, 71, 79; Henry James, "The Art of Fiction" (1884), in *The Portable Henry James*, ed. John Auchard (New York: Penguin, 2004), 430.

23. See, for instance, Patrick Brantlinger, *The Reading Lesson: The Threat of Mass Literacy in Nineteenth-Century British Fiction* (Bloomington: Indiana University Press, 1998); and Nicholas Dames, *The Physiology of the Novel: Reading, Neural Science, and the Form of Victorian Fiction* (Oxford: Oxford University Press, 2007).

24. "Robinson Crusoe," *Littell's Living Age*, December 3, 1859, 610. For an overview of *Robinson Crusoe*'s publication record in Britain, see William St. Clair, *The Reading Nation in the Romantic Period* (Cambridge: Cambridge University Press, 2004), 507–8. Shawn Thompson counts 122 distinct American printings of *Robinson Crusoe* between 1840 and 1860 (*The Fortress of Solitude: Robinson Crusoe in Antebellum Culture* [Madison, NJ: Fairleigh Dickinson University Press, 2010]).

25. John Lubbock, "A Song of Books," in *In Praise of Books: A Vade Mecum for Book-Lovers* (New York: Perkins, 1901), 84.

26. Untitled review, *New York Review*, January 1842, 144.

27. Thompson, *Fortress of Solitude*; Patricia Crain, *Reading Children: Literacy, Property, and the Dilemmas of Childhood in Nineteenth-Century America* (Philadelphia: University of Pennsylvania Press, 2016). See also Gillian Silverman, *Bodies and Books: Reading and the Fantasy of Communion in Nineteenth-Century America* (Philadelphia: University of Pennsylvania Press, 2012). Silverman's account of intimate reading has similarities with deserted island reading, though her emphasis on embodiment and intersubjectivity is different.

28. Ruskin quoted in Elizabeth Carolyn Miller, *Slow Print: Literary Radicalism and Late Victorian Print Culture* (Stanford, CA: Stanford University Press, 2013), 3; John Ruskin, "Of Kings' Treasuries" (1865), in *The Genius of John Ruskin: Selections from His Writings*, ed. John D. Rosenberg (Charlottesville: University of Virginia Press, 1964), 297; Ruskin, "The Cestus of Aglaia" (1866), in *The Complete Works of John Ruskin*, vol. 27 (New York: T. Y. Crowell, 1885), 359.

29. Crain, *Reading Children*, 109.

30. Inscriptions appear in the following editions of *Robinson Crusoe*: New Haven, CT: Sidney's Press for Cooke, 1807 (Coleman); Exeter, NH: Abel Brown, 1828 (Anderson); Philadelphia: Key and Mielke, 1831 (Gardiner; Gardner).

31. Daniel Defoe, *Robinson Crusoe* (New York: Kearny, 1844); n.a., *Stories for a Good Child* (Providence, RI: Kendall and Stillwell, 1831).

32. John Guillory, "The Ethics of Reading," in *The Turn to Ethics*, ed. Marjorie Garber, Beatrice Hanssen, Rebecca Walkowitz (New York: Routledge, 2000), 29–46; Rita Felski, *The Uses of Literature* (Malden, MA: Blackwell, 2008), 51–76.

33. "Robinson Crusoe," *American Monthly Magazine*, January 1836, 108.

34. Daniel Defoe, *The Life and Surprising Adventures of Robinson Crusoe*, vol. 1 (London: John Major, 1831), unnumbered prefatory materials. Cowper's lines here refer to *Pilgrim's Progress*, but Major's reference to Cowper's "Tirocinium" (1785) is also apt, as the poem contrasts the simplicity of youth to the burdens of formal schooling.

35. "Robinson Crusoe," *Era*, November 24, 1839, 2.

36. Edgar Allan Poe, review of *Crusoe*, *Southern Literary Messenger*, January 1836, 127, rpt. in *Edgar Allan Poe: Essays and Reviews* (New York: Library of America, 1984), 201–2.

37. For Poe, numbers, and mass print, see Maurice S. Lee, "Poe by the Numbers: Odd Man Out?," in *Remapping Antebellum Culture: Poe at 200*, ed. J. Gerald Kennedy (Baton Rouge: Louisiana State University Press, 2013), 227–44.

38. Edgar Allan Poe, "Marginalia," in *The Works of Edgar Allan Poe*, vol. 3, ed. John H. Ingram (London: A. and C. Black, 1899), 412.

39. Charles Dickens, *A Christmas Carol* (1843; London: Chapman and Hall, 1907), 63–64.

40. For a compatible argument that takes *Crusoe* as a site for reflections on mass print, see Price, *How to Do Things with Books*, 82, 207–8.

41. Annie Carey, *The History of a Book* (London: Cassell, Petter, and Galpin, 1873), 10. Subsequent references to this volume cited parenthetically. For It-Narratives and print culture with attention to Carey, see Price, *How to Do Things with Books*, 107–38.

42. Miller, *Slow Print*.

43. Harry Lyman Koopman, *The Mastery of Books: Hints on Reading and the Use of Libraries* (New York: American Book, 1896), 5, 128, 47, 80.

44. Harry Lyman Koopman, *The Librarian of the Desert and Other Poems* (Boston: Everett, 1908), 1–14.

45. *The Collected Works of Samuel Taylor Coleridge: Marginalia II*, ed. George Whalley (Princeton, NJ: Princeton University Press, 1984), 159. See also Patrick Keene, *Coleridge's Submerged Politics: The Ancient Mariner and Robinson Crusoe* (Columbia: University of Missouri Press, 1994), esp. 45–54.

46. Cleanth Brooks and Robert Penn Warren, *Understanding Poetry* (1938), in *The Lyric Theory Reader: A Critical Anthology*, ed. Virginia Jackson and Yopie Prins (Baltimore: Johns Hopkins University Press, 2014), 180. For a metacritical account of Coleridge's use by the New Criticism, see Jonathan Arac, "Repetition and Exclusion: Coleridge and New Criticism Reconsidered," *boundary 2* 8:1 (1979), 261–74. For the New Critics as hostile to data and information, see Andrew Kopec, "The Digital Humanities, Inc.: Literary Criticism and the Fate of a Profession," *PMLA* 131:2 (2016), 324–39. None of this is to suggest that Coleridge invented close reading; see, for instance, Maureen

N. McLane, "Mediating Antiquarians in Britain, 1760-1830: The Invention of Oral Tradition; or, Close Reading before Coleridge," in *This Is Enlightenment*, 247-64.

47. Jon Klancher, *The Making of English Reading Audiences, 1790-1832* (Madison: University of Wisconsin Press, 1987).

48. Lucy Newlyn, *Reading, Writing, and Romanticism: The Anxiety of Reception* (Oxford: Oxford University Press, 2000), 49-90; St. Clair, *Reading Nation in the Romantic Period*.

49. F. O. Matthiessen, *American Renaissance: Art and Expression in the Age of Emerson and Whitman* (Oxford: Oxford University Press, 1941), esp. 133-40; *The Transcendentalists: An Anthology*, ed. Perry Miller (Cambridge, MA: Harvard University Press, 1950), 34-38, 66-71; Laura Dassow Walls, *Emerson's Life in Science: The Culture of Truth* (Ithaca, NY: Cornell University Press, 2003).

50. Quoted in John Beer's introduction to *The Collected Works of Samuel Taylor Coleridge: Aids to Reflection*, vol. 9, ed. John Beer (Princeton, NJ: Princeton University Press, 1995), cxxviii.

51. Samuel Taylor Coleridge, *The Collected Works of Samuel Taylor Coleridge: Biographia Literaria*, 2 vols., ed. James Engell and W. Jackson Bate (Princeton, NJ: Princeton University Press, 1983), 1:289. Subsequent references to this work cited parenthetically.

52. For Kant and print culture, see Helge Jordheim, "The Present of Enlightenment: Temporality and Mediation in Kant, Foucault, and Jean Paul," in *This Is Enlightenment*, esp. 199-202.

53. Wellmon, *Organizing Enlightenment*, 123-50 (Kant), 170-75 (Schelling); Jonah Siegel, *Desire and Excess: The Nineteenth-Century Culture of Art* (Princeton, NJ: Princeton University Press, 2000), esp. 73-75.

54. Dames, *Physiology of the Novel*, 177.

55. Joshua King, "Coleridge's *Aids to Reflection*, Print Culture, and Mediated Spiritual Community," *European Romantic Review* 23:1 (2012), 43-62.

56. Scott Hess, "The Wedding Guest as Reader: 'The Rime of the Ancyent Marinere' as a Dramatization of Print Circulation and the Authorial Self," *Nineteenth Century Studies* 15 (2001), 19-36.

57. Samuel Taylor Coleridge, *A Dissertation on the Science of Method* (1818; London: Richard Griffin, 1854), 72. Note that this intended introduction was published separately as a book. See also Seth Rudy, *Literature and Encyclopedism in Enlightenment Britain: The Pursuit of Complete Knowledge* (Basingstoke, UK: Palgrave Macmillan, 2014), 148-50.

58. Quoted in William Hazlitt, *Johnson's Lives of the British Poets*, vol. 4 (London: Nathaniel Cooke, 1854), 187.

59. Samuel Taylor Coleridge, *The Collected Works of Samuel Taylor Coleridge: The Friend*, 2 vols., ed. Barbara E. Rooke (London: Routledge and Kegan Paul, 1969), 2:16.

60. St. Clair, *Reading Nation in the Romantic Period*, 164.

61. Theo Davis, *Ornamental Aesthetics: The Poetry of Attending in Thoreau, Dickinson, and Whitman* (Oxford: Oxford University Press, 2016).

62. S. T. Coleridge to Thomas Poole, January 28, 1810, in *Letters of Samuel Taylor Coleridge*, vol. 2, ed. Ernest Hartley Coleridge (London: William Heinemann, 1895), 557.

63. *Coleridge's Notebooks: A Selection*, ed. Seamus Perry (Oxford: Oxford University Press, 2002), 98.

64. Samuel Taylor Coleridge, *On the Constitution of the Church and State*, ed. Henry Nelson Coleridge (1830; New York: Harper and Brothers, 1884), 110.

65. Harold Bloom, "Coleridge: The Anxiety of Influence," *Diacritics* 2:1 (1972), 36–41; Newlyn, *Reading, Writing, and Romanticism*, 49–90.

66. De Quincey anecdotes from *Confessions of an English Opium-Eater* (1821; Boston: James R. Osgood, 1873), 219, 104.

67. Henry David Thoreau, *Walden, or Life in the Woods* (1854; New York: Penguin, 2004), 84, 81; and *Selections from the Journal*, ed. Walter Harding (Mineola, NY: Dover, 1995), 17.

68. Deidre Lynch, "'Wedded to Books': Bibliomania and the Romantic Essayists," *Romantic Circles*, https://www.rc.umd.edu/praxis/libraries/lynch/lynch.html. See also Ina Ferris, "Bibliographic Romance: Bibliophilia and the Book-Object," *Romantic Circles*, https://www.rc.umd.edu/praxis/libraries/ferris/ferris.html; and Jon Klancher, *Transfiguring the Arts and Sciences: Knowledge and Cultural Authority in the Romantic Age* (New York: Cambridge University Press, 2013), 85–106.

69. *Ballads of Books*, ed. Brander Matthews (New York: George J. Coombes, 1887).

70. David Lodge, *Changing Places: A Tale of Two Campuses* (New York: Penguin, 1975), 135.

71. Garrett Stewart, *Dear Reader: The Conscripted Audience in Nineteenth-Century British Fiction* (Baltimore: Johns Hopkins University Press, 1996), 113–32; Brantlinger, *Reading Lesson*, 49–69; Andrew Burkett, "Mediating Monstrosity: Media, Information, and Mary Shelley's *Frankenstein*," *Studies in Romanticism* 51:4 (2012), 579–605; Michele Turner Sharp, "If It Be a Monster Birth: Reading and Literary Property in Mary Shelley's 'Frankenstein,'" *South Atlantic Review* 66:4 (2001), 70–93.

72. Mary Shelley, *The Last Man*, ed. Anne McWhir (Orchard Park, NY: Broadview, 1996), 367.

73. Michel de Certeau, *The Practice of Everyday Life*, trans. Steven Randall (Berkeley: University of California Press, 1984), 174.

74. Ralph Waldo Emerson, *Emerson in His Journals*, ed. Joel Porte (Cambridge, MA: Harvard University Press, 1982), 296.

75. Ralph Waldo Emerson, "Domestic Life," in *The Collected Works of Ralph Waldo Emerson*, vol. 7, *Society and Solitude*, ed. Ronald A. Bosco and Douglas Emory Wilson (Cambridge, MA: Harvard University Press, 2007), 54.

76. Ronald Zboray and Mary Zboray, "Nineteenth-Century Print Culture," in *The Oxford Handbook of Transcendentalism*, ed. Joel Myerson, Sandra Harbert Petrulionis, and Laura Dassow Walls (New York: Oxford University Press, 2010), 103.

77. Ralph Waldo Emerson, "Books" (1858), in *The Collected Works of Ralph Waldo Emerson*, vol. 2, *Essays: First Series*, ed. Joseph Slater, Alfred R. Ferguson, and Jean Ferguson Carr (Cambridge, MA: Harvard University Press, 1979), 99; "Spiritual Laws" (1841), in Ralph Waldo Emerson, *Essays and Lectures* (New York: Library of America, 1983), 317.

78. Ralph Waldo Emerson, "Progress of Culture," in *The Collected Works of Ralph Waldo Emerson*, vol. 8, *Letters and Social Aims*, ed. Ronald A. Bosco, Glen M. Johnson, and Joel Myerson (Cambridge, MA: Harvard University Press, 2010), 123.

79. Emerson to Carlyle, April 29, 1843, in *The Correspondence of Emerson and Carlyle*, ed. Joseph Slater (New York: Columbia University Press, 1964), 342–43. See also Barbara Packer, "Forgiving the Giver: Emerson, Carlyle, Thoreau," in *Emerson and Thoreau: Figures of Friendship*, ed. John Lysaker and William Rossi (Bloomington: Indiana University Press, 2010), 33–50.

80. Meredith McGill, *American Literature and the Culture of Reprinting, 1834–1853* (Philadelphia: University of Pennsylvania Press, 2002).

81. Ralph Waldo Emerson, "The American Scholar," in *Essays and Lectures*, 54, 55. Subsequent references to this volume cited parenthetically.

82. Robert Belknap, *The List: The Uses and Pleasures of Cataloguing* (New Haven, CT: Yale University Press, 2004), 36–72.

83. Walls, *Emerson's Life in Science*.

84. Emerson, "Books," 97. Subsequent references to this text cited parenthetically.

85. Jonathan Kramnick, *Making the English Canon: Print-Capitalism and the Cultural Past, 1700–1770* (Cambridge: Cambridge University Press, 1999).

86. Simon Eliot and Andrew Nash, "Mass Markets: Literature," in *The Cambridge History of the Book in Britain*, vol. 6, *1830–1914*, ed. David McKitterick (Cambridge: Cambridge University Press, 2009), esp. 439–42.

87. St. Clair, *Reading Nation in the Romantic Period*, 392.

88. Ronald J. Zboray, *A Fictive People: Antebellum Economic Development and the American Reading Public* (New York: Oxford University Press, 1993), esp. 3–16 (Putnam quoted page 3).

89. Thomas De Quincey, *Letters to a Young Man Whose Education Has Been Neglected, and Other Papers* (London: James Hogg and Sons, 1860), 44. W. P. Atkinson, *Books and Reading: A Lecture* (Boston: Crosby, Nichols, Lee, 1860), 7. William Gladstone, *On Books and the Housing of Them* (New York: Dodd, Mead, 1891), 6. William Mathews, *Hours with Men and Books* (Chicago: S. C. Griggs, 1877), 143.

90. Herman Melville, *Moby-Dick*, in *Redburn, White-Jacket, Moby-Dick* (New York: Library of America, 1983), 846. Thanks to Christopher Bartlett for pointing out this passage to me.

91. Francis Bacon, "Of Studies," in *The Essays* (New York: Penguin, 1986), 209.

92. James Elliot Cabot, *A Memoir of Ralph Waldo Emerson* (Cambridge, MA: Riverside, 1887), 292; Charles Woodbury, "Emerson's Talks with a College Boy," *Century Illustrated Monthly* 39 (London: T. Fisher Unwin, 1890), 622; Lawrence Buell, *Emerson* (Cambridge, MA: Harvard University Press, 2003), 201. See also Robert D. Richardson, *First We Read, Then We Write: Emerson on the Creative Process* (Iowa City: University of Iowa Press, 2009), esp. 7–18.

93. For speed reading in the late nineteenth century, see Dames, *Physiology of the Novel*, 207–46.

94. William Law Symonds, "The Cadmean Madness," *Atlantic Monthly*, September 1864, 271, 268, 272, 271, 281. For biographical information, see *The Life and Writings of William Law Symonds*, ed. William Winter (n.p.: Joseph W. Symonds, 1908), 17–41.

95. Wai Chee Dimock, *Through Other Continents: American Literature across Deep Time* (Princeton, NJ: Princeton University Press, 2006), 23–51.

96. *Parnassus*, ed. Ralph Waldo Emerson (Boston: Houghton, Mifflin, 1874), v.

97. Meredith McGill, comments at "Interacting with Print Symposium," Montreal, April 2016.

98. Emerson, *Emerson in His Journals*, 547.

99. Here I concur with Nancy Glazener's distinction between Coleridge's interpretive literary criticism and Emerson's more epigrammatic practices. See Glazener, *Literature in the Making: A History of U.S. Literary Culture in the Long Nineteenth Century* (New York: Oxford University Press, 2016), 114–15.

100. All quotes from "Address at the Opening of the Concord Free Public Library" appear in *The Complete Works of Ralph Waldo Emerson: Miscellanies*, 2nd ed., ed. Joel Myerson (Brooklyn, NY: AMS, 1979), 507–8.

101. Christopher Hanlon, *Emerson's Memory Loss: Originality, Communality, and the Late Style* (New York: Oxford University Press, 2018).

102. For Emerson's canonization, see Randall Fuller, *Emerson's Ghosts: Literature, Politics, and the Making of Americanists* (New York: Oxford University Press, 2007).

103. Emerson, *Essays and Lectures*, 59.

104. Ralph Waldo Emerson, "Quotation and Originality" (1868), in *Emerson's Prose and Poetry*, ed. Joel Porte and Saundra Morris (New York: W. W. Norton, 2001), 326.

105. Emerson's formulation (with "carry out") takes on a meme-like life after "The American Scholar," appearing in Google Books over 650 times between 1838 and 2013, often without reference to Emerson.

106. For Johnson as "fungible," see John Plotz, *Portable Property: Victorian Culture on the Move* (Princeton, NJ: Princeton University Press, 2008), 11.

107. Ellen Gruber Garvey, *Writing with Scissors: American Scrapbooks from the Civil War to the Harlem Renaissance* (New York: Oxford University Press, 2012).

108. Jay Grossman, *Reconstituting the American Renaissance: Emerson, Whitman, and the Politics of Representation* (Durham, NC: Duke University Press, 2003), 116–19.

109. Lawrence Rosenwald, *Emerson and the Art of the Diary* (Oxford: Oxford University Press, 1988), esp. 29–60.

110. *The Journals and Miscellaneous Notebooks of Ralph Waldo Emerson, 1838–1842*, ed. A. W. Plumstead and Harrison Hayford (Cambridge, MA: Harvard University Press, 1969), 302.

111. Blake Bronson-Bartlett, "From Loose Leaves to Readymades: Manuscript Books in the Age of Emerson and Whitman," *J19* 6 (2018), 259–84.

112. *The Journals and Miscellaneous Notebooks of Ralph Waldo Emerson, 1824–1838*, vol. 6, ed. W. H. Gilman (Cambridge, MA: Harvard University Press, 1966), 222; *The Journals and Miscellaneous Notebooks of Ralph Waldo Emerson, 1841–1843*, vol. 8, 23.

113. Cary Wolfe, "The Eye Is the First Circle: Emerson's 'Romanticism,' Cavell's Skepticism, Luhmann's Modernity," in *The Other Emerson*, ed. Branka Arsić and Cary Wolfe (Minneapolis: University of Minnesota Press, 2010), 271–300.

114. Rob Chodat, *The Matter of High Words: Naturalism, Normativity, and the Postwar Sage* (Oxford: Oxford University Press, 2017).

115. Paul Grimstad, *Experience and Experimental Writing: Literary Pragmatism from Emerson to the Jameses* (New York: Oxford University Press, 2013), 25.

116. Emerson, *Essays and Lectures*, 10.

117. Quoted in Ronald A. Bosco's "Historical Introduction" to *Letters and Social Aims*, clxii.

118. Ralph Waldo Emerson, *Emerson: Collected Poems and Translations*, ed. Harold Bloom and Paul Kane (New York: Library of America, 1994), 411.

119. Daniel Defoe, *The Farther Adventures of Robinson Crusoe* (1719; London: J. M. Dent, 1895), 167.

120. Ralph Waldo Emerson, "Experience," *Essays and Lectures*, 491.

121. Quoted in Darnton, *Case for Books*, xxii.

122. N. Katherine Hayles, *How We Became Posthuman: Virtual Bodies in Cybernetics, Literature, and Informatics* (Chicago: University of Chicago Press, 1999), 13; Plotz, *Portable Property*, xiv.

Chapter Two. Searching

1. Charles Dickens (with William Henry Wills), "The Doom of English Wills," *Household Words*, September 28, 1850, 211–12, 214, 217.

2. Michel Foucault, *The Order of Things: An Archaeology of the Human Sciences* (New York: Vintage, 1994), xv.

3. Claude E. Shannon, "The Mathematical Theory of Communication" (1948), in Claude E. Shannon and Warren Weaver, *The Mathematical Theory of Communication* (1949; Urbana: University of Illinois Press, 1963), 3.

4. N. Katherine Hayles, "The Materiality of Information," *Configurations* 1:1 (1993), 147–70; Alan Liu, *Local Transcendence: Essays on Postmodern Historicism and the Database* (Chicago: University of Chicago Press, 2008); Mark Gobles, *Beautiful Circuits: Modernism and the Mediated Life* (New York: Columbia University Press, 2010), esp. 225–44.

5. Leah Price, *How to Do Things with Books in Victorian Britain* (Princeton, NJ: Princeton University Press, 2012).

6. Andrew Piper, *Dreaming in Books: The Making of the Bibliographic Imagination in the Romantic Age* (Chicago: University of Chicago Press, 2009), 25.

7. Walter Benjamin, "Ninth Thesis on the Philosophy of History" (1940) and "The Storyteller: Reflections on the Works of Nikolai Leskov" (1936), in *Illuminations*, trans. Harry Zohn, ed. Hannah Arendt (New York: Schocken Books, 1968), 83–110, 196–209.

8. Lev Manovich, *The Language of New Media* (Cambridge: MIT Press, 2001). See also "Remapping Genre," ed. Wai Chee Dimock, special issue of *PMLA* 122:5 (October 2007), 1571–612 (respondents include Hayles, Jerome McGann, Meredith McGill, Jonathan Freedman, and Peter Stallybrass).

9. Ted Underwood, "Theorizing Research Practices We Forgot to Theorize Twenty Years Ago," *Representations* 127:1 (2014), 64–72. See also Alan Bilansky, "Search, Reading, and the Rise of Database," *Digital Scholarship in the Humanities* 32:3 (2017), 511–27; Max Kemman, Martijn Kleppe, and Stef Scagliola, "Just Google It—Digital Research Practices of Humanities Scholars," https://arxiv.org/abs/1309.2434; and Patrick Leary, "Googling the Victorians," *Journal of Victorian Culture* 10:1 (2005), 72–86. For work on searching Victorian archives (but not on Victorian searching methods themselves), see *Virtual Victorians: Networks,*

Connections, Technologies, ed. Veronica Alfano and Andrew Stauffer (New York: Palgrave Macmillan, 2015).

10. Herman Melville, "Hawthorne and His Mosses" (1850), in *Herman Melville: Pierre, Israel Potter, The Piazza Tales, The Confidence-Man, Uncollected Prose, Billy Budd, Sailor* (New York: Library of America, 1984), 1168.

11. See, for instance, Nicholas Carr, *The Shallows: What the Internet Is Doing to Our Brains* (New York: Norton, 2010); N. Katherine Hayles, "Hyper and Deep Attention: The Generational Divide in Cognitive Modes," *Profession*, 2007, 187–99.

12. Liu, *Local Transcendence*, 6.

13. Dominick LaCapra, "Ideology and Critique in Dickens's *Bleak House*," *Representations* 6 (Spring 1984), 116–23; D. A. Miller, "Under Capricorn," *Representations* 6 (Spring 1984), 124–29; Frederick Crews, "Whose American Renaissance," *New York Review of Books*, October 27, 1988, 68–77. For retrospection, see Catherine Gallagher and Stephen Greenblatt, *Practicing New Historicism* (Chicago: University of Chicago Press, 2000), 1–19; and Donald E. Pease, "9/11: When Was 'American Studies after the New Americanists'?," *boundary 2* 33:3 (Fall 2006), 73–101. Carolyn Porter, "History and Literature: 'After the New Historicism,'" *New Literary History* 21:2 (1990), 253–72; Brook Thomas, *The New Historicism and Other Old-Fashioned Topics* (Princeton, NJ: Princeton University Press, 1991). William James to Theodore Flournoy, March 26, 1907, *The Letters of William James*, vol. 2, ed. Henry James (Boston: Atlantic Monthly Press, 1920), 268.

14. Michael Warner, "Literary Studies and the History of the Book," *Book* 12 (July 1987), 5; Fredric Jameson, *Postmodernism; or, The Cultural Logic of Late Capitalism* (Durham, NC: Duke University Press, 1991), 190.

15. Hayden White, "New Historicism: A Comment," in *The New Historicism*, ed. H. Aram Veeser (New York: Routledge, 1989), 293–302; F. R. Ankersmit, "An Appeal from the New to the Old Historicists," *History and Theory* 42:2 (May 2003), 253–70. See also Thomas's *New Historicism and Other Old-Fashioned Topics*, which placed New Historicism within American historiographical traditions, as well as Stanley Fish, who called the New Historicism "merely another move in the practice of history as it has always been done" ("Commentary: The Young and the Restless," in *New Historicism*, 313).

16. Elizabeth Fox-Genovese, "Literary Criticism and the Politics of the New Historicism," in *New Historicism*, 213–24; Lynn Hunt, "History as Gesture: or, The Scandal of History," in *Consequences of Theory*, ed. Jonathan Arac and Barbara Johnson (Baltimore: Johns Hopkins University Press, 1991), 91–107; John H. Zammito, "Are We Being Theoretical Yet? The New Historicism, the New Philosophy of History, and 'Practicing Historians,'" *Journal of Modern History* 65:4 (1993), 783–814.

17. For a compatible formulation, see Stephen Ramsay, *Reading Machines: Toward an Algorithmic Criticism* (Champaign: University of Illinois Press, 2011): "The scientist is right to say that the plural of anecdote is not data, but in literary criticism an abundance of anecdote is precisely what allows discussion to move forward" (9).

18. Joel Fineman, "The History of the Anecdote: Fiction and Fiction," in *New Historicism*, 49–76; Gallagher and Greenblatt, *Practicing New Historicism*, 49–74.

19. Catherine Gallagher, *The Industrial Reformation of English Fiction: Social Discourse and Narrative Form, 1832–1867* (Chicago: University of Chicago Press, 1985)

(economics and procreation); Michael Paul Rogin, *Subversive Genealogy: The Politics and Art of Herman Melville* (New York: Knopf, 1983), 135–40 (sermons on King Ahab); Shirley Samuels, "The Identity of Slavery," in *The Culture of Sentiment: Race, Gender, and Sentimentality in Nineteenth-Century America*, ed. Shirley Samuels (Oxford: Oxford University Press, 1992), 157–71 (dolls); Walter Benn Michaels, *The Gold Standard and the Logic of Naturalism: American Literature at the Turn of the Century* (Berkeley: University of California Press, 1987) (monetary policy).

20. Walter Cohen, "Political Criticism of Shakespeare," in *Shakespeare Reproduced: The Text in History and Ideology*, ed. Jean E. Howard and Marion F. O'Connor (New York: Methuen, 1987), 34. Cohen quoted in Porter, "History and Literature: 'After the New Historicism,'" 261; and Thomas, *New Historicism and Other Old-Fashioned Topics*, 151.

21. Leary, "Googling the Victorians," 73.

22. Jonathan Gottschall, *Literature, Science, and a New Humanities* (New York: Palgrave Macmillan, 2008).

23. Sianne Ngai, "Merely Interesting," *Critical Inquiry* 34:4 (2008), 771–817; Stephen Burt, "Without Evidence," *PN Review 201* 38:1 (2011), 57–59; Franco Moretti, *Distant Reading* (New York: Verso, 2013).

24. Stanley Cavell, *The World Viewed: Reflections on the Ontology of Film* (Cambridge, MA: Harvard University Press, 1979), 9.

25. Barbara Herrnstein Smith, "Belief and Resistance: A Symmetrical Account," *Critical Inquiry* 18:1 (1991), 126.

26. Bruno Latour, "Why Has Critique Run Out of Steam? From Matters of Fact to Matters of Concern," *Critical Inquiry* 30 (Winter 2004), 239. See also Jennifer Fleissner, "Historicism Blues," *American Literary History* 25:4 (2013), 699–717.

27. Jean Fagan Yellin, "Hawthorne and the American National Sin," in *The Green American Tradition: Essays and Poems for Sherman Paul*, ed. H. Daniel Peck (Baton Rouge: Louisiana State University Press, 1989), 75–97; F. O. Matthiessen, *American Renaissance: Art and Expression in the Age of Emerson and Whitman* (Oxford: Oxford University Press, 1941), 275–81; Michael Colacurcio, "'Such Ancestors': The Spirit of History in *The Scarlet Letter*," introduction to Nathaniel Hawthorne, *The Scarlet Letter* (Cambridge, MA: Harvard University Press, 2009), esp. xxxii. See also Laura Korobkin, "The Scarlet Letter of the Law: Hawthorne and Criminal Justice," NOVEL (Winter 1997), 193–217.

28. Jonathan Arac, "The Politics of *The Scarlet Letter*," in *Ideology and Classic American Literature*, ed. Sacvan Bercovitch and Myra Jehlen (Cambridge: Cambridge University Press, 1986), 262; Sacvan Bercovitch, *The Office of the Scarlet Letter* (Baltimore: Johns Hopkins University Press, 1991), 87–112.

29. Jay Grossman, "'A' Is for Abolition? Race, Authorship, *The Scarlet Letter*," *Textual Practice* 7:1 (Spring 1993), 13–30. See also Teresa Goddu, "Letters Turned to Gold: Hawthorne, Authorship, and Slavery," *Studies in American Fiction* 29:1 (Spring 2001), 49–76.

30. William Yates, "Slavery and Colored People in Delaware," *Colored American*, August 12, 1837, n.p.

31. "Ministers of the Gospel," *Liberator*, July 26, 1839, 4.

32. Peter Tosh, "Babylon Queendom," on *Equal Rights*, Columbia Records, 1977, http://lyrics.wikia.com/wiki/Peter_Tosh:Babylon_Queendom; Eddie Glaude

Jr., *Exodus! Religion, Race, and Nation in Early Nineteenth-Century Black America* (Chicago: University of Chicago Press, 2000).

33. Liu, *Local Transcendence*, 258–62.

34. Jacques Derrida, *Archive Fever: A Freudian Impression*, trans. Eric Prenowitz (Chicago: University of Chicago Press, 1995), 15–17; Derrida quoted in Michael Naas, *The End of the World and Other Teachable Moments: Jacques Derrida's Final Seminar* (New York: Fordham University Press, 2015), 125; McGann, Hayles, and McGill's comments appear in *PMLA* 122:5 (October 2007), 1588–96, 1603–8.

35. Franco Moretti, *Graphs, Maps, Trees: Abstract Models for a Literary History* (New York: Verso, 2005), 9.

36. For electronic database searches as testing but not initiating critical intuitions, see Susan Hockey, *Electronic Texts in the Humanities: Principles and Practice* (Oxford: Oxford University Press, 2000), 75.

37. Nathaniel Hawthorne, *The Scarlet Letter* (New York: Library of America, 1990), 117. Subsequent references to this volume cited parenthetically.

38. Gallagher and Greenblatt, *Practicing New Historicism*, 15–16.

39. Charles Peirce, "On the Logic of Drawing History from Ancient Documents, Especially from Testimonies" (1906), in *The Essential Peirce: Selected Philosophical Writings*, vol. 2, *1893–1913*, ed. Nathan Houser et al. (Bloomington: Indiana University Press, 1998), 79, 106–9.

40. Michael Colacurcio, *The Province of Piety: Moral History in Hawthorne's Early Tales* (Cambridge, MA: Harvard University Press, 1984), 1; James Chandler, *England in 1819: The Politics of Literary Culture and the Case of Romantic Historicism* (Chicago: University of Chicago Press, 1998).

41. Patricia Crain, *The Story of A: The Alphabetization of America from* The New England Primer *to* The Scarlet Letter (Stanford, CA: Stanford University Press, 2003), 79–83.

42. Joseph Felt, *Annals of Salem*, vol. 2, 2nd ed. (Salem, MA: W. and S. B. Ives, 1849), 13–14.

43. Nathaniel Hawthorne, preface to the 1851 edition of *Twice-Told Tales*, in *Selected Tales and Sketches*, ed. Hyatt H. Waggoner (New York: Holt, Rinehart, and Winston, 1950), 584. For marginalization, see Michael Gilmore, *American Romanticism and the Marketplace* (Chicago: University of Chicago Press, 1985), 71–112. For savvy, see Meredith McGill, *American Literature and the Culture of Reprinting, 1834–1853* (Philadelphia: University of Pennsylvania Press, 2003), 218–69; Richard Brodhead, *The School of Hawthorne* (Oxford: Oxford University Press, 1986); and Joseph Rezek, *London and the Making of Provincial Literature: Aesthetics and the Transatlantic Book Trade, 1800–1850* (Philadelphia: University of Pennsylvania Press, 2015), 185–98.

44. Nathaniel Hawthorne, "The Old Manse," in *Selected Tales and Sketches*, 569, 570.

45. Ibid., 570.

46. See, for instance, John Carlos Rowe, "The Internal Conflict of Romantic Narrative: Hegel's Phenomenology and Hawthorne's *The Scarlet Letter*," *MLN* 95:5 (1980), 1203–31.

47. Chad Wellmon, *Organizing Enlightenment: Information Overload and the Invention of the Modern Research University* (Baltimore: Johns Hopkins University Press, 2015).

48. Immanuel Kant, "An Answer to the Question: What Is Enlightenment" (1784), in *The Cambridge Edition of the Works of Immanuel Kant: Practical Philosophy*, ed. and trans. Mary J. Gregor (Cambridge: Cambridge University Press, 1996), 11–22; Max Weber, *The Theory of Social and Economic Organization*, trans. A. M. Henderson and Talcott Parsons (New York: Free Press, 1947).

49. McGill, *American Literature and the Culture of Reprinting*, 233–41.

50. Peter West, *The Arbiters of Reality: Hawthorne, Melville, and the Rise of Mass Information Culture* (Columbus: Ohio State University Press, 2008), 42–68.

51. Nathaniel Hawthorne, "The Devil in Manuscript," in *Tales and Sketches* (New York: Library of America, 1982), 330, 332, 337.

52. George Foster, *New York in Slices: By an Experienced Carver* (New York: W. F. Burgess, 1849), 40. Joel Ross, *What I Saw in New-York: or, A Bird's Eye View of City Life* (Auburn, NY: Derby and Miller, 1851), 144–45. See also Brian P. Luskey, "Special Marts: Intelligence Offices, Labor Commodification, and Emancipation in Nineteenth-Century America," *Journal of the Civil War Era* 3:3 (2013), 360–91. For how intelligence offices gave laborers access to information, see Vanessa H. May, *Unprotected Labor: Household Workers, Politics, and Middle-Class Reform in New York, 1870–1940* (Chapel Hill: University of North Carolina Press, 2011), 24–26, 60–63.

53. Ralph Waldo Emerson, *Essays and Lectures* (New York: Library of America, 1983), 221.

54. Nathaniel Hawthorne, "The Intelligence Office," in *Tales and Sketches* (New York: Library of America, 1982), 873, 875.

55. Ibid., 882, 883, 884.

56. Hsuan L. Hsu, "Counting On: Hendiadys and the Mathematical Sublime in *The Marble Faun*," *CEA Critic* 64:2–3 (2002), 47–62; Reed Gochberg, *Novel Objects: Museums and Scientific Knowledge in Nineteenth-Century American Literature* (PhD diss., Boston University, 2016).

57. For Hawthorne defending his customhouse work, see Stephen Nussbaum, "The Firing of Nathaniel Hawthorne," *Essex Institute Historical Collections* 114 (1978), 57–86; and Bryce Traister, "The Bureaucratic Origins of *The Scarlet Letter*," *Studies in American Fiction* 29:1 (2001), 77–92. Studies of antebellum civil service tend to focus solely on political controversies over the spoils system rather than on the bureaucratic challenge of managing information: William E. Nelson, *The Roots of American Bureaucracy, 1830–1900* (Cambridge, MA: Harvard University Press, 1982), 9–40; Brian J. Cook, *Bureaucracy and Self-Government: Reconsidering the Role of Public Administration in American Politics* (Baltimore: Johns Hopkins University Press, 1996), 49–64.

58. "Mr. Dickens's Romance of a Dust-Heap," *Eclectic and Congregational Review*, November 1865, 475.

59. George Henry Lewes, "Dickens in Relation to Criticism," *Fortnightly Review*, February 1, 1872, 151.

60. Jay Clayton, *Charles Dickens in Cyberspace: The Afterlife of the Nineteenth Century in Postmodern Culture* (Oxford: Oxford University Press, 2003), 1; Richard Menke, *Telegraphic Realism: Victorian Fiction and Other Information Systems* (Stanford, CA: Stanford University Press, 2008), 1; Kevin McLaughlin, *Paperwork: Fiction and Mass Mediacy in the Paper Age* (Philadelphia: University of Pennsylvania Press,

2005), 80; Juliet Johns, *Dickens and Mass Culture* (Oxford: Oxford University Press, 2010), 8.

61. Daniel Hack, *The Material Interests of the Victorian Novel* (Charlottesville: University of Virginia Press, 2005), 38; Price, *How to Do Things with Books*; McGill, *American Literature and the Culture of Reprinting*, esp. 132–40. For additional work on Dickens and textual excess, see Robert L. Patten, *Charles Dickens and His Publishers* (Oxford: Oxford University Press, 1978); David Vincent, "Dickens's Reading Public," in *Palgrave Advances in Charles Dickens Studies*, ed. John Bowen and Robert L. Patten (New York: Palgrave Macmillan, 2006), 176–97; Patrick Brantlinger, *The Reading Lesson: The Threat of Mass Literacy in Nineteenth-Century British Fiction* (Bloomington: Indiana University Press, 1998), 69–91; and Andrew Stauffer, "Ruins of Paper: Dickens and the Necropolitan Library," *Erudit: Romanticism and Victorianism on the Net* 47 (August 2007), https://www.erudit.org/en/journals/ravon/2007-n47-ravon1893/016700ar/.

62. Sean Grass, *Charles Dickens's* Our Mutual Friend: *A Publishing History* (Farnham, UK: Ashgate, 2014), 102–4.

63. Charles Dickens, *The Pickwick Papers*, ed. James Kinsley (Oxford: Oxford University Press, 2008), 1. Subsequent references to this volume cited parenthetically.

64. Richard Altick, *The English Common Reader: A Social History of the Mass Reading Public, 1800–1900* (Chicago: University of Chicago Press, 1957), esp. 279, 291.

65. Charles Dickens, *Martin Chuzzlewit*, ed. Margaret Cardwell (Oxford: Oxford University Press, 1982), 64.

66. Devin Griffiths, "The Radical's Catalogue: Antonio Panizzi, Virginia Woolf, and the British Museum Library's *Catalogue of Printed Books*," *Book History* 18 (2015), 134–65.

67. J. Hillis Miller, introduction to Charles Dickens, *Bleak House*, ed. Norman Page (New York: Penguin, 2003), 11.

68. D. A. Miller, *The Novel and the Police* (Berkeley: University of California Press, 1988), 67.

69. Dickens, *Bleak House*, 922, 615.

70. Ibid., 921.

71. Clay Shirky, "Ontology Is Overrated: Categories, Links, and Tags," http://www.shirky.com/writings/ontology_overrated.html?goback=.gde_1838701_member_179729766.

72. Dickens, *Bleak House*, 757–76.

73. Charles Dickens, "A Detective Police Party" (1850), in *Dickens' Journalism*, vol. 2, *"The Amusements of the People" and Other Papers: Reports, Essays and Reviews, 1834–51*, ed. Michael Slater (London: Dent, 1996), 269.

74. Franco Moretti, "Network Theory, Plot Analysis," *New Left Review* 68 (2011), 80–102; Jonathan H. Grossman, *Charles Dickens's Networks: Public Transport and the Novel* (Oxford: Oxford University Press, 2012); Anna Gibson, "*Our Mutual Friend* and Network Form," *Novel* 48:1 (May 2015), 63–84; Caroline Levine, *Forms: Whole, Rhythm, Hierarchy, Network* (Princeton, NJ: Princeton University Press, 2015), esp. 112–31.

75. R. H. Horne, "Dust; or Ugliness Redeemed," *Household Words*, July 13, 1850, 380.

76. Charles Dickens, *Our Mutual Friend*, ed. Michael Cotsell (Oxford: Oxford University Press, 1989), 49–50. Subsequent references to this volume cited parenthetically.

77. George Eliot, *Middlemarch* (New York: Barnes and Noble Classics, 2003), 24.

78. Johns, *Dickens and Mass Culture*, 1–10.

79. For the composition and reception of *Our Mutual Friend*, including reprinted reviews, see Grass, *Charles Dickens's* Our Mutual Friend.

80. Hannah More, *The Works of Hannah More*, vol. 3, *Containing Strictures on the Modern System of Female Education* (London: Henry G. Bohn, 1853), 118; Lydia Sigourney, *Letters to Young Ladies*, 3rd ed. (New York: Harper and Brothers, 1837), 137, 146.

81. Toni Weller, "The Puffery and Practicality of Etiquette Books: A New Take on Victorian Information Culture," *Library Trends* 62:3 (2014), 663–80.

82. Price, *How to Do Things with Books*, 97. See also *Literary Secretaries/Secretarial Culture*, ed. Leah Price and Pamela Thurschwell (Burlington, VT: Ashgate, 2005).

83. Kate Flint, *The Woman Reader, 1837–1914* (Oxford: Oxford University Press, 1993), esp. 163–83; Susan P. Casteras, "Reader, Beware: Representations of the Victorian Female and Books," *Nineteenth-Century Gender Studies* 3:1 (2007). See also James W. Cortada, *All the Facts: A History of Information in the United States since 1870* (Oxford: Oxford University Press, 2016), 49–67.

84. Eric Naiman, "When Dickens Met Dostoevsky," *Times Literary Supplement*, April 10, 2013, https://www.the-tls.co.uk/articles/public/when-dickens-met-dostoevsky/. For simultaneous reading, see Johns, *Dickens and Mass Culture*, 1–10.

85. Michael Slater, *Charles Dickens* (New Haven, CT: Yale University Press, 2009), 228, 230.

86. Benjamin Disraeli, *Sybil, or The Two Nations*, ed. Thom Braun (New York: Penguin, 1980), 308, 486.

87. Herman Melville, *Moby-Dick*, in *Redburn, White-Jacket, Moby-Dick* (New York: Library of America, 1983), 1165.

88. See, for instance, "The Woman in White," *Saturday Review*, August 25, 1860, 249–50; "Wilkie Collins," *Illustrated Review*, July, 1873, 29–37; and "Recent Popular Novels," *Dublin University Magazine*, February, 1861, esp. 200.

89. Eliot, *Middlemarch*, 469. For *Middlemarch*'s desire to circumscribe interpretation under conditions of mass print, see Elaine Freedgood, *The Ideas in Things: Fugitive Meaning in the Victorian Novel* (Chicago: University of Chicago Press, 2006), 111–39. For Eliot and the circulation of information, see Alexander Welsh, *George Eliot and Blackmail* (Cambridge, MA: Harvard University Press, 1985).

90. Yuval Noah Harari, *Sapiens: A Brief History of Humankind* (New York: HarperCollins, 2015), 119–26.

91. Ann Blair, *Too Much to Know: Managing Scholarly Information before the Modern Age* (New Haven, CT: Yale University Press, 2011). See also Roger Chartier, *The Order of Books* (Stanford, CA: Stanford University Press, 1992); Peter Stallybrass, "Navigating the Bible: Books and Scrolls," in *Books and Readers in Early Modern England: Material Studies*, ed. Jennifer Anderson and Elizabeth Sauer (Philadelphia: University of Pennsylvania Press, 2002), 42–79.

92. Jon Klancher, *Transfiguring the Arts and Sciences: Knowledge and Cultural Authority in the Romantic Age* (New York: Cambridge University Press, 2013), 85–98; Robert Darnton, "What Is the History of Books," *Daedalus* (Summer 1982), 65–83;

Geoffrey Nunberg, "Farewell to the Information Age," in *The Future of the Book*, ed. Geoffrey Nunberg (Berkeley: University of California Press, 1996), 115.

93. William Frederick Poole, *An Index to Periodical Literature* (New York: Charles Norton, 1853), v.

94. Wellmon, *Ordering the Enlightenment*; quotations are from reviews of Thomas Frognall Dibdin's *The Bibliomania; or Book-Madness; Containing Some Account of the History, Symptoms and Cure of this Fatal Disease* (1809), quoted in Ina Ferris, "Bibliographic Romance: Bibliophilia and the Book-Object," *Romantic Circles*, https://www.rc.umd.edu/praxis/libraries/ferris/ferris.html. For complaints about the informationalism of encyclopedists, see William Hazlitt, "On Genius and Common Sense," in *Table-Talk, or, Original Essays* (London: John Warren, 1821), esp. 104–8.

95. William Thoms, n.t., *Notes and Queries* 1:1 (November 1849), 1–2; W. D., "Useful versus Useless Learning," *Notes and Queries* 2:49 (October 5, 1850), 293.

96. Noah Heringman, *Sciences of Antiquity: Romantic Antiquarianism, Natural History, and Knowledge Work* (Oxford: Oxford University Press, 2013).

97. Anthony Grafton, *The Footnote: A Curious History* (Cambridge, MA: Harvard University Press, 1997), esp. 35–39; Andrew Piper, *Book Was There: Reading in Electronic Times* (Chicago: University of Chicago Press, 2012), 20.

98. Emerson, *Essays and Lectures*, 716–17.

99. Friedrich Nietzsche, *Untimely Meditations*, ed. Daniel Breazeale (1876; New York: Cambridge University Press, 1997), 57–124.

100. "Notes and Queries: 'When Found, Make a Note Of,'" *Literary World*, June 28, 1851, 515.

101. Merton M. Sealts Jr., *Melville's Reading: Revised and Enlarged Edition* (Columbia: University of South Carolina Press, 1966), 193.

102. Melville, *Moby-Dick*, 782.

103. Henry Chorley, *London Athenaeum*, October 25, 1851, 1112.

104. Evert A. Duyckinck, review of *Moby-Dick*, *Literary World*, November 22, 1851, 403–4.

105. Samuel Otter, "Reading *Moby-Dick*," *The New Cambridge Companion to Herman Melville*, ed. Robert S. Levine (New York: Cambridge University Press, 2014), 70.

106. George Frederick Holmes, "Present Condition of Letters," *Southern Literary Messenger*, November 1844, 673.

107. John Ward Dean, "Preface," *Historical Magazine, and Notes and Queries concerning the Antiquities, History, and Biography of America*, December 1857, iii.

108. Nancy Glazener, *Literature in the Making: A History of U.S. Literary Culture in the Long Nineteenth Century* (New York: Oxford University Press, 2016).

109. Michel Foucault, "Nietzsche, Genealogy, History" (1971), in *The Foucault Reader*, ed. Paul Rabinow (New York: Pantheon, 1984), 76.

110. "The Manifesto of the V21 Collective" (2015), http://v21collective.org/manifesto-of-the-v21-collective-ten-theses/.

111. Quoted in Grafton, *Footnote*, 39.

112. For biographical information on Bartlett, see Michael Hancher, "Familiar Quotations," *Harvard Library Bulletin* 14:2 (Summer 2003), 13–53.

113. John Bartlett, [List: of books read: manuscript], Houghton Library, Harvard University (c. 1900).

114. Blair, *Too Much to Know*; Leah Price, *The Anthology and the Rise of the Novel: From Richardson to George Eliot* (Cambridge: Cambridge University Press, 2000), 5. Altick, *English Common Reader*, 44. For poetic extracts in the nineteenth century, see Glazener, *Literature in the Making*, 27–29. See also Alexandra Socarides, "Making and Unmaking a Canon: American Women's Poetry and the Nineteenth-Century Anthology," in *A History of Nineteenth-Century American Women's Poetry*, ed. Jennifer Putzi and Alexandra Socarides (New York: Cambridge University Press, 2017), 186–202.

115. Sarah Josepha Hale, *A Complete Dictionary of Poetical Quotations Comprising the Most Excellent and Appropriate Passages in the Old British Poets; with Choice and Copious Selections from the Best Modern British and American Poets* (1849; Philadelphia: J. B. Lippincott, 1860), n.p.; Isabella Rushton Preston, *Handbook of Familiar Quotations, Chiefly from English Authors* (London: John Murray, 1853), vii.

116. John Bartlett, "Mr. Bartlett's and Mr. Friswell's Familiar Quotations," *Nation*, February 7, 1867, 115.

117. John Bartlett, *A Collection of Familiar Quotations: With Complete Indices of Authors and Subjects* (Cambridge, MA: John Bartlett, 1855), iii; John Bartlett, *A Collection of Familiar Quotations: With Complete Indices of Authors and Subjects* (Cambridge, MA: John Bartlett, 1856), iii.

118. R.G.W., "Familiar Quotations," *Galaxy*, October 1868, 571.

119. John Bartlett, *Familiar Quotations* (1856), iii.

120. Nancy Bentley, *Frantic Panoramas: American Literature and Mass Culture, 1870–1920* (Philadelphia: University of Pennsylvania, 2009).

121. *Familiar Quotations*, ed. John Bartlett (Boston: Little, Brown, 1863), v.

122. Ellen Gruber Garvey, *Writing with Scissors: American Scrapbooks from the Civil War to the Harlem Renaissance* (Oxford: Oxford University Press, 2013).

123. E. D. Hirsch Jr., *Cultural Literacy: What Every American Needs to Know* (New York: Houghton Mifflin, 1987), xiii–xiv.

124. Quoted in Blair, *Too Much to Know*, 254.

125. More, *Works of Hannah More*, vol. 3, *Containing Strictures on the Modern System of Female Education*, 119.

126. "Objectionable Books," *Blackwood's Edinburgh Magazine*, February 1859, 164–65.

127. Charlotte Brontë, *Villette* (New York: Barnes and Noble Books, 2005), 398.

128. Price, *Anthology and the Rise of the Novel*, 2; Ralph Waldo Emerson, "Quotation and Originality" (1868), in *Emerson's Prose and Poetry*, ed. Joel Porte and Saundra Morris (New York: W. W. Norton, 2001), 326. According to one remembrance, Emerson once advised a college student to burn his literary compendia (Charles Woodbury, "Emerson's Talks with a College Boy," *Century Illustrated Monthly* 39 [London: T. Fisher Unwin, 1890], 621–22).

129. Sarah Morgan, *The Civil War Diary of a Southern Woman*, ed. Charles East (New York: Simon and Schuster, 1991), 575. Thanks to Julia Nitz for this reference.

130. "The College Boy's Oration," *Puck*, May 28, 1890, 213.

131. Michael David Cohen, "Bartlett's Familiar Quotations: 'A Glancing Bird's Eye View' by a 'Morbid Scholiast,'" *Harvard Library Bulletin* 14:2 (Summer 2003), 55–74. Cohen also notes how *Bartlett's* in the twentieth century becomes more committed to

quotes that are not only familiar but also interesting; Jeanette Gilder, "The Lounger," *Critic*, March 1906, 206.

132. Edith Wharton, *The Custom of the Country* (New York: Charles Scribner's Sons, 1914), 550.

133. Bentley, *Frantic Panoramas*, 57.

134. *Choice Thoughts from Shakespeare*, ed. John Bartlett (London: Whittaker, 1861), v.

135. John Bartlett, *New and Complete Concordance, or Verbal Index to Words, Phrases, and Passages in the Dramatic Works of Shakespeare* (London: Macmillan, 1894), n.p. A similar lack of aesthetic commentary is evident in Bartlett's 123-word preface to the 1,034-page *The Shakespeare Phrase Book* (Boston: Little, Brown, 1880).

136. "Books and Authors: Bartlett's Shakespeare Concordance," *Outlook*, August 17, 1895, 267.

Chapter Three. Counting

1. Johanna Drucker, "What Distant Reading Isn't," *PMLA* 132:3 (2017), 632.

2. Theodore Porter, *Trust in Numbers: The Pursuit of Objectivity in Science and Public Life* (Princeton, NJ: Princeton University Press, 1995), 49, 74. See also Thomas Kuhn's claim that "after science has become thoroughly technical, particularly mathematically technical, its role as a force of intellectual history becomes relatively insignificant" ("The Relations between History and the History of Science," *Daedalus* 100 [1977], 277).

3. Rita Felski, *The Uses of Literature* (Oxford: Blackwell, 2008), 51–76; Nancy Bentley, "Introduction," "The Spirit of the Thing: Critique as Enchantment," forum in *J19* 1:1 (2013), 147–53; Christopher Castiglia, "Twists and Turns," in *Turns of Event: Nineteenth-Century American Literary Studies in Motion*, ed. Hester Blum (Philadelphia: University of Pennsylvania Press, 2016), esp. 70.

4. Felski, *Uses of Literature*, 53–54.

5. Philip Fisher, *Wonder, the Rainbow, and the Aesthetics of Rare Experience* (Cambridge, MA: Harvard University Press, 1998), 131.

6. Jane Bennett, *The Enchantment of Modern Life: Attachments, Crossings, and Ethics* (Princeton, NJ: Princeton University Press, 2001); Simon During, *Modern Enchantments: The Cultural Power of Secular Magic* (Cambridge, MA: Harvard University Press, 2002), esp. 14–27.

7. Max Weber, "Science as a Vocation," in *From Max Weber: Essays in Sociology*, ed. and trans. H. H. Gerth and C. Wright Mills (New York: Routledge, 2009), 155, 139. For a similar view of Weber, see Felski, *Uses of Literature*, 59.

8. Gilbert German, *A Discourse on Disenchantment: Reflections on Politics and Technology* (Albany: State University of New York Press, 1993), 26–30. See also Bennett, *Enchantment of Modern Life*, 57–65.

9. Weber, "Science as a Vocation," 135–36; Max Weber, *The Protestant Ethic and the "Spirit" of Capitalism and Other Writings*, ed. and trans. Peter Baehr and Gordon C. Wells (New York: Penguin Books, 2002), 23.

10. Max Horkheimer and Theodor Adorno, *Dialectic of Enlightenment*, trans. John Cumming (1944; New York: Continuum, 1969), 6; Walter Benjamin, "The Storyteller:

Reflections on the Works of Nikolai Leskov" (1936), in *Illuminations*, trans. Harry Zohn, ed. Hannah Arendt (New York: Schocken Books, 1968), esp. 89.

11. Michel Foucault, *The Order of Things: An Archaeology of the Human Sciences* (New York: Vintage, 1994), xvi.

12. Michael Saler, "Modernity and Enchantment: A Historiographic Review," *American Historical Review* 111 (2006), 692–716.

13. Jane Bennett, *Vibrant Matter: A Political Ecology of Things* (Durham, NC: Duke University Press, 2010), 63.

14. For juvenile nostalgia and adventure fiction in general, see Joseph Bristow, *Empire Boys: Adventures in a Man's World* (London: HarperCollins, 1991), esp. 127–69.

15. For the stubborn presence of adult content and control in children's literature, see Marah Gubar, *Artful Dodgers: Reconceiving the Golden Age of Children's Literature* (Oxford: Oxford University Press, 2009); and Jacqueline Rose, *The Case of Peter Pan, or The Impossibility of Children's Fiction* (Philadelphia: University of Pennsylvania Press, 1984). For the ideology of adventure novels, see (among others) Diane Loxley, *Problematic Shores: The Literature of Islands* (New York: St. Martin's, 1990); Bristow, *Empire Boys*; and Louis Chude-Sokei, *The Sound of Culture: Diaspora and Black Technopoetics* (Middletown, CT: Wesleyan University Press, 2016), 100–27.

16. Kenneth Grahame, *The Golden Age* (New York: John Lane, 1906), 215.

17. Mary Poovey, *Genres of the Credit Economy: Mediating Value in Eighteenth- and Nineteenth-Century Britain* (Chicago: University of Chicago Press, 2008), and *A History of the Modern Fact: Problems of Knowledge in the Sciences of Wealth and Society* (Chicago: University of Chicago Press, 1998).

18. An accessible overview is I. B. Cohen's *The Triumph of Numbers: How Counting Shaped Modern Life* (New York: Norton, 2005).

19. J. L. Heilbron, "Introductory Essay," in *The Quantifying Spirit in the 18th Century*, ed. Tore Frängsmyr, J. L. Heilbron, and Robin E. Rider (Berkeley: University of California Press, 1990), 1–25; Ian Hacking, *The Taming of Chance* (Cambridge: Cambridge University Press, 1990), 2. See also Theodore Porter, *The Rise of Statistical Thinking, 1820–1900* (Princeton, NJ: Princeton University Press, 1986); Patricia Cline Cohen, *A Calculating People: The Spread of Numeracy in Early America* (Chicago: University of Chicago Press, 1982).

20. Andrew Piper, *Book Was There: Reading in Electronic Times* (Chicago: University of Chicago Press, 2012), 131–33.

21. Friedrich Kittler, "Number and Numeral," *Theory, Culture, and Society* 23:7–8 (2016), 51–61.

22. William Dean Howells, *Literature and Life* (New York: Harper and Brothers, 1902), 12.

23. *The Portable Mark Twain*, ed. Bernard De Voto (New York: Penguin Books, 1977), 541.

24. Gubar, *Artful Dodgers*. See also Steven Mintz, *Huck's Raft: A History of American Childhood* (Cambridge, MA: Harvard University Press, 2014).

25. [Elizabeth Rigby], "Early Lessons," *Quarterly Review* 74 (June 1844), 1–2; Charlotte Yonge, "Children's Literature of the Last Century," *Macmillan's Magazine*, July 1869, 229.

26. Yonge, "Children's Literature of the Last Century," 237.

27. Matthew Grenby, *The Child Reader, 1700–1840* (Cambridge: Cambridge University Press, 2011); Kate Douglas Wiggin, *Children's Rights: A Book of Nursery Logic* (Boston: Houghton, Mifflin, 1892), 79.

28. See especially Twain's "The Story of the Bad Little Boy" (1875) and "The Story of the Good Little Boy" (1875), in *Sketches: New and Old* (Hartford: American, 1893), 37–51.

29. Gretchen R. Galbraith, *Reading Lives: Reading Childhood, Books, and Schools in Britain, 1870–1920* (New York: St. Martin's, 1997), esp. 45–47.

30. "Contemporary Literature," *Blackwood's*, August 1879, 253.

31. James Russell Lowell, *A Fable for Critics*, in *Poems*, vol. 3 (Boston: Houghton, Mifflin, 1891), 22.

32. For quantitative tracking of literacy in the 1830s and 1840s, see Stephen Colclough and David Vincent, "Reading," in *The Cambridge History of the Book in Britain*, vol. 6, *1830–1914*, ed. David McKitterick (Cambridge: Cambridge University Press, 2009), 284–85, 297–99.

33. Charles Dickens, *The Works of Charles Dickens*, vol. 27, *Sketches by Boz*, ed. Andrew Lang (New York: Charles Scribner's Sons, 1900), 364–65.

34. Charles Henry Timperley, *The Dictionary of Printers and Printing, with the Progress of Literature* (London: H. Johnson, 1839), 957.

35. For the numbering impulse in children's literature and its industry, see Seth Lerer, *Children's Literature: A Reader's History, from Aesop to Harry Potter* (Chicago: University of Chicago Press, 2008), 4–8.

36. For guides to reading, see Philip Waller, *Writers, Readers, and Reputations: Literary Life in Britain, 1870–1918* (Oxford: Oxford University Press, 2006), 68–115; Kate Flint, *The Woman Reader, 1837–1914* (Oxford: Oxford University Press, 1993), 84–91; David McKitterick, "Organising Knowledge in Print," in *The Cambridge History of the Book in Britain*, vol. 6, 552–53.

37. Frederic Harrison, *The Choice of Books and Other Literary Pieces* (New York: Macmillan, 1899), 1–3.

38. Waller, *Writers, Readers, and Reputations*, 68–72; Donald Foster, "100 Best Books," *Renaissance Quarterly* 8:1 (Fall 1968), 20–22; Clare Hutton, "'The Promise of Literature in the Coming Days': The Best Hundred Irish Books Controversy of 1886," *Victorian Literature and Culture* 39:2 (2001), 581–92.

39. John Lubbock, *The Choice of Books* (Philadelphia: Henry Altemus, 1896), 9.

40. Ryan Cordell, "Reprinting, Circulation, and the Network Author in Antebellum Newspapers," *American Literary History* 27:3 (2015), 417–45.

41. "Gossip," in *Progress*, vol. 6 (London: Progressive, 1886), 91. For an early retrospective on the mania for best book lists, see Edmund Gosse, "The Best Books," *Lippincott's Monthly Magazine*, December 1901, 737–43.

42. Jay Hubbell synopsizes a number of late nineteenth-century polls in *Who Are the Major American Writers? A Study of the Changing Literary Canon* (Durham, NC: Duke University Press, 1972), 80–90. The earliest example I have found is Clara E. Laughlin's "American Literature" from *Interior* (August 10, 1893, 8–9), in a which a reader poll renders the following rankings of best books by number of votes:

Emerson's Essays—512

Hawthorne's "The Scarlet Letter"—493
Longfellow's Poems—444
Stowe's "Uncle Tom's Cabin"—434
Holmes' "Autocrat at the Breakfast Table"—388
Irving's "Sketchbook"—307
Lowell's Poems—269
Whittier's Poems—256
Wallace's "Ben Hur"—250
Motley's "Rise of the Dutch Republic"—246. (8)

After the results were published, some readers complained about the absence of Poe.

43. Edward Dowden, "The Interpretation of Literature," *Contemporary Review*, May 1886, 701.

44. Robert E. Belknap, *The List: The Uses and Pleasures of Cataloguing* (New Haven, CT: Yale University Press, 2004); Umberto Eco, *The Infinity of Lists*, trans. Alastair McEwen (New York: Rizzoli, 2009), esp. 17.

45. "The Best Hundred Books for Boys," *Pall Mall Budget*, June 24, 1886, 13.

46. George Hardy, *Five Hundred Books for the Young: A Graded and Annotated List* (New York: Charles Scribner's Sons, 1892), 16.

47. Edward Salmon, *Juvenile Literature as It Is* (London: Henry J. Drane, 1888), 9, 12.

48. "Current Educational Topics," *Public-School Journal*, May 1897, 517-19.

49. Kathleen McDowell, "Toward a History of Children as Readers, 1890-1930," *Book History* 12 (2009), 240-65. See also Flint, *Woman Reader*, 155-62.

50. Leslie Butler, *Critical Americans: Victorian Intellectuals and Transatlantic Liberal Reform* (Chapel Hill: University of North Carolina Press, 2007), 153-64.

51. Nicholas Dames, *The Physiology of the Novel* (Oxford: Oxford University Press, 2007), 37-48; Thomas Carlyle, *Sartor Resartus: The Life and Opinions of Herr Teufelsdröckh* (1834; London: Chapman and Hall, 1904), 53; John Dewey, *Art as Experience* (1934; New York, Perigee, 1980), 44; W. H. Auden, "Under Which Lyre" (1946), in *Collected Poems*, ed. Edward Mendelson (New York: Modern Library, 1976), 338; F. R. Leavis, *Two Cultures? The Significance of C. P. Snow* (1962; Cambridge: Cambridge University Press, 1962), 65-66.

52. Geoffrey Harpham, "Finding Ourselves: The Humanities as a Discipline," *American Literary History* 25:3 (2013), 518; Stephen Marche, "Literature Is Not Data: Against Digital Humanities," *Los Angeles Review of Books*, October 28, 2012, https://lareviewofbooks.org/article/literature-is-not-data-against-digital-humanities/#!; Caleb Crain, "Counter Culture: Fighting for Literature in an Age of Algorithms," *Harper's Magazine*, July 2015, 8. See also Gary Hall, "Toward a Postdigital Humanities: Cultural Analytics and the Computational Turn to Data-Driven Scholarship," *American Literature* 85:4 (2013), 781-809.

53. Among the scholarship that takes Busa as a starting point for DH are Susan Hockey, "A History of Humanities Computing," in *A Companion to Digital Humanities*, ed. Susan Schreibman, Ray Siemens, and John Unsworth (Oxford: Oxford University Press, 2004), 3-19; Stephen Ramsay, *Reading Machines: Toward an Algorithmic Criticism* (Champaign: University of Illinois Press, 2011), 1; and Matthew Jockers, *Macroanalysis: Digital Methods and Literary History* (Chicago: University of Illinois Press, 2013), 3.

54. Lucius Adelno Sherman, *Analytics of Literature: A Manual for the Objective Study of English Prose and Poetry* (Boston: Ginn, 1893), xiii.

55. L. A. Sherman to E. C. Stedman, June 2, 1893 (manuscript inserted into title pages of Sherman, *Analytics of Literature*, Harvard University Library).

56. *Willa Cather in Person: Interviews, Speeches, and Letters*, ed. L. Brent Bohlke (Lincoln: University of Nebraska Press, 1986), 111; Andrew Jewell and Brian L. Pytlik Zillig, "'Counted Out at Last': Text Analysis on the *Willa Cather Archive*," in *The American Literature Scholar in the Digital Age*, ed. Amy E. Earhart and Andrew Jewell (Ann Arbor: University of Michigan Press, 2011), esp. 167–70.

57. Crane quoted in Paul Sorrentino, *Stephen Crane: A Life of Fire* (Cambridge, MA: Harvard University Press, 2014), 154.

58. Frank Norris, "The 'English Courses' of the University of California," in *Novels and Essays: Vandover and the Brute, McTeague, The Octopus, Essays* (New York: Library of America, 1986), 1110–11.

59. "Educational Literature," *Critic*, June 10, 1893, 380; "The Objective Study of English Literature," *Dial*, June 1, 1893, 343; "Analytics of Literature," *Literary World*, August 26, 1893, 268.

60. T. C. Mendenhall, "The Characteristic Curves of Composition," *Science*, March 11, 1887, 237–46. For responses, see "Notes" in *Critic*, March 26, 1887, 159; "Literary Notes," *Shakespeariana*, July 1, 1887, 334; and Joel Benton, "The Word-Curve," *Christian Union*, September 8, 1887, 223. See also Jason Camlot, *Style and the Nineteenth-Century British Critic: Sincere Mannerisms* (Burlington, VT: Ashgate, 2008), 142–46.

61. Benjamin Morgan, *The Outward Mind: Materialist Aesthetics in Victorian Science and Literature* (Chicago: University of Chicago Press, 2017), 219–54; Yohei Igarashi, "Statistical Analysis at the Birth of Close Reading," *New Literary History* 46:3 (2015), 485–504. Note that Richards's mentor, William Empson, began as a student of mathematics before writing *Seven Types of Ambiguity* (London: Chatto and Windus, 1930).

62. I. A. Richards, *Practical Criticism: A Study of Literary Judgement* (New York: Harcourt, Brace, and World, 1929), 321–22.

63. Robert Louis Stevenson, "Ordered South," in *The Travels and Essays of Robert Louis Stevenson* (New York: Charles Scribner's Sons, 1918), 87, 89.

64. Robert Louis Stevenson, *Essays in the Art of Writing* (London: Chatto and Windus, 1905), 49.

65. Robert Louis Stevenson, "Letter to a Young Gentleman Who Proposes to Embrace the Career of Art" (1888), in *Across the Plains, with Other Memories and Essays* (Leipzig: Bernhard Tauchnitz, 1892), 259–60.

66. Stephen Arata, "Stevenson's Careful Observances," *Romanticism and Victorianism on the Net* 47 (2007), https://www.erudit.org/en/journals/ravon/2007-n47-ravon1893/016704ar/. Robert Louis Stevenson, *The Wrecker* (New York: Jefferson, 1891), 486.

67. For Stevenson and Defoe in general, see John Robert Moore, "Defoe, Stevenson, and the Pirates," *ELH* 10:1 (March 1943), 35–60; and Lerer, *Children's Literature*, 129–50. For competing accounts of *Treasure Island* and imperialism, see (for instance), Bristow, *Empire Boys*, 109–23; and Gubar, *Artful Dodgers*, 70–92. For a broader account of deserted (or castaway) fiction and imperialism, see Rebecca

Weaver-Hightower, *Empire Islands: Castaways, Cannibals, and Fantasies of Conquest* (Minneapolis: University of Minnesota Press, 2007).

68. "Robert Louis Stevenson," *The Living Age* (Boston: Living Age, 1897), 189. See also Bradley Deane, "Imperial Boyhood: Piracy and the Play Ethic," *Victorian Studies* 53:3 (2011), 689–714.

69. Henry James, *Partial Portraits* (1888; London: Macmillan, 1899), 168. For the porous boundary between adult and children's literature in the Victorian age, see Beverly Lyon Clark, *Kiddie Lit: The Cultural Construction of Children's Literature in America* (Baltimore: Johns Hopkins University Press, 2004). Clark also discusses James's general dislike of children's literature. For a reading of James and *Treasure Island* that emphasizes camaraderie over coercion, see Patricia Crain, *Reading Children: Literacy, Property, and the Dilemmas of Childhood in Nineteenth-Century America* (Philadelphia: University of Pennsylvania Press, 2016), 147–55.

70. Bill Brown, *The Material Unconscious: American Amusement, Stephen Crane, and the Economies of Play* (Cambridge, MA: Harvard University Press, 1996), 170.

71. "Schoolroom Classics in Fiction—a Survey," *Edinburgh Review*, October 1901, 414.

72. Fredric Jameson, *Postmodernism; or, The Cultural Logic of Late Capitalism* (Durham, NC: Duke University Press, 1991), 279–96.

73. Robert Louis Stevenson, *Treasure Island* (New York: Charles Scribner's Sons, 1901), ix. Subsequent references cited parenthetically.

74. Cannon Schmitt, "Technical Maturity in Robert Louis Stevenson," *Representations* 125:1 (2014), 54–79; Ian Duncan, "Stevenson and Fiction," in *The Edinburgh Companion to Robert Louis Stevenson*, ed. Penny Fielding (Edinburgh: Edinburgh University Press, 2010), 11–26; Rosalind Williams, *The Triumph of Human Empire: Verne, Morris, and Stevenson at the End of the World* (Chicago: University of Chicago Press, 2013), 237–59.

75. Robert Louis Stevenson, "A Gossip on Romance" (1882), in *The Works of Robert Louis Stevenson: Miscellanies*, vol. 1 (Edinburgh: Longmans Green, 1894), 260.

76. For Stevenson and bureaucracy, see Christopher Parkes, "*Treasure Island* and the Romance of the British Civil Service," *Children's Literature Association Quarterly* 31:4 (2006), 332–45.

77. Walter Benn Michaels, *The Gold Standard and the Logic of Naturalism: American Literature at the Turn of the Century* (Berkeley: University of California Press, 1988); Matthew Kaiser, *The World in Play: Portraits of a Victorian Concept* (Stanford, CA: Stanford University Press, 2011) 117–45.

78. John Guillory, *Cultural Capital: The Problem of Literary Canon Formation* (Chicago: University of Chicago Press, 1993).

79. Bristow, *Empire Boys*.

80. Here I follow other scholars in considering the immensely influential Verne as part of an English-language canon (he published many of his books serially in the *Boy's Own Paper*). For Verne, science, and knowledge acquisition, see Loxley, *Problematic Shores*, esp. 16–33. Verne reportedly hoped to summarize in his writings "all the geographical, geological, physical, [and] astronomical knowledge amassed by modern science," and he created over twenty-five thousand bibliographic cards, which he carefully organized (Loxley, *Problematic Shores*, 16).

81. H. Rider Haggard, *King Solomon's Mines* (London: Cassell, 1907), 280. For how the map of *King Solomon's Mines* reflects an uneasiness with modernity, see Nicholas Daly, *Modernism, Romance, and the* Fin de Siècle: *Popular Fiction and British Culture* (New York: Cambridge University Press, 1999), 58–61.

82. H. Rider Haggard, *Mr. Meeson's Will* (London: Spencer Blackett, 1888), 20.

83. Ibid., 142.

84. Garrett Stewart, *Dear Reader: The Conscripted Audience in Nineteenth-Century British Fiction* (Baltimore: Johns Hopkins University Press, 1996).

85. Ross Forman, "Room for Romance: Playing with Adventure in Arthur Conan Doyle's *The Lost World*," *Genre* 43:1–2 (2010), 27–59. See also Ian Duncan's introduction to *The Lost World* (Oxford: Oxford University Press, 1998).

86. Arthur Conan Doyle, *The Lost World* (New York: Hodder and Stoughton, 1912), 85.

87. Ibid., 289.

88. Amanda Claybaugh, "Bureaucracy in America: De Forest's Paperwork," *Studies in American Fiction* 37:2 (2010), 203–23.

89. Thomas Augst, *The Clerk's Tale: Young Men and Moral Life in 19th Century America* (Chicago: University of Chicago Press, 2003); Ceri Sullivan, *Literature in the Public Service: Sublime Bureaucracy* (New York: Palgrave Macmillan, 2013).

90. Ronald Zboray, *A Fictive People: Antebellum Economic Development and the American Reading Public* (Oxford: Oxford University Press, 1993), 124. See also Ben Kafka, "Paperwork: The State of the Discipline," *Book History* 12 (2009), 340–53.

91. Henry W. Bellows, *The Leger and the Lexicon; or, Business and Literature in Account with American Education* (Cambridge, MA: John Bartlett, 1853), 31.

92. John F. Kasson, *Houdini, Tarzan, and the Perfect Man: The White Male Body and the Challenge of Modernity in America* (New York: Hill and Wang, 2001), 169–79.

93. Mark Seltzer, *Bodies and Machines* (New York: Routledge, 1992); Martha Banta, *Taylored Lives: Narrative Productions in the Age of Taylor, Veblen, and Ford* (Chicago: University of Chicago Press, 1993).

94. For London, see Seltzer, *Bodies and Machines*, 14.

95. Edgar Rice Burroughs, *The Monster Men* (CreateSpace, 2013), 181; also at http://www.gutenberg.org/files/96/96.txt.

96. Edgar Rice Burroughs, *The Efficiency Expert*, http://www.gutenberg.org/ebooks/3475.

97. For Tarzan and literacy, see, for instance, Eric Cheyfitz, *The Poetics of Imperialism: Translation and Colonization from* The Tempest *to* Tarzan (New York: Oxford University Press, 1991), 11–21.

98. John Locke, *Essay concerning Human Understanding* (New York: Penguin, 1998), 197.

99. For a typical popular account of Tylor's work, see "The Art of Counting," *Oliver Optic's Magazine*, July 1874, 558–59. Note that Tylor published portions of his work on numbers as early as 1868 in proceedings from the Royal Institution and Smithsonian Institution. For Tylor's influence on James Frazer, see Frazer's *Questions on the Customs, Beliefs, and Languages of Savages* (1907; Cambridge: Cambridge University Press, 1916), 34–35. For the "egalitarian basis" of Tylor's anthropology, see Gillian

Beer, *Darwin's Plots: Evolutionary Narrative in Darwin, George Eliot and Nineteenth-Century Fiction* (Cambridge: Cambridge University Press, 1983), 109.

100. Levi Conant, *The Number Concept: Its Origin and Development* (New York: Macmillan, 1931), 73.

101. For popular accounts, see James Weir, "The Faculty of Computing in Animals," *Lippincott's Monthly Magazine*, May 1898, 677–81; and Th. Ribot [Thédole-Armand], "The Intelligence of Animals," *Open Court*, February 1899, 85–97.

102. John Lubbock, *On the Senses, Instincts, and Intelligence of Animals* (New York: Appleton, 1894), 285.

103. Quoted in Diana Seitler, *Atavistic Tendencies: The Culture of Science in American Modernity* (Minneapolis: University of Minnesota Press, 2008), 141; Edgar Rice Burroughs, *Tarzan of the Apes* (New York: A. L. Burt, 1914), 82. Subsequent references cited parenthetically.

104. *Literary Secretaries/Secretarial Culture*, ed. Leah Price and Pamela Thurschwell (Burlington, VT: Ashgate, 2005).

105. Andrew Piper, *Enumerations: Data and Literary Study* (Chicago: University of Chicago Press, 2018), esp. 1–21. See also Mary Poovey, *A History of the Modern Fact: Problems of Knowledge in the Sciences of Wealth and Society* (Chicago: University of Chicago Press, 1998): "figures of arithmetic had more in common with figures of speech in the early nineteenth century than most of the practitioners of either 'science' or 'art' liked to acknowledge" (325).

106. J. M. Barrie, *Peter and Wendy* (New York: Charles Scribner's Sons, 1911), 3–4.

107. Ibid., 258.

108. Rose, *Case of Peter Pan*, esp. 78–80. Rose also relates how children's editions of *Peter and Wendy* reflect a broader desire in British culture and educational policy to separate factual and enchanted reading.

109. Jonathan Gottschall, *Literature, Science, and a New Humanities* (New York: Palgrave Macmillan, 2008).

110. Gerald Graff, "New Preface," in *Professing Literature: An Institutional History, Twentieth Anniversary Edition* (Chicago: University of Chicago Press, 2007), xviii.

111. Jerome McGann, *Radiant Textuality: Literature after the World Wide Web* (New York: Palgrave Macmillan, 2001), xi–xii.

112. Franco Moretti, *Distant Reading* (New York: Verso, 2013), 204.

113. Hayles in Patricia Tomaszek, "Conference Review: *Reading Digital Literature* at Brown University, October 4–7, 2007," *Digital Humanities Quarterly* 2:1 (Summer 2008), 5.

114. Jockers, *Macroanalysis*, 7.

115. Frederick Gibbs and Daniel Cohen, "A Conversation with Data: Prospecting Victorian Words and Ideas," *Victorian Studies* 54:1 (2011), 76–77.

116. Ramsay, *Reading Machines*.

117. Lev Manovich, "Trending: The Promises and the Challenges of Big Social Data" (2011), http://manovich.net/content/04-projects/066-trending-the-promises-and-the-challenges-of-big-social-data/64-article-2011.pdf.

118. For the difficulties of distinguishing genre in nineteenth-century literary history, see James Machor, *Reading Fiction in Antebellum America: Informed Response*

and Reception Histories, 1820–1865 (Baltimore: Johns Hopkins University Press, 2011), 299–321.

119. Ted Underwood, Michael L. Black, Loretta Auvil, and Boris Capitanu, "Mapping Mutable Genres in Structurally Complex Volumes" (2013), https://arxiv.org/pdf/1309.3323v2.pdf. This article also briefly notes the high frequency of numbers in Robinsonade narratives.

120. Most of the texts were obtained from Project Gutenberg, to which we made a modest donation through the Hariri Foundation.

121. *Raw Data Is an Oxymoron*, ed. Lisa Gitelman (Cambridge: MIT Press, 2013); Porter, *Trust in Numbers*; Warren Weaver, "Recent Contributions to the Mathematical Theory of Communication" (1949), in Claude Shannon and Warren Weaver, *The Mathematical Theory of Communication* (1949; Urbana: University of Illinois Press, 1963), 116–17.

122. According to the 1897 survey of children's reading in the *Public-School Journal* ("Current Educational Topics"), the adventure genre constituted 13.2 percent of reading by boys and 1.7 percent of reading by girls.

123. Gibbs and Cohen, "Conversation with Data," 70; Ramsay, *Reading Machines*, 16.

124. Robert Frost, *Collected Poems, Prose, and Plays* (New York: Library of America, 1995), 122.

125. Semir Zeki, John Paul Romaya, Dionigi M. T. Benincasa, and Michael F. Atiyah, "The Experience of Mathematical Beauty and Its Neural Correlates," *Frontiers in Human Neuroscience* 8 (2014), 68.

126. Henry Morton Stanley, "Mr. H. M. Stanley," in *Best Hundred Books: Containing an Article on the Choice of Books* (London: Pall Mall Gazette Office, 1886), 21–22.

127. Stephen Greenblatt, *Shakespearian Negotiations* (Berkeley: University of California Press, 1988), 161–64.

128. Henry Morton Stanley, *Through the Dark Continent*, 2 vols. (New York: Harper and Brothers, 1878), 2:386.

129. For Stanley's influence, see Marianna Torgovnick, *Gone Primitive: Savage Intellects, Modern Lives* (Chicago: University of Chicago Press, 1990), 26–34.

130. Daniel Bivona, *British Imperial Literature, 1870–1940: Writing and the Administration of Empire* (Cambridge: Cambridge University Press, 1998), esp. 40–68; Stanley, *Through the Dark Continent*, 1:87.

131. Jon Agar, *The Government Machine: A Revolutionary History of the Computer* (Cambridge, MA: MIT Press, 2003), 118.

132. H. T. De La Bache, *How to Observe: Geology* (London: Charles Knight, 1835), iv.

133. Stanley, *Through the Dark Continent*, 1:2.

134. Hester Blum, *The News at the Ends of the Earth: The Print Culture of Polar Exploration* (Durham, NC: Duke University Press, 2019); Adriana Craciun, *Writing Arctic Disaster: Authorship and Exploration* (New York: Cambridge University Press, 2016).

135. Matthew Rubery, "A Transatlantic Sensation: Stanley's Search for Livingstone and the Anglo-American Press," in *The Oxford History of Popular Print Culture*, vol. 6, *US Popular Print Culture, 1860–1920*, ed. Christine Bold (Oxford: Oxford University Press, 2012), 510–17; Jennifer Greeson, "Expropriating the Great South and Exporting 'Local Color': Global and Hemispheric Imaginaries of the First Reconstruction," *American Literary History* 18:3 (Fall 2006), 496–520.

136. Stanley, *Through the Dark Continent*, 1:65.

137. Pascale Casanova, *The World Republic of Letters*, trans. Malcolm DeBevoise (Cambridge, MA: Harvard University Press, 2007); Elaine Freedgood, "Literary Debt," *PMLA* 131:5 (2016), 1480–88.

138. Stanley, "Mr. H. M. Stanley," 22.

139. Friedrich Kittler, *Discourse Networks 1800/1900*, trans. Michael Metteer, with Chris Cullens (1985; Stanford, CA: Stanford University Press, 1990), 352–56. For a corrective to Kittler regarding the gendering of information, see Jennifer Fleissner, "Dictation Anxiety: The Stenographer's Stake in *Dracula*," in *Literary Secretaries/Secretarial Culture*, 63–90.

140. Paul Barber, *Vampires, Burial, and Death: Folklore and Reality* (New Haven, CT: Yale University Press, 1988), 55, 83.

141. Such alliances are all to varying degrees recognized in Said's *Orientalism* (New York: Pantheon, 1978) and have since been widely elaborated. Especially relevant books include: Thomas Richards, *The Imperial Archive: Knowledge and the Fantasy of Empire* (New York: Verso, 1986); C. A. Bailey, *Empire and Information: Intelligence Gathering and Social Communication in India, 1780–1870* (Cambridge: Cambridge University Press, 1996); and Ian Baucom, *Specters of the Atlantic: Finance, Capital, Slavery, and the Philosophy of History* (Durham, NC: Duke University Press, 2005).

142. Arnold White, *Efficiency and Empire* (London: Methuen, 1901).

143. Joseph Conrad, *Heart of Darkness*, ed. Robert Kimbrough, 3rd ed. (New York: Norton, 1988), 21. Subsequent references cited parenthetically.

144. Joseph Conrad, "Geography and Some Explorers" (1924), in *The Cambridge Edition of the Works of Joseph Conrad: Last Essays*, ed. Harold Ray Stevens and J. H. Stape (Cambridge: Cambridge University Press, 2010), 14.

145. Ibid., 3–4.

146. For an exceptionalist account of American Robinsonades, see Leslie Fiedler, *Love and Death in the American Novel* (New York: Criterion Books, 1960), 366–68. For studies emphasizing the influence of *Robinson Crusoe* in American literature and culture, see Martin Green, *Dreams of Adventure, Deeds of Empire* (New York: Basic Books, 1979), esp. 129–32; and Shawn Thompson, *The Fortress of Solitude: Robinson Crusoe in Antebellum Culture* (Madison, NJ: Fairleigh Dickinson University Press, 2010).

147. John Carlos Rowe, *The New American Studies* (Minneapolis: University of Minnesota Press, 2002); Amy Kaplan, *The Anarchy of Empire in the Making of U.S. Culture* (Cambridge, MA: Harvard University Press, 2002); Jennifer Greeson, *Our South: Geographic Fantasy and the Rise of National Literature* (Cambridge, MA: Harvard University Press, 2010); Williams, *Triumph of Human Empire*, 9.

148. Frederick Jackson Turner, "The Significance of the Frontier in American History" (1893), in *The Frontier in American History* (New York: Henry Holt, 1920), 1–38. The best background for stadialism remains George Dekker, *The American Historical Romance* (Cambridge: Cambridge University Press, 1987).

149. Turner, *Frontier in American History*, 312. For Turner as methodological pioneer, see Allan Bogue, "The Quest for Numeracy: Data and Methods in American Political History," *Journal of Interdisciplinary History* 21 (1990), 89–116.

150. Lawrence Scaff, *Max Weber in America* (Princeton, NJ: Princeton University Press, 2011), esp. 73–97. See also Christian F. Feest, "Germany's Indians in a European Perspective," in *Germans and Indians: Fantasies, Encounters, Projections*, ed. Colin G. Calloway and Gerd Gemünden (Lincoln: University of Nebraska Press, 2002), esp. 34.

151. Owen Wister, *The Virginian: A Horseman of the Plains* (New York: Penguin Books, 1988), 83, 94. Subsequent references cited parenthetically.

152. Mark Twain, *The Adventures of Huckleberry Finn* (1884; New York: Signet Classic, 1959), 248. That Tom Sawyer wants the imprisoned Jim to file the stolen spoon into a pen so as to write a rescue note in iron-rust and tears suggests a satire of both the stirring enumerations and the atavistic texts of adventure fiction.

153. The list of authors Molly receives includes "Shakespeare, Tennyson, Browning, Longfellow; and a number of novels by Scott, Thackeray, George Eliot, Hawthorne, and lesser writers; some volumes of Emerson; and Jane Austen complete" (Wister, *Virginian*, 106–7).

154. Max Horkheimer and Theodor Adorno, *Dialectic of Enlightenment*, trans. John Cumming (1944; New York: Continuum, 1969), 164.

155. Bennett, *Enchantment of Modern Life*, 104–10

Chapter Four. Testing

1. Bill Readings, *The University in Ruins* (Cambridge, MA: Harvard University Press, 1996), esp. 130–34, 150–65.

2. Michel Foucault, *The Order of Things: An Archeology of the Human Sciences* (New York: Random House, 1971), 55.

3. Michel Foucault, *Discipline and Punish: The Birth of the Prison* (New York: Verso, 1977), 184–94.

4. Foucault, *Order of Things*, 300. For a compatible narrative about how literary-critical hermeneutics were historically constructed in juxtaposition to philology—but also how such juxtaposition need not lead to an informational/literary divide—see Jerome McGann, *A New Republic of Letters: Memory and Scholarship in the Age of Digital Reproduction* (Cambridge, MA: Harvard University Press, 2014).

5. Edward A. Freeman, "Literature and Language," *Contemporary Review*, December 1887, 562.

6. John Churton Collins, *The Study of English Literature: A Plea for Its Recognition and Organization at the Universities* (London: Macmillan, 1891), 113. For an account of Collins, see Alvin B. Kernan, *The Death of Literature* (New Haven, CT: Yale University Press, 1990), 36–40. For related responses to Freeman, see also Henry Latham, *On the Action of Examinations Considered as a Means of Selection* (Boston: Willard Small, 1886).

7. J. C. Collins, *Study of English Literature*, 48.

8. William Symington M'Cormick, "English Literature and University Education" (1887), in *Three Lectures on English Literature* (London: Alexander Gardner, 1889), 31. Here M'Cormick is paraphrasing Freeman's view. See also Collins's preface to *Ephemera Critica: Or Plain Truths about Current Literature* (New York: E. P. Dutton, 1902), 3–8.

9. D. J. Palmer, *The Rise of English Studies* (London: Oxford University Press, 1965); Thomas Heyck, *The Transformation of Intellectual Life in Victorian England* (London: Croom Helm, 1982); Gerald Graff, *Professing Literature: An Institutional History* (Chicago: University of Chicago Press, 1987); Terry Eagleton, *Literary Theory: An Introduction* (Oxford: Blackwell, 1983); Ian Hunter, *Culture and Government: The Emergence of Literary Education* (London: Macmillan, 1988); Gauri Viswanathan, *Masks of Conquest: Literary Study and British Rule in India* (New York: Columbia University Press, 1989); John Guillory, *Cultural Capital: The Problem of Literary Canon Formation* (Chicago: University of Chicago Press, 1993); David Shumway, *Creating American Civilization: A Genealogy of American Literature as an Academic Discipline* (Minneapolis: University of Minnesota Press, 1994).

10. Eagleton, *Literary Theory*, 20.

11. Palmer, *Rise of English Studies*, 16.

12. Elizabeth Renker, *The Origins of American Literature Studies: An Institutional History* (New York: Cambridge University Press, 2007); Nancy Glazener, *Literature in the Making: A History of U.S. Literary Culture in the Long Nineteenth Century* (Oxford: Oxford University Press, 2016); Jon Klancher, *Transfiguring the Arts and Sciences: Knowledge and Cultural Institutions in the Romantic Age* (Cambridge: Cambridge University Press, 2013).

13. Cathy Shuman, *Pedagogical Economies: The Examination and the Victorian Literary Man* (Stanford, CA: Stanford University Press, 2002); Jennifer Ruth, *Novel Professions: Interested Disinterest and the Making of the Professional in the Victorian Novel* (Columbus: Ohio State University Press, 2006).

14. See, for example, Cathy Davidson, *The New Education: How to Revolutionize the University to Prepare Students for a World in Flux* (New York: Basic Books, 2017); and Richard J. Shavelson, *Measuring College Learning Responsibly: Accountability in a New Era* (Stanford, CA: Stanford University Press, 2010).

15. Geoffrey Holmes, *Augustan England: Professions, State and Society, 1680–1730* (London: George Allen, 1982).

16. Raymond Williams, *The Long Revolution* (London: Chatto and Windus, 1961), 137–40; John Roach, *Public Examinations in England, 1850–1900* (Cambridge: Cambridge University Press, 1971).

17. Mark Garrison, *A Measure of Failure: The Political Origins of Standardized Testing* (Albany: State University of New York Press, 2009); Leslie Butler, *Critical Americans: Victorian Intellectuals and Transatlantic Liberal Reform* (Chapel Hill: University of North Carolina Press, 2007), esp. 8–10; Cindy Sondik Aron, *Ladies and Gentlemen of the Civil Service: Middle-Class Workers in Victorian America* (New York: Oxford University Press, 1987); Ari Hoogenboom, "Thomas A. Jenckes and Civil Service Reform," *Mississippi Valley Historical Review* 47:4 (March 1961), 636–58.

18. One present-day definition of standards largely compatible with nineteenth-century examination practices includes the following criteria: (1) "agreed-upon rules"; (2) "spans more than one community of practice . . . over time"; (3) works "over distance" and across "heterogeneous metrics"; (4) enforceable; (5) not based on "natural law"; (6) "significant inertia" (Geoffrey C. Bowker and Susan Leigh Star, *Sorting Things Out: Classification and Its Consequences* [Cambridge, MA: MIT Press, 1999], 13).

19. Thomas Stantial, *A Test-Book for Students; Comprising Sets of Examination Papers upon Language and Literature, History and Geography, and Mathematical and Physical Sciences, Designed for Students Preparing for the Universities or for Appointments in the Army and Civil Service* (London: Bell and Daldy, 1859), iv.

20. Elaine Hadley, *Living Liberalism: Practical Citizenship in Mid-Victorian Britain* (Chicago: University of Chicago Press, 2010), esp. 49–56.

21. William Gladstone in an 1854 letter happily predicted that, in addition to their "natural gifts," the "acquired advantages" of English gentlemen would lift their scores above those of "the mass" (William Gladstone to Lord John Russell, quoted in Peter Hennessy, *Whitehall* [Charlottesville: University of Virginia Press, 1989], 44).

22. J. P. Mahaffy, *Report of the Commissioners . . . to Inquire in to the Endowments, Funds, and Actual Condition of All Schools Endowed for the Purpose of Education in Ireland*, vol. 1 (Dublin: Alex. Thom, 1881), 256; *Education and Examination* (New York: Leonard Scott, 1889), 2; "Memoir, Letters, and Remains of Alexis de Tocqueville," *Littell's Living Age*, December 14, 1861, 492.

23. Thomas Henry Farrar, *The Sacrifice of Education to Examination: Letters from "All Sorts and Conditions of Men,"* ed. Auberon Herbert (London: Williams and Norgate, 1889), 2.

24. Mary Poovey, *Genres of the Credit Economy: Mediating Value in Eighteenth- and Nineteenth-Century Britain* (Chicago: University of Chicago Press, 2008); John Guillory, "The Memo and Modernity," and "Literary Study and the Modern System of the Disciplines," in *Disciplinarity at the Fin de Siècle*, ed. Amanda Anderson and Joseph Valente (Princeton, NJ: Princeton University Press, 2001), 19–43. For modern coordinates, see Robert Orrill, "Humanism and Quantitative Literacy," in *Calculation vs. Context: Quantitative Literacy and Its Implications for Teacher Education*, ed. Bernard L. Madison and Lynn Arthur Steen (Washington, DC: Mathematical Association of America, 2007), 45–58.

25. Catherine Robson, *Heart Beats: Everyday Life and the Memorized Poem* (Princeton, NJ: Princeton University Press, 2012), 55–67.

26. John Henry Newman, *The Idea of a University*, ed. Martin J. Svaglic (Notre Dame, IN: University of Notre Dame Press, 1982), 109, 96.

27. Richard D. Altick *The English Common Reader: A Social History of the Mass Reading Public, 1800–1900* (Chicago: University of Chicago Press, 1957), 182–84.

28. Henry Moseley, *Report on the Examination for Appointments in the Royal Artillery and Engineers* (London: Pall Mall, 1855), 80.

29. Arthur Hugh Clough, "A Passage upon Oxford Studies," in *Prose Remains of Arthur Hugh Clough*, ed. Blanche Smith Clough (London: Macmillan, 1888), 402.

30. Quoted in Robert Demaus, *English Literature and Composition: A Guide to Candidates in Those Departments in the Indian Civil Service, with Examination-Papers and Specimens of Answers* (London: Longmans, Green, 1866), 54. See also Robert Johnston, *Civil Service Guide* (London: Longmans, Green, 1869), 154.

31. *Fourth Report of Her Majesty's Civil Service Commissioners* (London: Eyre and Spottiswoode, 1859), 253–60.

32. Demaus, *English Literature and Composition*, x, 8–9.

33. *Questions for Examination in English Literature*, ed. Walter William Skeat (London: Bell and Daldy, 1873), ix.

34. Matthew Arnold, *Higher Schools and Universities in Germany* (London: Macmillan, 1882), 428.

35. Ibid., 55.

36. Robert Lowe, *On the Revised Code* (London: James Ridgway, 1862), 21–22.

37. *Matthew Arnold and the Education of the New Order*, ed. Peter Smith and Geoffrey Summerfield (Cambridge: Cambridge University Press, 1969), 171.

38. Ibid., 199, 206, 202, 208, 212, 217. Note, too, that Arnold's father made similar arguments at Rugby and Oxford when defending oral examinations against the rising practice of written tests (Arthur Stanley, *The Life and Correspondence of Thomas Arnold* [1844; New York: Scribner, Armstrong, 1877], 112).

39. *Matthew Arnold and the Education of the New Order*, 227, 225.

40. Ibid., 214–15.

41. Hunter, *Culture and Government*, 113–15 (grammar). Mary Poovey, "The Model System of Contemporary Literary Criticism," *Critical Inquiry* 27 (2001), 424. For how Arnold believed that poetry recitation could not teach taste but might provide a foundation for it, see Robson, *Heart Beats*, 43; and Shuman, *Pedagogical Economies*, 52.

42. John Forster, *The Life of Charles Dickens* (1872; London: Chapman and Hall, 1892), 23; Charles Dickens, "Address to the Birmingham Polytechnic Institution" (1844), in *The Works of Charles Dickens: Letters and Speeches*, vol. 2 (London: Chapman and Hall, 1908), 366.

43. Charles Dickens, *Dombey and Son* (Oxford: Oxford University Press, 1974), 65, 152.

44. For Dickens's autobiographical fragment, see Forster, *Life of Charles Dickens*, 47–69.

45. James L. Hughes, *Dickens as an Educator* (1902; New York: Haskell House, 1971), 2; Philip Collins, *Dickens and Education* (London: Macmillan, 1963); Amanda Claybaugh, *The Novel of Purpose: Literature and Social Reform in the Anglo-American World* (Ithaca, NY: Cornell University Press, 2006), esp. 53–54.

46. Quoted in Leon Litvak, "Education," in *The Oxford Companion to Charles Dickens: Anniversary Edition*, ed. Paul Schlicke (Oxford: Oxford University Press, 2011), 215; Dickens to Angela Burdett Coutts, September 5, 1857, *The Selected Letters of Charles Dickens*, ed. Jenny Hartley (Oxford: Oxford University Press, 2012), 324.

47. *Minutes of the Committee of Council on Education: Correspondence, Financial Statements, and Reports by Her Majesty's Inspectors of Schools, 1854-5* (London: George Eyre and William Spottiswoode, 1855), 20. See also Palmer, *Rise of English Studies*, 46–48.

48. Charles Dickens, *Hard Times* (New York: Penguin, 1995), 10.

49. James Kay-Shuttleworth, *Four Periods of Public Education* (London: Longman, Green, Longman, and Roberts, 1862), 330.

50. Ibid., 575.

51. Lauren M. E. Goodlad, *Victorian Literature and the Victorian State: Character and Governance in a Liberal Society* (Baltimore: Johns Hopkins University Press, 2003), 118–58.

52. Charles Dickens, *Our Mutual Friend*, ed. Michael Cotsell (Oxford: Oxford University Press, 1989), 217. Subsequent references cited parenthetically. For Dickens, Kay-Shuttleworth, and rote memorization, see Sarah Winter, *The Pleasures of*

Memory: Learning to Read with Charles Dickens (New York: Fordham University Press, 2011), 226–69.

53. For a compatible reading of this passage that focuses on examinations as a social sorting mechanism, see Shuman, *Pedagogical Economies*, 155.

54. Elisa Tamarkin, *Anglophilia: Deference, Devotion, and Antebellum America* (Chicago: University of Chicago Press, 2007), 247–324. For other American coordinates, see Helen Horowitz, *Campus Life: Undergraduate Cultures from the End of the Eighteenth Century to the Present* (New York: Knopf, 1987), 23–55.

55. *Reports from Committees: Chain Cables and Anchors Bill; Dockyards; Public Accounts; Thames Conservancy Bill; Weighing of Grain (Port of London) Bill* (London: House of Commons, 1864), esp. 37–40. For problems of standardized metrics in general, see Theodore Porter, *Trust in Numbers: The Pursuit of Objectivity in Science and Public Life* (Princeton, NJ: Princeton University Press, 1995), 21–29.

56. George Levine, *Dying to Know: Scientific Epistemology and Narrative in Victorian England* (Chicago: University of Chicago Press, 2002); Amanda Anderson, *The Powers of Distance: Cosmopolitanism and the Cultivation of Detachment* (Princeton, NJ: Princeton University Press, 2001).

57. Charles Dickens, *The Uncommercial Traveler*, in *The Works of Charles Dickens*, vol. 29 (London: Chapman and Hall, 1868), 247–48.

58. For education theory, see Hunter, *Culture and Government*, 59–64.

59. Charles Dickens, "In and Out of School," *All the Year Round*, October 19, 1861, 77–80; P. Collins, *Dickens and Education*, 34, 43. See also Charles Dickens, "Official Flags" (1862), published in *All the Year Round*, which lightly satirizes civil service examinations but still favorably contrasts bureaucratic meritocracy to patronage abuses.

60. Cathie Jo Martin, "Imagine All the People: Literature, Society, and Cross-National Variation in Education Systems," *World Politics* 70:3 (2018), 1–45.

61. Joseph Bristow, *Empire Boys: Adventures in a Man's World* (London: HarperCollins, 1991), 53–92. Shuman, *Pedagogical Economies*; Ruth, *Novel Professions*.

62. Friedrich Kittler, *Discourse Networks 1800/1900*, trans. Michael Metteer, with Chris Cullens (1985; Stanford, CA: Stanford University Press, 1990), esp. 76.

63. "School and College Life: Its Romance and Reality," *Blackwood's Edinburgh Review*, February 1861, 145.

64. For Farrar as educator and novelist, see A. N. Wilson, *The Victorians* (New York: Norton, 2003), 88–90; and Bristow, *Empire Boys*, 70–75.

65. Frederic Farrar, *Julian Home: A Tale of College Life* (London: Adam and Charles Black, 1895), 6. Subsequent references cited parenthetically.

66. John Seeley, "Liberal Education in Universities," in *Essays on Liberal Education*, ed. Frederic Farrar (London: Macmillan, 1867), 156.

67. William Johnson Cory, "On the Education of the Reasoning Faculties," in *Essays on Liberal Education*, 334–35.

68. Thomas Hughes, *Tom Brown at Oxford* (New York: Harper and Brothers, 1871), 9. Subsequent references cited parenthetically.

69. L.W.B. Brockliss, *The University of Oxford: A History* (Oxford: Oxford University Press, 2016), 349–60.

70. One review that identified mischaracterizations in Hughes's novel was titled "Oxford as It Is Not" (*Leisure Hour*, August 15, 1861, 517–18). Note, too, that Hardy,

for all his meritocratic beliefs, says nothing of plucking nobleman, who ranked above gentlemen-commoners.

71. Quoted in N. John Hall, *Trollope: A Biography* (Oxford: Oxford University Press, 1991), 8.

72. James W. Cortada, *All the Facts: A History of Information in the United States since 1870* (Oxford: Oxford University Press, 2016), 49–67; Toni Weller, "The Puffery and Practicality of Etiquette Books: A New Take on Victorian Information Culture," *Library Trends* 62:3 (2014), 663–80; *Literary Secretaries/Secretarial Culture*, ed. Leah Price and Pamela Thurschwell (Burlington, VT: Ashgate, 2005).

73. Kate Flint, *The Woman Reader, 1837–1914* (Oxford: Oxford University Press, 1993), 118–36.

74. Yonge, a supporter of the Oxford movement, may have had the experience of John Henry Newman in mind, though it was not unusual for young men to break down during examinations.

75. Charlotte Yonge, *The Daisy Chain, or Aspirations* (London: Macmillan, 1892), 93. Subsequent references cited parenthetically.

76. For Yonge and credentialing, see Charlotte Yonge, *Womankind* (1876; New York: Macmillan, 1890), 91.

77. Melissa Schaub, "'Worthy Ambition': Religion and Domesticity in *The Daisy Chain*," *Studies in the Novel* 39:1 (March, 2007); Talia Schaffer, "The Mysterious Magnum Bonum: Fighting to Read Charlotte Yonge," *Nineteenth-Century Literature* 55 (2000), 244–75. Yonge objected to the founding of Girton women's college at Oxford (Laura Morgan Green, *Educating Women: Cultural Conflict and Victorian Literature* [Athens: Ohio University Press, 2001], 85).

78. Elizabeth Gaskell, *The Life of Charlotte Brontë*, ed. Elisabeth Jay (1857; New York: Penguin Books, 1997), 82.

79. Ibid., 390.

80. Charlotte Brontë, *Villette* (New York: Barnes and Noble Books, 2005), 394. Subsequent references cited parenthetically.

81. Charlotte Brontë, *Jane Eyre* (New York: Penguin, 2006), 67.

82. Charlotte Brontë, *Shirley* (New York: Penguin, 2006), 75, 87, 521.

83. Gaskell, *Life of Charlotte Brontë*, 369.

84. For a compatible account of the feminine reading practices of such characters (excepting Ruth Hall), see Jed Deppman, *Trying to Think with Emily Dickinson* (Amherst: University of Massachusetts Press, 2008), 154–83.

85. Readings, *University in Ruins*, 164–65.

86. Quoted in Hall, *Trollope*, 71.

87. Ibid., 72. Trollope also wrote in his *Autobiography* that in comparison to his schoolmates, "I could have given a fuller list of the names of the poets of all countries, with their subjects and periods—and probably of historians,—than many others" (Anthony Trollope, *An Autobiography and Other Writings*, ed. Nicholas Shrimpton [Oxford: Oxford University Press, 2014], 32).

88. Goodlad, *Victorian Literature and the Victorian State*, 118–58; Jon Agar, *The Government Machine: A Revolutionary History of the Computer* (Cambridge, MA: MIT Press, 2003), 55–56; Ceri Sullivan, *Literature in the Public Service: Sublime Bureaucracy* (New York: Palgrave Macmillan, 2013), 65–113.

89. Richard Menke, *Telegraphic Realism: Victorian Fiction and Other Information Systems* (Stanford, CA: Stanford University Press, 2008), 54–67.

90. Anthony Trollope, *Three Clerks* (Oxford: Oxford University Press, 1989), 129, 125. Subsequent references cited parenthetically. Jobbles is a stand-in for Trevelyan's ally Benjamin Jowett, who also supported standardized examinations in the civil service.

91. George Cornewall Lewis, House of Commons, July 9, 1856 (*Hansard's Parliamentary Debates*, 3rd ser., vol. 147 [London: Cornelius Buck, 1856], 527); "Reports of Committees of Inquiry into Public Offices," *Quarterly Review*, October 1860, esp. 590–91. See also Shuman, *Pedagogical Economies*, 111–13.

92. Anthony Trollope, "The Civil Service as a Profession," *Cornhill Magazine*, February 1861, 214–28; Hadley, *Living Liberalism*, 36.

93. Nicholas Dames, "Trollope and the Career: Vocational Trajectories and the Management of Ambition," *Victorian Studies* 45:2 (2003), 258.

94. Trollope to G. H. Lewes, August 9, 1860, *The Letters of Anthony Trollope*, ed. N. John Hall (Stanford, CA: Stanford University Press, 1983), 118.

95. Sullivan, *Literature in the Public Service*, 6, 79–92. See also Anne Frey, *British State Romanticism: Authorship, Agency, and Bureaucratic Nationalism* (Palo Alto, CA: Stanford University Press, 2010).

96. Samuel Smiles, *Self-Help* (London: John Murray, 1859), 194.

97. Trollope, *Autobiography*, 133.

98. Ibid., 170.

99. Samuel Taylor Coleridge, *The Collected Works of Samuel Taylor Coleridge: Biographia Literaria*, 2 vols., ed. James Engell and W. Jackson Bate (Princeton, NJ: Princeton University Press, 1983), 1:38; "Books of the Hour," *Chambers's Edinburgh Journal* 20 (London: William and Robert Chambers, 1854), 328; Herman Melville, "Bartleby, the Scrivener," in *Pierre, Israel Potter, The Piazza Tales, The Confidence-Man, Uncollected Prose, Billy Budd, Sailor* (New York: Library of America, 1984), 642.

100. "New York Literary Correspondence," *Ladies' Repository*, August 1860, 506.

101. George Trevelyan, *The Competition Wallah* (London: Macmillan, 1866), 3. Subsequent references cited parenthetically.

102. For connections between civil service reform and Indian educational policy, see Charles Trevelyan, *On the Education of the People of India* (London: Longman, Orme, Brown, Green, and Longmans, 1838).

103. Viswanathan, *Masks of Conquest*, 134–38.

104. Philip Hartog, *Examinations and Their Relation to Culture and Efficiency* (London: Constable, 1918), 8.

105. William Huntting Howell, *Against Self Reliance: The Arts of Dependence in the Early United States* (Philadelphia: University of Pennsylvania Press, 2015).

106. Susan Ikenberry, "Education for Fun and Profit: Traditions of Popular College Fiction in the United States, 1875–1945," in *Imagining the Academy: Higher Education and Popular Culture*, ed. Susan Edgerton, et al. (New York: Routledge, 2005), 51–65; Christopher Findeisen, "Injuries of Class: Mass Education and the American Campus Novel," *PMLA* 130:2 (March 2015), 284–98, esp. 286.

107. Burt L. Standish, *Frank Merriwell at Yale* (Philadelphia: David McKay, 1903), 12.

108. Horatio Alger, *Strive and Succeed, or, The Progress of Walter Conrad* (New York: New York Publishing, 1872), 55–61; and T*he New Schoolma'am, or, A Summer in North Sparta* (Boston: Loring, 1877), 24–26.

109. Mann wrote in 1837: "Even the choicest literature should be taken as the condiment, and not as the sustenance, of life. It should be neither the warp nor the woof of existence, but only the flowery edging upon its borders" (*Thoughts: Selected from the Writings of Horace Mann* [Boston: Lee and Shepard, 1872], 105).

110. Ralph Waldo Emerson, *Essays and Lectures* (New York: Library of America, 1983), 55–56. Emerson had a high opinion of Mann throughout his life but found that his commitment to systematic education betrayed a lack of faith in human nature.

111. "English Literature in High Schools," *Massachusetts Teacher and Journal of Home and School Education*, April 1863, 117.

112. A. S. Hill, "An Answer to the Cry for More English" (1879), and L.B.R. Bridge, "The Harvard Admission Examination in English" (1888), in *Twenty Years of School and College English* (Cambridge, MA: Harvard University, 1896), 6–16, 17–32. *Examination and Education*, ed. Charles Kendall Adams (New York: Leonard Scott, 1889). Thorstein Veblen, *The Higher Learning in America: A Memorandum on the Conduct of Universities by Business Men* (New York: B. W. Huebsch, 1918).

113. Jeannette Marks, "The American College Girl's Ignorance of Literature," *Critic* 47:4 (October 1905), 312 ("very quantity"); all other quotations from 314. Thanks to Eloise Lawrence for this reference.

114. Cathy Davidson, *Revolution and the Word: The Rise of the Novel in America* (Oxford: Oxford University Press, 1988).

115. Lara Langer Cohen, *Material Texts: The Fabrication of American Literature: Fraudulence and Antebellum Print Culture* (Philadelphia: University of Pennsylvania Press, 2011), 133–61.

116. James Parton, *Fanny Fern: A Memorial Volume* (New York: G. W. Carleton, 1873), 38–42.

117. Fanny Fern, *Ruth Hall: A Domestic Tale of the Present Time* (New York: Penguin Books, 1997), 189. Subsequent references cited parenthetically.

118. Joyce Warren, *Fanny Fern: An Independent Woman* (New Brunswick, NJ: Rutgers University Press, 1992), 82–83.

119. Louisa May Alcott, *Little Women, or, Meg, Jo, Beth, and Amy* (Boston: Roberts Brothers, 1880), 29; and *Little Men: Life at Plumfield with Jo's Boys* (Boston: Roberts Brothers, 1871), 136, 225. Subsequent references to *Little Men* cited parenthetically.

120. Louisa May Alcott, *Jo's Boys: And How They Turned Out* (Boston: Roberts Brothers, 1891), 188.

121. Kimberley Johnson, "'The First New Federalism' and the Development of the Administrative State, 1883–1929," in *The Oxford Handbook of American Bureaucracy*, ed. Robert F. Durant (New York: Oxford University Press, 2010), 52–76.

122. Dorman Eaton, *The "Spoils" System and Civil Service Reform in the Custom-House and Post-Office* (New York: Putnam's, 1881), 55, 114.

123. Shumway, *Creating American Civilization*.

124. Francis Ellington Leupp, *How to Prepare for a Civil Service Examination, with Recent Questions and Answers* (New York: Hinds, Noble, and Eldredge, 1898), 2.

125. See, for example, "Lessons for Use by Teachers in the Service," *Indian School Journal* 7:2 (1906), 5; and "The Chilocco Normal Course," *Indian School Journal* 6:8 (1906), 39–40. See also David Wallace Adams, *Education for Extinction: American Indians and the Boarding School Experience, 1875–1928* (Lawrence: University of Kansas Press, 1995), esp. 72; and K. Tsianina Lomawaima, *They Called It Prairie Light: The Story of Chilocco Indian School* (Lincoln: University of Nebraska Press, 1994), esp. 34–46.

126. Silko quoted in Amelia V. Katanski, *Learning to Write 'Indian': The Boarding-School Experience and American Indian Literature* (Norman: University of Oklahoma Press, 2006), 20.

127. *Annual Report of the Commissioner of Indian Affairs for the Year 1894* (Washington, DC: Government Printing Office, 1894), 359.

128. *Manual of Examination for the Classified Civil Service of the United States* (Washington, DC: Government Printing Office, 1901), 75. For copies of civil service examination questions, see the Civil Service Commission's *Manual of Examination*, first published in 1898 and regularly thereafter. For a somewhat later example of the BIA's ambivalence toward literary aesthetics, see *Books for Indian School Libraries* (Washington, DC: Government Printing Office, 1913), which emphasizes vocational and informational texts but also includes canonical novels, as well as books that focus on Native American history and (in the case of Charles Eastman) experience.

129. For *Kathrina*, see Mary Loeffelholz, "Mapping the Cultural Field: *Aurora Leigh* in America," in *The Traffic in Poems: Nineteenth-Century Poetry and Transatlantic Exchange*, ed. Meredith L. McGill (New Brunswick, NJ: Rutgers University Press, 2008), 141–48.

130. See, for instance, William E. Sedlacek, *Beyond the Big Test: Noncognitive Assessment in Higher Education* (San Francisco: Jossey-Bass, 2004).

131. Kenneth W. Warren, *What Was African American Literature?* (Cambridge, MA: Harvard University Press, 2011).

132. Thomas Jefferson, *Writings* (New York: Library of America, 1984), 269.

133. Eli Cook, *The Pricing of Progress: Economic Indicators and the Capitalization of American Life* (Cambridge, MA: Harvard University Press, 2017), 11; Oz Frankel, *States of Inquiry: Social Investigations and Print Culture in Nineteenth-Century Britain and the United States* (Baltimore: Johns Hopkins University Press, 2006), 204–33. See also Maurice S. Lee, *Uncertain Chances: Science, Skepticism, and Belief in Nineteenth-Century American Literature* (Oxford: Oxford University Press, 2012), 102–5.

134. Frederick Douglass, *The Frederick Douglass Papers*, ser. 1, vol. 3, *Speeches, Debates, and Interviews, 1855–1863*, ed. John Blassingame (New York: Yale University Press, 1986), 502.

135. For *Beloved*, Schoolteacher, and sociology, see Avery Gordon, *Ghostly Matters: Haunting and the Sociological Imagination*, 2nd ed. (Minneapolis: University of Minnesota Press, 2008), 184–90.

136. "Noble Examples," *Provincial Freeman*, December 9, 1854, [3]. For a more comprehensive view, see William C. Nell, "Improvement of Colored People," *Liberator*, August 24, 1855, 134, later reprinted in the *Provincial Freeman*, August 29, 1855, 74.

137. *Argument of Charles Sumner, Esq., before the Supreme Court of Massachusetts in the Case of Sarah C. Roberts vs. the City of Boston* (Washington, DC: Rivers and Bailey, 1870), 12.

138. "Civil Service Reform," *Christian Recorder*, August 30, 1883, [2]. See also "The Workings of the Civil Service Examination Promises Well," *Christian Recorder*, August 16, 1883, [2].

139. Kepler, "Our Special Letter," *Christian Recorder*, March 27, 1884, [2]; D. T. McDaniel, "Merit vs. Favoritism," *Christian Recorder*, June 17, 1897, [1].

140. Anna Julia Cooper, *A Voice from the South* (Oxford: Oxford University Press, 1988), 229, 283, 284.

141. For Du Bois, sociology, and quantification, see Ross Posnock, *Color and Culture: Black Writers and the Making of the Modern Intellectual* (Cambridge, MA: Harvard University Press, 1998), 114–21; and Sarah Wilson, "Black Folk by the Numbers: Quantification in Du Bois," *American Literary History* 28 (2016), 27–45.

142. W.E.B. Du Bois, "The Black North: A Social Study" (1901), in *Selection from His Writings*, ed. Bob Blaisdell (New York: Dover, 2014), 27; W.E.B. Du Bois, *Black Folk Then and Now: An Essay in the History and Sociology of the Negro Race*, ed. Henry Louis Gates, introduction by Wilson J. Moses (New York: Oxford University Press, 2007), 85.

143. W.E.B. Du Bois, *The Souls of Black Folk* (New York: Penguin, 1996), 4, 9, 12.

144. See, for example, selections from *The New Negro: Readings on Race, Representation, and African American Culture, 1892–1938*, ed. Henry Louis Gates Jr. and Gene Andrew Jarrett (Princeton, NJ: Princeton University Press, 2007).

145. Langston Hughes, "The Negro Artist and the Racial Mountain" (1926), in *The Collected Works of Langston Hughes*, vol. 9, *Essays on Art, Race, Politics, and World Affairs*, ed. Christopher C. De Santis (Columbia, Missouri: University of Missouri Press, 2002), 32.

146. Laura Korobkin, "Avoiding 'Aunt Tomasina': Charles Dickens Responds to Harriet Beecher Stowe's Black American Reader, Mary Webb," *ELH* 82:1 (2015), 115–40. For what we know of Webb's biography, see Eric Gardner, "'A Gentleman of Superior Cultivation and Refinement': Recovering the Biography of Frank J. Webb," *African American Review* 35:2 (2001), 297–308.

147. Frank Webb, *The Garies and Their Friends*, ed. William Huntting Howell and Megan Walsh (Peterborough, Ontario: Broadview, 2016), 249. Subsequent references cited parenthetically.

148. Samuel Otter, "Frank Webb's Still Life: Rethinking Literature and Politics through *The Garies and Their Friends*," *American Literary History* 20:4 (2008), 728–52.

149. For a brief history of segregated hospitals in America, see Sidney D. Watson, "Race, Ethnicity and Quality of Care: Inequalities and Incentives," *American Journal of Law and Medicine* 27 (2001), esp. 210–11. More specific to Philadelphia, one piece of evidence suggests that black victims of the 1849 election riot were taken to an integrated hospital ("The Riots—Deplorable Results," *North Star*, October 26, 1849, [1]), but even here race is a visible factor.

150. Gerald Graff and Cathy Birkenstein, "A Progressive Case for Educational Standardization: How Not to Respond to Calls for Common Standards," *Academe*,

May–June 2008, 217–26; Kathleen Woodward, "Work-Work Balance, Metrics, and Resetting the Balance," *PMLA* 127:4 (2012), 994–1000; John Guillory, "Literary Study and the Modern System of the Disciplines," in *Disciplinarity at the Fin de Siécle*, ed. Amanda Anderson and Joseph Valente (Princeton, NJ: Princeton University Press, 2002), 33.

151. Davidson, *New Education*; Christopher Newfield, "Yes to the New Education, but What Kind?," *PMLA* 133:3 (2018), 686–93.

152. Richard Arum and Josipa Roksa, *Academically Adrift: Limited Learning on College Campuses* (Chicago: University of Chicago Press, 2011), 21.

153. The CLA quoted in Shavelson, *Measuring College Learning Responsibly*, 39.

154. Farrar, *Sacrifice of Education to Examination*, 2.

155. *Graduate Record Examinations: Literature in English Test Practice Book* (Princeton, NJ: Educational Testing Service, 2010), 5.

156. For an inconclusive study in the case of English, see N. W. Burton and M. Wang, "Predicting Long-Term Success in Graduate School: A Collaborative Validity Study" (GRE Board Report No. 99-14R, 2005). For a critique of GRE scores, see Julie R. Posselt, *Inside Graduate Admissions: Merit, Diversity, and Faculty Gatekeeping* (Cambridge, MA: Harvard University Press, 2016), 7–8.

157. Michael Bérubé, "Testing the Test," *Chronicle of Higher Education*, February 6, 2009, B5.

158. Before giving my score, let me say that I did no exam preparation except for taking one practice test and studying literature full time for twenty-one years as a graduate student and professor. Also, the person behind me was a mouth breather. I'm not insensitive of my failure to review rhetorical terms such as *litotes*. And you'd think there'd be fewer Middle English translation questions, right? Yet if the value of the GRE subject test in English literature can be doubted, and if nothing besides pride was at stake for me when I took the exam, scores retain a kind of totemic power. (Recall how Adorno and Horkheimer compare "data" to "incantations.") I thus hesitate to report that my score was 710 out of 800 (ninety-fifth percentile), only seven percentile points higher than my effort in 1991 before applying to graduate school.

INDEX

Accessible Archives, 65, 68
accountability, in education, 170, 175, 177–78, 183, 188, 219
accounting of literature: adventure novels and, 17, 130–52, 163–64; criticisms of, 45, 113–14, 115–16, 122–23; DH experiment on, 141–52; examples of quantification in, 43–44; nineteenth-century emergence of, 43–44, 111, 113–23; reading practices influenced by, 44; *Robinson Crusoe* and, 22–23; *Treasure Island* and, 124–30; Trollope and, 195; and Victorian juvenile literature, 114–16, 119–20; in *The Virginian*, 161
ACT exams, 184
Adams, Henry, 208
Adorno, Theodor, 103, 110; "Culture Industry," 163
adventure novels, 17, 111–12, 130–52, 163–64
aesthetics: African Americans and, 211–12, 214–15, 218; autonomy of, 2, 6, 16, 32, 40, 103, 108, 120, 167, 169, 199, 202; *Bartlett's Familiar Quotations* and, 104–6; Coleridge's, 32–35; in intuitive search behaviors, 69–70, 73–75, 83, 89–91, 98; mass print's effect on, 35; New Historicism and, 69–70; quantification/calculation in relation to, 118–23, 128, 137, 154, 166–67, 218; romantic, 16. *See also* judgment
African Americans: and aesthetics, 211–12, 214–15, 218; assessments and measurements of, 212–15; and standardized testing, 212–18
Agar, Jon, 155
Alcott, Bronson, 207
Alcott, Louisa May, 9, 17, 54, 166, 205, 218; *Jo's Boys*, 208; *Little Men*, 207–8; *Little Women*, 9, 115, 207–8
Alger, Horatio, 203–4
Altick, Richard, 80, 84, 100
Amazon (company), 20

American Antiquarian Society, 26, 104
American Library Association, 119
American Periodical Series, 65, 68
American Statistical Association, 46
anecdotal method of interpretation, 11, 62–63, 65, 67–72, 74
anthologies, 100–102
antipositivism, 53, 181, 219
antiquarianism, 59, 72, 92–98
Appleton, Victor, *Tom Swift and His Big Tunnel*, 140
Appleton's American Cyclopaedia, 47
Arabian Nights, 130
Arac, Jonathan, 65
Arata, Stephen, 44, 124
Aristotle, 135
Arnold, Matthew, 48, 94, 101, 115, 119, 166, 175–76, 178, 191, 218; "The Twice-Revised Code," 175–76
Arsić, Branka, 53, 220
Arum, Richard, *Academically Adrift*, 219
assessment. *See* testing
assimilation, 209–10, 215–16
Associated Press, 76
Astor Library, New York, 46
Atkins, Frank, *The Devil-Tree of El Dorado*, 148, 150
Atkinson, W. P., 44
Atlantic Monthly (magazine), 42, 47
Auden, W. H., 120
Augst, Thomas, 133
Austen, Jane, 161; *Emma*, 102

Babbage, Charles, 46, 109, 155
Bacon, Francis, 46, 175
Bain, Alexander, 45
Ballantyne, R. M., *Coral Island*, 131, 145–46
Balzac, Honoré de, 83
Banta, Martha, 134
Barnard, Henry, 204
Barrie, J. M., *Peter and Wendy*, 138–39, 148

Bartlett, John, 57, 98–104; *Bartlett's Familiar Quotations*, 17, 46, 99–106; *Choice Thoughts from Shakespeare*, 103; "List: of Books Read," 98–100, 103–4; *New and Complete Concordance, or Verbal Index to Words, Phrases, and Passages in the Dramatic Works of Shakespeare*, 99, 103–4
Bateson, Gregory, 14–15
Beecher, Catherine, 206
Belknap, Robert, 119
Bellows, Henry W., 133–34
Benjamin, Walter, 59, 110
Bennett, Jane, 110, 111, 163
Bentley, Nancy, 101, 109
Bercovitch, Sacvan, 65
Bérubé, Michael, 220
Bible, 23–24, 32, 40, 54, 101, 128, 131, 153, 227n14
bibliography, 91
Binet, Alfred, 170
Birkenstein, Cathy, 219
Bivona, Daniel, 155
Blackwood's (magazine), 102, 114, 185
Blaine, James, 210
Blair, Ann, 21, 91, 100
Blair, Hugh, "Lectures on Belles Lettres," 191
Bloom, Harold, 36
Blum, Hester, 155
Blumenbach, Johann, 41
bookkeeping, 22–23
Books and Reading (anthology), 117
Boole, George, 109
Borges, Jorge Luis, 31, 58, 164
Boston Mercantile Library Association, 104–5
Boston Public Library, 46
Boswell, James, *The Life of Samuel Johnson*, 51
Bourdieu, Pierre, 169, 184
Brantlinger, Patrick, 38
Bristow, Joseph, 130
British Association for the Advancement of Science, 116
British Civil Service, 17, 189, 195–200
British Museum, 46, 47, 81
The British Prose Writers: Johnsoniana, 51
British Public Libraries Act (1850), 46
Brodhead, Richard, 72

Brontë, Charlotte, 7, 17, 166, 184, 191–94, 218; *Jane Eyre*, 156, 192; *The Professor*, 193, 194; *Shirley*, 192; *Villette*, 6, 102, 165, 191–95, 206
Brooks, Cleanth, 32
Brown, Bill, 125
Brown, Margaret Wise, *Goodnight Moon*, 126
Browning, Elizabeth Barrett, 119, 194
Browning, Robert, "Count Gismond," 122
Brown University Library, 46
Buell, Lawrence, 47
Bulwer-Lytton, Edward, 154; *Vril*, 139, 145–46, 150
bureaucracy: artistic imagination compared to, 6, 73–74; criticisms of, 13, 58, 72–73, 75; Dickens and, 79, 82; enchantment with, 163; information linked to, 2, 4, 8; literature in relation to, 199–200; in nineteenth century, 7, 17; *Raiders of the Lost Ark* and, 163–64
Bureau of Indian Affairs. *See* US Bureau of Indian Affairs
Burroughs, Edgar, 140, 154; *Efficiency Expert*, 134–35; *A Man without a Soul*, 134; *Tarzan of the Apes*, 135, 136–38, 145–46
Burt, Stephanie, 64
Busa, Roberto, 121
Buss, R. W., *Dickens' Dream*, 87–89
Butler, Leslie, 120

Cabot, James Elliot, 47
calculation, as source of enchantment, 6, 17, 162. *See also* quantification
Cameron, Sharon, 220
canon. *See* literary canon
Carey, Annie, *The History of a Book*, 29–31
Carlyle, Thomas, 41, 50, 120; "On the Choice of Books," 117
Carroll, Lewis (pen name of Charles Lutwidge Dodson), *Alice's Adventures in Wonderland*, 108, 111, 115
Casanova, Pascale, 156
Castiglia, Christopher, 109
Cather, Willa, 122; "He Took Analytics," 122
Cavell, Stanley, 51, 53, 64, 220
Certeau, Michel de, 39

Cervantes, Miguel de, *Don Quixote*, 130
Chandler, James, 71
Chartier, Roger, 21
childhood reading, enchantment of, 26, 28, 29, 111, 114–16, 125–26. *See also* juvenile literature
children's literature. *See* juvenile literature
Chilocco Indian Agricultural School, 209
Chinese Exclusion Act (United States, 1882), 210
Chorley, Henry, 95
Christian Recorder (newspaper), 213
Citizen Kane (film), 163
civil service: British, 17, 189, 195–200; Indian, 172–74, 200–201, 210; US, 203, 208–9, 213
classification schemes, 82
Claybaugh, Amanda, 177
Clayton, Jay, 78
close reading: Coleridge and, 16, 32, 36, 55; deserted island reading likened to, 16, 19–20, 28; digital technologies as threat to, 19; distant reading in relation to, 140–42, 145–48, 150–51; persistence of, 20, 56; and quantitative methods, 123; *Robinson Crusoe* linked to, 25–26, 28; textual excess in relation to, 37–38
Clough, Arthur Hugh, 172
Cobban, James, *The Tyrants of Kool-Sim*, 140
Cody, William Frederick "Buffalo Bill," 160
Cohen, Daniel, 141, 144, 150
Cohen, Lara Langer, 206
Cohen, Michael David, 102
Coke, Edward, 105
Colacurcio, Michael, 65, 71
Coleridge, Samuel Taylor, 7, 16, 32–39, 48, 50, 55, 74, 200; *Biographia Literaria*, 33–36, 38; *Encyclopedia Metropolitan*, 34; *Lyrical Ballads*, 34, 37
collectors, 37–38
College Entrance Examination Board, 170
College Learning Assessment (CLA) test, 219–20
Collins, John Churton, 168
Collins, Phillip, 177
Collins, Wilkie, 83, 119; *Hide and Seek*, 90; *The Moonstone*, 29, 90; *The Woman in White*, 90

Colored American (newspaper), 66
Common Core standards, 18
Conant, Levi, *The Number Concept*, 136
confirmation bias, 11, 64, 139
Confucius, *Analects*, 118
Conrad, Joseph: "Geography and Some Explorers," 158; *Heart of Darkness*, 157–58
Cook, Eli, 212
Cooper, Anna Julia, *A Voice from the South*, 213–14
Cooper, James Fenimore, 99, 113, 114, 155, 159; *The Crater*, 29, 139, 145–46; *The Deerslayer*, 113–14; *Leatherstocking Tales*, 160, 210; *The Spy*, 210
Cordell, Ryan, 118
Cory, William Johnson, 186
Council of India, 201
Coutts, Angela Burdett, 177
Cowper, William, 28
Crabbe, George, 25
Craciun, Adriana, 155
Crain, Caleb, 121
Crain, Patricia, 26, 71
Crane, Stephen, 122
Crews, Frederick, 61
Critic (journal), 204
Critic (magazine), 101, 102
Cruikshank, George, 28
cultural capital, 38, 101–3, 166, 169
Curtis, George William, 208

Daily Telegraph (London newspaper), 155
Damasio, Antonio, *Descartes' Error*, 150
Dames, Nicholas, 33, 120, 198
Darnton, Robert, 7, 21, 91
Darwin, Charles: *The Descent of Man*, 136; *On the Origin of Species*, 45
Darwinism, 130, 136. *See also* social Darwinism
Davidson, Cathy, 205, 219
Davis, Allison, 215
Davis, Lennard, 21
Davis, Theo, 35
Davy, Humphry, 34
Defoe, Daniel, 21–32, 114; *The Complete English Tradesman*, 22; *Essay upon Literature*, 24; *Essay upon Projects*, 21; *The Further Adventures of Robinson Crusoe*, 54; *Journal of the Plague*

Defoe, Daniel (cont.)
Year, 24, 39; *Robinson Crusoe*, 9, 16, 22–32, 40, 111, 120, 124, 125, 128, 130, 154; *Roxana*, 21
De Forest, John, 133
De la Beche, Henry, *How to Observe: Geology*, 155
DeLillo, Don, 164
Demaus, Robert, 175
De Quincey, Thomas, 37, 44
Derrida, Jacques, 68
deserted island novels, 130, 132, 141–52
deserted island reading: close reading likened to, 16, 19–20, 28; defined, 16; Emerson and, 43, 49; enchantment of literature in relation to, 110; institutionalization of children's literature and, 126; mass print contrasted with, 16, 55; paradox of, 25, 129; persistence of, 56; *Robinson Crusoe* and, 23–25, 29, 32, 40; Rousseau and, 24; as twentieth-century conceit, 24, 227n14. *See also* close reading
Dewey, John, 120
Dewey Decimal System, 101, 113
DH. *See* digital humanities
Dial (magazine), 41
Dickens, Charles, 5, 7, 16, 17, 46, 78–89, 106, 120, 123, 133, 156, 166, 191, 197, 199, 215, 218; *American Notes*, 133; *Bleak House*, 58, 81–83; "Bottled Information," 79; *A Christmas Carol*, 29; *David Copperfield*, 29, 117, 177; *Dombey and Son*, 96, 177; "The Doom of English Wills," 57–58, 79, 80, 92–93; "Full Report of the First Meeting of the Mudfog Association for the Advancement of Everything," 116–17; *Great Expectations*, 85; *Hard Times*, 115, 177–78, 180, 181, 183; *Martin Chuzzlewit*, 57, 80–81; "The Metropolitan Protectives," 79; *Nicholas Nickleby*, 177, 181; *Our Mutual Friend*, 78, 83–87, 178–84, 208; *The Pickwick Papers*, 79–80, 87; "The Short-Timers," 79, 182–83; "Valentine's Day at the Post-Office," 79
Dickens, Edward "Plorn," 184
Dickens, Henry, 183
Dickinson, Emily, 35, 52, 133, 194, 210

digital humanities (DH): applications of, 140–41; criticisms of, 10–11, 59; distant reading as application of, 3, 20, 59; experiment in, on deserted island and lost world novels, 141–52; *Frankenstein* as subject for, 38; historical foundations of, 11, 17, 22, 138, 142
Dilke, Lady (Emilia Francis Strong), 119
disenchantment: with American frontier, 159; information as source of, 2, 3; of literary critics, 28; mass print as source of, 26; Stevenson on, 124; Weber on, 28, 110, 129. *See also* enchantment
Disraeli, Benjamin, *Sybil*, 89–90, 93
distant reading: characteristics of, 141; characterization of, 20; close reading in relation to, 140–42, 145–48, 150–51; controversies over, 56, 59, 120, 123; as instance of DH, 3, 20, 59; precursors of, 10, 109, 123, 142; relation of, to conventional literary criticism, 10, 56, 141, 150–52
Dostoevsky, Fyodor, 87
Douglass, Frederick, 108, 212
Dowden, Edward, 119
Doyle, Arthur Conan, 119, 154; *The Lost World*, 132–34, 145–46
Drucker, Johanna, 109
Dryden, John, 119
Du Bois, W.E.B., 8, 214–15; *The Quest of the Silver Fleece*, 214; *The Souls of Black Folk*, 214–15
Dumas, Alexandre, 114
Duncan, Ian, 126
During, Simon, 110
Duyckinck, Evert, 94–96

Eagleton, Terry, 45, 169
Eastman, Mary, 135
Eaton, Dorman, 208–9
Eco, Umberto, 119, 164
Edinburgh Review (journal), 125
education: accountability initiatives in, 170, 175, 177–78, 183, 188, 219; controversy over nineteenth-century English literary studies, 167–68; Dickens and, 177–84; quantification in, 178; reading curriculum in nineteenth-century, 114–16; standardization of, 115, 177–80,

183, 204–5, 207; testing controversies in, 167–68, 172, 176; in Victorian era, 166–84; women and, 189, 191. *See also* standardized testing
Educational Testing Service, 220
1850 Commission (Oxford University), 186–88
Eliot, Charles Norton, 43
Eliot, George (pen name of Mary Ann Evans), 5, 8, 194; *Middlemarch*, 90–91, 190; *Romola*, 93
Eliot, T. S., 12
Emerson, Ellen, 49
Emerson, Ralph Waldo, 7, 9, 16, 39–56, 74, 93, 102, 121, 208, 260n110; "The American Scholar," 39, 41–42, 48, 50–51, 53, 115, 204; "Art," 48; "Books," 42–43, 45–47, 117; "Circles," 54; Concord Library speech (1873), 40, 49; *English Traits*, 50; "Experience," 54, 220–21; "Fate," 54; "Goethe, or the Writer," 48; "Illusions," 54; journals, 48–49, 51–52, 133; "Lecture on the Times," 50; "Literature," 48; *Nature*, 53; *Parnassus*, 48; "The Poet," 48, 54; "The Progress of Culture," 41; "Quotation and Originality," 48–49, 51; "Self-Reliance," 54; "Shakespeare, or the Poet," 48; *Society and Solitude*, 40; "Thoughts on Modern Literature," 48; "The *Times*," 50; World Wide journals, 51–52; "The Young American," 76
Emerson, William, 51
empiricism, 97–98
Empson, William, 247n61
enchantment: bureaucracy as source of, 163; calculation as source of, 6, 17, 162; childhood, in reading, 26, 28, 29, 111; information as source of, 111–12, 151, 161–62; recent critical emphasis on, 109–11; *Robinson Crusoe* as source of, 25, 29; science in relation to, 110–11; threats to, 22, 109, 110, 139; Weber on, 110. *See also* disenchantment; pleasure
Enlightenment, 33, 163, 211
evidence, in literary criticism, 60–64, 68–69
evolution, 136
Examination and Education (essay collection), 204

excess. *See* textual excess
extensive reading: in contemporary context, 55; defined, 25; emergence of, 25; Emerson and, 47, 48, 55–56; mass print linked to, 25, 28, 31, 34, 36, 38, 47–48, 124; as recommended tactic, 31, 47

falsifiability, 63–64, 139, 146
Farrar, Frederic, 184, 198, 218; *Essays on Liberal Education*, 186; *Julian Home*, 185–86
Felski, Rita, 28, 109–10
Felt, Joseph, *Annals of Salem*, 71
Fern, Fanny (pen name of Sara Payson Willis), 7, 17, 166, 194, 199, 205–7, 218; *Ruth Hall*, 45, 205–8; "Suggestions on Arithmetic," 206
Ferriar, John, "The Bibliomania," 38
Fichte, Johann Gottlieb, 33
Fisher, Philip, 110
Flint, Kate, 189
Floridi, Luciano, 13
florilegia, 91–92, 100–105
Ford, Harrison, 161
Ford, Henry, 134
Forster, John, 176
Foster, George, 76
Foster Wallace, David, 164
Foucault, Michel, 97, 110, 166–67, 169, 191, 208; *Discipline and Punish*, 58, 166–67; *The Order of Things*, 58, 166–67
Fourteenth Amendment, 213, 218
Frankel, Oz, 212
Frankfurt school, 5, 22, 134
Franklin, Benjamin, 28, 73, 208. *See also* Poor Richard
Frazer, James, 136
Freeman, E. A., 167–68, 172
Friswell, J. Hain, *Familiar Words*, 100
Frost, Robert, "Range-Finding," 151

Gallagher, Catherine, 69–70
Galton, Francis, 137
Garfield, James, 203, 210
Garvey, Ellen Gruber, 11, 51, 101
Gaskell, Elizabeth, 191
Geological Survey of Great Britain, 155
Gerwig, G. W., 123
Gibbs, Frederick, 141, 144, 150

Gibson, Anna, 83
Gilder, Jeannette, 102
Gilman, Charlotte Perkins, *Herland*, 149, 150, 157
Gissing, George, 5, 133; *New Grub Street*, 115
Gitelman, Lisa, 8, 10, 22, 147
Glazener, Nancy, 97, 169
Gobles, Mark, 58
Gochberg, Reed, 77
Goethe, Johann Wolfgang von, 41; *Faust*, 15
Goldsmith, Oliver, 201
Google, 82, 103
Google Books, 2, 20, 24
Gottschall, Jonathan, 64
Graff, Gerald, 139, 168–69, 219
Grafton, Anthony, 93
Grahame, Kenneth, *The Golden Age*, 111
Greenblatt, Stephen, 69–70, 109, 153
Greeson, Jennifer, 159
GRE Literature in English subject exam, 18, 172, 220–21
Grimstad, Paul, 53
Grossman, Jay, 65
Grossman, Jonathan, 83
Gruening, Martha, 215
Guillory, John, 28, 38, 128, 169, 171, 219

Habermas, Jürgen, 68
Hachette, 105
Hack, Daniel, 78
Hacking, Ian, 113
Hadley, Elaine, 171, 198
Haggard, H. Rider, 137, 154; *King Solomon's Mines*, 131, 145–46, 149; *Mr. Meeson's Will*, 132; *She*, 131–32, 145–46
Hale, Sarah Josepha, *Complete Dictionary of Poetical Quotations*, 100
Hall, Stuart, 14
Harari, Yuval Noah, 7, 91
Hardy, George, *Five Hundred Books for the Young*, 119
Harpham, Geoffrey, 120–21
Harrison, Frederic, *The Choice of Books*, 117
Hartley, David, 35
Hartog, Philip, 202
Harvard Classics, 43
Harvard University, 203, 204
HathiTrust, 19

Hawthorne, Nathaniel, 5, 7, 16, 71–72, 75, 79, 106; *American Claimant*, 77; British notebooks, 77; "Chiefly about War Matters," 67; "The Custom-House," introduction to *The Scarlet Letter*, 71–74, 77–78, 81, 200; "The Devil in Manuscript," 75; *The House of Seven Gables*, 75; "The Intelligence Office," 75–77; *The Marble Faun*, 77; *Mosses from an Old Manse*, 72; "Mr. Higginbotham's Catastrophe," 75; "Old News," 75; *The Scarlet Letter*, 17, 65–75, 77–78, 81, 93, 200; *The Story Teller*, 75; "A Visit to the Clerk of the Weather," 76
Hayles, N. Katherine, 15, 20, 55, 58, 68, 141
Hazlitt, William, Jr., 43
Heber, Reginald, 105
Heidegger, Martin, 36, 53
Hemans, Felicia Dorothea, 173
Heringman, Noah, 93
Herschel, Caroline, 189
Herschel, John, 155
Hervey, James, 227n14
Heyck, Thomas, 168
Hirsch, E. D., *Cultural Literacy*, 101
Historical Magazine, and Notes and Queries (magazine), 97
historicism, 60–62, 98, 107
Holland, Josiah, 210; *Kathrina*, 210
Holmes, George Frederick, 95
homologies, 62–63, 66
Hopkins, Pauline, *Of One Blood*, 149, 157
Horkheimer, Max, 103, 110; "Culture Industry," 163
Howell, William Huntting, 203
Howells, William Dean, 113
Hsu, Hsuan, 77
Hughes, Langston, 215
Hughes, Thomas, 166, 184, 191, 198, 218; *Tom Brown at Oxford*, 187–89; *Tom Brown's School Days*, 187
Humboldt, Alexander von, 41, 135
Hume, David, 45, 73
Hunter, Ian, 169
hyper reading, 20

Igarashi, Yohei, 123
imperialism, 127, 130, 153, 155–59
Indian Civil Service, 172–74, 200–201, 210

Indian Civil Service exams, 183
influence, Emerson and, 40, 42, 48–51
informational modernity, 5, 17, 29, 83, 86, 111, 114, 134, 154–55, 171, 206
information and the informational: adventure novels and, 111–12; aesthetic experience in relation to, 3, 110–11, 116, 119; ancient writing in relation to, 91; characteristics of, 4; context as important for, 14–15; data in relation to, 4, 12; enchantment in relation to, 111–12, 151, 161–62; gendering of, 189; genres of, 8; history of, 91–92; knowledge in relation to, 2, 12; literary criticism and, 2–4; literature in relation to, 1–6, 10–15, 22, 25, 32, 55–56, 58–59, 70, 73–74, 77–78, 85–87, 91–92, 95–98, 101–4, 106–7, 110, 120–23, 133–34, 152, 154, 157, 159, 172–76, 180, 194, 195, 205–8, 221–22; meanings of, 4, 12–16; in nineteenth century, 4, 6–7; pleasure derived from, 1, 17, 151; reading practices linked to, 2, 15; scholarship on, 9–15. *See also* informational modernity
information management: antiquarian journal as means of, 92–95; *Bartlett's Familiar Quotations* and, 100–101; Dickens and, 79–80, 82–89, 181; Emerson and, 39–40, 46, 52–55; Hawthorne and, 72–74; information overload as ironic result of, 9, 16–17, 31–32; literary studies and, 55; *Middlemarch* and, 90–91; *Moby-Dick* and, 90; necessity of, 15–16; in nineteenth century, 4, 58–59, 85–86, 91–92; reading lists as instance of, 117–18; romantics and, 91; *Three Clerks* and, 195–96; women and, 85–86, 206. *See also* information overload; textual excess
information overload: anxieties concerning, 20; Coleridge and, 34, 36; as intrinsic potential of information, 15; as ironic result of information management practices, 9, 16–17, 31–32; literary meaning in context of, 16; in nineteenth century, 4, 7, 58; as research issue, 9; *Robinson Crusoe* as counter to, 29; selection criteria in context of, 39, 70, 74, 92, 100–101, 103–4, 117–20; as threat to pleasure, 3.

See also information management; mass print; textual excess
intelligence offices, 75–76
IQ tests, 170
Irving, Washington, *The History of New York*, 96

Jackson, Shelley, *Patchwork Girl*, 38
James, Henry, 8, 25, 72, 103, 125; *In the Cage*, 14, 129; "Greville Fane," 207
James, William, 16, 53, 61
Jameson, Fredric, 62, 94, 125
Jefferson, Thomas, 211–12; *Notes on the State of Virginia*, 211
Jenckes Bill (United States), 208
Jewett, Charles Coffin, 46
Jobs, Steve, 5
Jockers, Matthew, 141, 142
Johns, Juliet, 78, 84
Johnson, Samuel, 25, 45, 51, 201
Jones, William, 135
Joyce, James, 15; *Finnegans Wake*, 13
judgment: of aesthetic/literary worth, 16, 45, 48, 64, 69, 103, 114, 168, 193, 194, 245n42; assessment of, 165; criteria for, in context of information overload, 39, 70, 74, 92, 100–101, 103–4, 117–20
juvenile literature, 111, 114–16, 119–20, 125. *See also* childhood reading

Kaiser, Matthew, 127
Kant, Immanuel, 5, 28, 33, 52, 74–75, 110, 135
Kaplan Amy, 159
Kay-Shuttleworth, James, 177–80, 191; *Four Periods of Public Education*, 177; *Public Education*, 177
Keats, John, 173
keyword frequencies, 142–49
Kindle, 39, 105
Kingsley, Charles, *Westward Ho!*, 154
Kipling, Rudyard: *Kim*, 156, 201
Kittler, Friedrich, 10, 14, 22, 24, 113, 156, 185
Klancher, Jon, 91, 169
knowledge: information in relation to, 2, 12; literary, 17–18, 115–16, 165–69, 172–76, 185–86, 191–94, 201, 204, 208–10, 219–22
Knox, Vicesimus, *Elegant Extracts*, 102

Koopman, Harry, 31–32
Koran, 118
Kramnick, Jonathan, 43

LaCapra, Dominick, 61
Laconics, or The Best Words of the Best Authors, 51
Lamb, Charles, 37
Latour, Bruno, 64–65
Laughlin, Clara E., "American Literature," 245n42
Leary, Patrick, 63
Leavis, F. R., 120
Lee, Vernon, 123
Leighton, Robert, "Too Many Books," 38
Leopold II, king of Belgium, 153, 158
Leupp, Francis, *How to Prepare for a Civil Service Examination*, 209
Levine, Caroline, 83
Lewes, George Henry, 78
Lewis, George Cornewall, 197, 199
Liberator (newspaper), 66, 67
literary canon, 8–9, 38, 43, 45, 168
literary criticism/studies: assessment in, 167–68, 172–76, 185–86, 191–94, 201, 204, 208–10, 219–22; computational, 121–23; criteria of evidence for, 63–65, 68–69, 168; Crusoe and, 23; Foucault on, 167; history of, 167–69; and information, 2–4; information management and, 55; philology in relation to, 167, 168; and quantitative methods, 151–52; searching technologies' effect on, 59–61, 63–70, 107; selection processes in, 139–40, 150; and textual excess, 59. *See also* close reading; digital humanities; literature
Literary World (magazine), 94–95, 101
literature: bureaucracy in relation to, 199–200; characteristics of, 4; data compared to, 3, 5; examinations on, 17–18, 165–69, 172–76, 185–86, 191–94, 201, 204, 208–10, 219–22; information in relation to, 1–6, 10–15, 22, 25, 32, 55–56, 58–59, 70, 73–74, 77–78, 85–87, 91–92, 95–98, 101–4, 106–7, 110, 120–23, 133–34, 152, 154, 157, 159, 172–76, 180, 194, 195, 205–8, 221–22; scholarship on, 9–12. *See also* literary criticism/studies

Little, Brown and Company, 99, 102, 105
"Little Red Riding Hood" (folktale), 9
Liu, Alan, 58, 60, 68
Livingstone, David, 152; *Missionary Travels and Researches in South Africa*, 154
Locke, Alain, 215
Locke, John, 35, 51, 135; *An Essay concerning Human Understanding*, 135
Lodge, David, 38
London, Jack, 134
Longfellow, Henry Wadsworth, 14
lost world novels, 130, 132–39, 141–52, 154
Lovelace, Ada, 189
Lowe, Robert, 175, 183
Lowell, James Russell, 227n14; *A Fable for Critics*, 115
Lubbock, John: "Hundred Best Books," 118, 152, 155; *On the Origin of Civilization*, 136; *On the Senses, Instincts, and Intelligence of Animals*, 136
Luhmann, Niklas, 14, 53
Lynch, Deidre, 37

Macaulay, Thomas Babington, 121, 201
Macy Conference, 14–15
Major, John, 28
Malthus, Thomas, 44
Manguel, Alberto, 23
"The Manifesto of the V21 Collective," 98
Mann, Horace, 115, 204, 260n110
Manovich, Lev, 59, 142
Marche, Stephen, 121
Marks, Jeannette, 204–5
Marryat, Frederick, 155; *Masterman Ready*, 131, 145–46
Marx, Karl, 22, 169
mass print: adventure novels and, 131–32; aesthetics affected by, 35; Coleridge and, 32–35; criticisms of, 26, 28, 29, 75; deserted island reading contrasted with, 16, 55; Dickens and, 78, 80, 88; Emerson and, 40–42, 49–50; expedition reports and, 155; extensive reading linked to, 25, 28, 31, 34, 36, 38, 47–48, 124; Hawthorne and, 71–72, 75; in nineteenth century, 7, 10; quantification in relation to, 117; reading practices affected by, 35–36, 44; *Robinson*

Crusoe as counter to, 22, 26, 28–30; romantic responses to, 32, 36–37; *Ruth Hall* and, 206–7; Stevenson and, 124; *Treasure Island* and, 128–30; *The Virginian* and, 161. *See also* information overload; textual excess
Mather, Cotton, *Magnalia Christi Americana*, 67
Mathews, William, 44
Matthews, Brander, *Ballads of Books*, 38
Matthiessen, F. O., 33, 65
McDowell, Paula, 24
McGann, Jerome, 10, 68, 140–41
McGill, Meredith, 11, 41, 48, 68, 72, 78
McKeon, Michael, 21, 23
McLaughlin, Kevin, 78
Mead, Margaret, 15
measurement. *See* quantification
Melville, Herman, 8, 46, 60, 133; "Bartleby, the Scrivener," 5, 13, 200; *Moby-Dick*, 1–2, 44, 62, 90, 94–96, 119; *Pierre*, 35, 45; *Typee*, 148
Mendenhall, T. C., 123
Menke, Richard, 11, 78, 196
Mercier, Louis Sébastien, *The Year 2440*, 43
meritocracy, 17, 118, 166, 170, 182, 184–85, 187–88, 191, 197–98, 200, 202, 206, 210, 213, 215–16
Merritt, Abraham, *The Moon Pool*, 139, 145–46
Michaels, Walter Benn, 127
military exams, in World War I, 170
Mill, James, 73
Mill, John Stuart, 115, 135
Miller, D. A., 61, 82
Miller, J. Hillis, 82
Miller, Perry, 33
Milton, John, 99; *Areopagitica*, 177; *Paradise Lost*, 177
Mitchell, Maria, 189
modernity: adventure novels and, 111, 155; informational excesses of, 5, 17, 29, 83, 86, 111, 114, 134, 154–55, 171, 206; juvenile literature and, 125; rejection of, 5, 17, 29, 111, 114, 125–26, 134–35, 138; standardized testing as aspect of, 171; *Tarzan of the Apes* and, 135, 137; Weber and, 28, 110
Modern Library One Hundred Best Novels, 118

Montaigne, Michel de, 101
Monthly Review (London journal), 24
More, Hannah, *Strictures on the Modern System of Female Education*, 86, 102
Moretti, Franco, 20, 64, 69, 83, 141
Morgan, Benjamin, 123
Morgan, Sarah, 102
Moritz, R. E., 123
Morris, William, 119
Morrison, Toni, *Beloved*, 212
Morton, Charles, 22
Mount Holyoke College, 204

New Americanists, 61
New Criticism, 5, 32, 141
Newfield, Christopher, 219
New Historicism, 5, 16, 60–63, 65, 67–71, 74, 83, 97, 107, 123, 141, 152
New Imperialism, 130
Newlyn, Lucy, 36
Newman, John Henry, 172, 192, 258n74
New Materialism, 61, 97
New Woman, 130
New York Herald (newspaper), 155
Ngai, Sianne, 64
Nietzsche, Friedrich, 5, 53, 93–94, 97, 110
Norris, Frank, 122
Northcote-Trevelyan Report, 196, 197, 200
Norton, Charles Eliot, 208
Notes and Queries (journal), 17, 92–98, 102, 106
Novak, Maximillian, 22
novels, criticisms of, 25, 33
numbers. *See* accounting of literature; quantification
numeracy, 135–38
Nunberg, Geoffrey, 15, 22, 91

Obama, Barack, 105
Oldbuck, Jonathan, 96
Otter, Samuel, 95, 216
Oxford University, 167–68

Packer, Barbara, 53, 220
Pall Mall Gazette (newspaper), 118, 119, 152–56
Palmer, D. J., 168, 169
Panizzi, Antonio, 46
Parker, Theodore, 62
Pater, Walter, 205

Peirce, Charles, 70
Pendleton Act (United States, 1883), 203, 208, 210, 213
People (magazine), 118
Perkins, Frederic, *The Best Reading*, 117
Pestalozzi, Johann, 207
philology, 15, 92, 94, 95, 167, 168, 177
Pickens, William, 215
Piper, Andrew, 10–11, 22, 59, 93, 138
play, 183
pleasure: aesthetic, 3, 4; in compilations, 100; information as source of, 1, 17, 151; textual excess as threat to, 3, 57. *See also* enchantment
Plessy vs. Ferguson (United States, 1896), 218
Pliny the Elder, 30, 175
Plotz, John, 55
Poe, Edgar Allan, 6, 8, 19, 28–29, 37, 48, 83, 210; "The Gold-Bug," 128, 129; *The Narrative of Arthur Gordon Pym*, 139, 145–46, 149; "The Purloined Letter," 89; "The Raven," 13
Poirier, Richard, 53
Poole, William, *Index to Periodical Literature*, 7, 46, 91, 101
Poor Richard (pseudonym of Benjamin Franklin), 105
Poovey, Mary, 11, 21, 24, 111–12, 127, 171, 176
Pope, Alexander, 99
Porter, Carolyn, 61
Porter, Jane, 99
Porter, Theodore, 109, 147
positivism, 5, 28, 62, 72, 98, 110, 151, 163, 168, 169, 183, 187, 193, 202, 204–5, 209, 210, 216. *See also* antipositivism
postcolonialism, 157
postmodernism, 62, 164
poststructuralism, 5, 63, 141
Pound, Ezra, 70
Pound, Louis, 123
Prescott, William, 209
Preston, Isabella Rushton, *Handbook of Familiar Quotations*, 100
Price, Leah, 11, 58, 78, 86, 100, 102
probability: in digital searching, 69–70; in information theory, 13, 15
Provincial Freeman (newspaper), 212
Public-School Journal, 120

Puck (magazine), 102
Putnam, George, 43–44
Pynchon, Thomas, 164

quantification: aesthetics in relation to, 118–23, 128, 137, 154, 166–67, 218; criticisms of, 181; DH experiment on, 143–52; in education, 178; enchanting/disenchanting effects of, 110–11; history of, 112–13; human capacity for, 135–37; literary criticism and, 151–52; of literary knowledge, 115–16, 166–68; mass print in relation to, 117; in *Treasure Island*, 126–30, 147. *See also* accounting of literature
Quetelet, Adolphe, 109
quotations: compilations of, 100–105; Emerson and, 48, 51, 54

Raiders of the Lost Ark (film), 8, 161–64
Ramsay, Stephen, 141, 146, 150
Ranke, Leopold von, 98
reading: Coleridge's critique of, 35; in contemporary context, 19–20; criteria for, in context of information overload, 39, 99, 117–20; digital practices in, 20, 38; in eighteenth century, 25; Emerson on, 40–43, 46–50, 55–56; information linked to practices of, 2, 15; mass print's effect on, 35–36, 44; in nineteenth-century curriculum, 114–16; quantitative approaches to, 44; recommendations for limiting, 43; textual excess/mass print linked to practices of, 2, 21, 25, 30. *See also* childhood reading; close reading; deserted island reading; extensive reading
Readings, Bill, 165, 194
Renker, Elizabeth, 169
Reuter, Paul Julius, 46
Reuters, 7, 76
Revised Code (England, 1862), 175, 178, 180, 183
Rezek, Joseph, 72
Richards, I. A., 123
Richardson, Charles Francis, *The Choice of Books*, 117
Riefenstahl, Leni, 162
Rigby, Elizabeth, 114
Right Reading (anthology), 117

Right Reading for Children (anthology), 117
Roberts vs. the City of Boston (United States, 1850), 212
Rockwell, Geoffrey, 143
Roksa, Josipa, *Academically Adrift*, 219
Romanes, George, *The Mental Evolution of Man*, 136
romanticism: aesthetics associated with, 16; convention as nemesis of, 194; and education, 183; Emerson and, 40; and information management, 91; and mass print, 32, 36–37
Roosevelt, Teddy, 159, 160
Rose, Jacqueline, 139
Rosenwald, Lawrence, 51, 52
Rousseau, Jean-Jacques, *Emile*, 24
Routledge, 119
Rowe, John Carlos, 159
Royal Artillery and Engineers Corps, 172
Ruskin, John, 26, 48, 94, 119, 192
Russell, William, *The Frozen Pirate*, 140
Ruth, Jennifer, 169

The Sacrifice of Education to Examination (essay collection), 171, 220
Said, Edward, 157, 169
Saler, Michael, 111
Salmon, Edward, *Juvenile Literature as It Is*, 120
sampling errors, 139–40
Sampson, Dominie, 96
Saramago, José, 164
SAT exams, 175, 184, 194, 220
Savage, Leonard, 15
Saxe, John Godfrey, 210
Schelling, F.W.J., 33, 74
Schlegel, A. W., 33
Schmitt, Cannon, 126
science, 5, 10, 110–11, 160
Science (magazine), 123
Scott, Walter, 25, 80, 99, 114, 154, 156; *The Antiquary*, 96; *Guy Mannering*, 96
Scribner's Monthly (magazine), 210
searching technologies: *Bartlett's Familiar Quotations* and, 101–2; counterfactual methods, 68; Dickens and, 82–83; failure to theorize, 59–60; Hawthorne and, 75–76; in intelligence offices, 76; literary criticism as affected by, 59–61, 63–70, 107; New Historicism in relation to, 60–61; role of intuition/aesthetic imagination in, 69–70, 73–75, 83, 89–91, 98; standards of evidence as issue for, 60–64; targeted searching, 60–61, 63, 67–68
Seltzer, Mark, 134
Seneca, 43
Shakespeare, William, 14, 15, 36, 92, 99, 101, 103–4, 153–54; *Hamlet*, 122; *Henry V*, 177; *Macbeth*, 168; *The Tempest*, 24, 153
Shannon, Claude, 13–15, 58
Sharp, Michele Turner, 38
Shelley, Mary, 2, 8, 19, 38–39; *Frankenstein*, 38–39; *The Last Man*, 39
Shelley, Percy Bysshe, *Alastor*, 122
Sherman, Lucius Adelno, *Analytics of Literature*, 121–23
Shuman, Cathy, 169, 198
Shumway, David, 169, 209
Siegel, Jonah, 33
Sigourney, Lydia, *Letters to Young Ladies*, 86
Silko, Leslie Marmon, 209
Silverman, Gillian, 228n27
Sinclair, Stéfan, 143
Sitting Bull, 160
Skeat, William, 175
slavery, 65–69
Smiles, Samuel, 199
Smith, Barbara Herrnstein, 64
Smithsonian Library, 46
Snow, C. P., 120
social Darwinism, 137
Society for Promoting Christian Knowledge, 114
Society for the Diffusion of Useful Knowledge, 114
Society of Antiquaries (London), 92
Somerville, Mary, 189
Sonnenschein, William: *The Best Books*, 117; *Guide to Best Books*, 117
Spencer, Herbert, 45
Spenser, Edmund, 121
Spielberg, Steven, 161
Sprague, Charles, 105
standardization of education, 115, 177–80, 183, 204–5, 207. *See also* standardized testing

standardized testing: African Americans and, 212–18; associated with modernity, 171; characteristics of, 170; criticisms of, 171–72, 175–76, 177–78, 180, 204, 211; history of, 165–70; in literary studies, 220; literature concerning, 184–208; purposes of, 170; subjectivity constructed on basis of, 191, 192; support/defense of, 184, 186–88, 190, 195, 200–202, 213; *Three Clerks* and, 195–98; in United States, 203–11; in Victorian era, 166–71, 175, 195; women and, 189–94. *See also* standardization of education

Standish, Burt, 203

Stanley, Arthur, *The Life and Correspondence of Thomas Arnold*, 191

Stanley, Henry Morton, 152–58; *Through the Dark Continent*, 153–57

statistics. *See* digital humanities; quantification

Stedman, E. C., 122

Stevenson, Robert Louis, 7, 14, 119; *Kidnapped*, 139, 145–46; "My First Book—'Treasure Island'", 126; *Treasure Island*, 8, 17, 108, 112, 124–30, 145–47; *The Wrecker*, 124

Stewart, Garrett, 38, 132

Stoker, Bram, 2; *Dracula*, 156

Stowe, Harriet Beecher, 5, 215; *Dred*, 29

study guides, 175

stylometric analysis, 20, 121–23

Sullivan, Ceri, 133, 195, 199

Sumner, Charles, 212

superabundance. *See* information overload; mass print; textual excess

surface data, 142

Swift, Jonathan, *Gulliver's Travels*, 43

Swinburne, Algernon, 119

Symonds, William Law, 47–48

System (magazine), 134

systems theory, 14, 53

Tamarkin, Elisa, 180

targeted searching, 60–61, 63, 67–68

Taunton Commission, 172

Taylor, Frederick Winslow, 134

Tennyson, Alfred, Lord, 173

testing: history of, 166–67, 170; of literary knowledge, 17–18, 165–69, 172–76, 185–86, 191–94, 201, 204, 208–10, 219–22; performance and, 182; study guides as preparation for, 175; subjectivity constructed on basis of, 166–67, 184, 191. *See also* standardized testing

textual excess: adventure novels and, 131, 149–51; anxieties concerning, 19–20, 44, 114, 117–18, 124, 131; close reading in relation to, 37–38; dangers of, 108; Dickens and, 79–84; in eighteenth century, 24–25; Emerson and, 39–40, 42–43, 45, 49, 53–56; excerpts and compilations as response to, 100–102; Hawthorne and, 71–72; historical occurrences of, 21; ironies of, 31–32; juvenile literature and, 114, 119, 125; management of, 17; *Moby-Dick* and, 96; in nineteenth century, 9, 21–22, 58–59; quantitative responses to, 44–45; reading practices linked to, 21, 23, 25, 30; as research issue, 8; *Robinson Crusoe* linked to, 24–26; in romantic period, 16; scholarship on, 11; as threat to pleasure, 3, 57; *Treasure Island* and, 124. *See also* information management; information overload; mass print

textuality, DH experiment on, 143–52

Thackeray, William Makepeace, 123; *The History of Henry Esmond*, 156; *Pendennis*, 45

This Is Spinal Tap (film), 105

Thomas, Brook, 61

Thomas, Clarence, 105

Thompson, Shawn, 26

Thoms, William, 92, 95–97

Thoreau, Henry David, 8, 37, 40, 48, 133; *Walden*, 2, 35, 37, 72, 115; *A Week on the Concord and Merrimack Rivers*, 37

Timperley, Charles Henry, *Dictionary of Printers and Printing, with the Progress of Literature*, 116

Tompkins, Jane, 45

Tosh, Peter, 67

transcendentalism, 33–34, 40, 45, 53, 72, 74

Trevelyan, Charles, 196

Trevelyan, George, 184; *The Competition Wallah*, 200–201

Trollope, Anthony, 2, 17, 133, 166, 184, 195, 198–200, 218; *American Senator*, 203; *Autobiography*, 195, 199–200; "The Civil Service as a Profession," 198; *North America*, 203; *Three Clerks*, 195–200, 206, 215

Trollope, Frances, 189

Trump, Donald, 78

Turing test, 13

Turner, Frederick Jackson, "The Significance of the Frontier in American History," 159–60

Twain, Mark: "Fenimore Cooper's Literary Offenses," 113–14; *Huckleberry Finn*, 114

Tylor, Edward, *Primitive Cultures*, 135–36

Underwood, Ted, 60, 142

United States: frontier of, 159–61; imperialism of, 159; racism in, 211–19; standardized testing in, 203–11

unity: as aesthetic component, 3, 4; in Coleridge's aesthetics, 32, 34–35, 41–42

US Bureau of Education, 44

US Bureau of Indian Affairs, 17, 209–11, 261n128

US Census, 211

US Civil Service, 203, 208–9, 213

utilitarianism, 192

Veblen, Thorstein, 204

Vendler, Helen, 142

Venn, John, 109

Verne, Jules, 248n80; *Mysterious Island*, 131, 145–46

Viswanathan, Gauri, 169, 201

Voyant, 143, 148

Wallace, Alfred Russell, 136

Walls, Laura Dassow, 33, 41

Warner, Michael, 61–62

Warren, Kenneth, 211; *What Was African American Literature?*, 218

Warren, Robert Penn, 32

Watt, Ian, 22

Weaver, Warren, 14–15, 147

Webb, Frank, 7, 9, 17, 166, 199; *The Garies and Their Friends*, 211, 215–19

Weber, Max, 5, 22, 28, 75, 110, 129, 134; *The Protestant Ethic and the Spirit of Capitalism*, 110, 159–60; "Science as a Vocation," 110, 160

Weitkamp, Carl, 143

Wellmon, Chad, 21, 33

West, Peter, 75

Wharton, Edith, 5, 133; *The Custom of the Country*, 103

Wheatley, Phillis, 212

Whewell, William, 135

White, Arnold, *Efficiency and Empire*, 157

Whitman, Walt, 41, 119; *Song of Myself*, 35

Wiener, Norbert, 15

Wiggin, Kate Douglas, *Children's Rights*, 114

Wikipedia, 102

Williams, Rosalind, 126

Williams, William Carlos, 70

Wills, William Henry, 57

Wilson, Woodrow, 213

Wister, Owen, *The Virginian*, 159, 160–61

Wittgenstein, Ludwig, 53

Wolfe, Cary, 53

women: and education, 189, 191; and gendered critique of adventure novels, 149; and information management, 85–86, 206; and standardized testing, 189–94

Woodward, Kathleen, 219

Wordsworth, William, 50, 105, 173; *Excursion*, 177; *Prelude*, 35; "We Are Seven," 111

Wright, J. J., *So Many Books! So Little Time! What to Do?*, 44

Wyss, Johann David, *Swiss Family Robinson*, 131, 145–46, 150

Yahoo, 82

Yellin, Jean Fagan, 65

Yonge, Charlotte, 9, 17, 184, 198, 207, 218, 258n74; "Children's Literature of the Last Century," 114; *The Daisy Chain, or Aspirations*, 189–91

Young, Edward, *Night-Thoughts*, 177

Zboray, Mary, 40

Zboray, Ronald, 40, 133

A NOTE ON THE TYPE

THIS BOOK has been composed in Miller, a Scotch Roman typeface designed by Matthew Carter and first released by Font Bureau in 1997. It resembles Monticello, the typeface developed for The Papers of Thomas Jefferson in the 1940s by C. H. Griffith and P. J. Conkwright and reinterpreted in digital form by Carter in 2003.

Pleasant Jefferson ("P. J.") Conkwright (1905–1986) was Typographer at Princeton University Press from 1939 to 1970. He was an acclaimed book designer and AIGA Medalist.

The ornament used throughout this book was designed by Pierre Simon Fournier (1712–1768) and was a favorite of Conkwright's, used in his design of the *Princeton University Library Chronicle*.

GPSR Authorized Representative: Easy Access System Europe - Mustamäe tee 50, 10621 Tallinn, Estonia, gpsr.requests@easproject.com